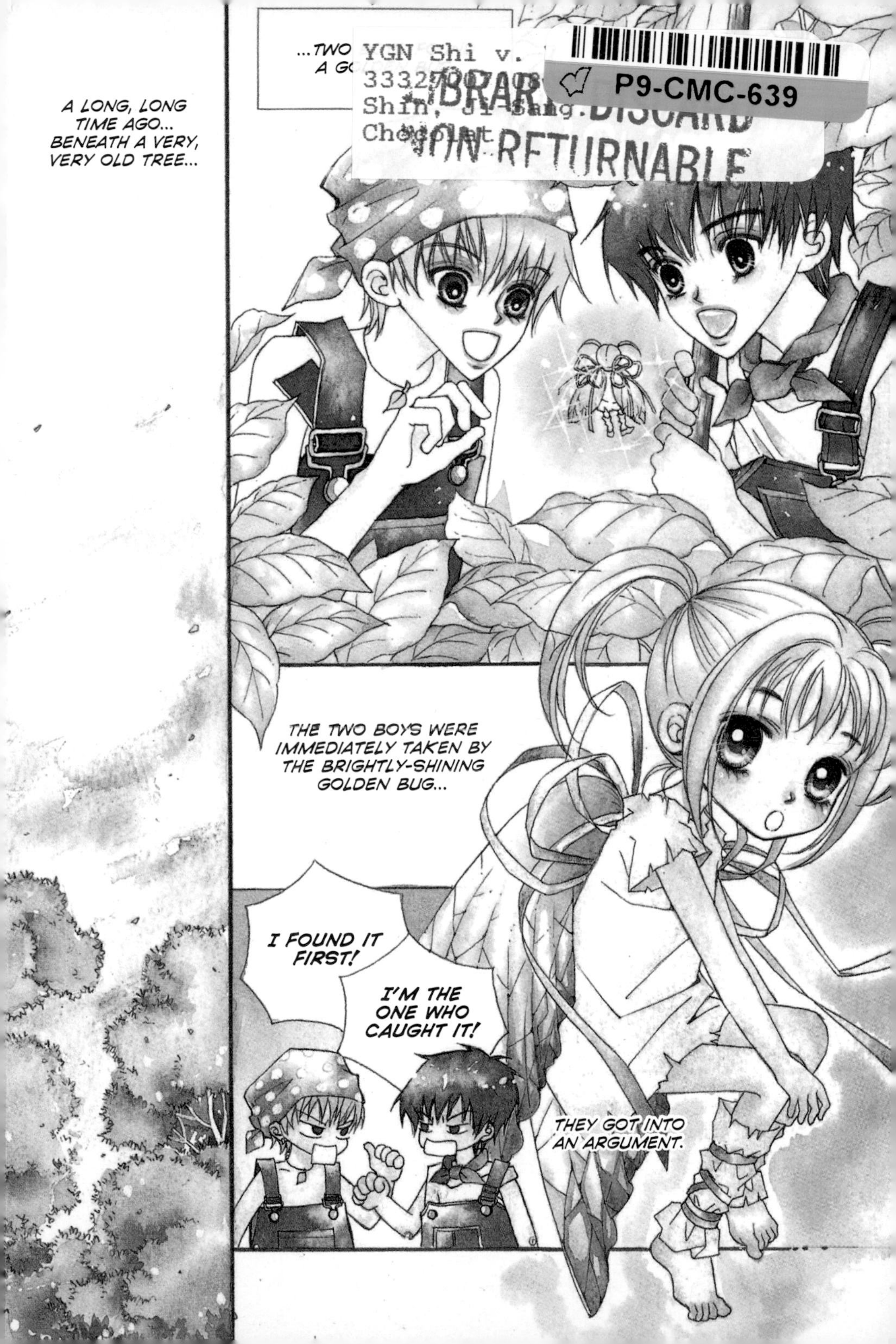
A LONG, LONG TIME AGO... BENEATH A VERY, VERY OLD TREE...
...TWO
A GO
THE TWO BOYS WERE IMMEDIATELY TAKEN BY THE BRIGHTLY-SHINING GOLDEN BUG...
I FOUND IT FIRST!
I'M THE ONE WHO CAUGHT IT!
THEY GOT INTO AN ARGUMENT.

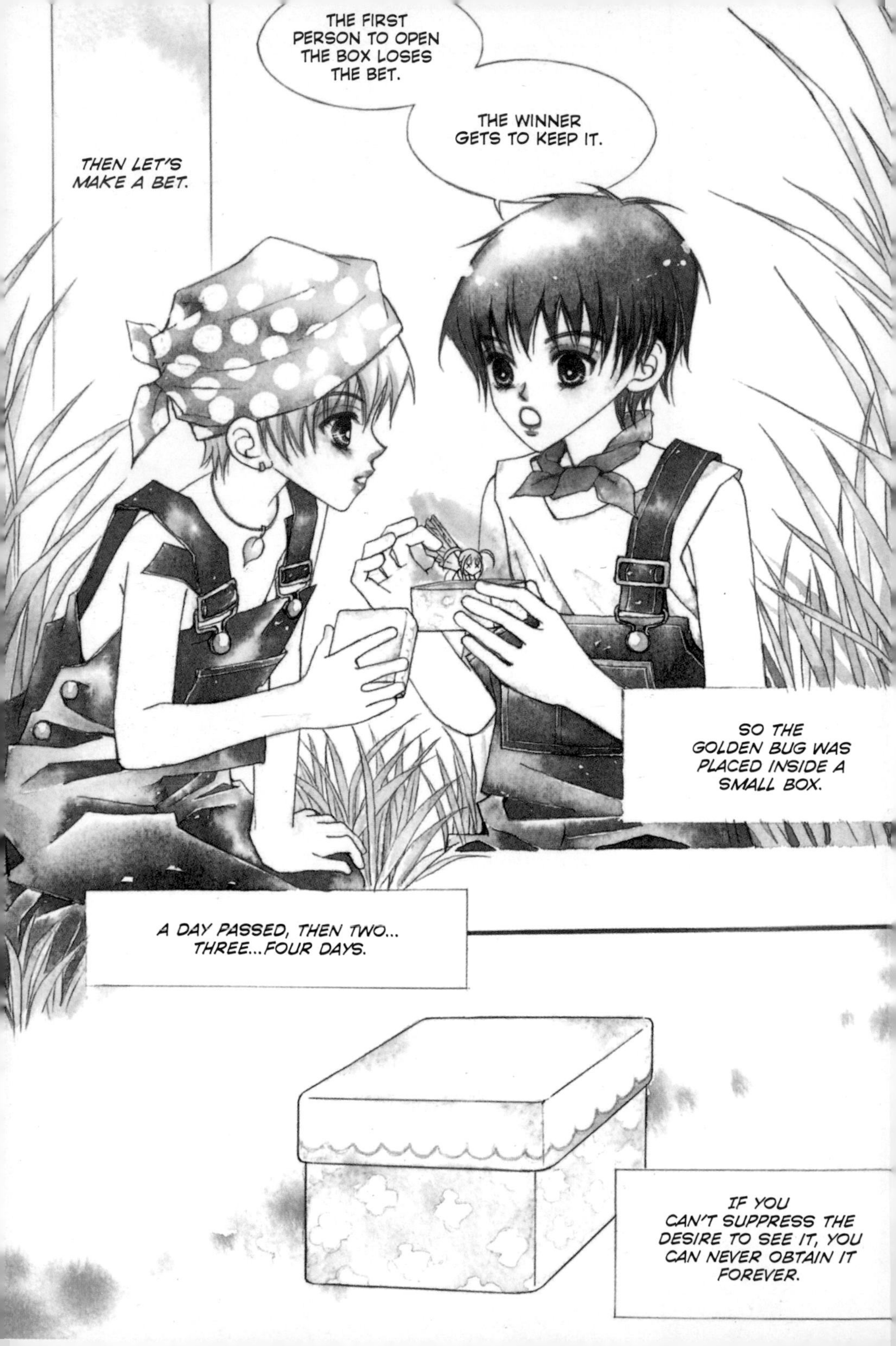
THEN LET'S MAKE A BET.
THE FIRST PERSON TO OPEN THE BOX LOSES THE BET.
THE WINNER GETS TO KEEP IT.
SO THE GOLDEN BUG WAS PLACED INSIDE A SMALL BOX.
A DAY PASSED, THEN TWO... THREE...FOUR DAYS.
IF YOU CAN'T SUPPRESS THE DESIRE TO SEE IT, YOU CAN NEVER OBTAIN IT FOREVER.

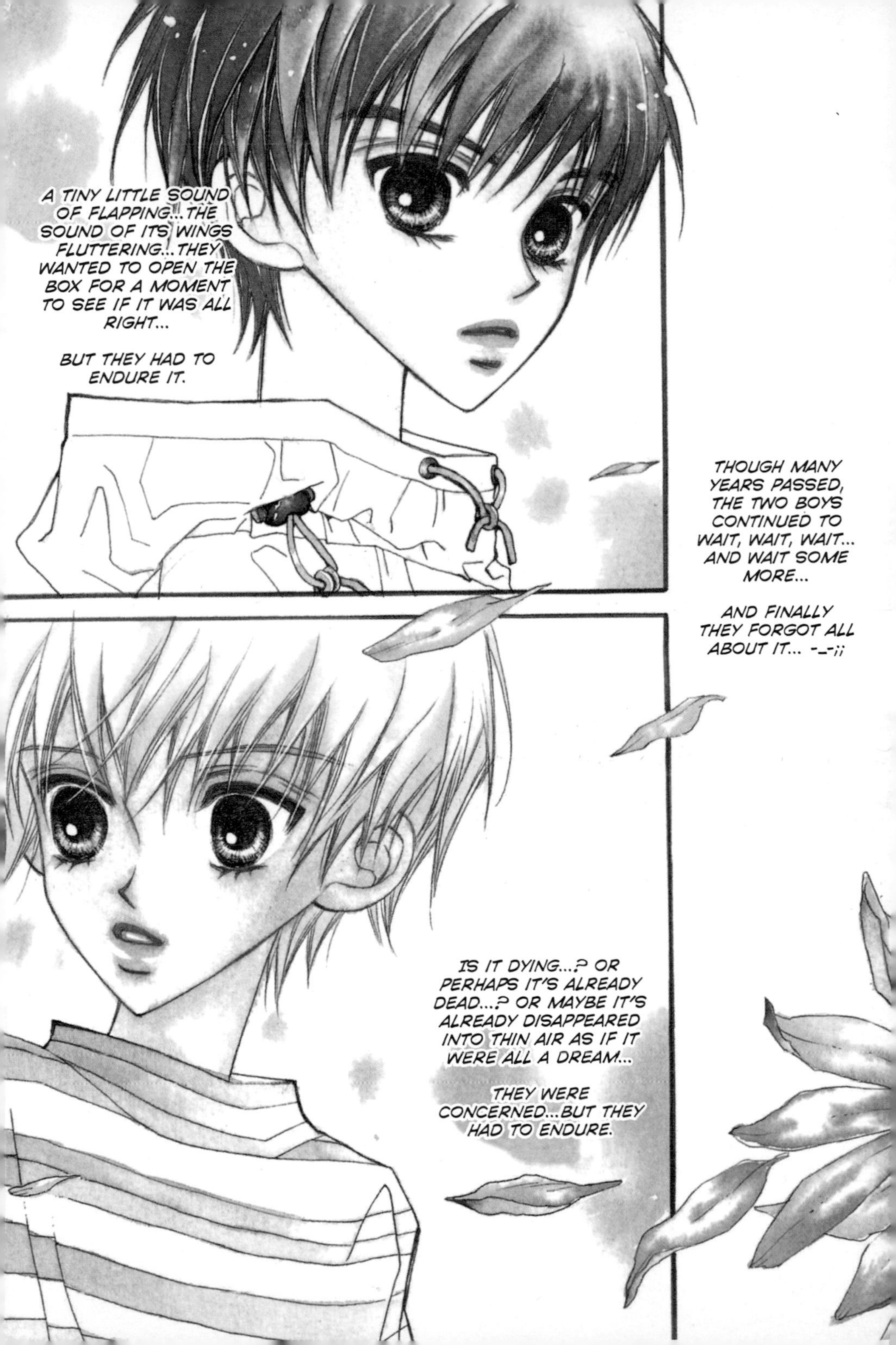
A TINY LITTLE SOUND OF FLAPPING...THE SOUND OF ITS WINGS FLUTTERING...THEY WANTED TO OPEN THE BOX FOR A MOMENT TO SEE IF IT WAS ALL RIGHT...
BUT THEY HAD TO ENDURE IT.
THOUGH MANY YEARS PASSED, THE TWO BOYS CONTINUED TO WAIT, WAIT, WAIT... AND WAIT SOME MORE...
AND FINALLY THEY FORGOT ALL ABOUT IT... -_-;;
IS IT DYING...? OR PERHAPS IT'S ALREADY DEAD...? OR MAYBE IT'S ALREADY DISAPPEARED INTO THIN AIR AS IF IT WERE ALL A DREAM...
THEY WERE CONCERNED...BUT THEY HAD TO ENDURE.

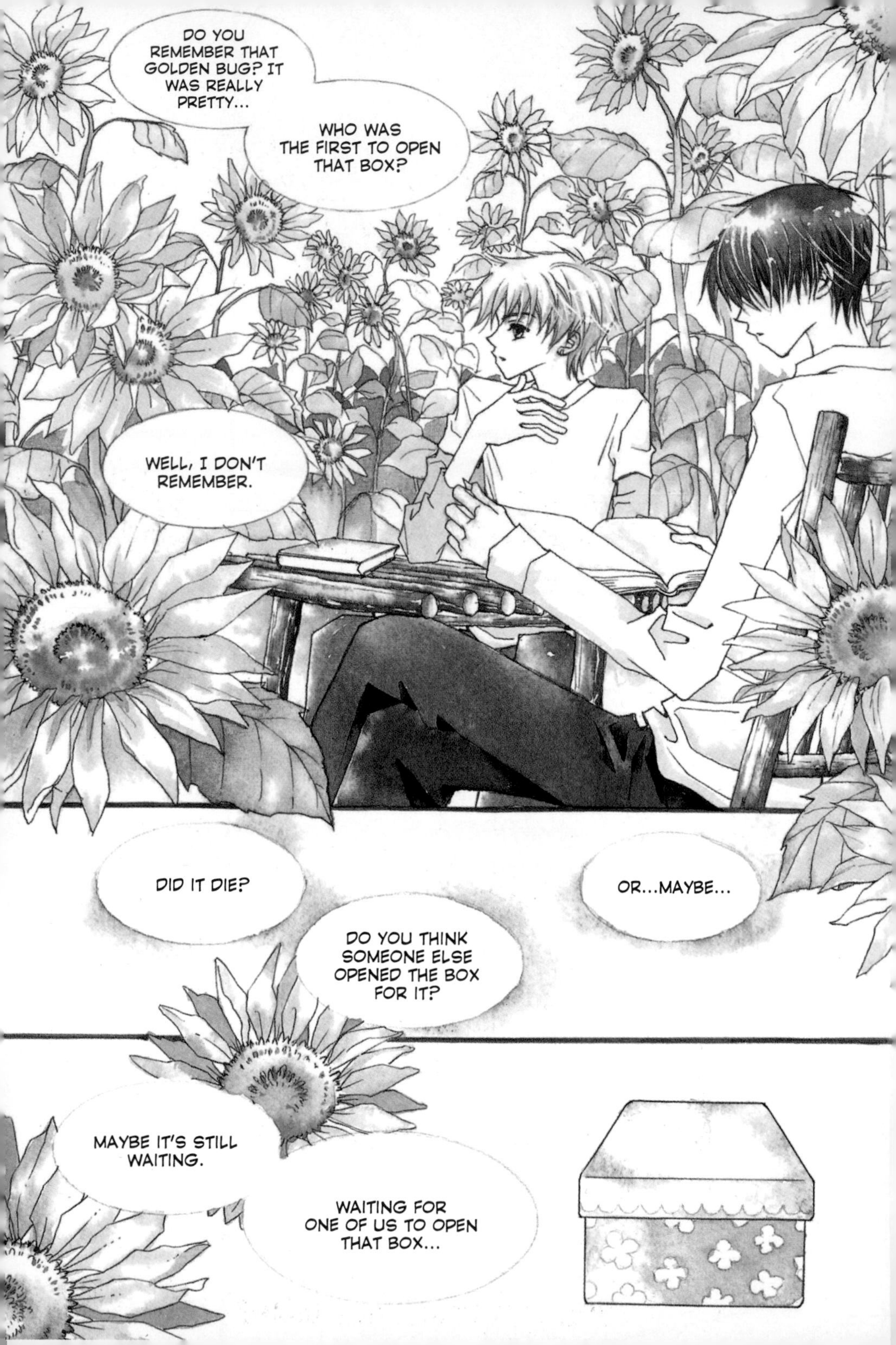

DO YOU REMEMBER THAT GOLDEN BUG? IT WAS REALLY PRETTY...
WHO WAS THE FIRST TO OPEN THAT BOX?
WELL, I DON'T REMEMBER.
DID IT DIE?
DO YOU THINK SOMEONE ELSE OPENED THE BOX FOR IT?
OR...MAYBE...
MAYBE IT'S STILL WAITING.
WAITING FOR ONE OF US TO OPEN THAT BOX...

CHOCOLAT

vol. 7

Shin JiSang · Geo

Yen
Press

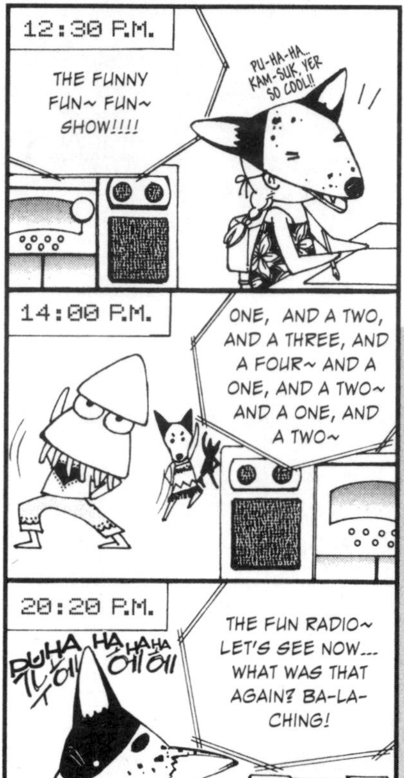
12:30 P.M.
THE FUNNY FUN~ FUN~ SHOW!!!!
PU-HA-HA.. KAM-SUK, YER SO COOL!!
14:00 P.M.
ONE, AND A TWO, AND A THREE, AND A FOUR~ AND A ONE, AND A TWO~ AND A ONE, AND A TWO~
20:20 P.M.
THE FUN RADIO~ LET'S SEE NOW... WHAT WAS THAT AGAIN? BA-LA-CHING!
PUHA HA HAHA
DAE-HUNG~ YER SO CUTE~
01:00 A.M.
HELLO...I HAVE THIS PROBLEM. LIKE, THERE'S THIS PERSON, LIKE, I WANNA KILL, AND LIKE... OMG...
I THINK YOU'VE DONE ENOUGH ALREADY!
AND WHILE LISTENING, ANOTHER DAY HAS PASSED IN THE CHOCOLAT STUDIO.

WORDS FROM THE CREATORS

FOR MANY YEARS, WE DIDN'T LISTEN TO THE RADIO. BUT RECENTLY, WE STARTED TO LISTEN TO IT AGAIN DUE TO THE FACT THAT WE'RE NOT CURRENTLY HOOKED ON ANY RECENT SOAP OPERAS.

EVEN THOUGH MANY YEARS HAVE PASSED, NOT MUCH HAS CHANGED ON THE RADIO. ON THE AM DIAL, THERE'S STILL...THE SMELL OF SWEAT FROM THE HARD-WORKING MEN AND WOMEN OF THIS LAND, AND ON THE FM CHANNELS, THERE ARE WHISPERS OF PEOPLE DRUNK WITH MUSIC, THE NIGHT, AND LOVE. THE THEMES HAVEN'T CHANGED MUCH, AND EVEN TEN OR SO YEARS LATER, IT FEELS LIKE THE MUSIC IS THE SAME TONIGHT AS IT WAS MANY YEARS AGO—THE SAME FEEL, THE SAME HEART.

THINKING BACK, WE BELIEVE THERE'S POWER IN HOW CULTURE CAN TRANSCEND TIME. BOOKS ARE LIKE THAT...SO IS THE RADIO. AND THEY'RE ALL STRENGTHS PRESERVED IN TIME. ANYONE CAN GO BACK TO THAT TIME...WHENEVER AND WHEREVER THEY MIGHT BE. IT'S ALL VERY NOSTALGIC.

WE THINK WE'VE SAID TOO MUCH. -_-;; ALL WE WANTED TO SAY...WAS THAT WE WISH THAT ***CHOCOLAT*** WILL BE LIKE THAT. MANY YEARS FROM NOW, WHEN ALL OF YOU ACCIDENTALLY COME ACROSS THIS BOOK AND OPEN IT ONCE MORE, THERE'LL BE A FLOOD OF MEMORIES BRINGING YOU BACK TO THIS DAY...TO THIS MOMENT... BACK TO THIS AGE...AND YOU'LL SAY, "AH, IT WAS LIKE THAT BACK THEN...I REMEMBER," AND SMILE ONCE AGAIN FONDLY...

JI-SANG SHIN & GEO

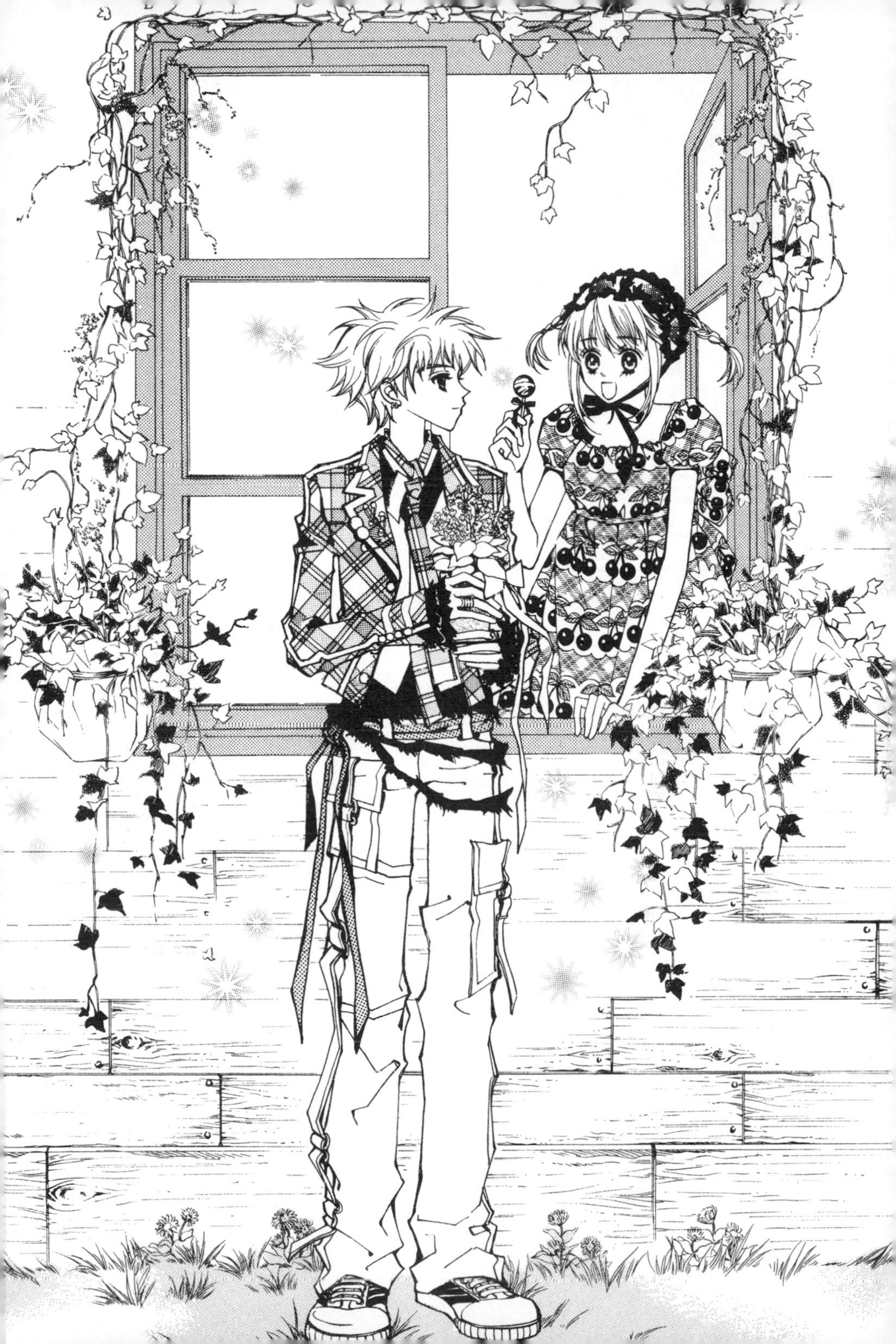

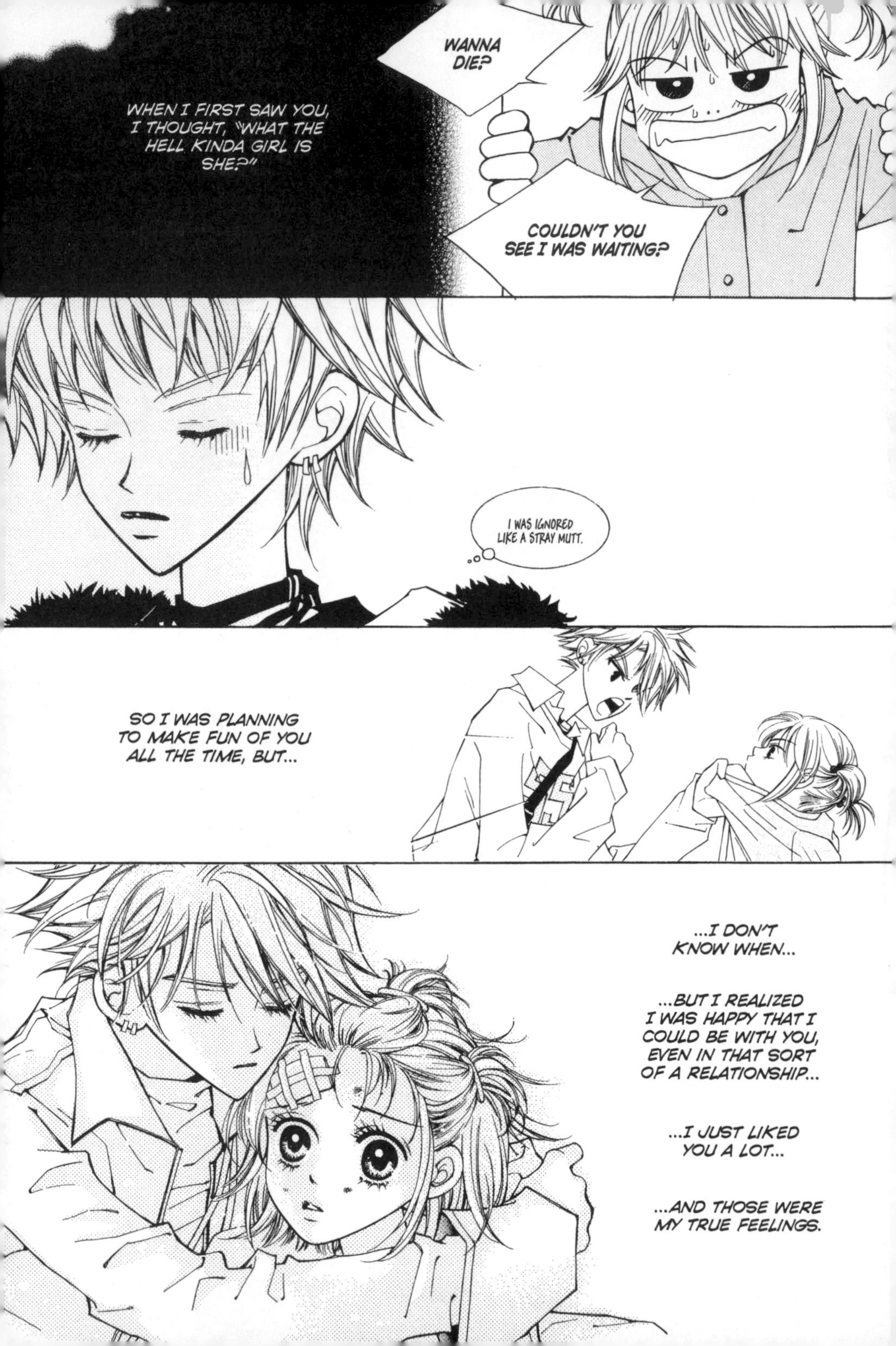
WHEN I FIRST SAW YOU, I THOUGHT, "WHAT THE HELL KINDA GIRL IS SHE?"
WANNA DIE?
COULDN'T YOU SEE I WAS WAITING?
I WAS IGNORED LIKE A STRAY MUTT.
SO I WAS PLANNING TO MAKE FUN OF YOU ALL THE TIME, BUT...
...I DON'T KNOW WHEN...
...BUT I REALIZED I WAS HAPPY THAT I COULD BE WITH YOU, EVEN IN THAT SORT OF A RELATIONSHIP...
...I JUST LIKED YOU A LOT...
...AND THOSE WERE MY TRUE FEELINGS.

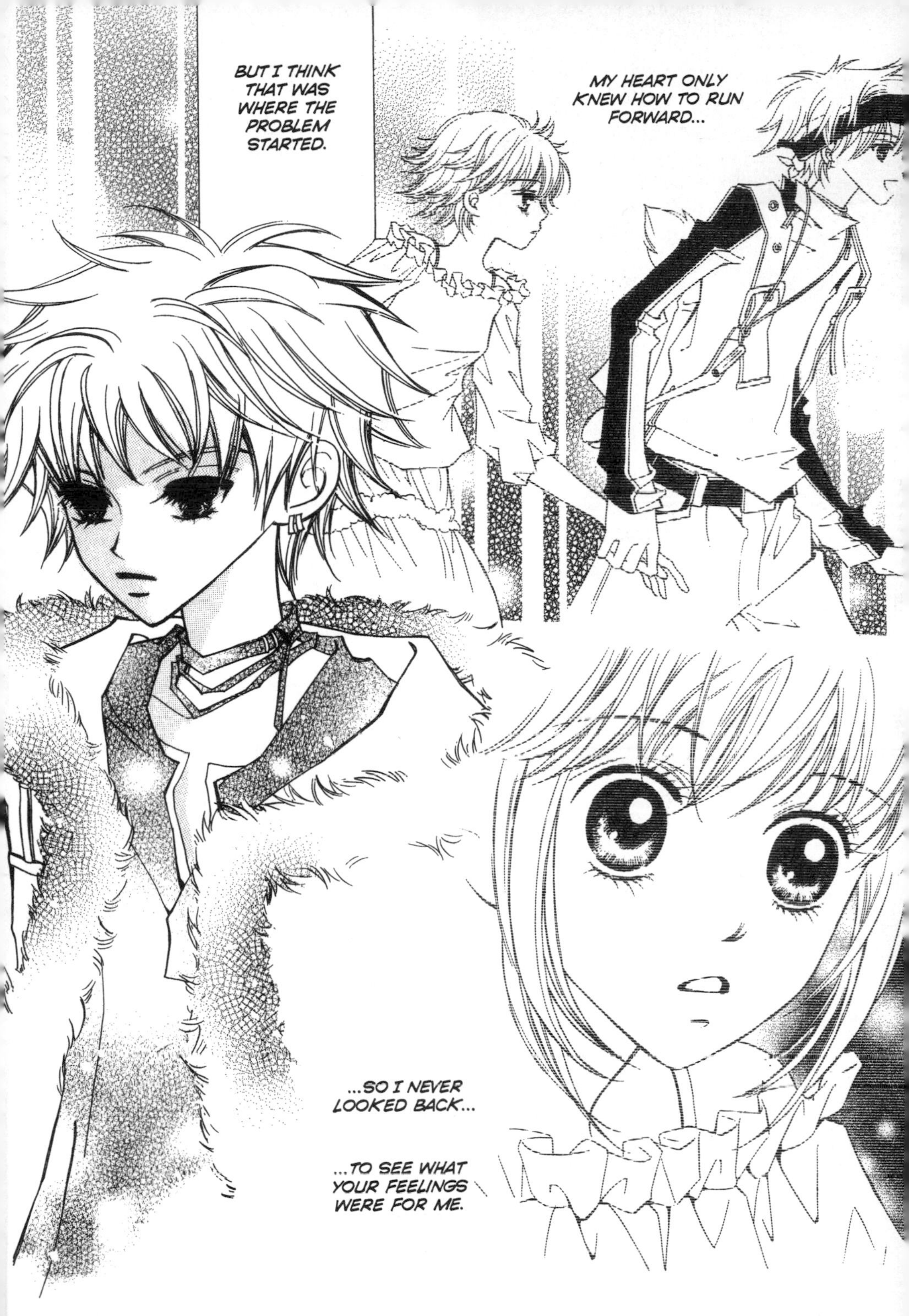
BUT I THINK THAT WAS WHERE THE PROBLEM STARTED.
MY HEART ONLY KNEW HOW TO RUN FORWARD...
...SO I NEVER LOOKED BACK...
...TO SEE WHAT YOUR FEELINGS WERE FOR ME.

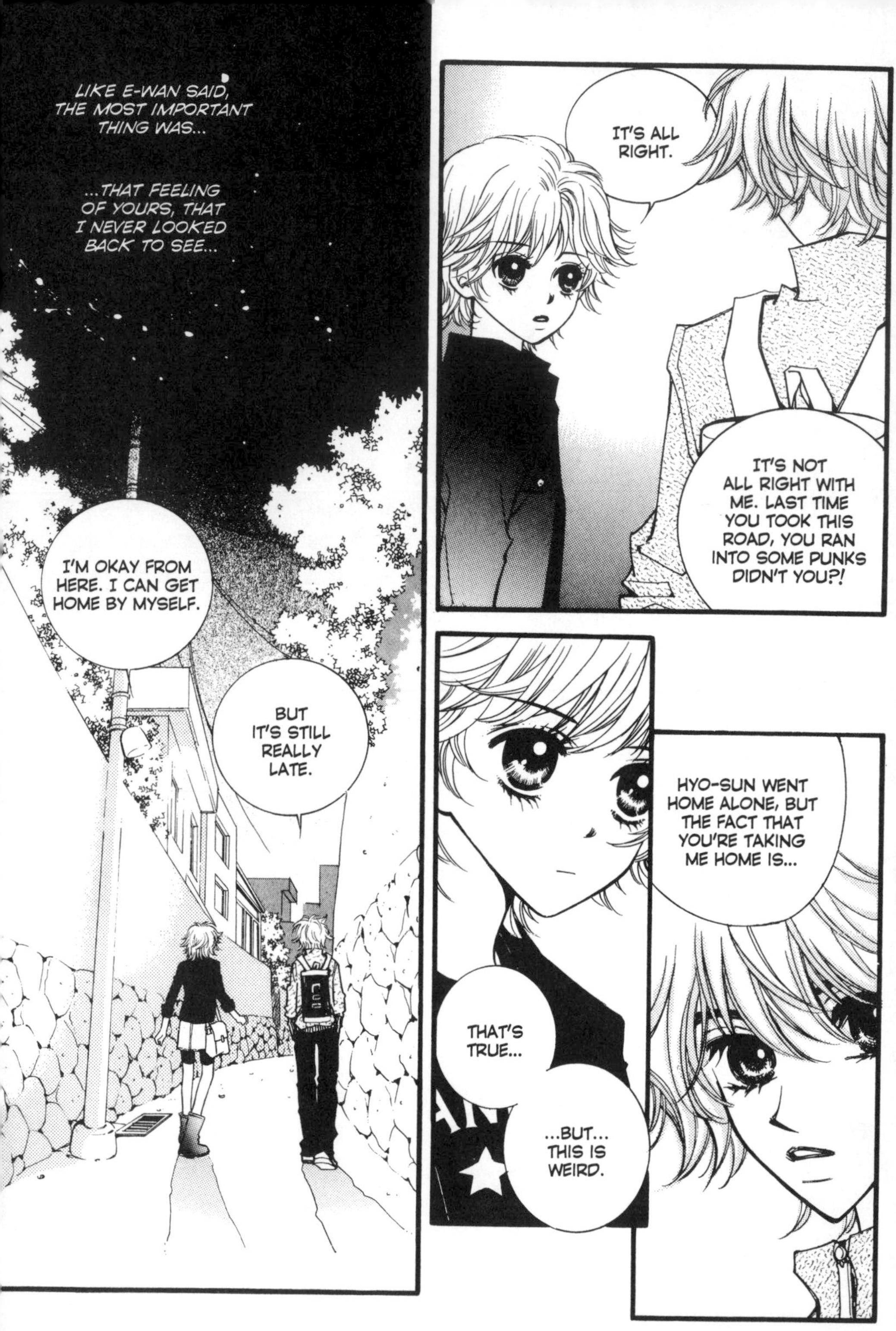
LIKE E-WAN SAID, THE MOST IMPORTANT THING WAS...
...THAT FEELING OF YOURS, THAT I NEVER LOOKED BACK TO SEE...
I'M OKAY FROM HERE. I CAN GET HOME BY MYSELF.
BUT IT'S STILL REALLY LATE.
IT'S ALL RIGHT.
IT'S NOT ALL RIGHT WITH ME. LAST TIME YOU TOOK THIS ROAD, YOU RAN INTO SOME PUNKS DIDN'T YOU?!
HYO-SUN WENT HOME ALONE, BUT THE FACT THAT YOU'RE TAKING ME HOME IS...
THAT'S TRUE...
...BUT... THIS IS WEIRD.

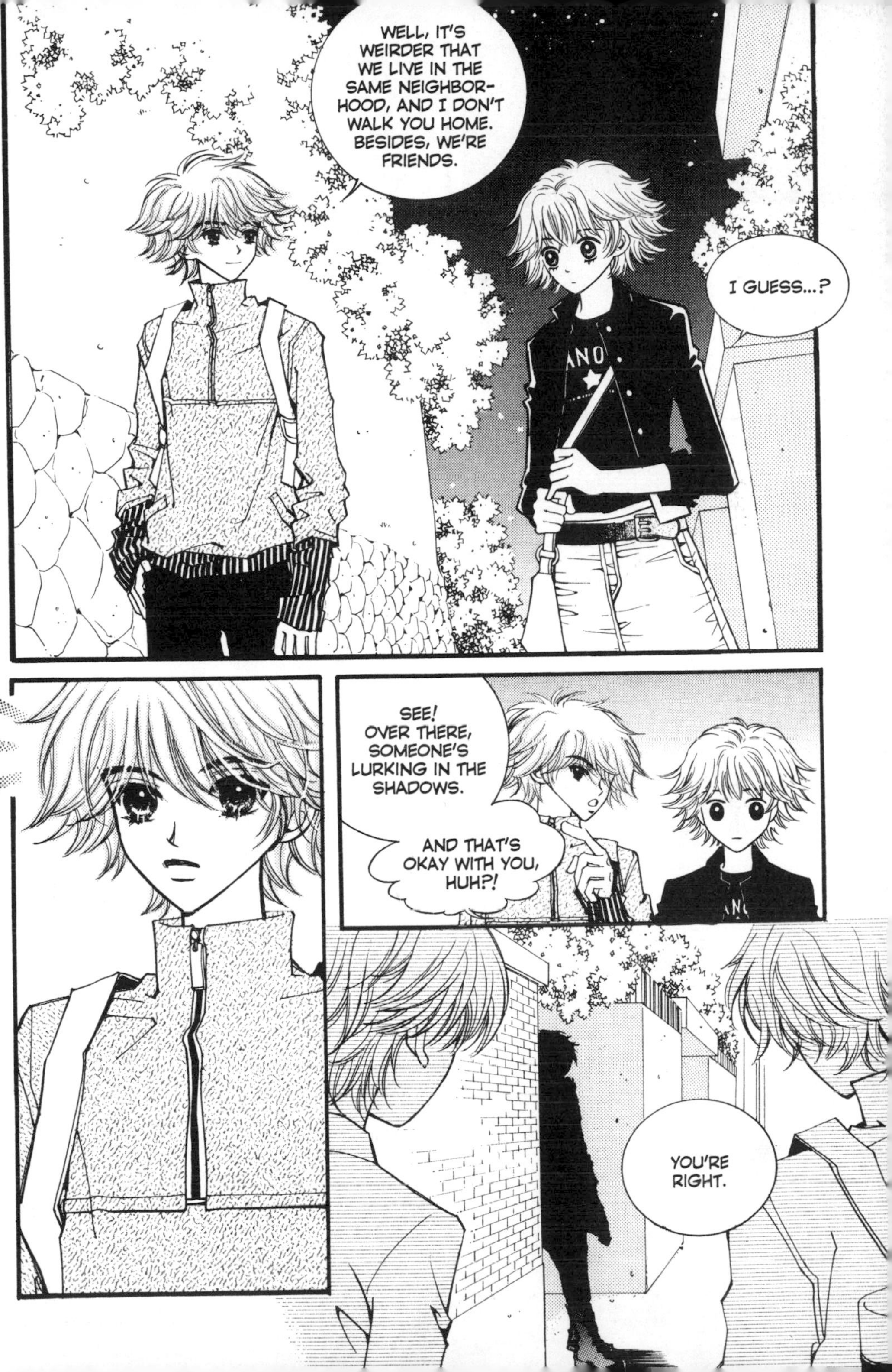
WELL, IT'S WEIRDER THAT WE LIVE IN THE SAME NEIGHBOR-HOOD, AND I DON'T WALK YOU HOME. BESIDES, WE'RE FRIENDS.
I GUESS...?
SEE! OVER THERE, SOMEONE'S LURKING IN THE SHADOWS.
AND THAT'S OKAY WITH YOU, HUH?!
YOU'RE RIGHT.

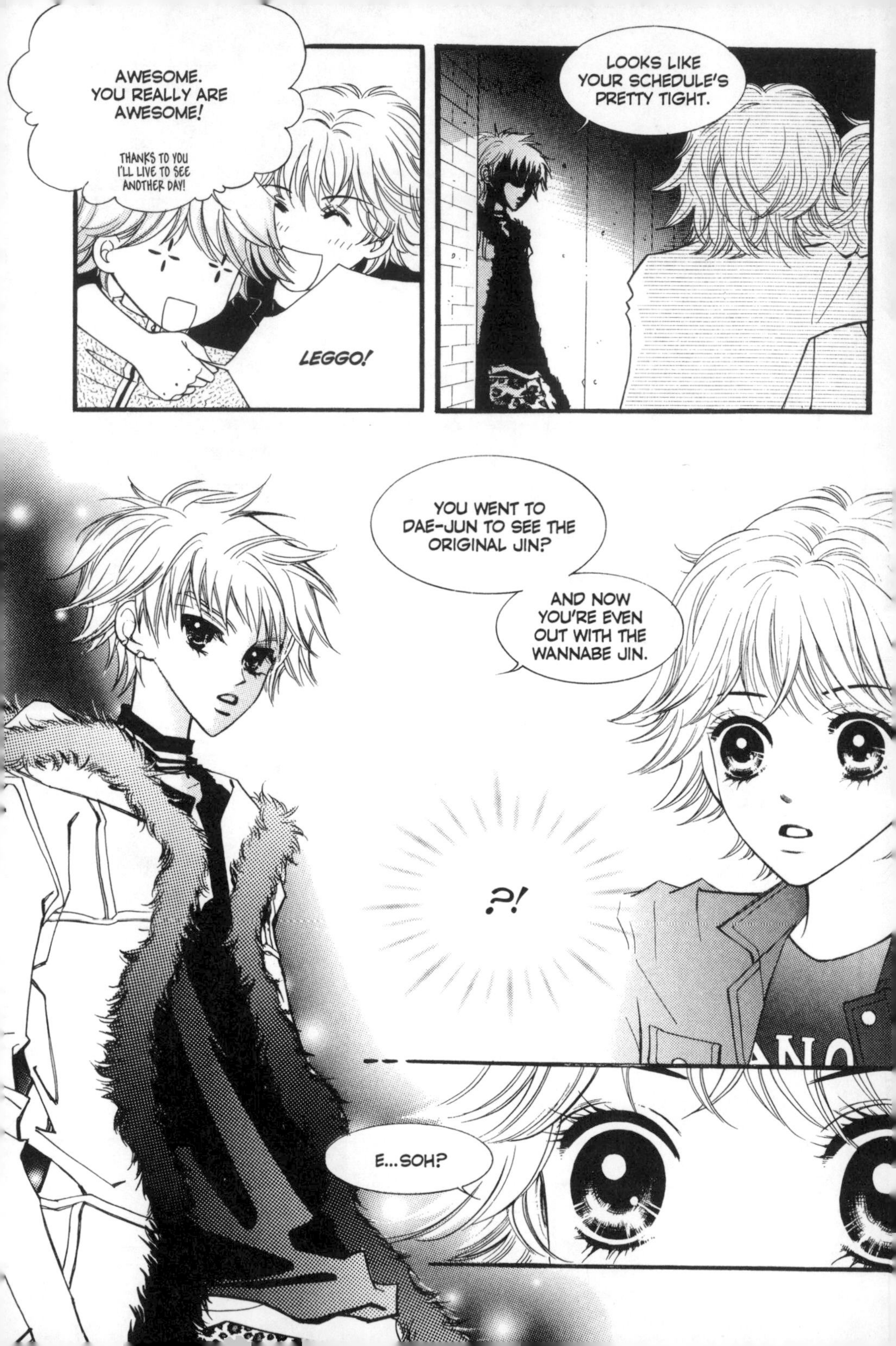

AWESOME. YOU REALLY ARE AWESOME!
THANKS TO YOU I'LL LIVE TO SEE ANOTHER DAY!
LEGGO!
LOOKS LIKE YOUR SCHEDULE'S PRETTY TIGHT.
YOU WENT TO DAE-JUN TO SEE THE ORIGINAL JIN?
AND NOW YOU'RE EVEN OUT WITH THE WANNABE JIN.
?!
E...SOH?

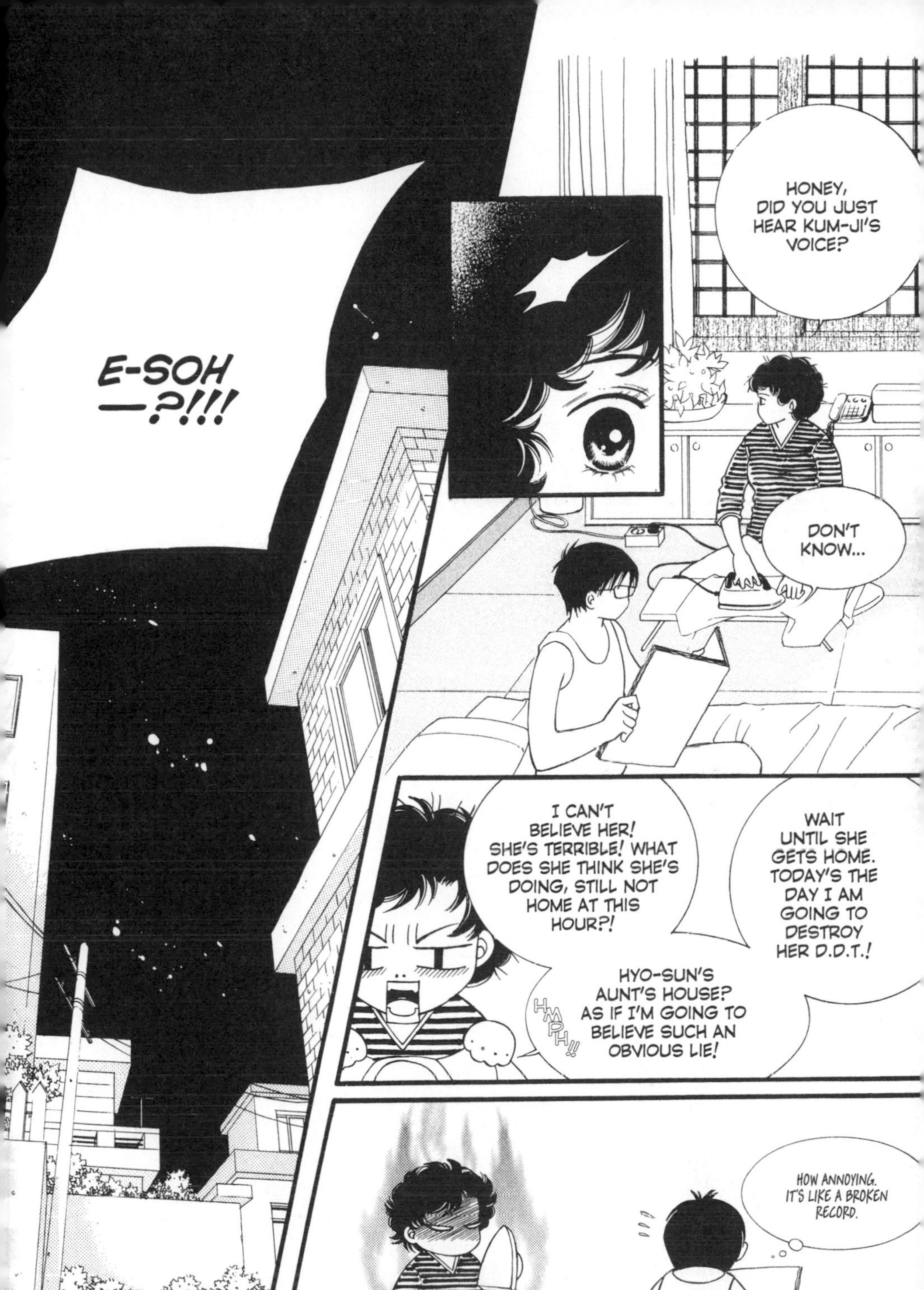
E-SOH —?!!!
HONEY, DID YOU JUST HEAR KUM-JI'S VOICE?
DON'T KNOW...
I CAN'T BELIEVE HER! SHE'S TERRIBLE! WHAT DOES SHE THINK SHE'S DOING, STILL NOT HOME AT THIS HOUR?!
WAIT UNTIL SHE GETS HOME. TODAY'S THE DAY I AM GOING TO DESTROY HER D.D.T.!
HMPH!!
HYO-SUN'S AUNT'S HOUSE? AS IF I'M GOING TO BELIEVE SUCH AN OBVIOUS LIE!
HOW ANNOYING. IT'S LIKE A BROKEN RECORD.

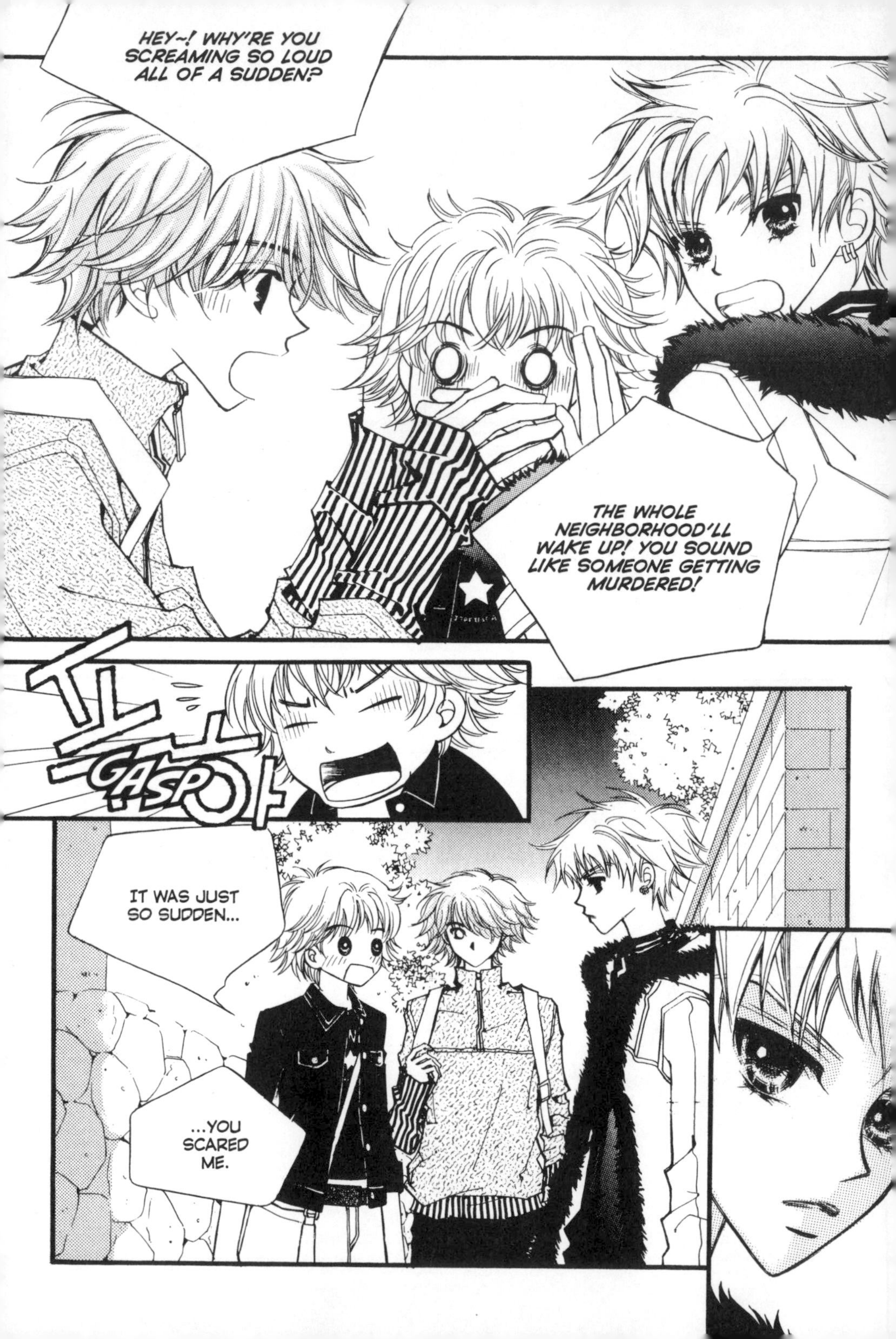
HEY~! WHY'RE YOU SCREAMING SO LOUD ALL OF A SUDDEN?
THE WHOLE NEIGHBORHOOD'LL WAKE UP! YOU SOUND LIKE SOMEONE GETTING MURDERED!
GASP
IT WAS JUST SO SUDDEN...
...YOU SCARED ME.

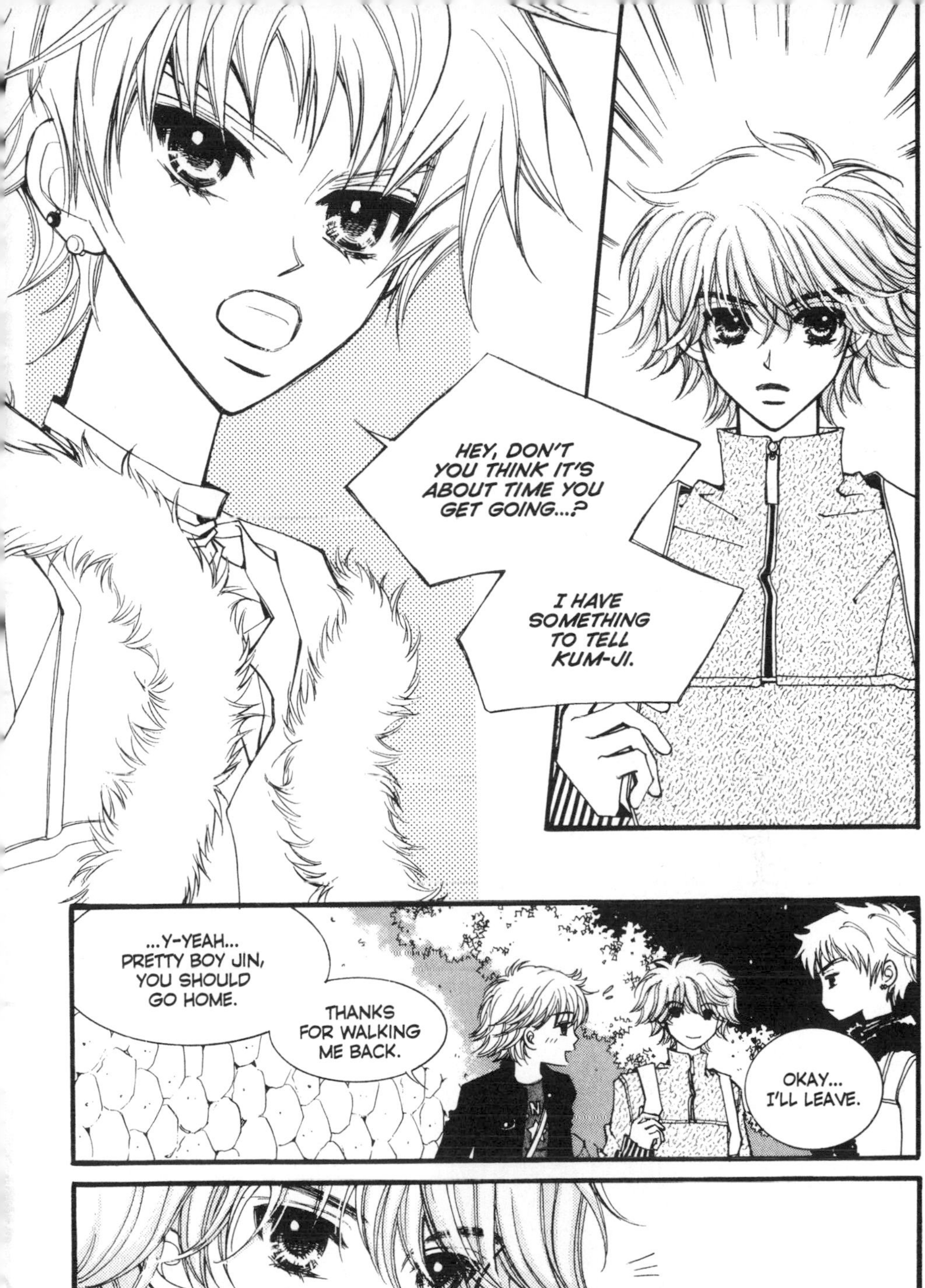
HEY, DON'T YOU THINK IT'S ABOUT TIME YOU GET GOING...?
I HAVE SOMETHING TO TELL KUM-JI.
...Y-YEAH... PRETTY BOY JIN, YOU SHOULD GO HOME.
THANKS FOR WALKING ME BACK.
OKAY... I'LL LEAVE.

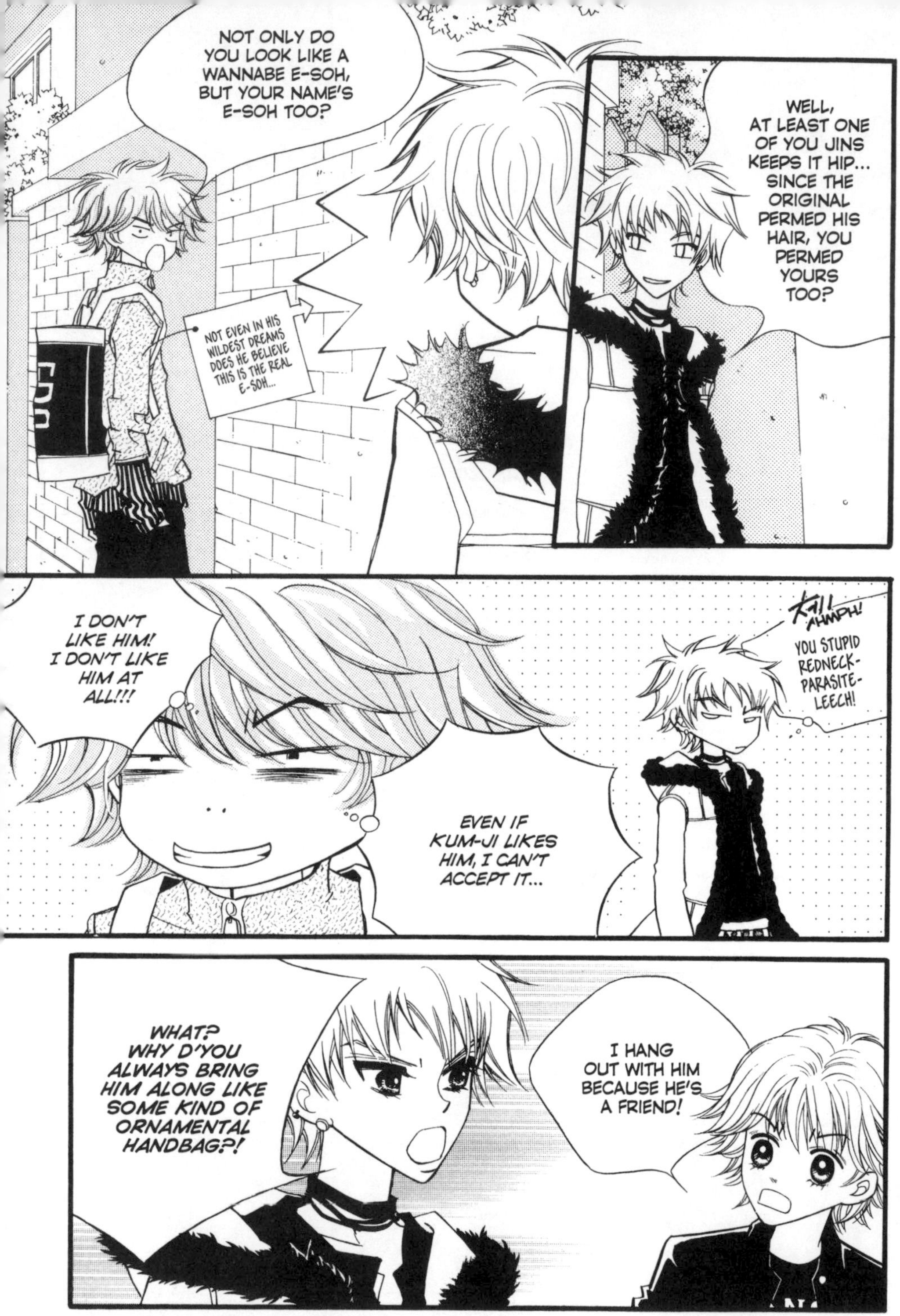
NOT ONLY DO YOU LOOK LIKE A WANNABE E-SOH, BUT YOUR NAME'S E-SOH TOO?
NOT EVEN IN HIS WILDEST DREAMS DOES HE BELIEVE THIS IS THE REAL E-SOH...
WELL, AT LEAST ONE OF YOU JINS KEEPS IT HIP... SINCE THE ORIGINAL PERMED HIS HAIR, YOU PERMED YOURS TOO?
I DON'T LIKE HIM! I DON'T LIKE HIM AT ALL!!!
EVEN IF KUM-JI LIKES HIM, I CAN'T ACCEPT IT...
AHMPH!
YOU STUPID REDNECK-PARASITE-LEECH!
WHAT? WHY D'YOU ALWAYS BRING HIM ALONG LIKE SOME KIND OF ORNAMENTAL HANDBAG?!
I HANG OUT WITH HIM BECAUSE HE'S A FRIEND!

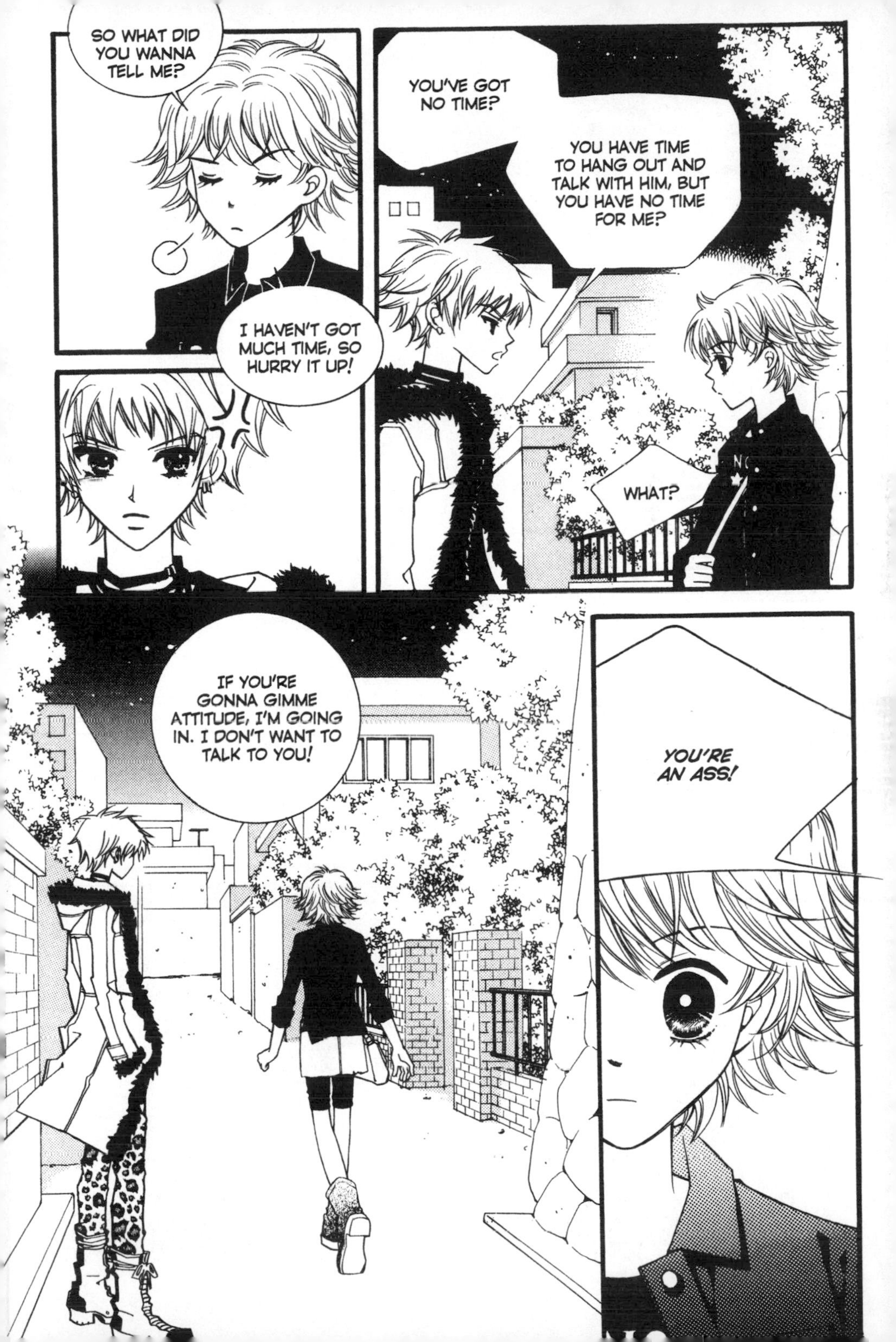
SO WHAT DID YOU WANNA TELL ME?
I HAVEN'T GOT MUCH TIME, SO HURRY IT UP!
YOU'VE GOT NO TIME?
YOU HAVE TIME TO HANG OUT AND TALK WITH HIM, BUT YOU HAVE NO TIME FOR ME?
WHAT?
IF YOU'RE GONNA GIMME ATTITUDE, I'M GOING IN. I DON'T WANT TO TALK TO YOU!
YOU'RE AN ASS!

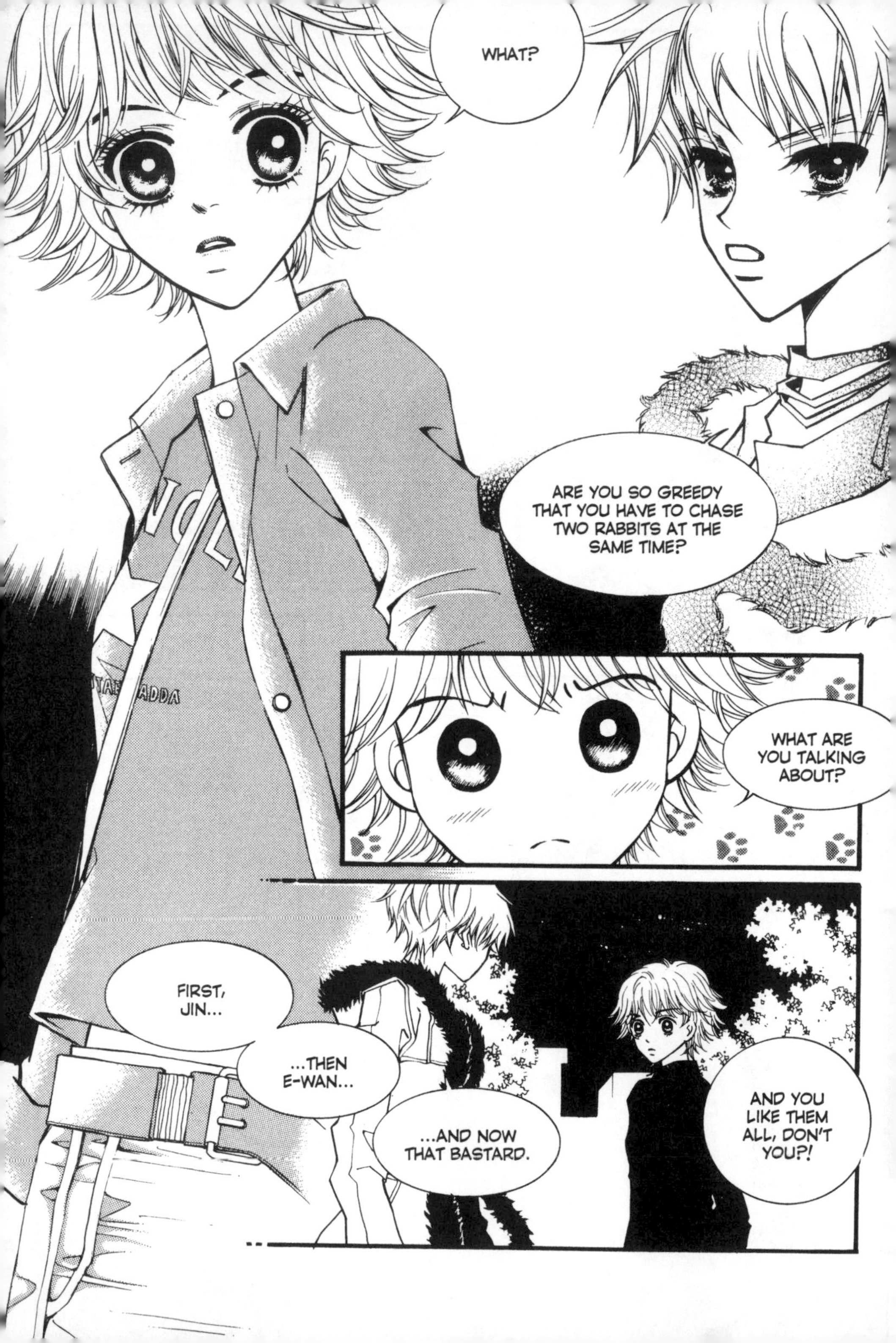
WHAT?
ARE YOU SO GREEDY THAT YOU HAVE TO CHASE TWO RABBITS AT THE SAME TIME?
WHAT ARE YOU TALKING ABOUT?
FIRST, JIN...
...THEN E-WAN...
...AND NOW THAT BASTARD.
AND YOU LIKE THEM ALL, DON'T YOU?!

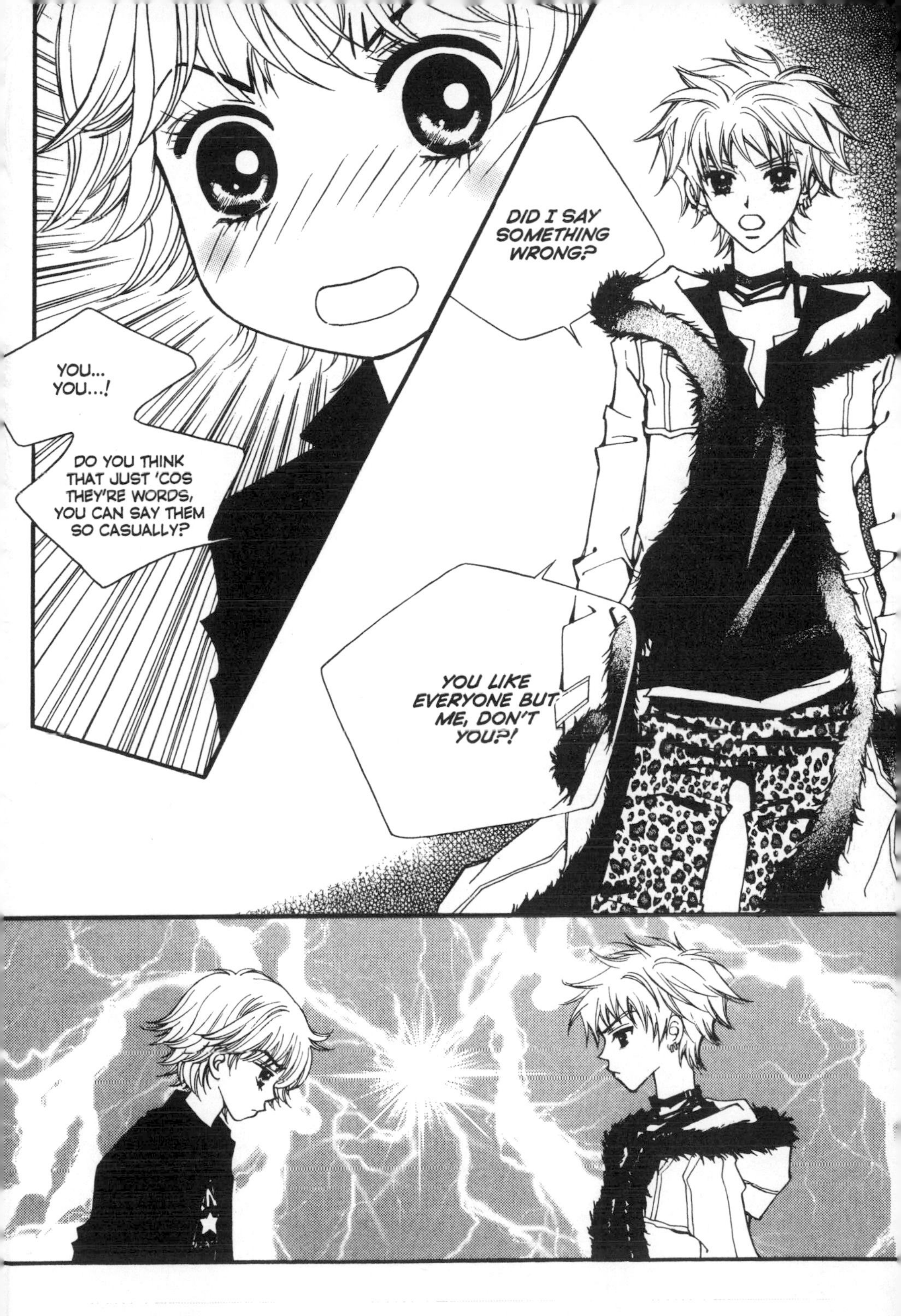
YOU... YOU...!
DO YOU THINK THAT JUST 'COS THEY'RE WORDS, YOU CAN SAY THEM SO CASUALLY?
DID I SAY SOMETHING WRONG?
YOU LIKE EVERYONE BUT ME, DON'T YOU?!

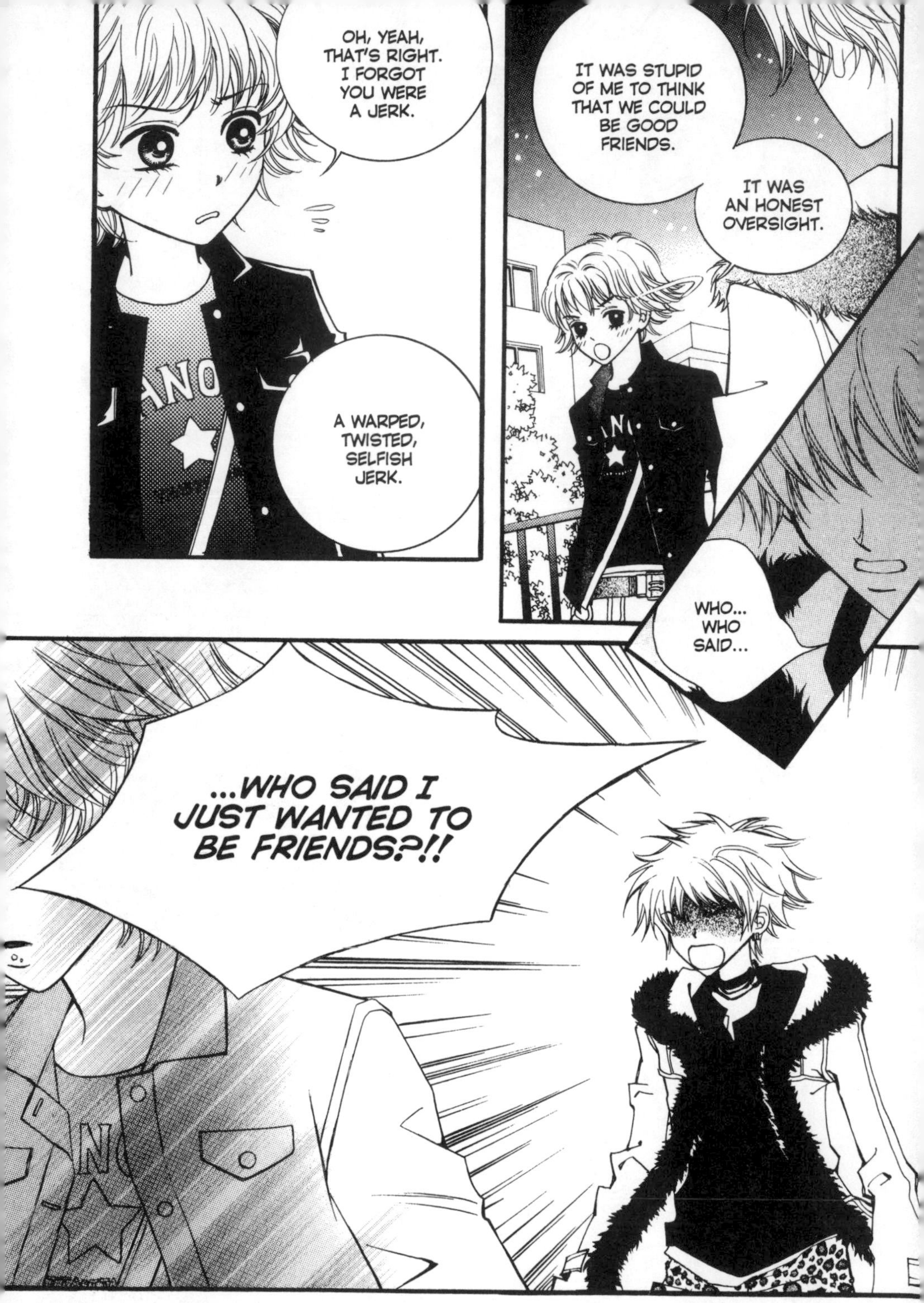
OH, YEAH, THAT'S RIGHT. I FORGOT YOU WERE A JERK.
A WARPED, TWISTED, SELFISH JERK.
IT WAS STUPID OF ME TO THINK THAT WE COULD BE GOOD FRIENDS.
IT WAS AN HONEST OVERSIGHT.
WHO... WHO SAID...
...WHO SAID I JUST WANTED TO BE FRIENDS?!!

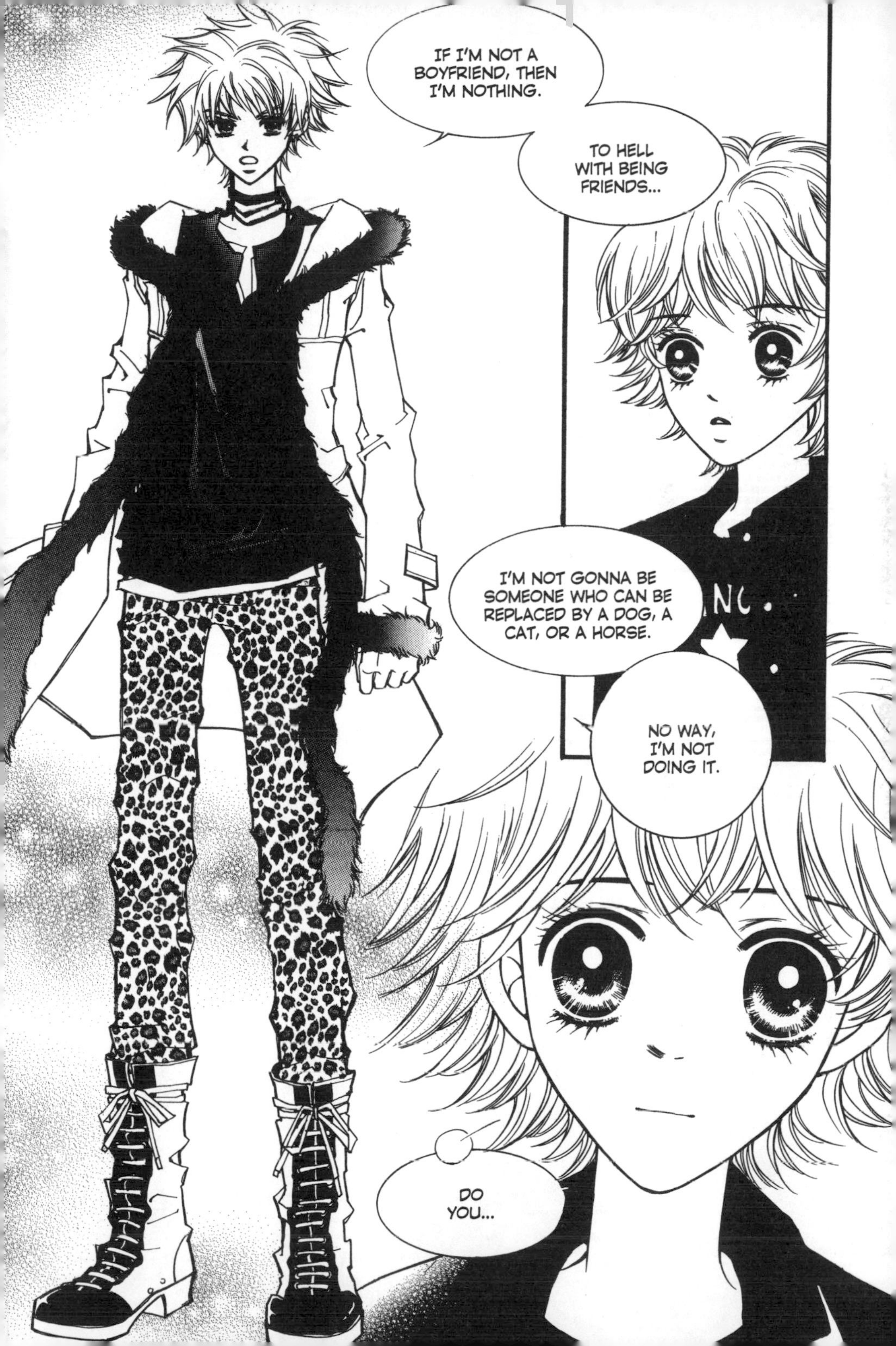
IF I'M NOT A BOYFRIEND, THEN I'M NOTHING.
TO HELL WITH BEING FRIENDS...
I'M NOT GONNA BE SOMEONE WHO CAN BE REPLACED BY A DOG, A CAT, OR A HORSE.
NO WAY, I'M NOT DOING IT.
DO YOU...

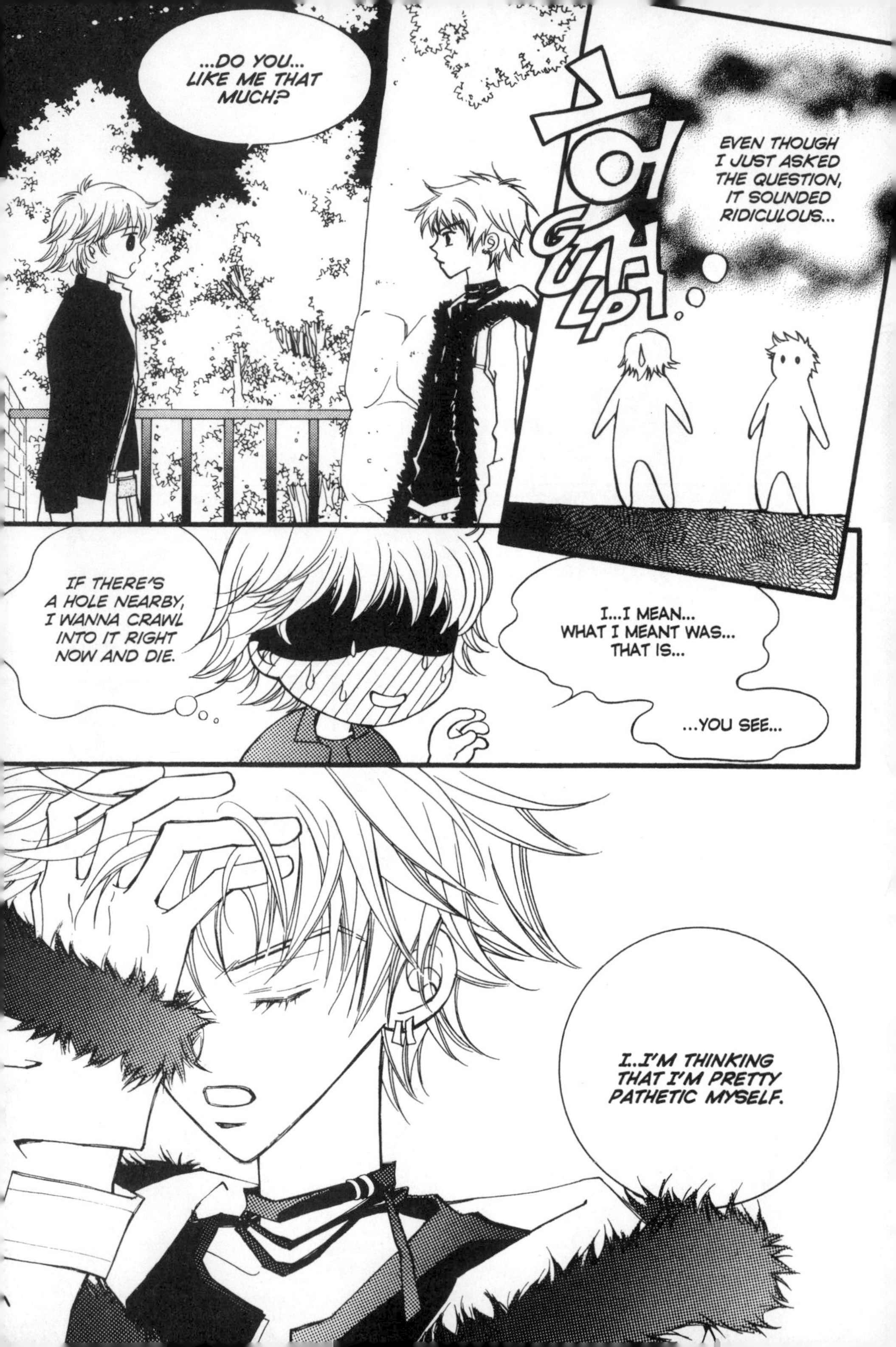
...DO YOU... LIKE ME THAT MUCH?
GULP!
EVEN THOUGH I JUST ASKED THE QUESTION, IT SOUNDED RIDICULOUS...
IF THERE'S A HOLE NEARBY, I WANNA CRAWL INTO IT RIGHT NOW AND DIE.
I...I MEAN... WHAT I MEANT WAS... THAT IS...
...YOU SEE...
I..I'M THINKING THAT I'M PRETTY PATHETIC MYSELF.

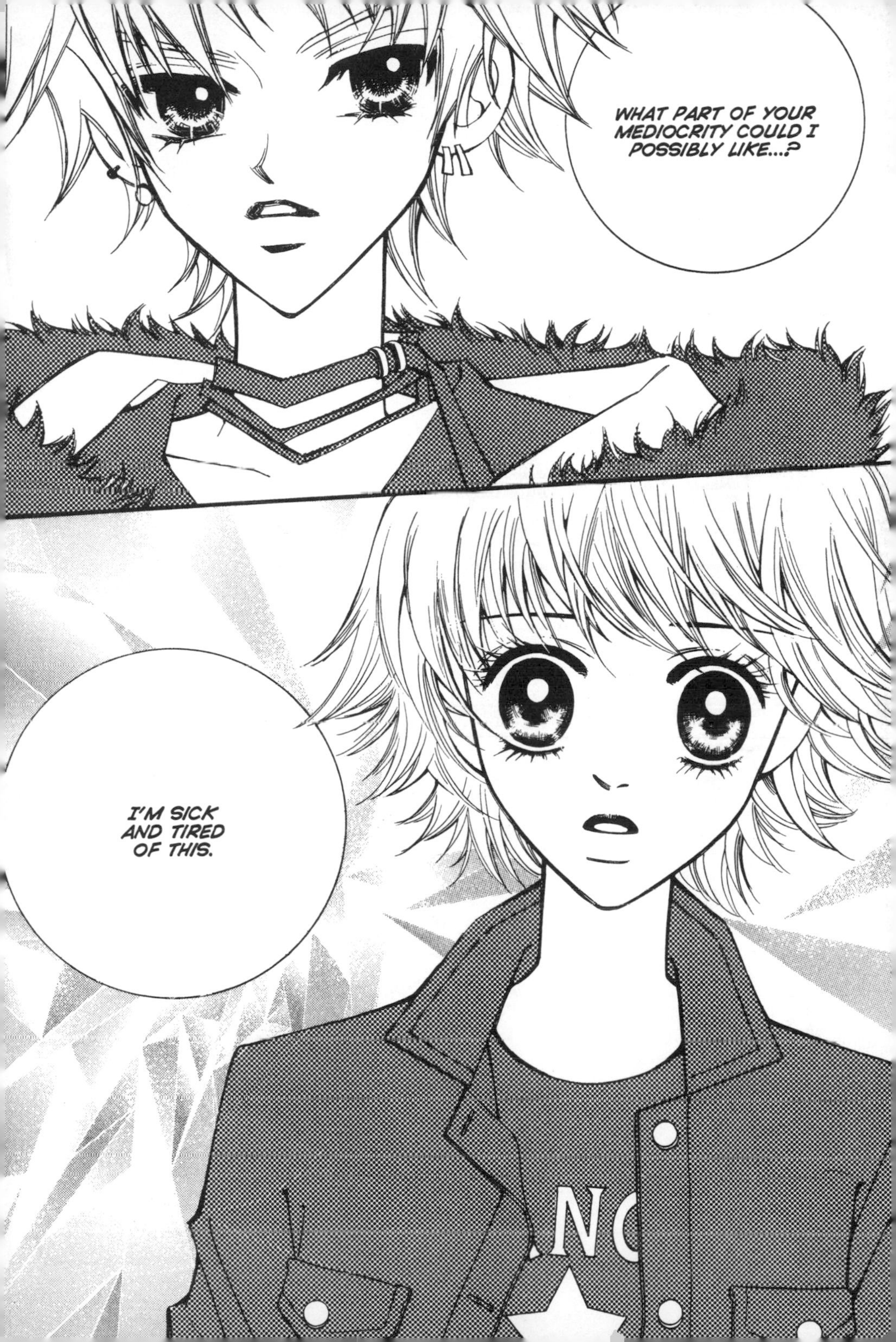
WHAT PART OF YOUR MEDIOCRITY COULD I POSSIBLY LIKE...?
I'M SICK AND TIRED OF THIS.

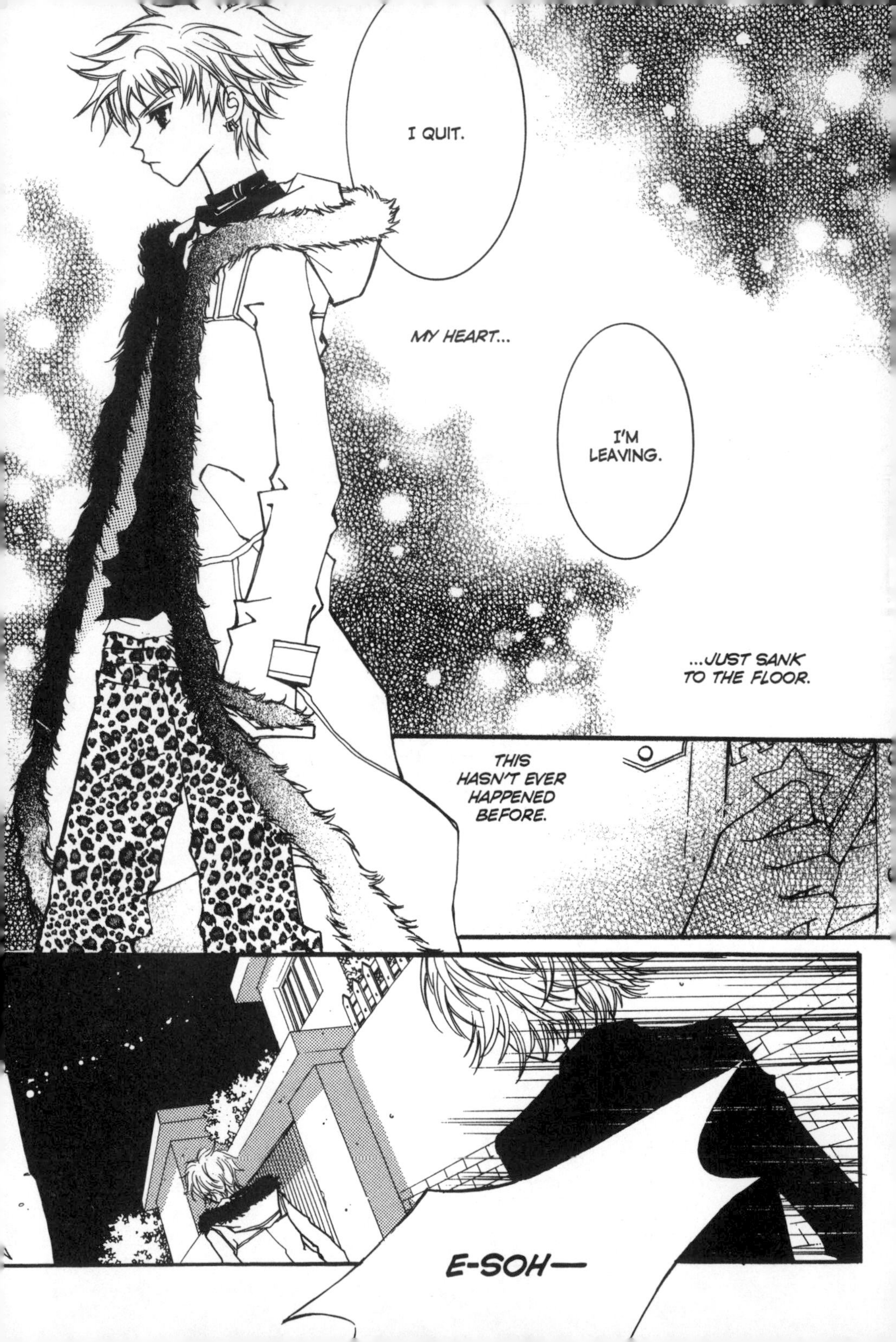
I QUIT.
MY HEART...
I'M LEAVING.
...JUST SANK TO THE FLOOR.
THIS HASN'T EVER HAPPENED BEFORE.
E-SOH—

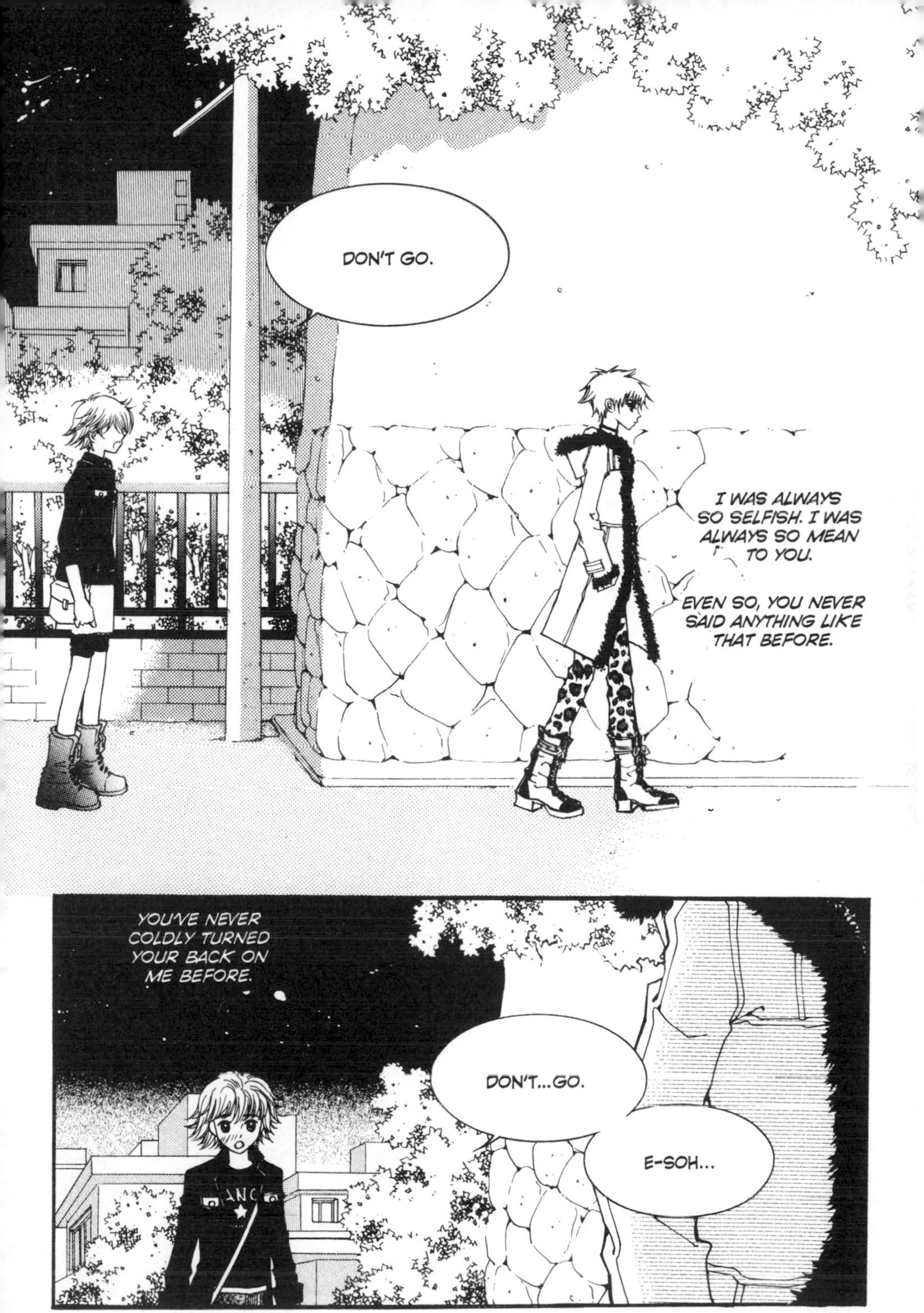
DON'T GO.
I WAS ALWAYS SO SELFISH. I WAS ALWAYS SO MEAN TO YOU.
EVEN SO, YOU NEVER SAID ANYTHING LIKE THAT BEFORE.
YOU'VE NEVER COLDLY TURNED YOUR BACK ON ME BEFORE.
DON'T...GO.
E-SOH...

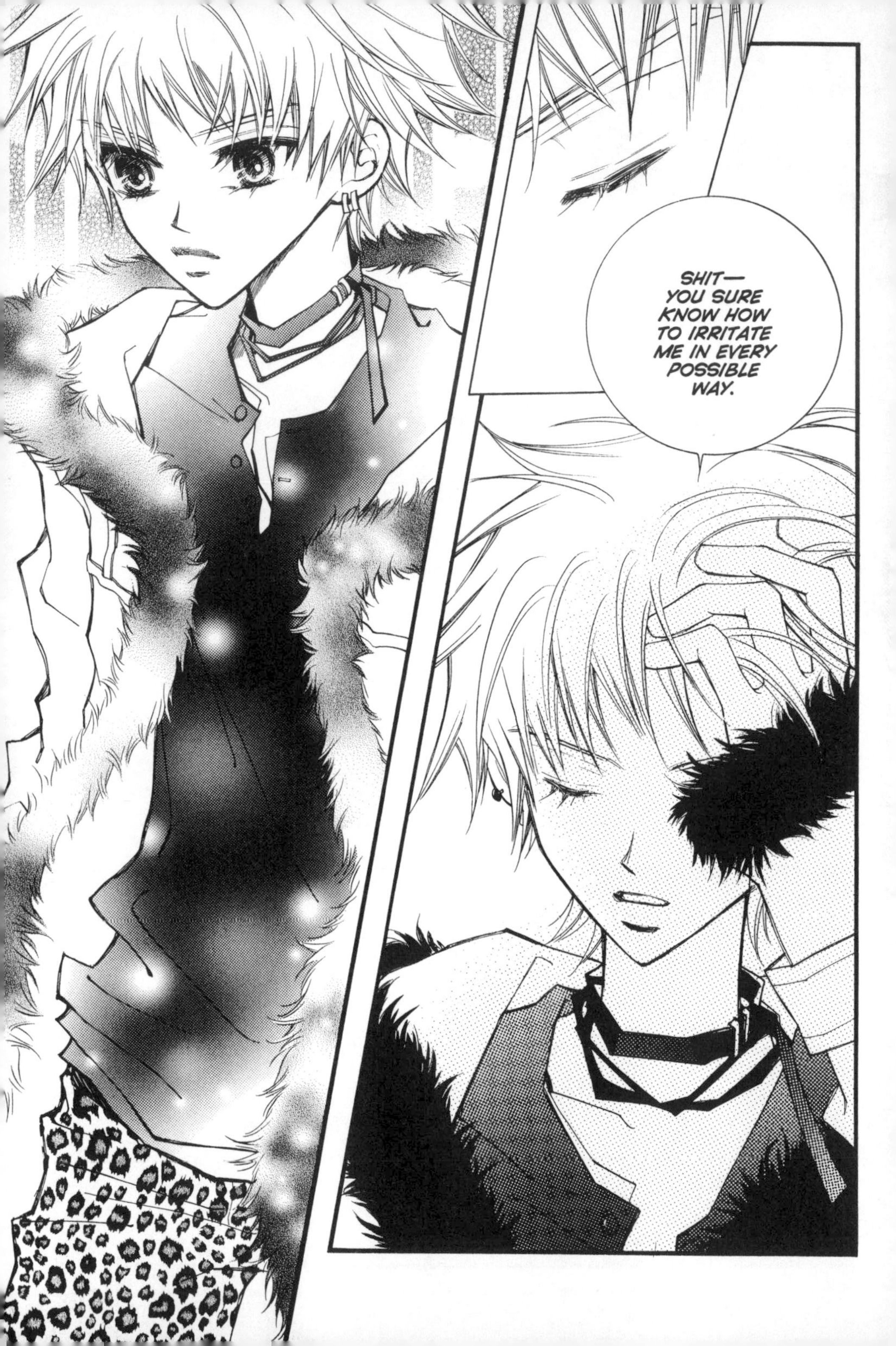
SHIT—YOU SURE KNOW HOW TO IRRITATE ME IN EVERY POSSIBLE WAY.

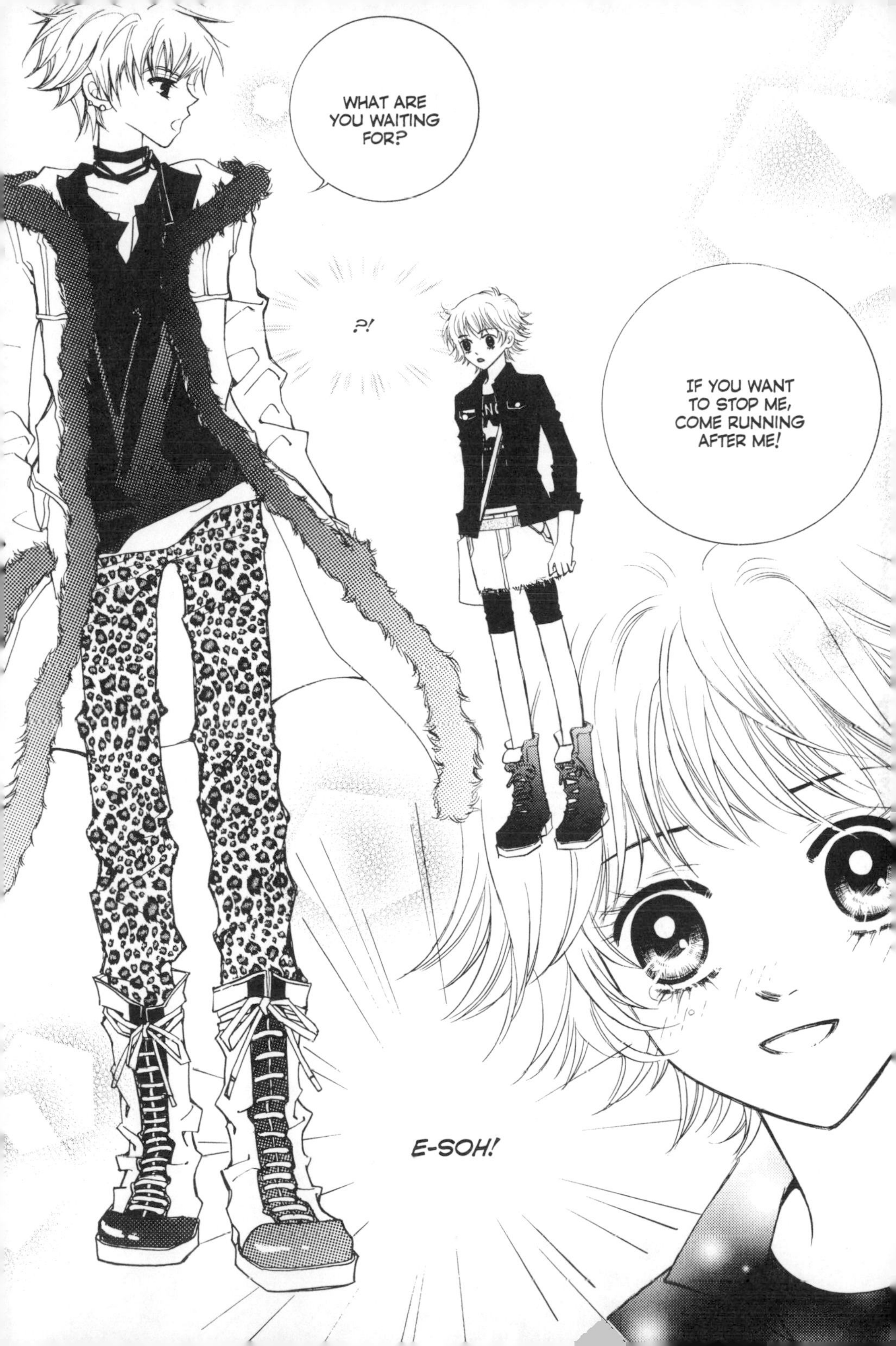

WHAT ARE YOU WAITING FOR?
?!
IF YOU WANT TO STOP ME, COME RUNNING AFTER ME!
E-SOH!

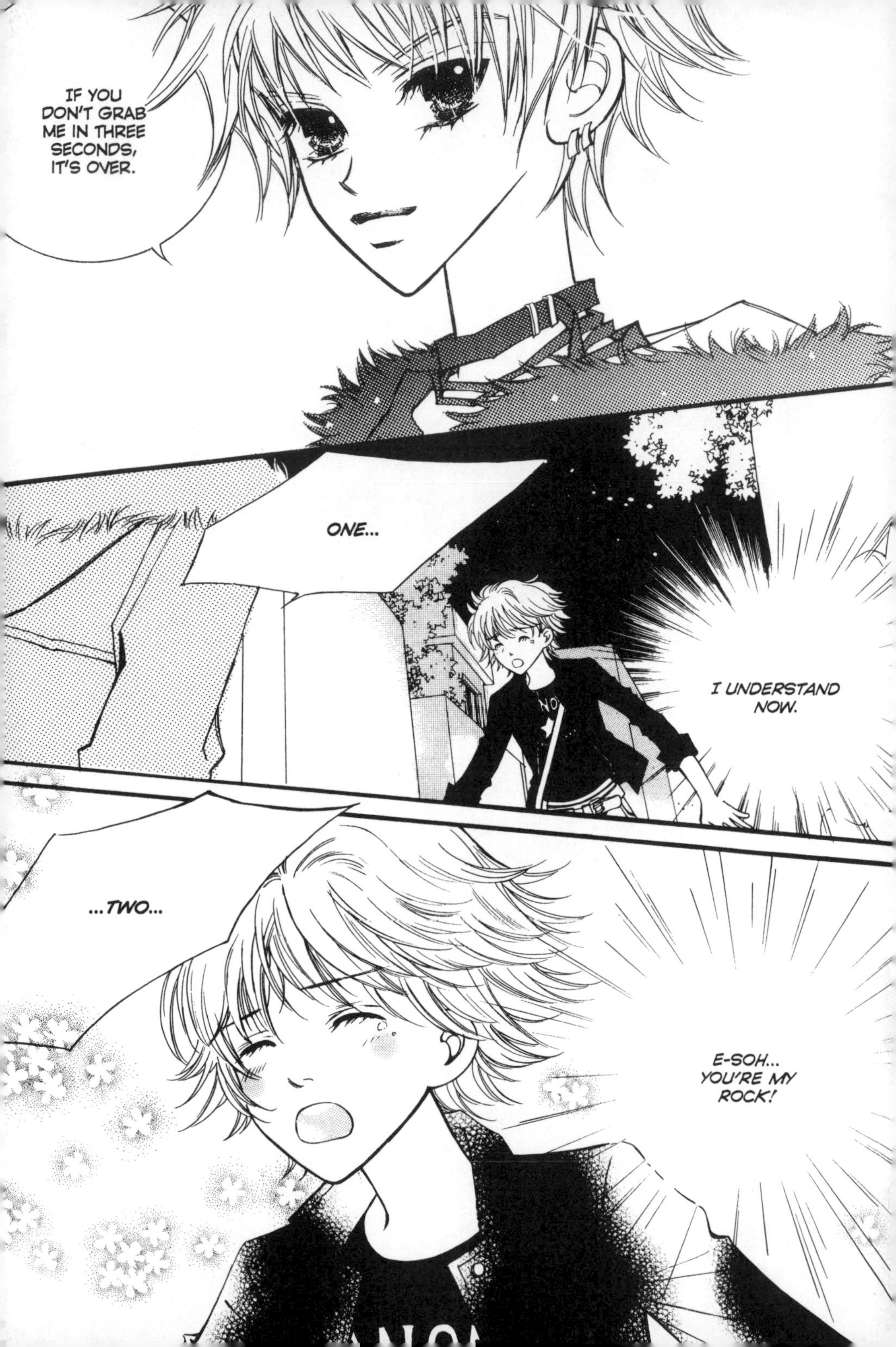
IF YOU DON'T GRAB ME IN THREE SECONDS, IT'S OVER.
ONE...
I UNDERSTAND NOW.
...TWO...
E-SOH... YOU'RE MY ROCK!

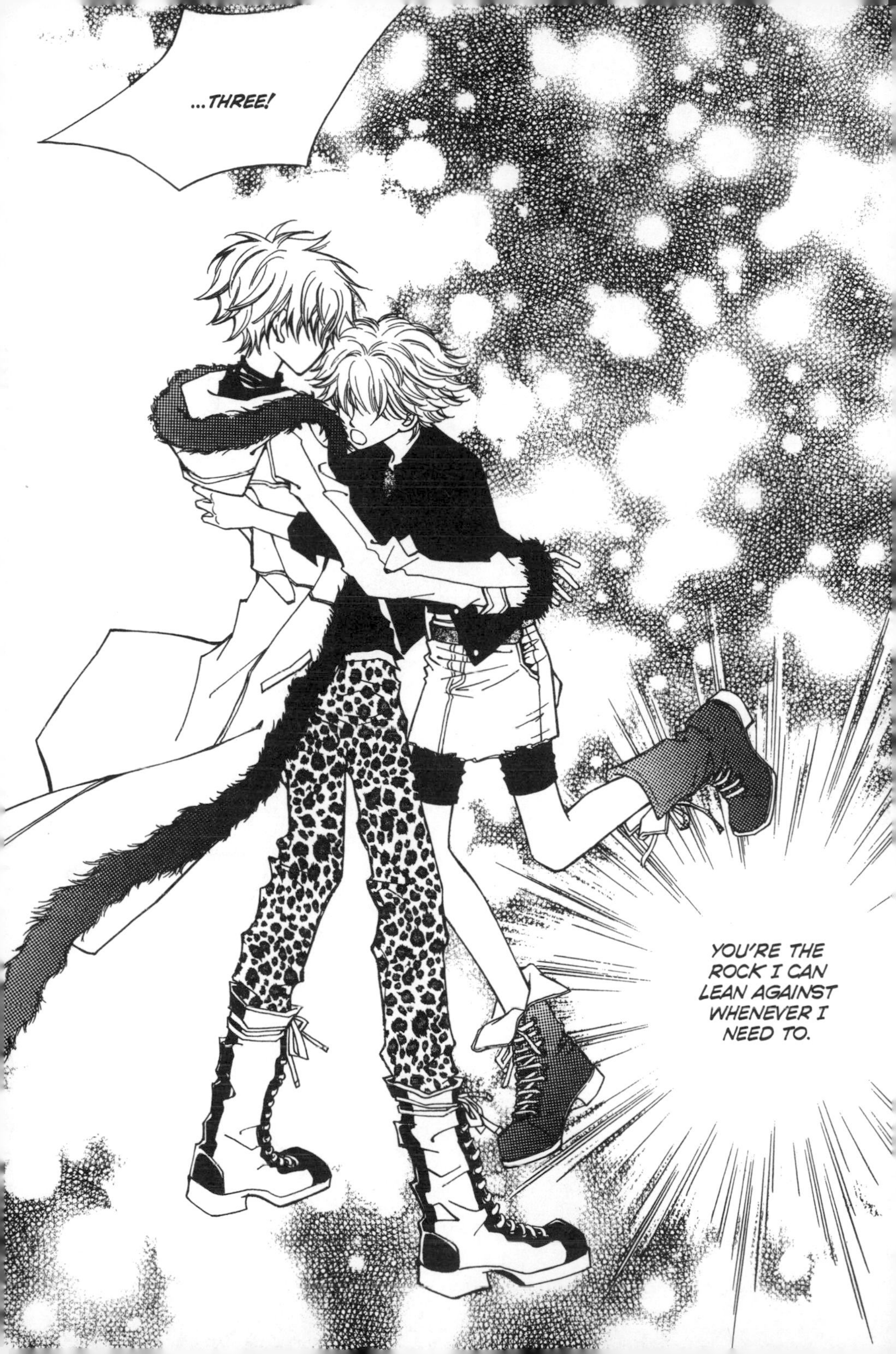
...THREE!
YOU'RE THE ROCK I CAN LEAN AGAINST WHENEVER I NEED TO.

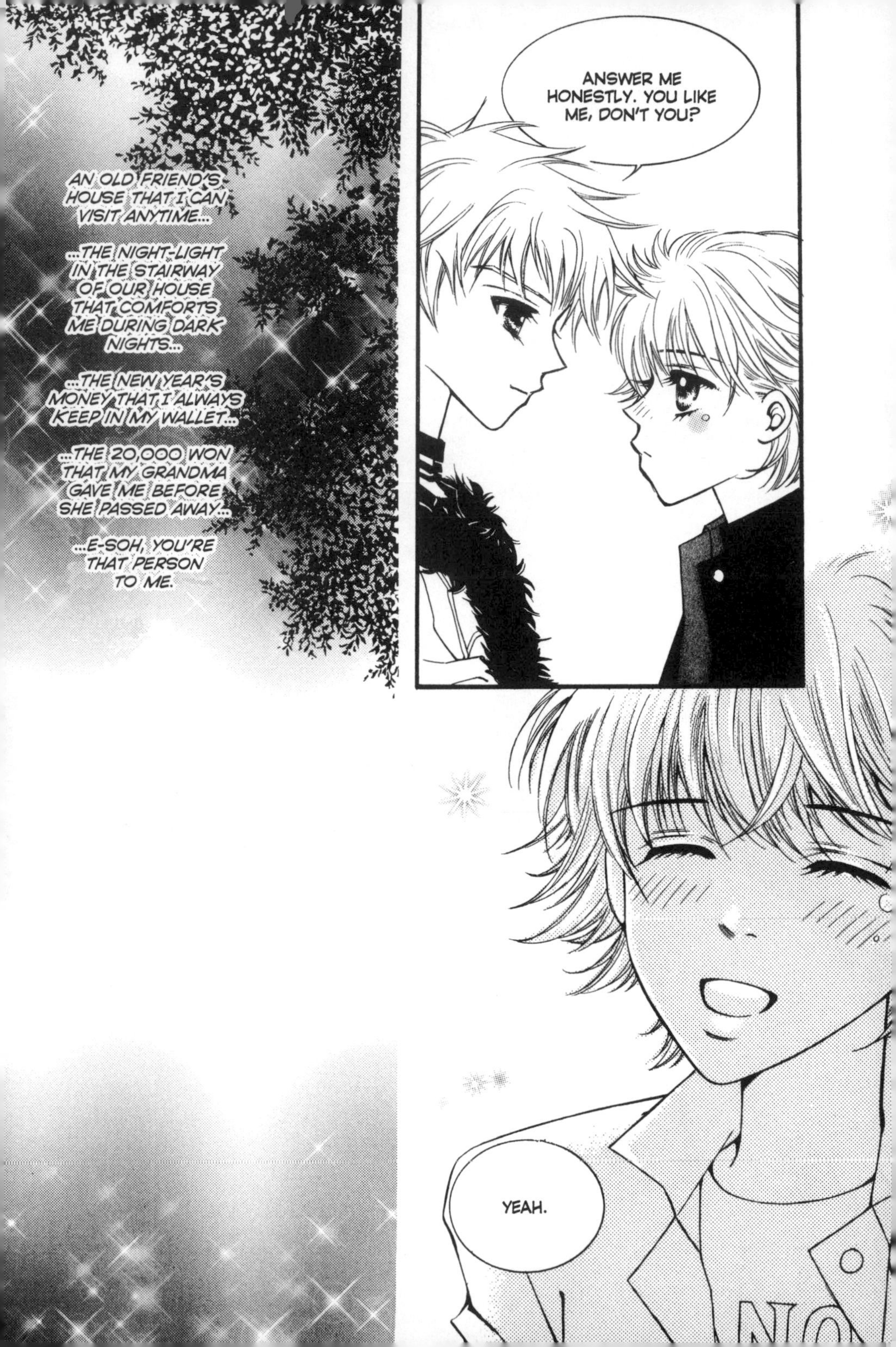
AN OLD FRIEND'S HOUSE THAT I CAN VISIT ANYTIME...
...THE NIGHT-LIGHT IN THE STAIRWAY OF OUR HOUSE THAT COMFORTS ME DURING DARK NIGHTS...
...THE NEW YEAR'S MONEY THAT I ALWAYS KEEP IN MY WALLET...
...THE 20,000 WON THAT MY GRANDMA GAVE ME BEFORE SHE PASSED AWAY...
...E-SOH, YOU'RE THAT PERSON TO ME.
ANSWER ME HONESTLY. YOU LIKE ME, DON'T YOU?
YEAH.

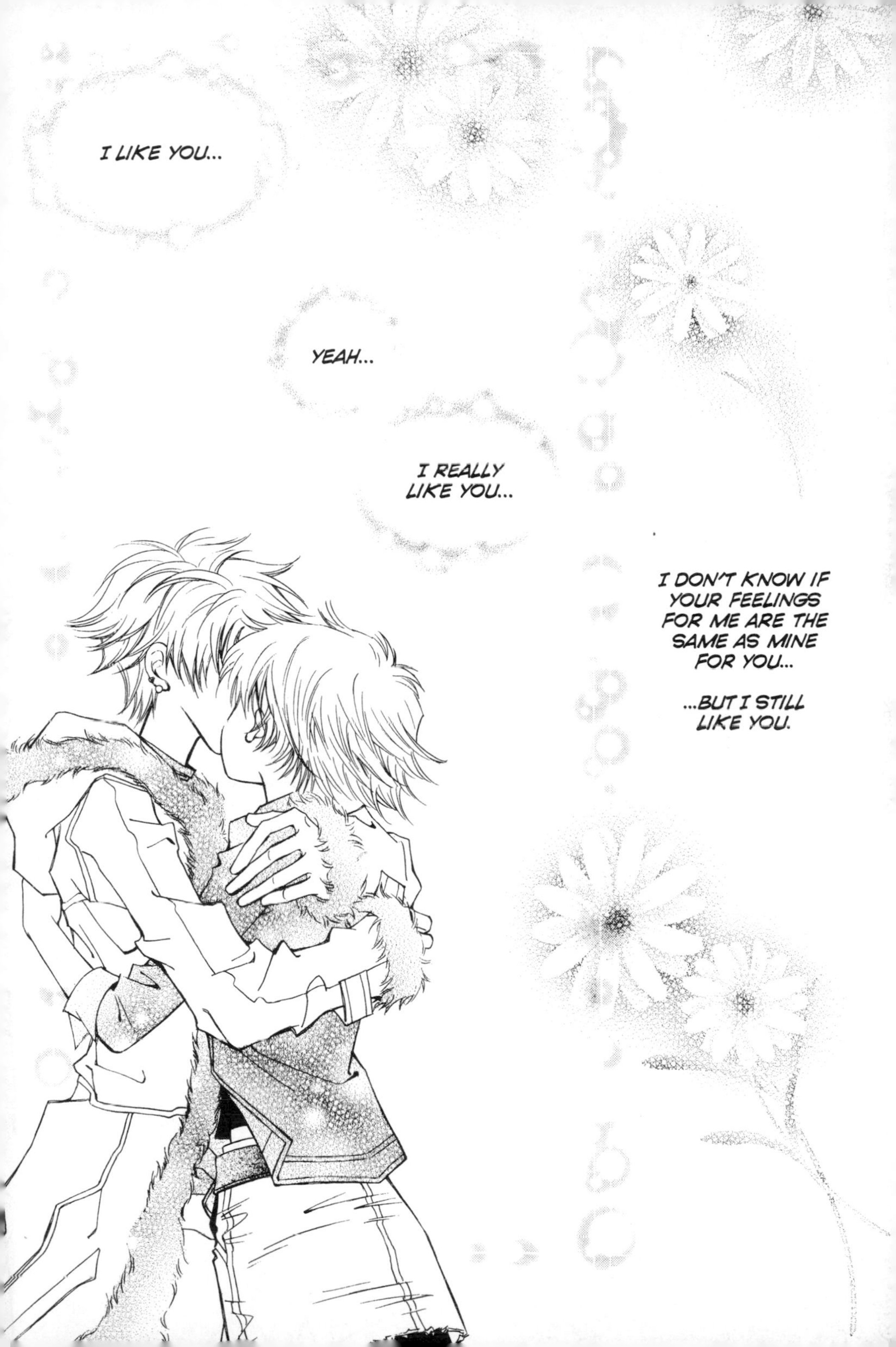
I LIKE YOU...
YEAH...
I REALLY LIKE YOU...
I DON'T KNOW IF YOUR FEELINGS FOR ME ARE THE SAME AS MINE FOR YOU...
...BUT I STILL LIKE YOU.

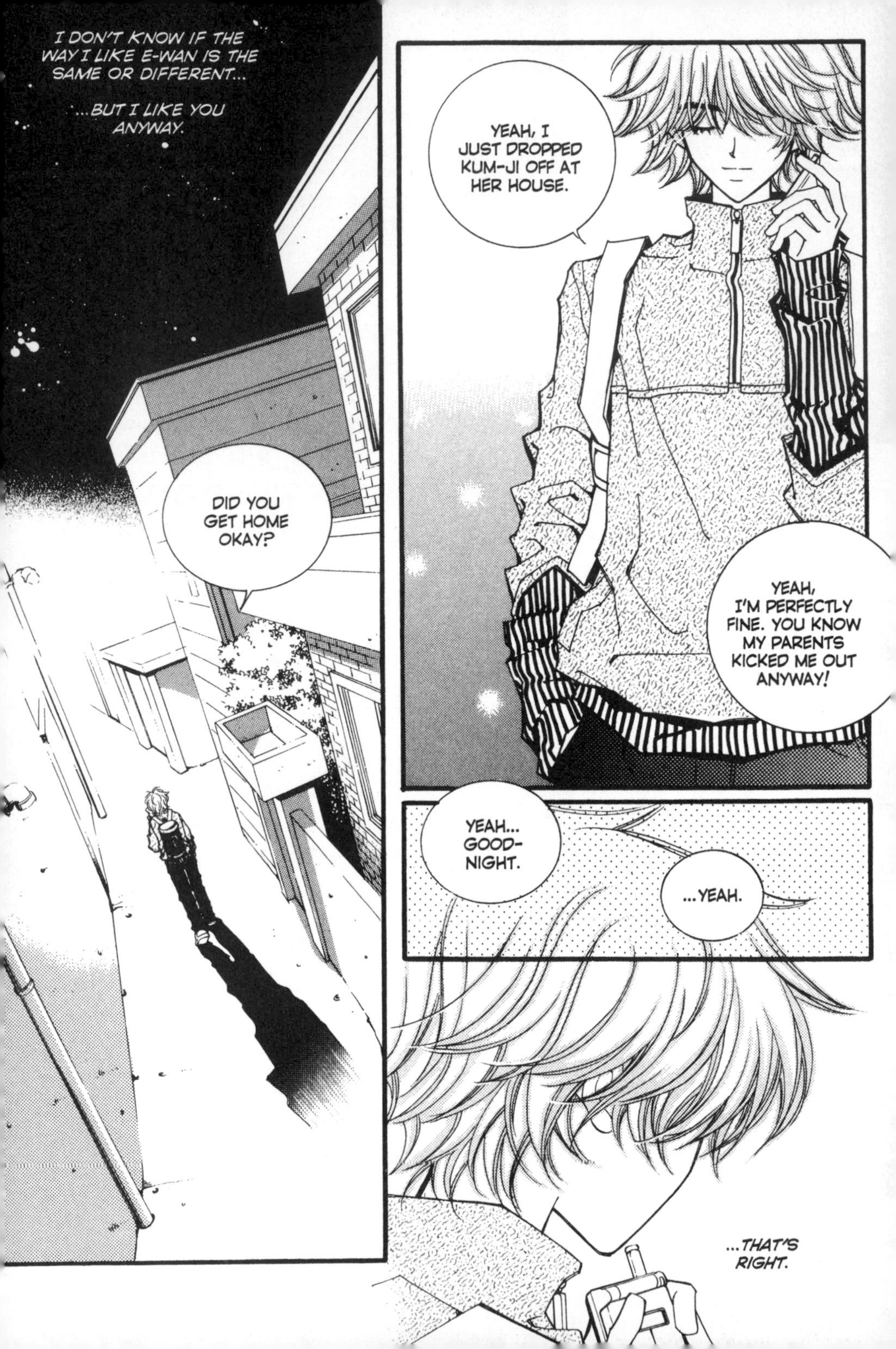
I DON'T KNOW IF THE WAY I LIKE E-WAN IS THE SAME OR DIFFERENT...
...BUT I LIKE YOU ANYWAY.
DID YOU GET HOME OKAY?
YEAH, I JUST DROPPED KUM-JI OFF AT HER HOUSE.
YEAH, I'M PERFECTLY FINE. YOU KNOW MY PARENTS KICKED ME OUT ANYWAY!
YEAH... GOOD-NIGHT.
...YEAH.
...THAT'S RIGHT.

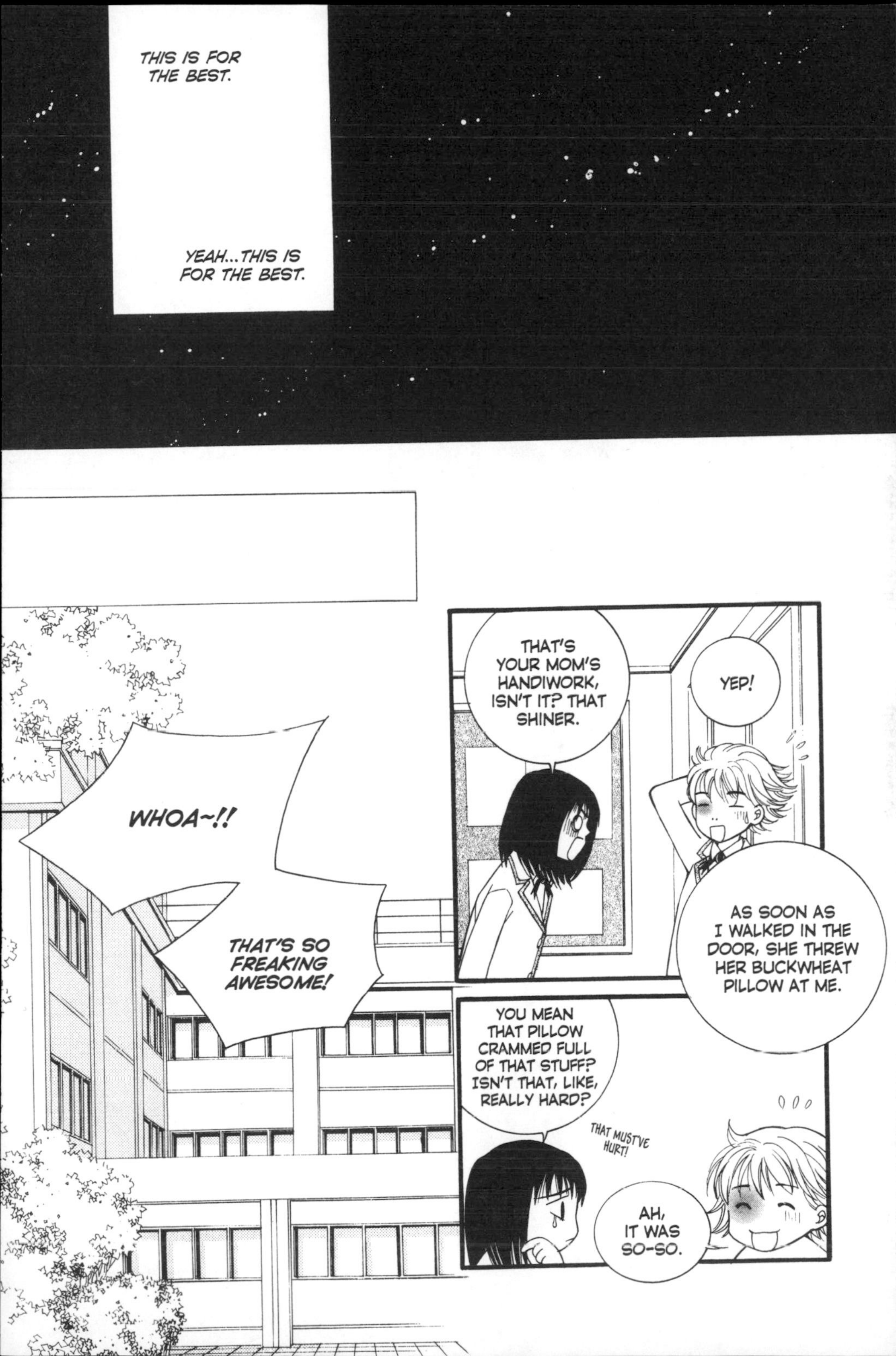
THIS IS FOR THE BEST.
YEAH...THIS IS FOR THE BEST.
WHOA~!!
THAT'S SO FREAKING AWESOME!
THAT'S YOUR MOM'S HANDIWORK, ISN'T IT? THAT SHINER.
YEP!
AS SOON AS I WALKED IN THE DOOR, SHE THREW HER BUCKWHEAT PILLOW AT ME.
YOU MEAN THAT PILLOW CRAMMED FULL OF THAT STUFF? ISN'T THAT, LIKE, REALLY HARD?
THAT MUST'VE HURT!
AH, IT WAS SO-SO.

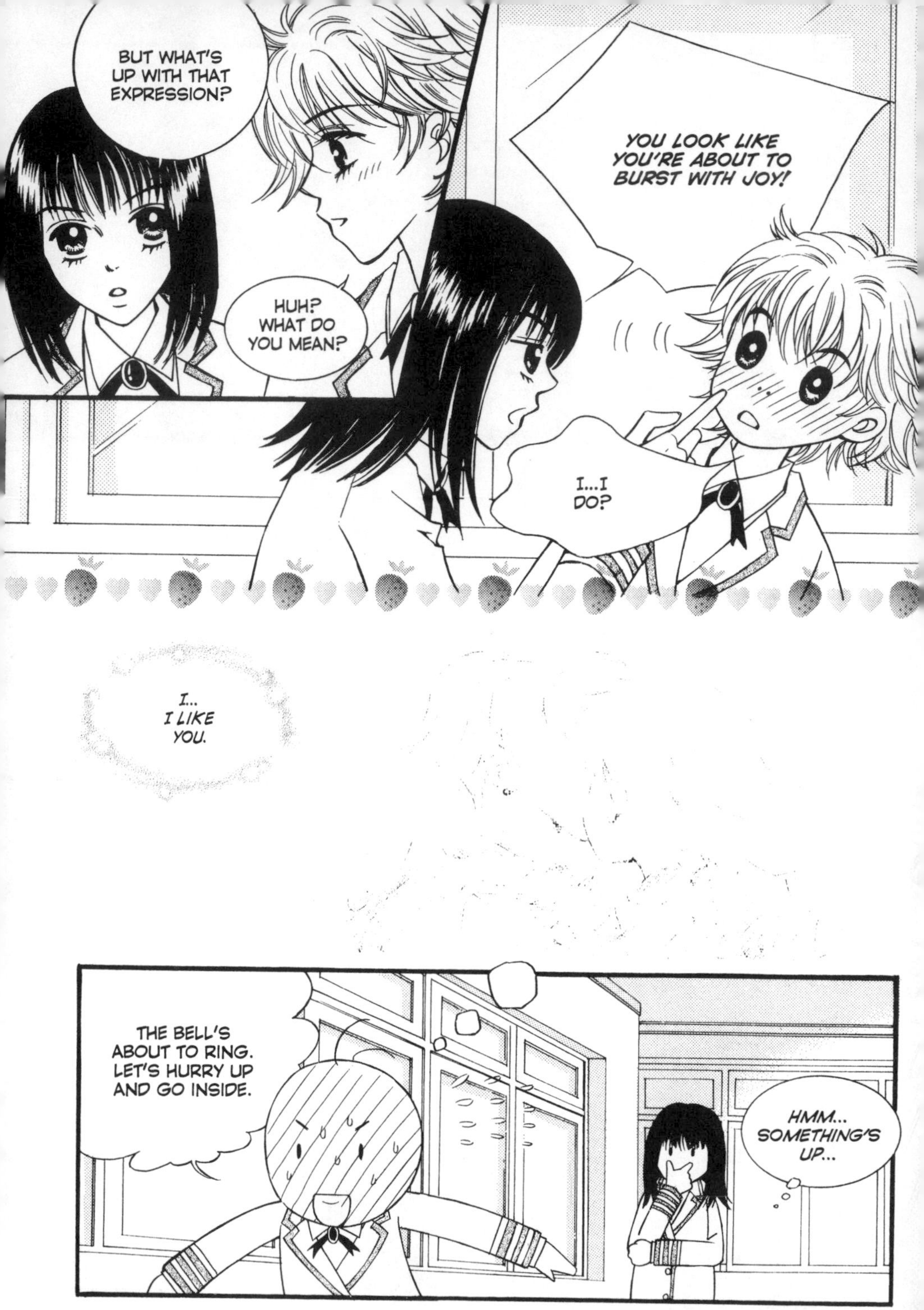

BUT WHAT'S UP WITH THAT EXPRESSION?
HUH? WHAT DO YOU MEAN?
YOU LOOK LIKE YOU'RE ABOUT TO BURST WITH JOY!
I...I DO?
I... I LIKE YOU.
THE BELL'S ABOUT TO RING. LET'S HURRY UP AND GO INSIDE.
HMM... SOMETHING'S UP...

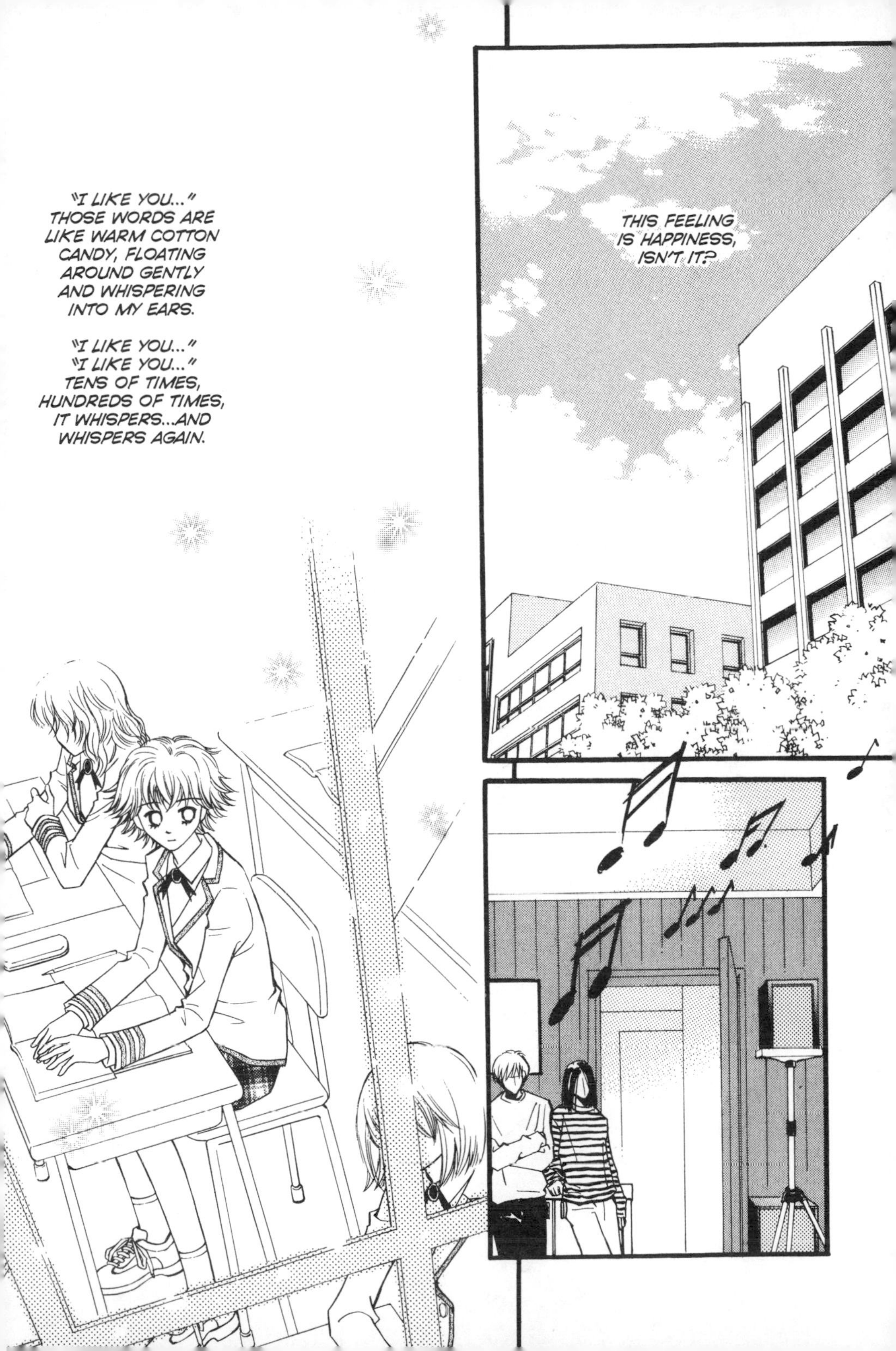
"I LIKE YOU..." THOSE WORDS ARE LIKE WARM COTTON CANDY, FLOATING AROUND GENTLY AND WHISPERING INTO MY EARS.
"I LIKE YOU..." "I LIKE YOU..." TENS OF TIMES, HUNDREDS OF TIMES, IT WHISPERS...AND WHISPERS AGAIN.
THIS FEELING IS HAPPINESS, ISN'T IT?

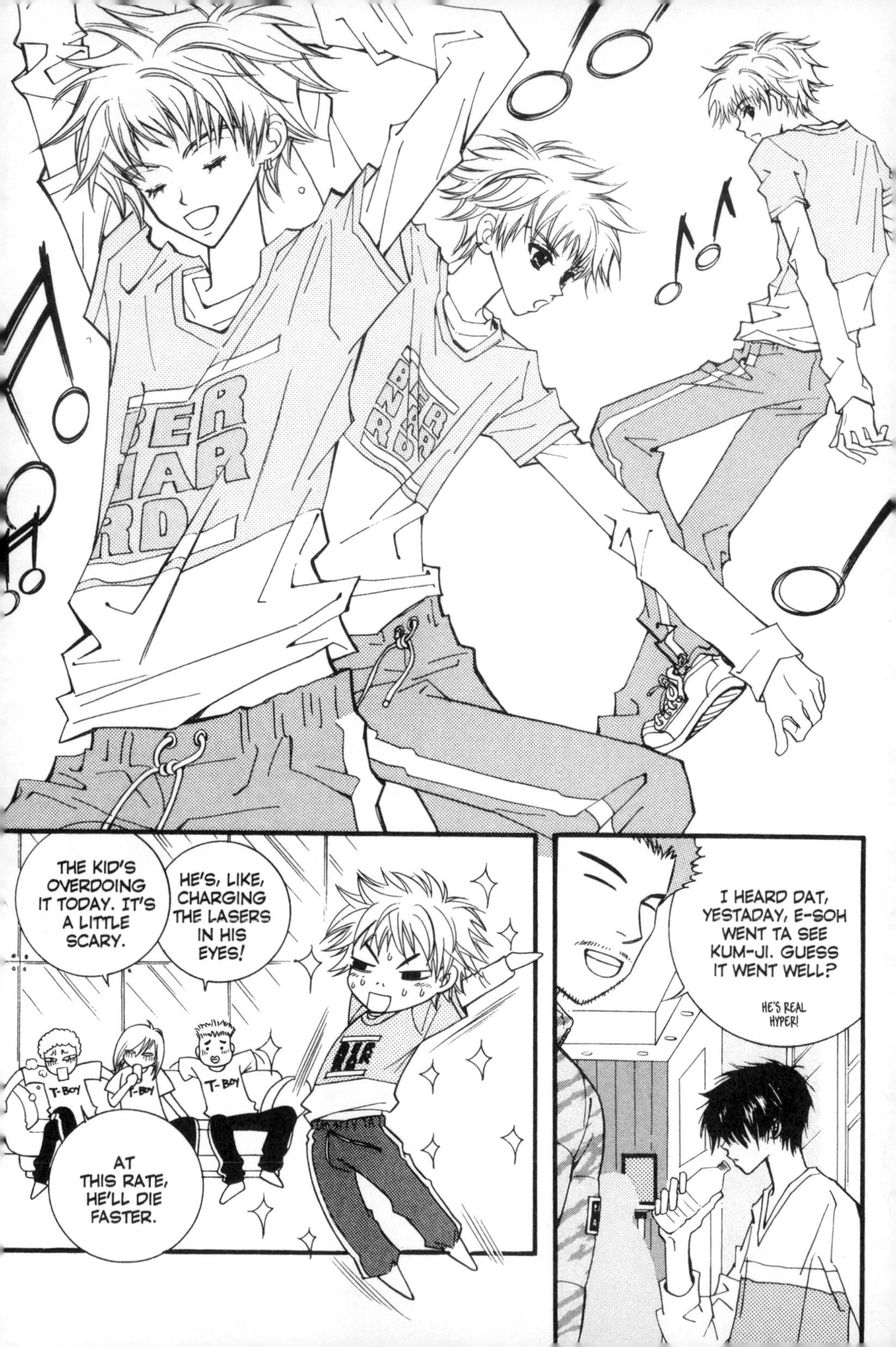

THE KID'S OVERDOING IT TODAY. IT'S A LITTLE SCARY.
HE'S, LIKE, CHARGING THE LASERS IN HIS EYES!
T-BOY
T-BOY
T-BOY
AT THIS RATE, HE'LL DIE FASTER.
I HEARD DAT, YESTADAY, E-SOH WENT TA SEE KUM-JI. GUESS IT WENT WELL?
HE'S REAL HYPER!

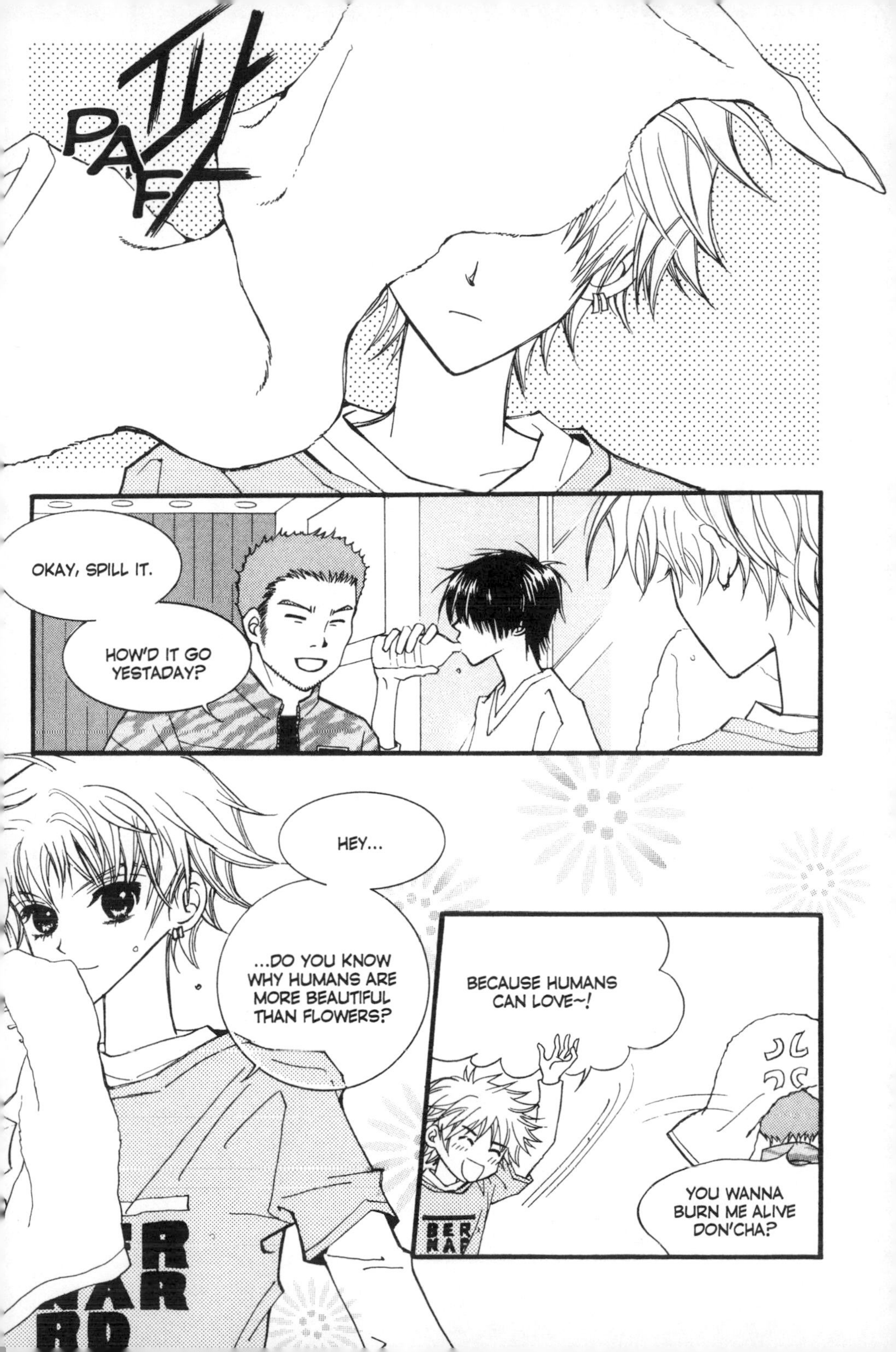
PAFF
OKAY, SPILL IT.
HOW'D IT GO YESTADAY?
HEY...
...DO YOU KNOW WHY HUMANS ARE MORE BEAUTIFUL THAN FLOWERS?
BECAUSE HUMANS CAN LOVE~!
YOU WANNA BURN ME ALIVE DON'CHA?

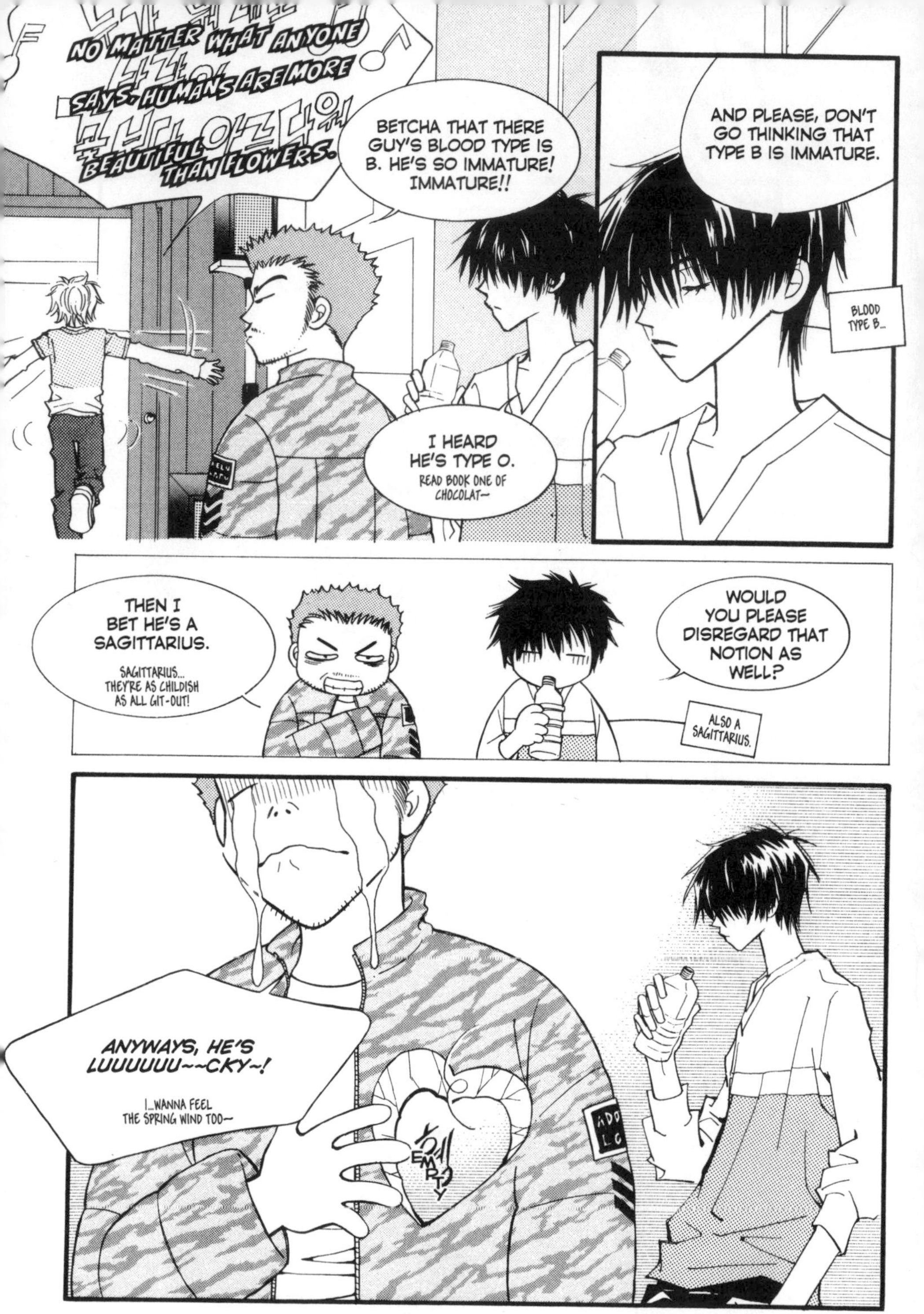
NO MATTER WHAT ANYONE SAYS, HUMANS ARE MORE BEAUTIFUL THAN FLOWERS.
BETCHA THAT THERE GUY'S BLOOD TYPE IS B. HE'S SO IMMATURE! IMMATURE!!
I HEARD HE'S TYPE O.
READ BOOK ONE OF CHOCOLAT~
AND PLEASE, DON'T GO THINKING THAT TYPE B IS IMMATURE.
BLOOD TYPE B...
THEN I BET HE'S A SAGITTARIUS.
SAGITTARIUS... THEY'RE AS CHILDISH AS ALL GIT-OUT!
WOULD YOU PLEASE DISREGARD THAT NOTION AS WELL?
ALSO A SAGITTARIUS.
ANYWAYS, HE'S LUUUUUU~~CKY~!
I...WANNA FEEL THE SPRING WIND TOO~
EMPTY

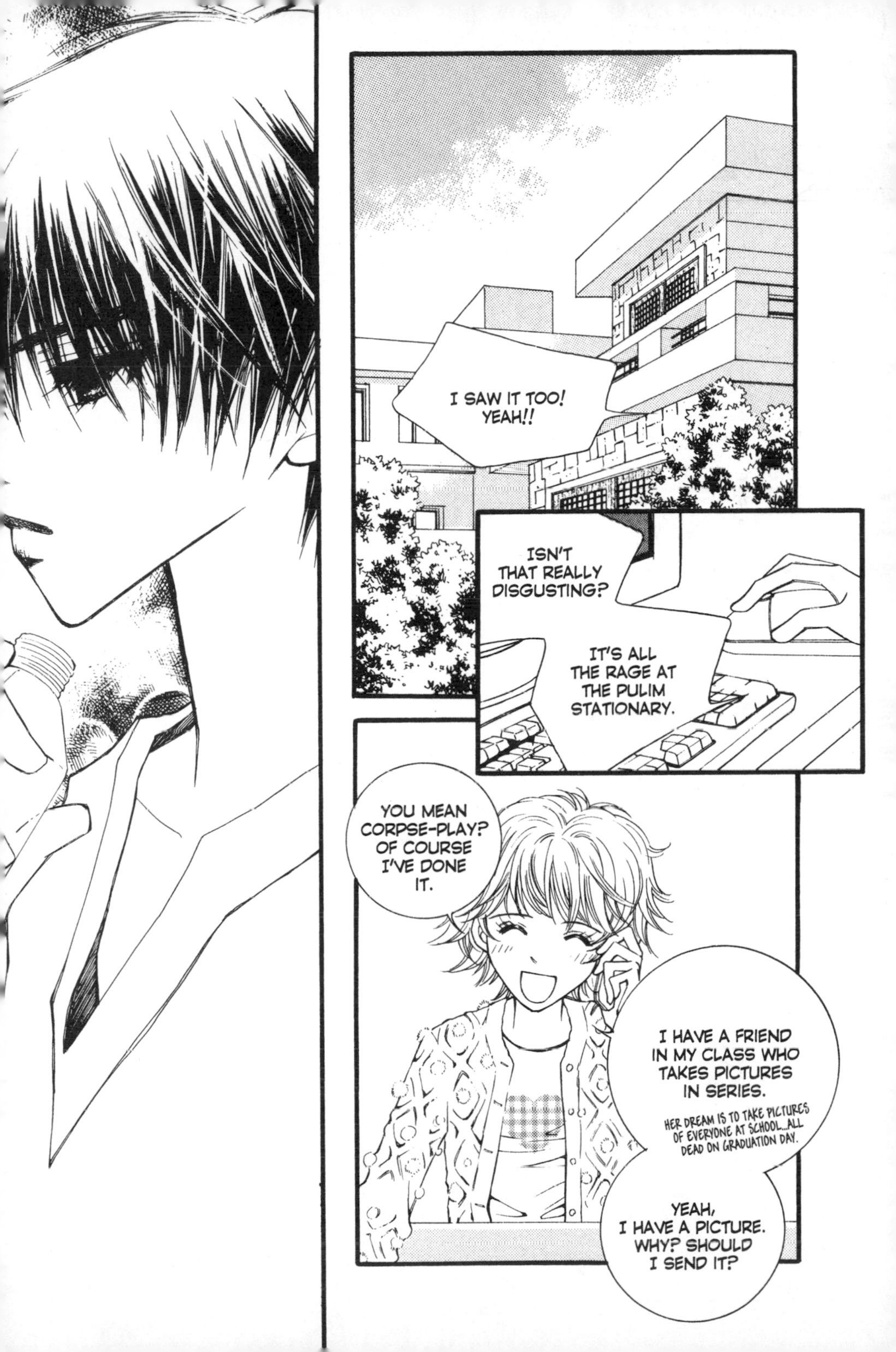
I SAW IT TOO! YEAH!!
ISN'T THAT REALLY DISGUSTING?
IT'S ALL THE RAGE AT THE PULIM STATIONARY.
YOU MEAN CORPSE-PLAY? OF COURSE I'VE DONE IT.
I HAVE A FRIEND IN MY CLASS WHO TAKES PICTURES IN SERIES.
HER DREAM IS TO TAKE PICTURES OF EVERYONE AT SCHOOL...ALL DEAD ON GRADUATION DAY.
YEAH, I HAVE A PICTURE. WHY? SHOULD I SEND IT?

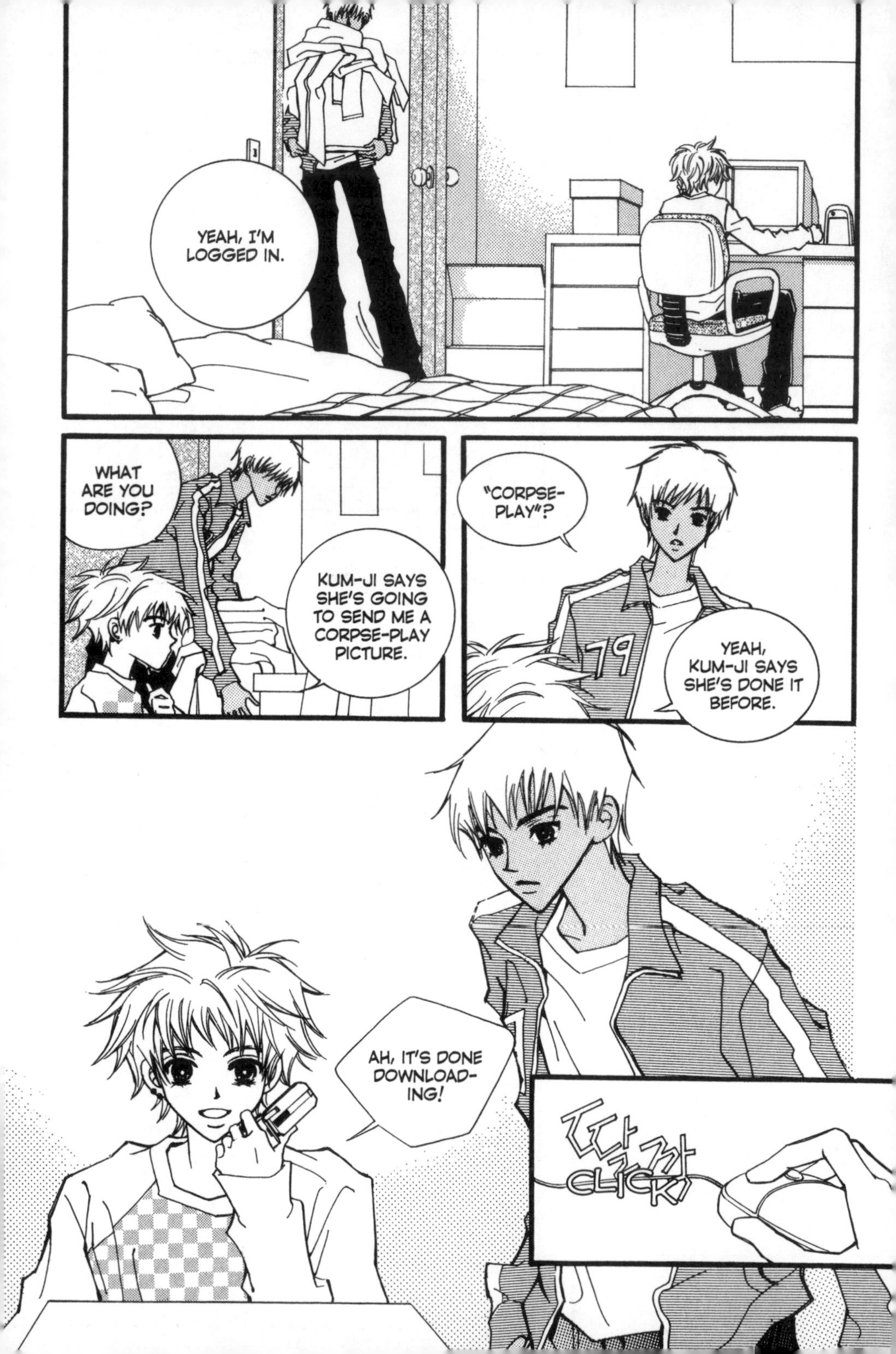
YEAH, I'M LOGGED IN.
WHAT ARE YOU DOING?
KUM-JI SAYS SHE'S GOING TO SEND ME A CORPSE-PLAY PICTURE.
"CORPSE-PLAY"?
YEAH, KUM-JI SAYS SHE'S DONE IT BEFORE.
AH, IT'S DONE DOWNLOAD-ING!
CLICK!

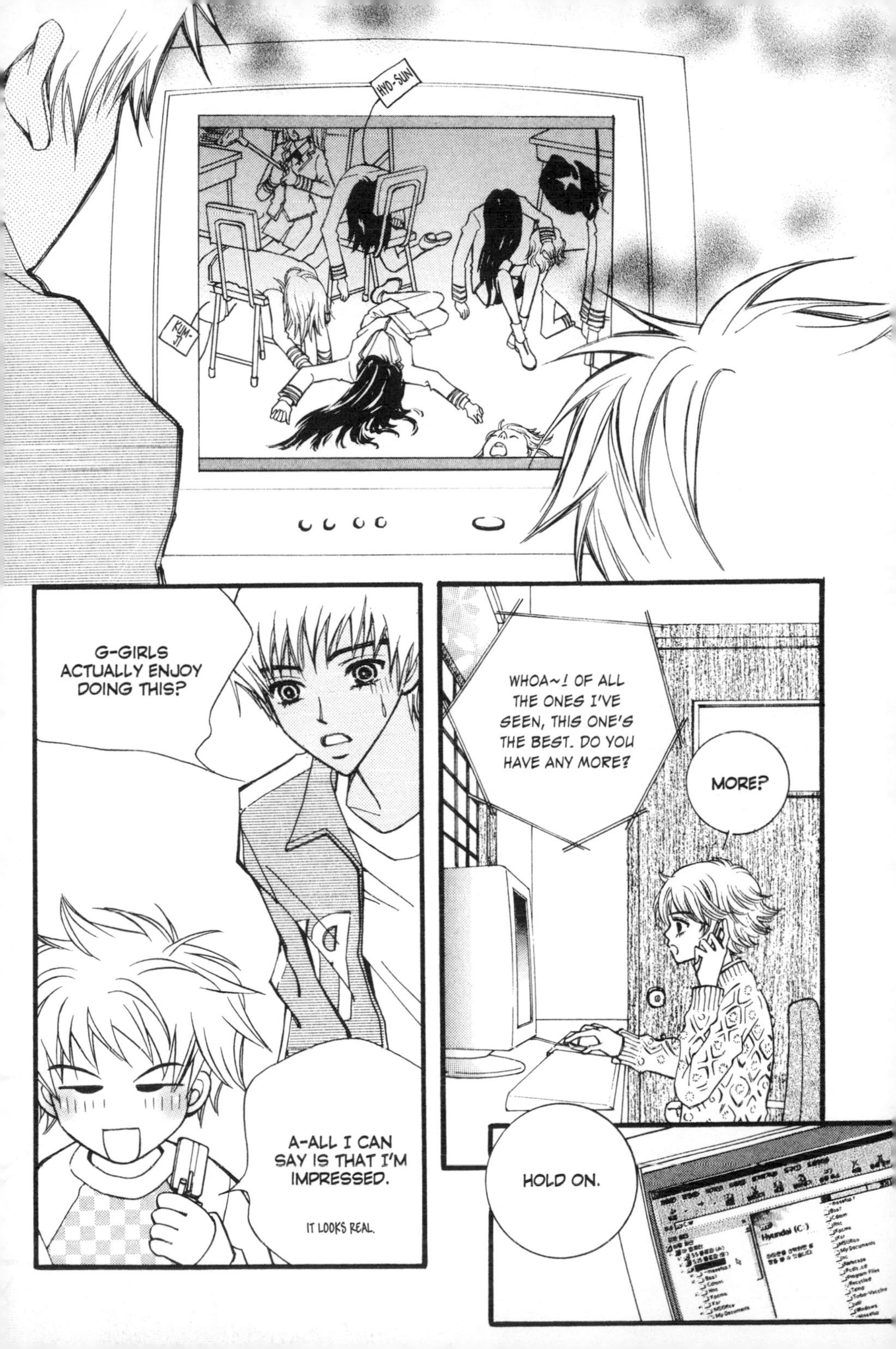
HYO-SUN
KUM-JI
G-GIRLS ACTUALLY ENJOY DOING THIS?
A-ALL I CAN SAY IS THAT I'M IMPRESSED.
IT LOOKS REAL.
WHOA~! OF ALL THE ONES I'VE SEEN, THIS ONE'S THE BEST. DO YOU HAVE ANY MORE?
MORE?
HOLD ON.
Hyundai (C:)

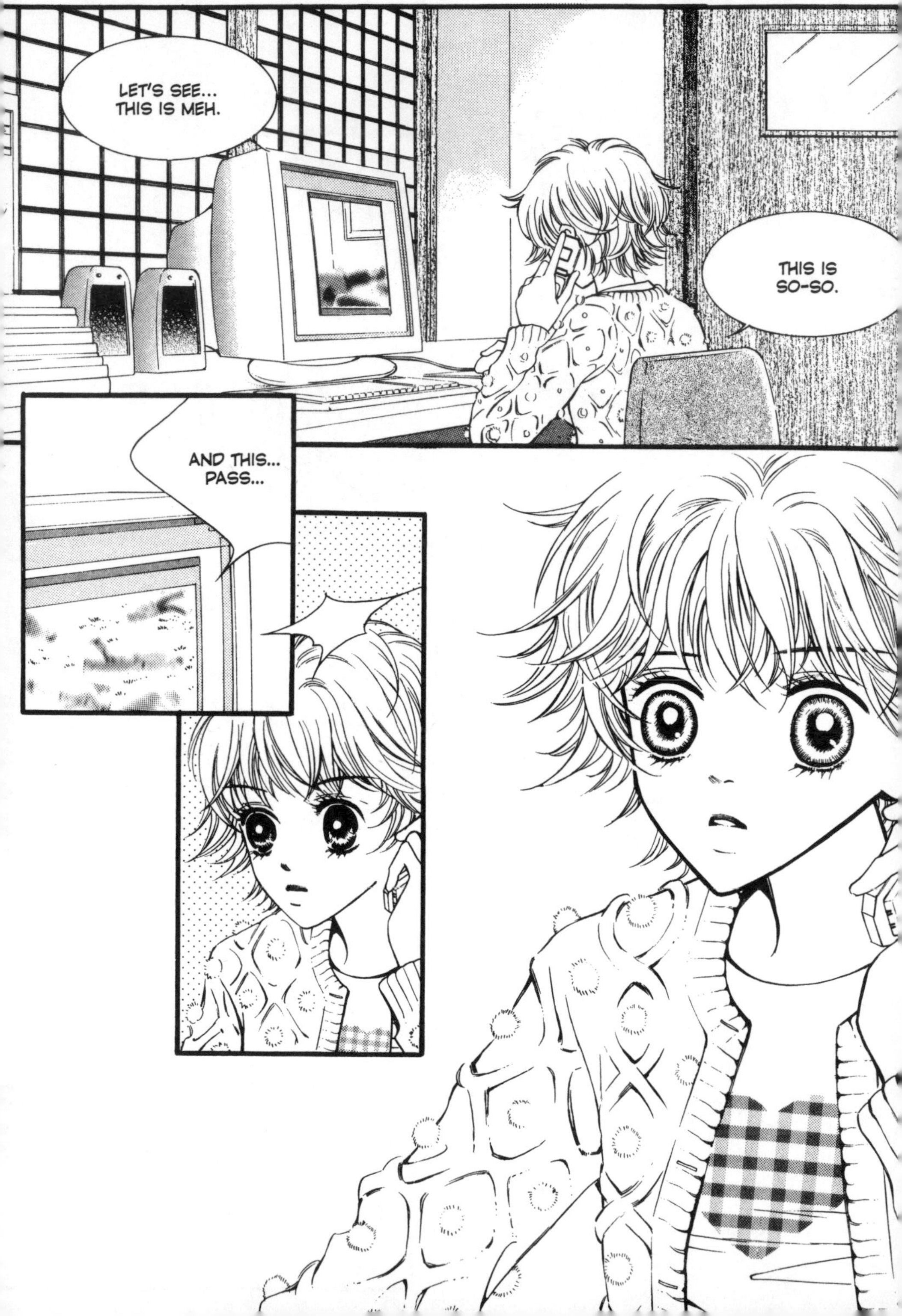
LET'S SEE... THIS IS MEH.
THIS IS SO-SO.
AND THIS... PASS...

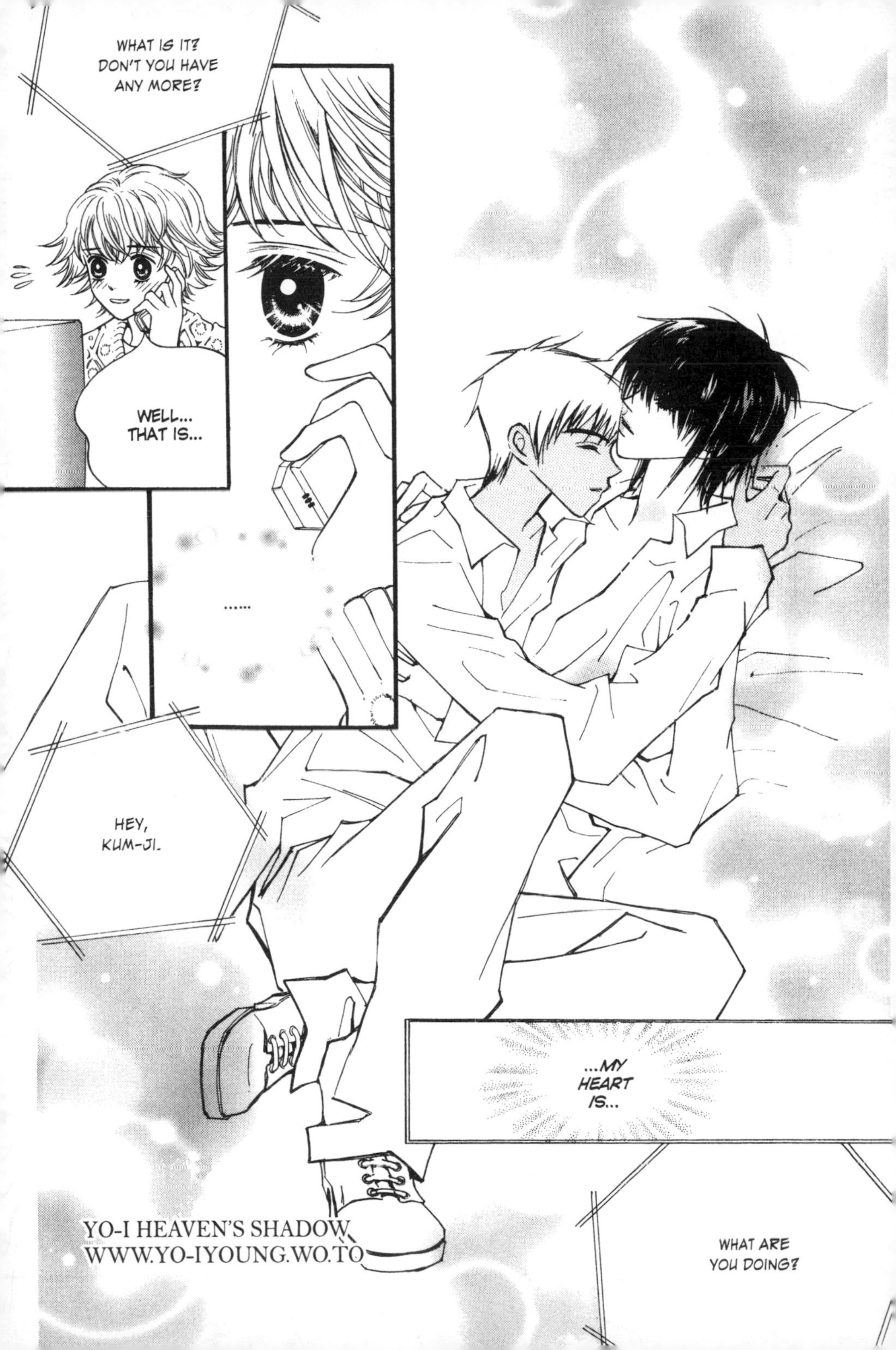
WHAT IS IT? DON'T YOU HAVE ANY MORE?
WELL... THAT IS...
......
HEY, KUM-JI.
...MY HEART IS...
WHAT ARE YOU DOING?
YO-I HEAVEN'S SHADOW
WWW.YO-IYOUNG.WO.TO

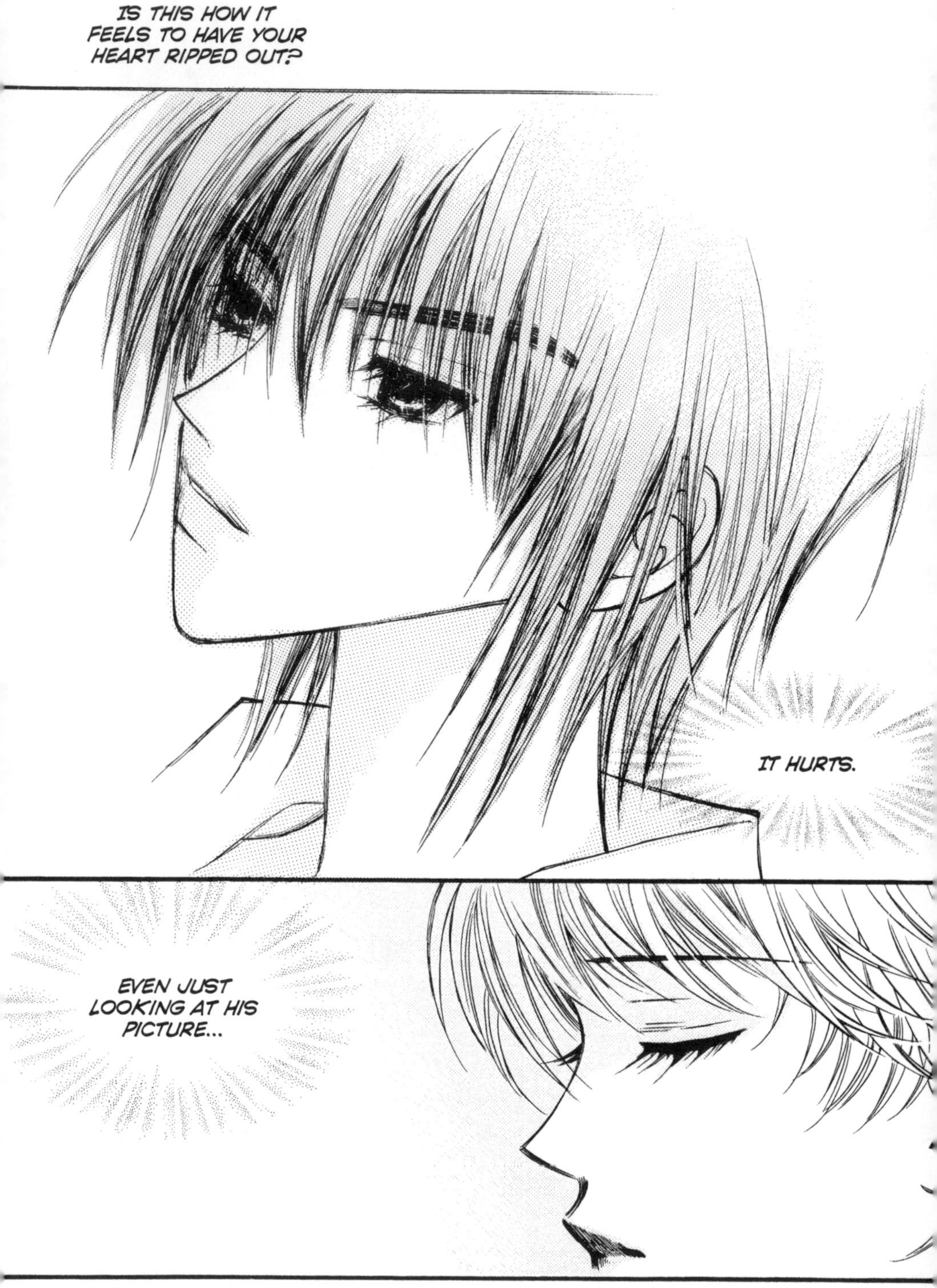
IS THIS HOW IT FEELS TO HAVE YOUR HEART RIPPED OUT?
IT HURTS.
EVEN JUST LOOKING AT HIS PICTURE...

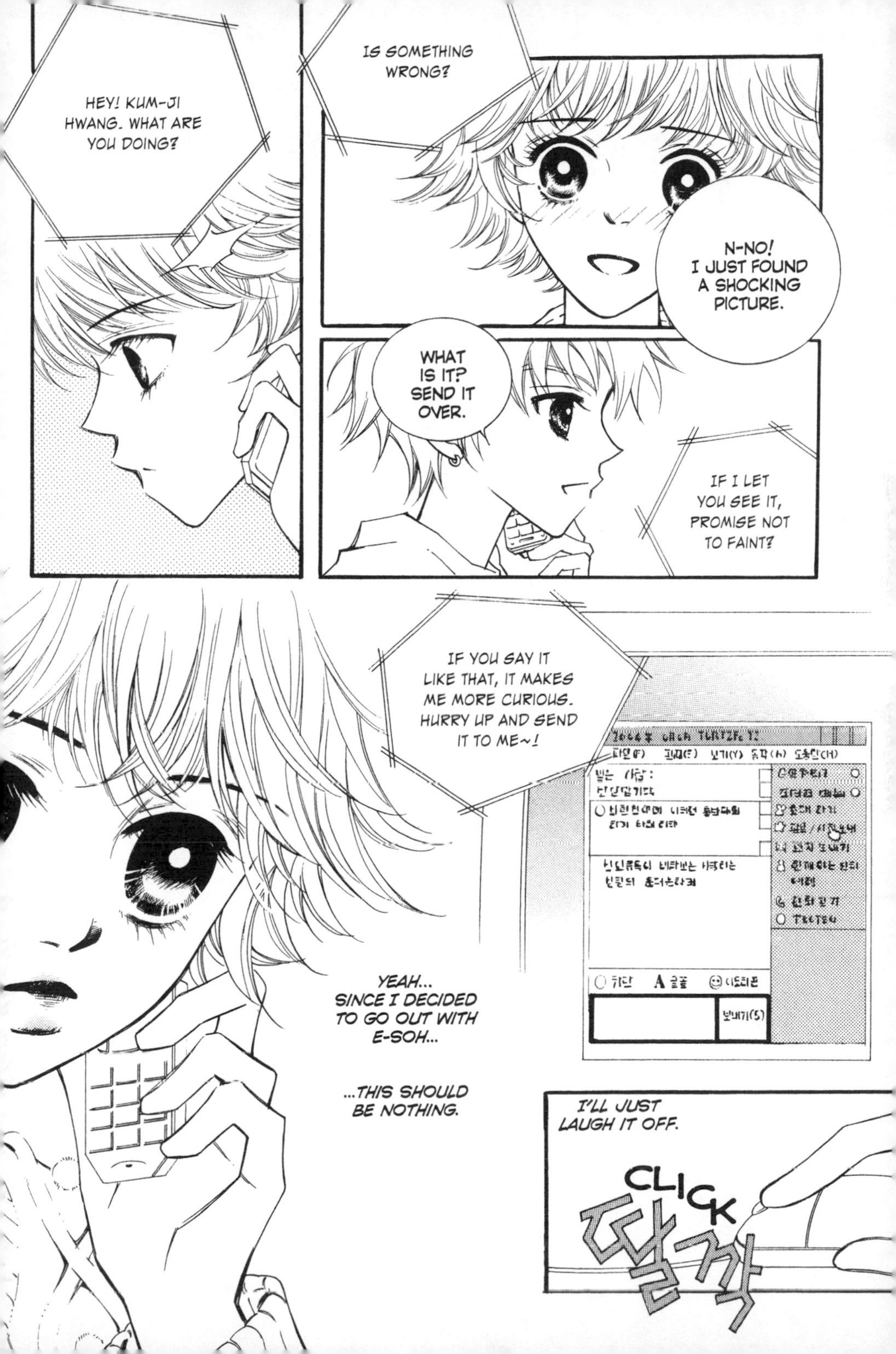

HEY! KUM-JI HWANG. WHAT ARE YOU DOING?
IS SOMETHING WRONG?
N-NO! I JUST FOUND A SHOCKING PICTURE.
WHAT IS IT? SEND IT OVER.
IF I LET YOU SEE IT, PROMISE NOT TO FAINT?
IF YOU SAY IT LIKE THAT, IT MAKES ME MORE CURIOUS. HURRY UP AND SEND IT TO ME~!
YEAH... SINCE I DECIDED TO GO OUT WITH E-SOH...
...THIS SHOULD BE NOTHING.
I'LL JUST LAUGH IT OFF.
CLICK
딸깍

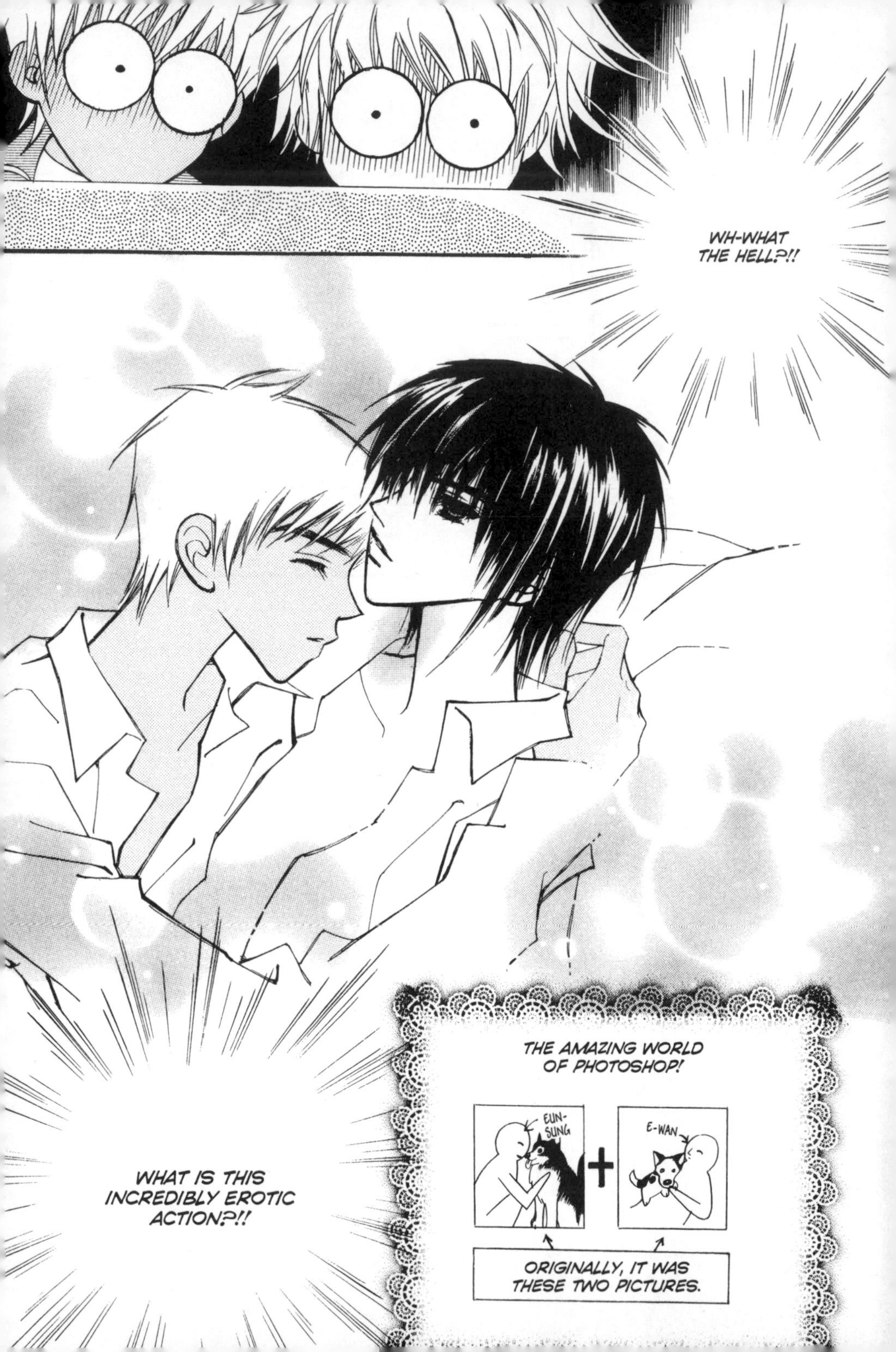

WH-WHAT THE HELL?!!
WHAT IS THIS INCREDIBLY EROTIC ACTION?!!
THE AMAZING WORLD OF PHOTOSHOP!
EUN-SUNG
E-WAN
ORIGINALLY, IT WAS THESE TWO PICTURES.

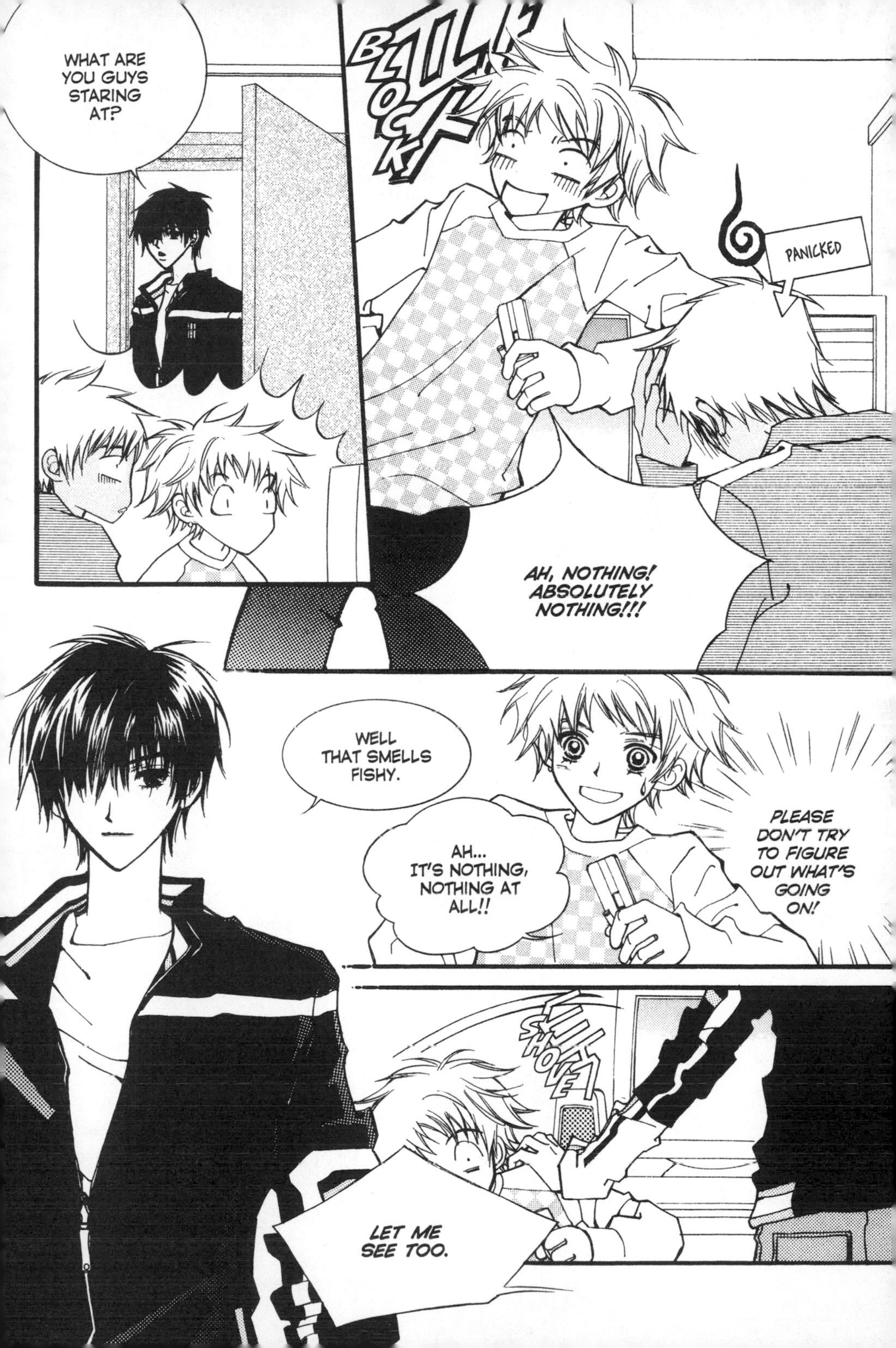
WHAT ARE YOU GUYS STARING AT?
BLOCK
PANICKED
AH, NOTHING! ABSOLUTELY NOTHING!!!
WELL THAT SMELLS FISHY.
AH... IT'S NOTHING, NOTHING AT ALL!!
PLEASE DON'T TRY TO FIGURE OUT WHAT'S GOING ON!
SHOVE
LET ME SEE TOO.

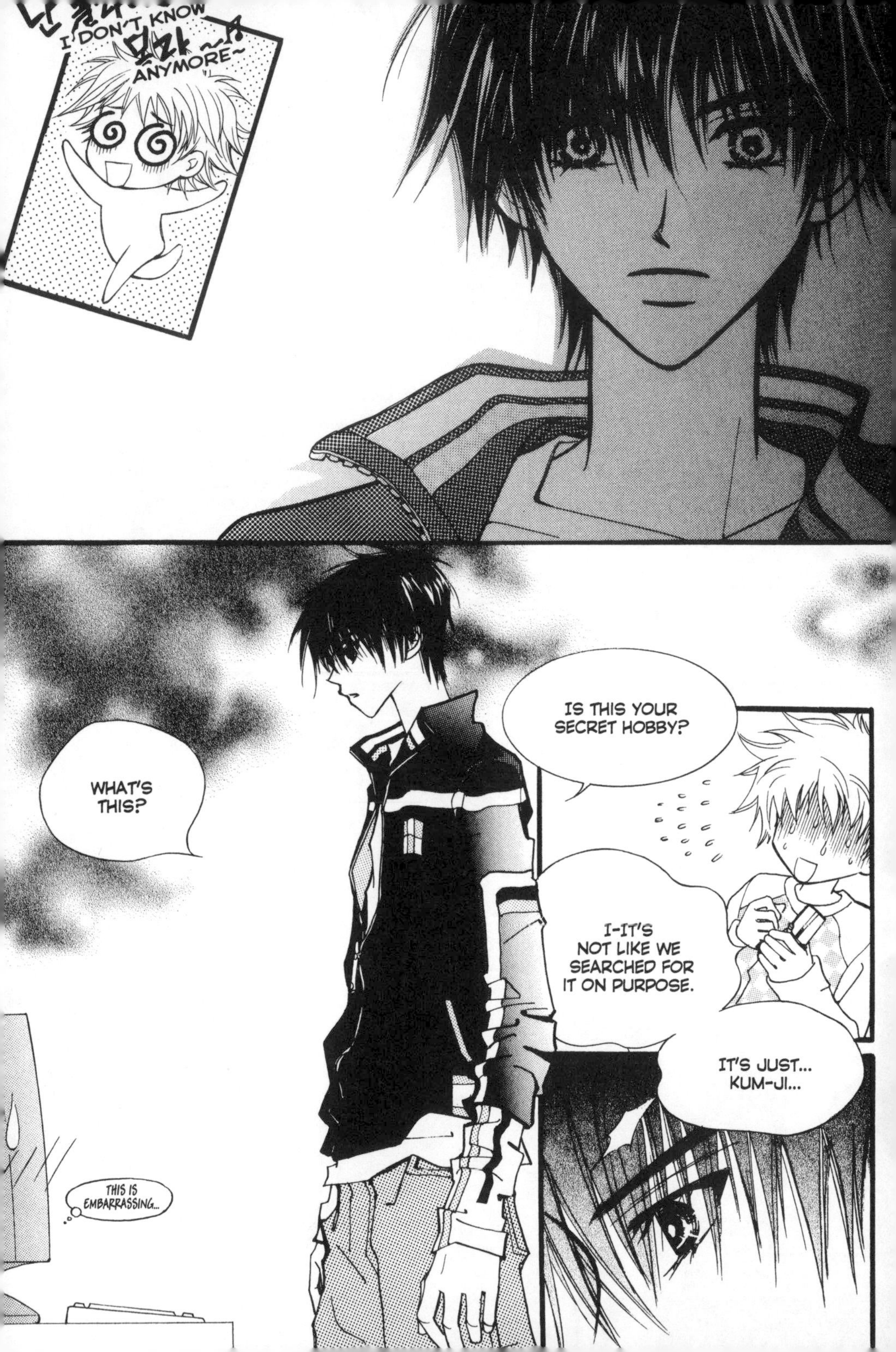
I DON'T KNOW ANYMORE~
WHAT'S THIS?
THIS IS EMBARRASSING...
IS THIS YOUR SECRET HOBBY?
I-IT'S NOT LIKE WE SEARCHED FOR IT ON PURPOSE.
IT'S JUST... KUM-JI...

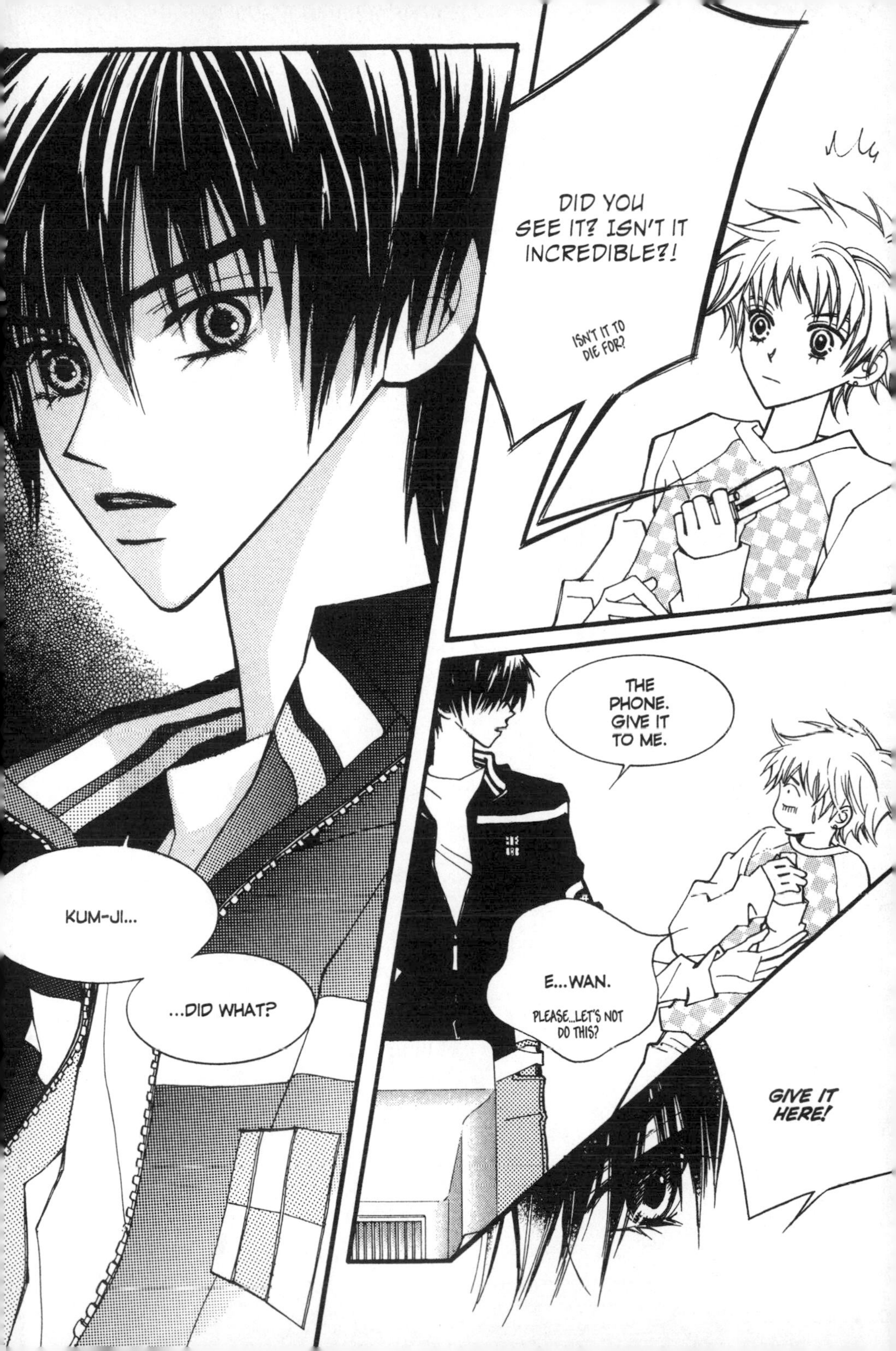
KUM-JI...
...DID WHAT?
DID YOU SEE IT? ISN'T IT INCREDIBLE?!
ISN'T IT TO DIE FOR?
THE PHONE. GIVE IT TO ME.
E...WAN.
PLEASE...LET'S NOT DO THIS?
GIVE IT HERE!

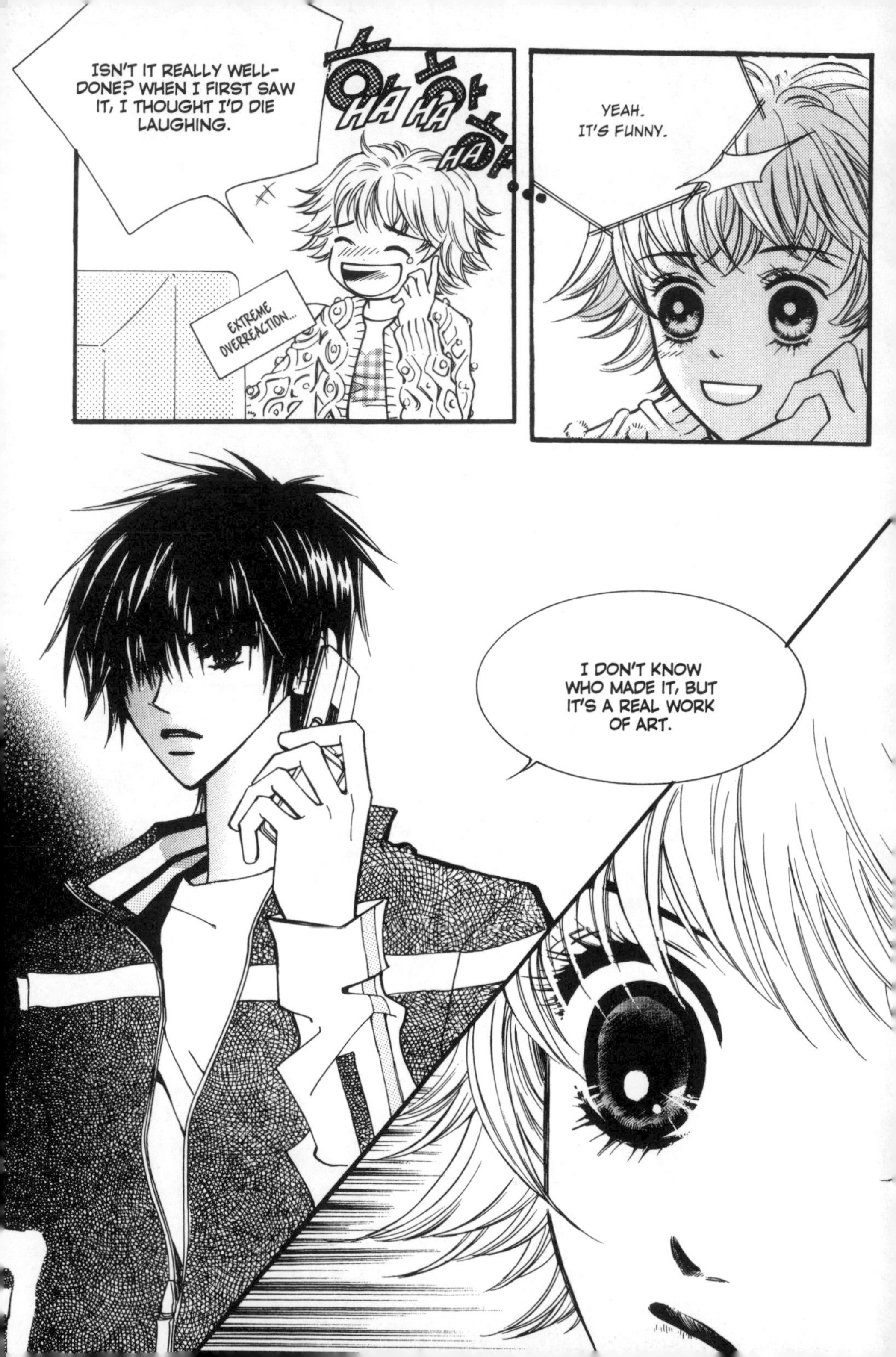
ISN'T IT REALLY WELL-DONE? WHEN I FIRST SAW IT, I THOUGHT I'D DIE LAUGHING.
HA HA HA...
EXTREME OVERREACTION...
YEAH. IT'S FUNNY.
I DON'T KNOW WHO MADE IT, BUT IT'S A REAL WORK OF ART.

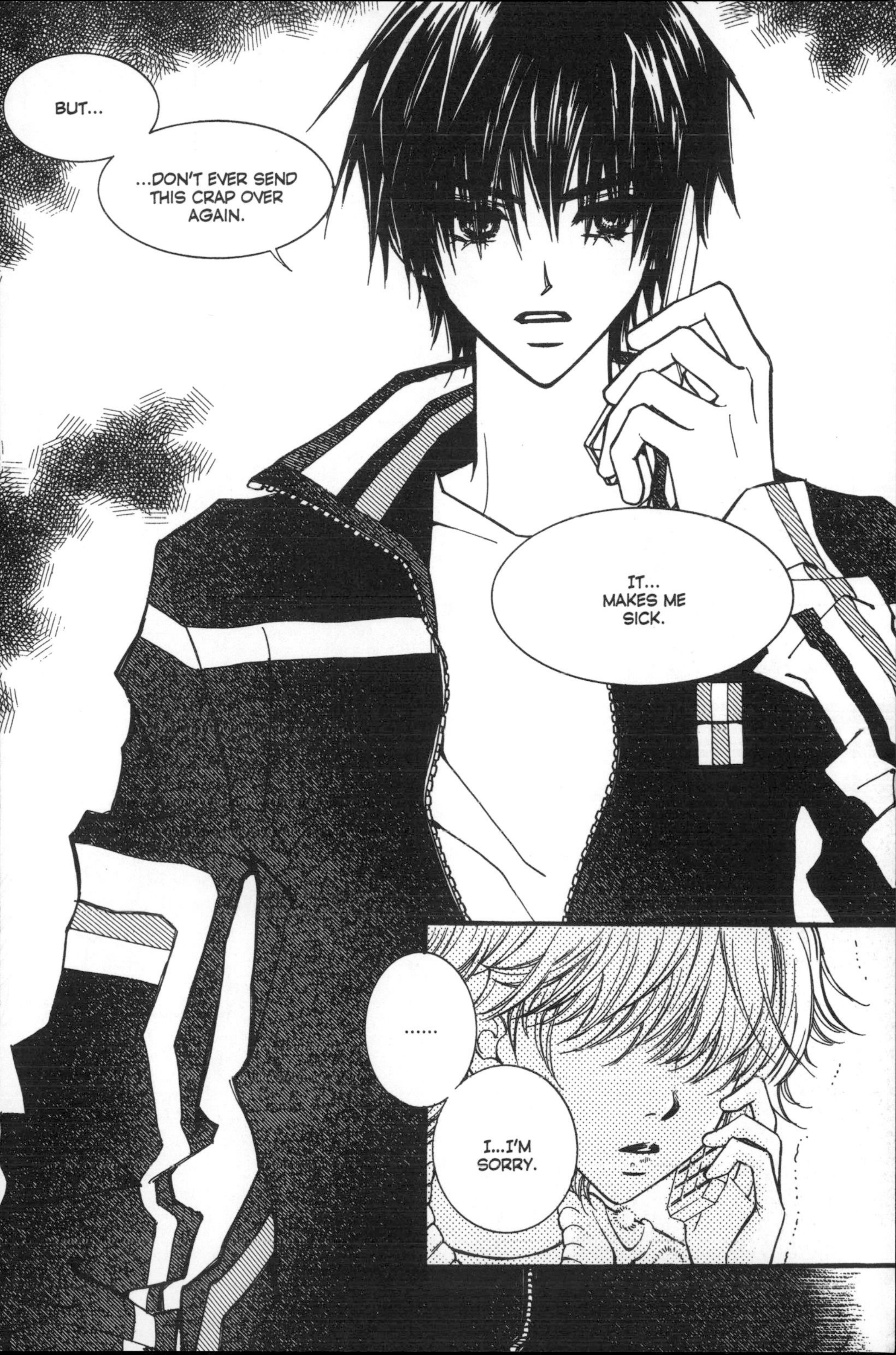
BUT...
...DON'T EVER SEND THIS CRAP OVER AGAIN.
IT... MAKES ME SICK.
......
I...I'M SORRY.

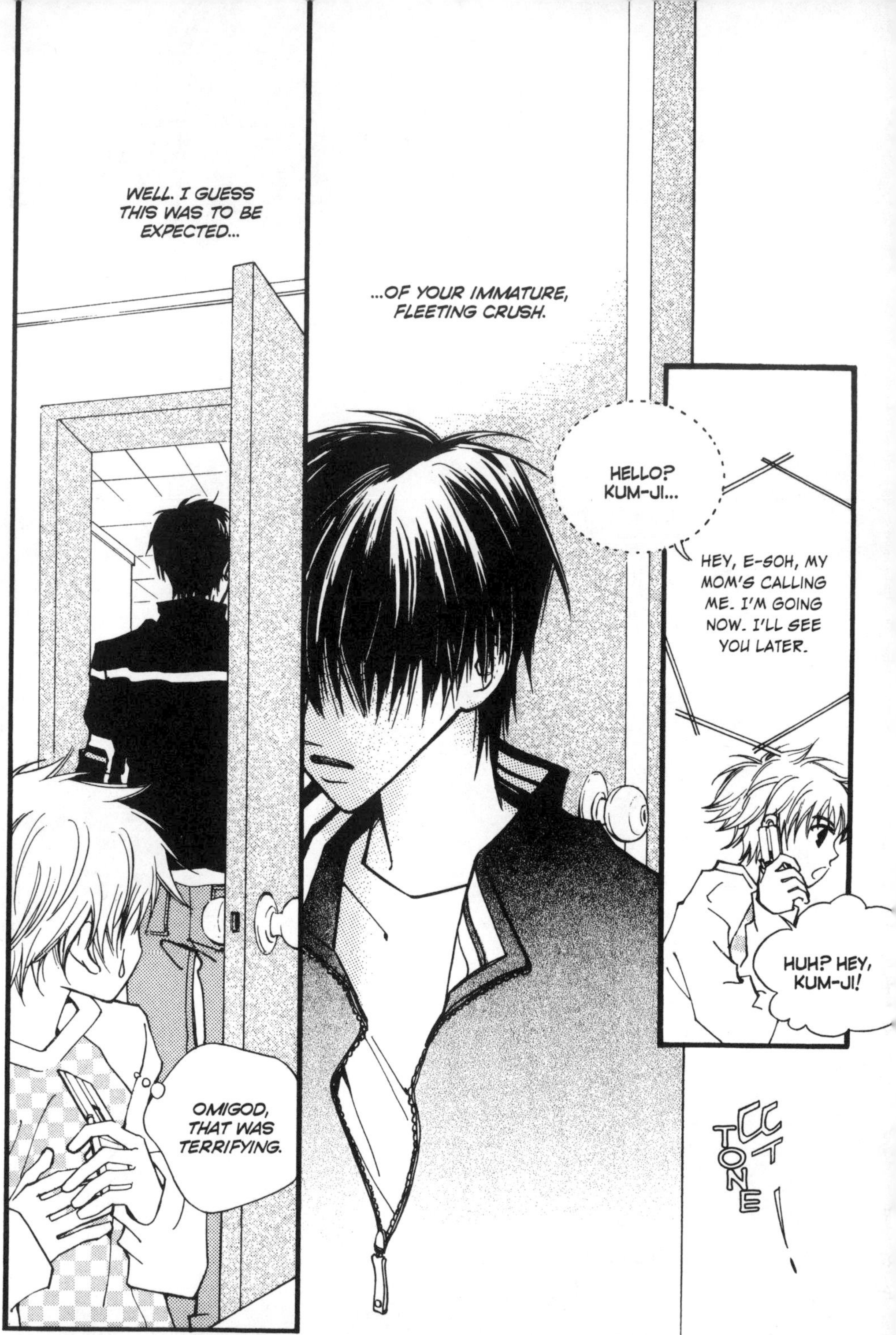
WELL. I GUESS THIS WAS TO BE EXPECTED...
OMIGOD, THAT WAS TERRIFYING.
...OF YOUR IMMATURE, FLEETING CRUSH.
HELLO? KUM-JI...
HEY, E-SOH, MY MOM'S CALLING ME. I'M GOING NOW. I'LL SEE YOU LATER.
HUH? HEY, KUM-JI!
CCT
TONE

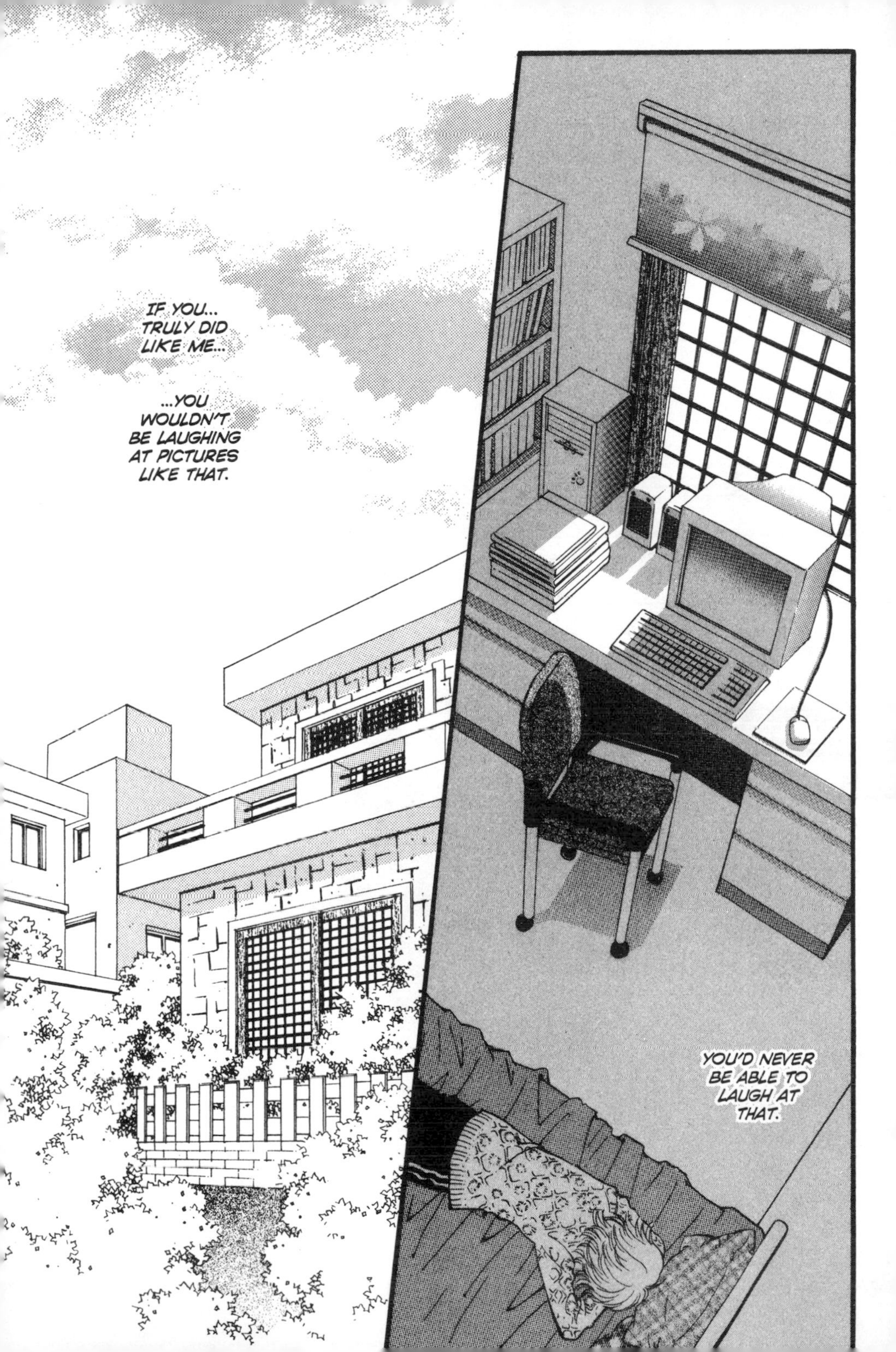
IF YOU... TRULY DID LIKE ME...
...YOU WOULDN'T BE LAUGHING AT PICTURES LIKE THAT.
YOU'D NEVER BE ABLE TO LAUGH AT THAT.

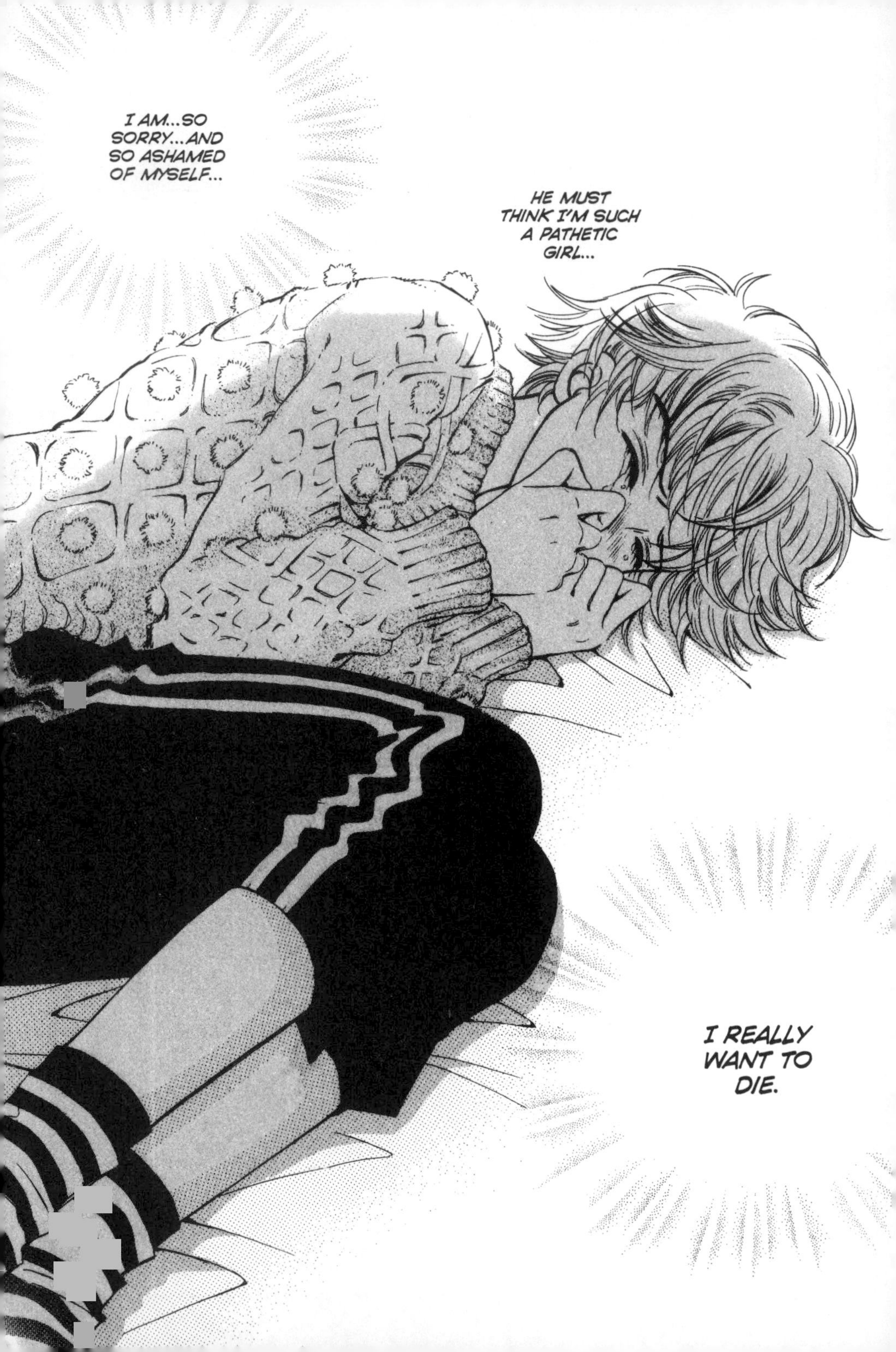
I AM...SO SORRY...AND SO ASHAMED OF MYSELF...
HE MUST THINK I'M SUCH A PATHETIC GIRL...
I REALLY WANT TO DIE.

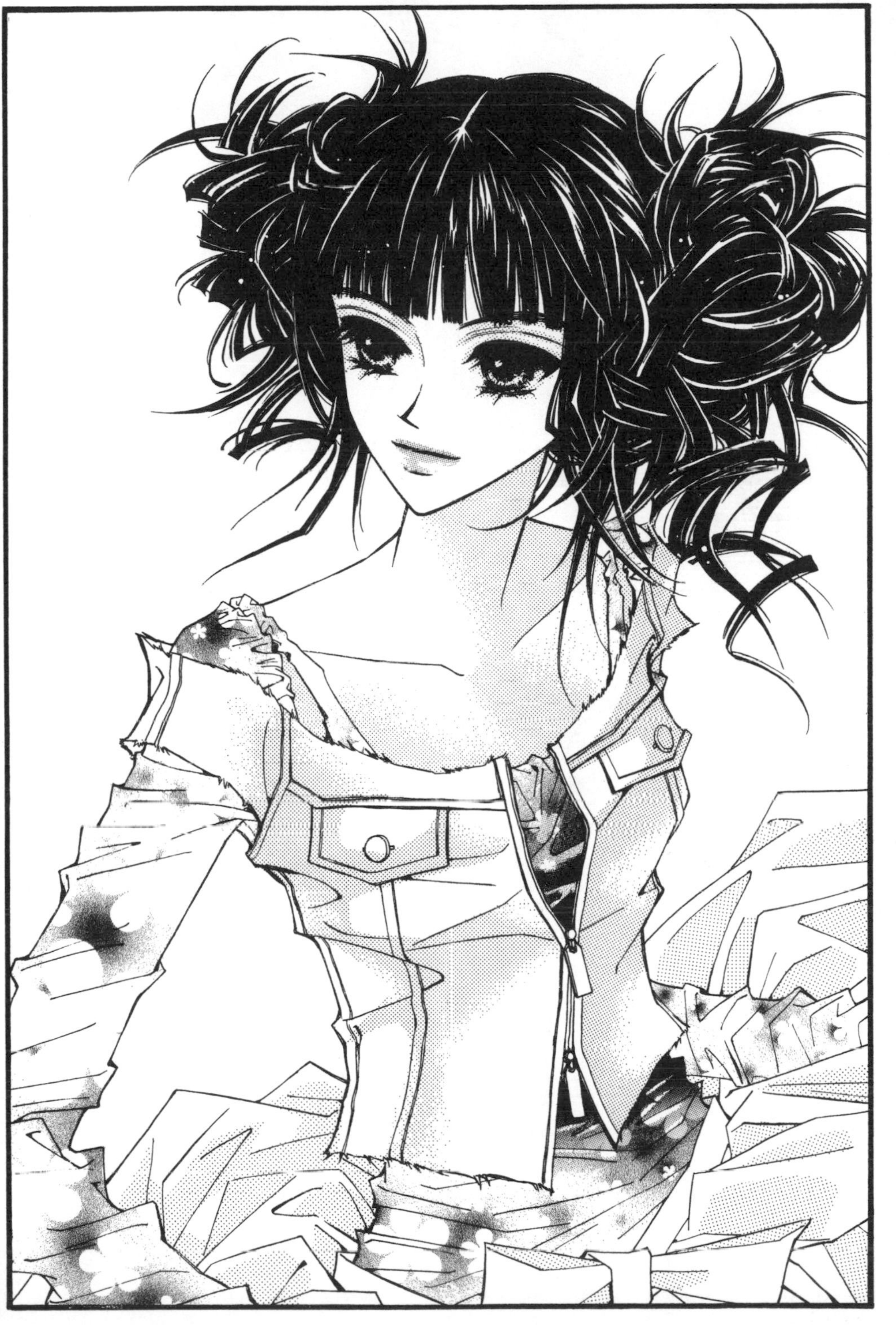

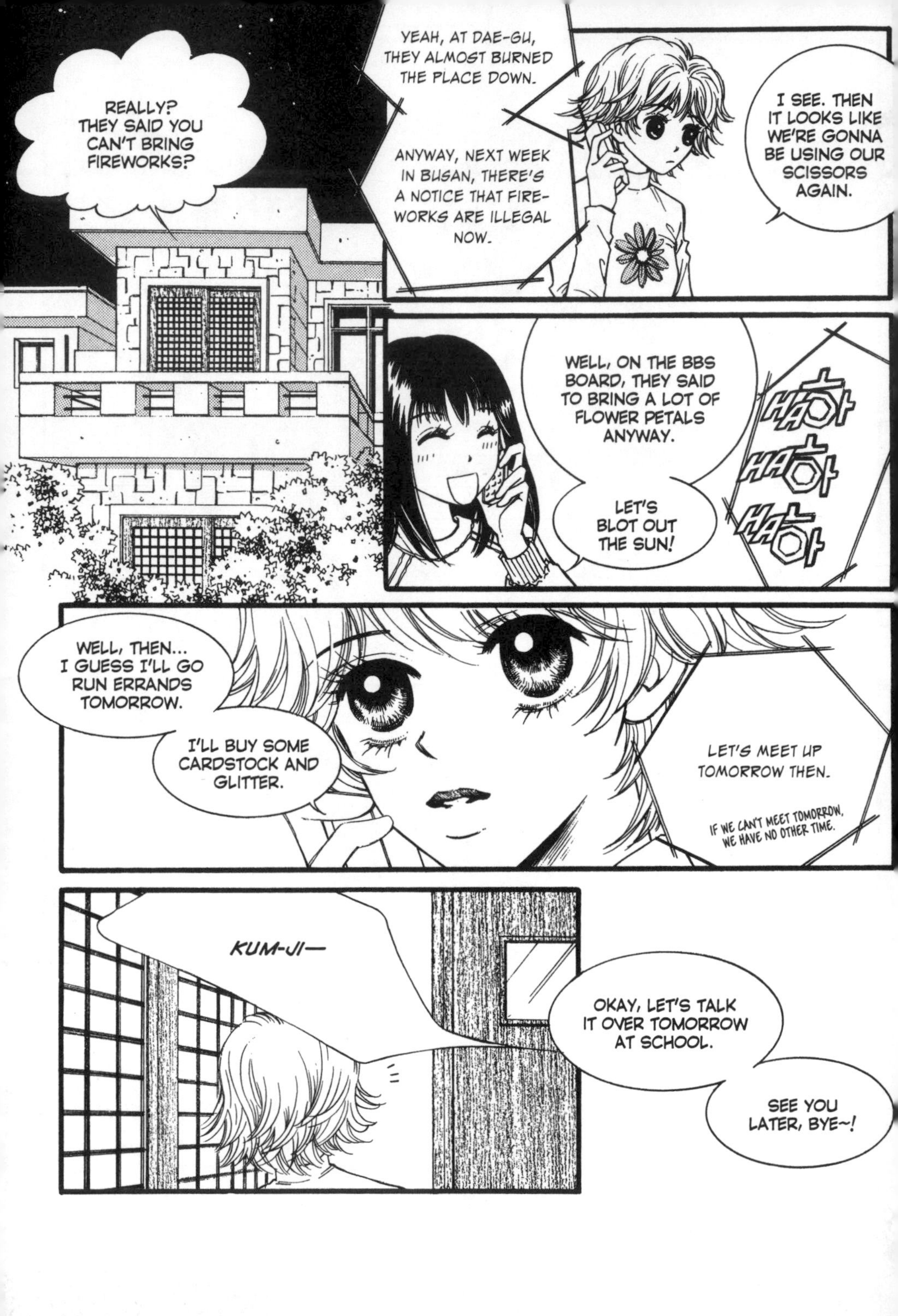
REALLY? THEY SAID YOU CAN'T BRING FIREWORKS?
YEAH, AT DAE-GU, THEY ALMOST BURNED THE PLACE DOWN.
ANYWAY, NEXT WEEK IN BUSAN, THERE'S A NOTICE THAT FIRE-WORKS ARE ILLEGAL NOW.
I SEE. THEN IT LOOKS LIKE WE'RE GONNA BE USING OUR SCISSORS AGAIN.
WELL, ON THE BBS BOARD, THEY SAID TO BRING A LOT OF FLOWER PETALS ANYWAY.
LET'S BLOT OUT THE SUN!
HA하 HA하 HA하
WELL, THEN... I GUESS I'LL GO RUN ERRANDS TOMORROW.
I'LL BUY SOME CARDSTOCK AND GLITTER.
LET'S MEET UP TOMORROW THEN.
IF WE CAN'T MEET TOMORROW, WE HAVE NO OTHER TIME.
KUM-JI—
OKAY, LET'S TALK IT OVER TOMORROW AT SCHOOL.
SEE YOU LATER, BYE~!

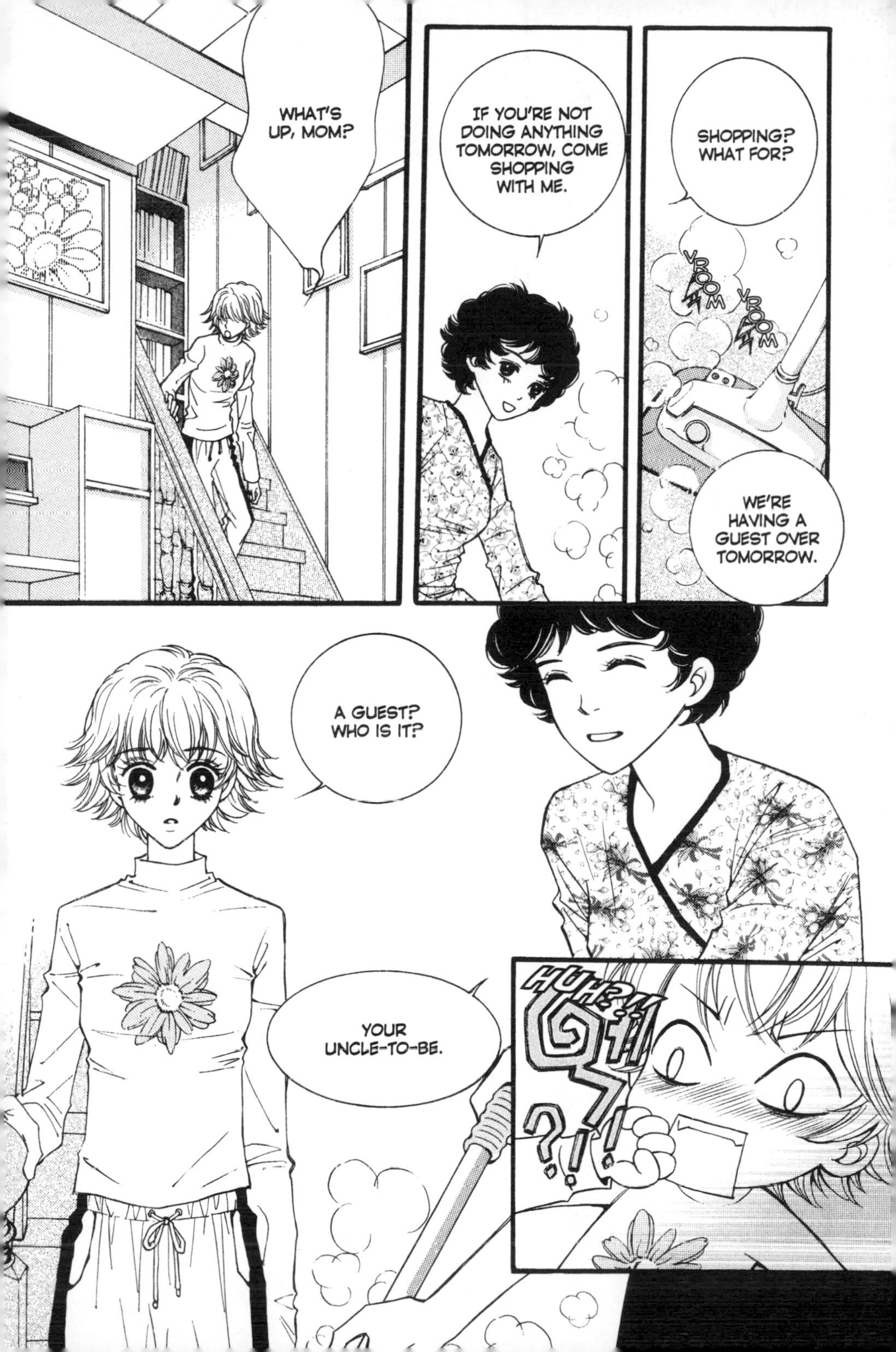
WHAT'S UP, MOM?
IF YOU'RE NOT DOING ANYTHING TOMORROW, COME SHOPPING WITH ME.
SHOPPING? WHAT FOR?
VROOM
VROOM
WE'RE HAVING A GUEST OVER TOMORROW.
A GUEST? WHO IS IT?
YOUR UNCLE-TO-BE.
HUH?!!

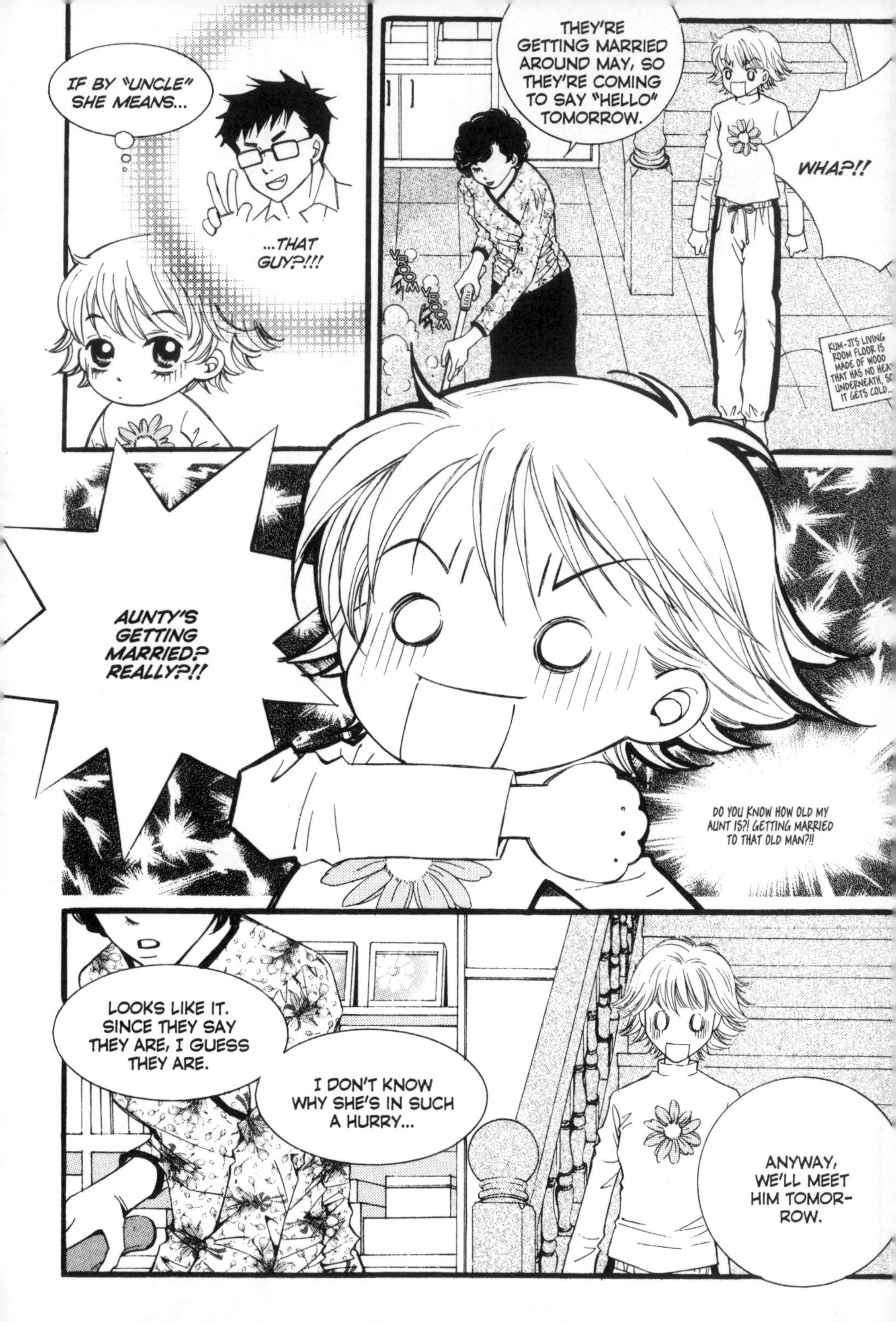
IF BY "UNCLE" SHE MEANS...
...THAT GUY?!!!
THEY'RE GETTING MARRIED AROUND MAY, SO THEY'RE COMING TO SAY "HELLO" TOMORROW.
VROOM VROOM
WHA?!!
KUM-JI'S LIVING ROOM FLOOR IS MADE OF WOOD THAT HAS NO HEAT UNDERNEATH, SO IT GETS COLD.
AUNTY'S GETTING MARRIED? REALLY?!!
DO YOU KNOW HOW OLD MY AUNT IS?! GETTING MARRIED TO THAT OLD MAN?!!
LOOKS LIKE IT. SINCE THEY SAY THEY ARE, I GUESS THEY ARE.
I DON'T KNOW WHY SHE'S IN SUCH A HURRY...
ANYWAY, WE'LL MEET HIM TOMORROW.

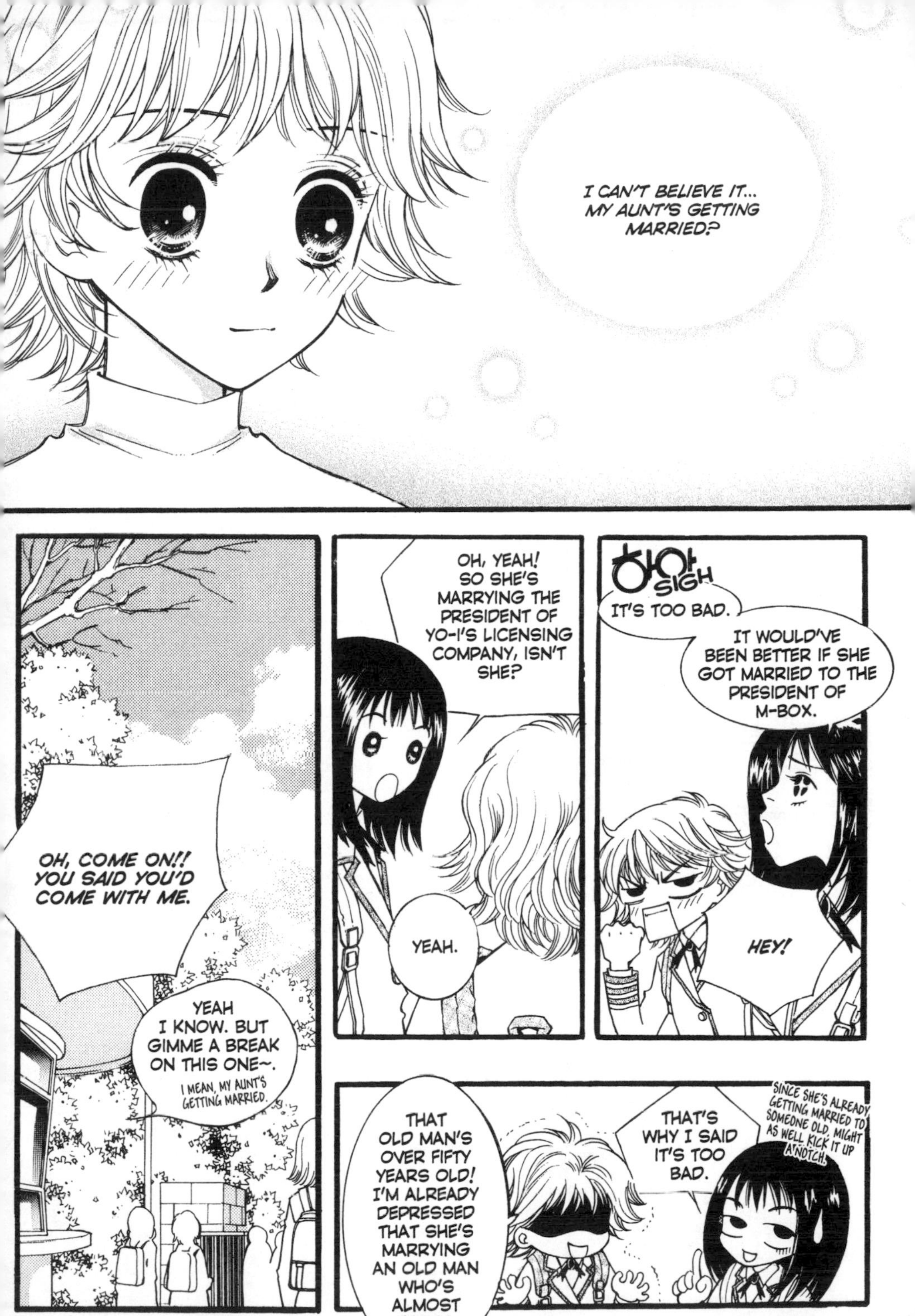
I CAN'T BELIEVE IT... MY AUNT'S GETTING MARRIED?
OH, COME ON!! YOU SAID YOU'D COME WITH ME.
YEAH I KNOW. BUT GIMME A BREAK ON THIS ONE~.
I MEAN, MY AUNT'S GETTING MARRIED.
OH, YEAH! SO SHE'S MARRYING THE PRESIDENT OF YO-I'S LICENSING COMPANY, ISN'T SHE?
YEAH.
SIGH
IT'S TOO BAD.
IT WOULD'VE BEEN BETTER IF SHE GOT MARRIED TO THE PRESIDENT OF M-BOX.
HEY!
THAT OLD MAN'S OVER FIFTY YEARS OLD! I'M ALREADY DEPRESSED THAT SHE'S MARRYING AN OLD MAN WHO'S ALMOST FORTY.
THAT'S WHY I SAID IT'S TOO BAD.
SINCE SHE'S ALREADY GETTING MARRIED TO SOMEONE OLD, MIGHT AS WELL KICK IT UP A NOTCH.

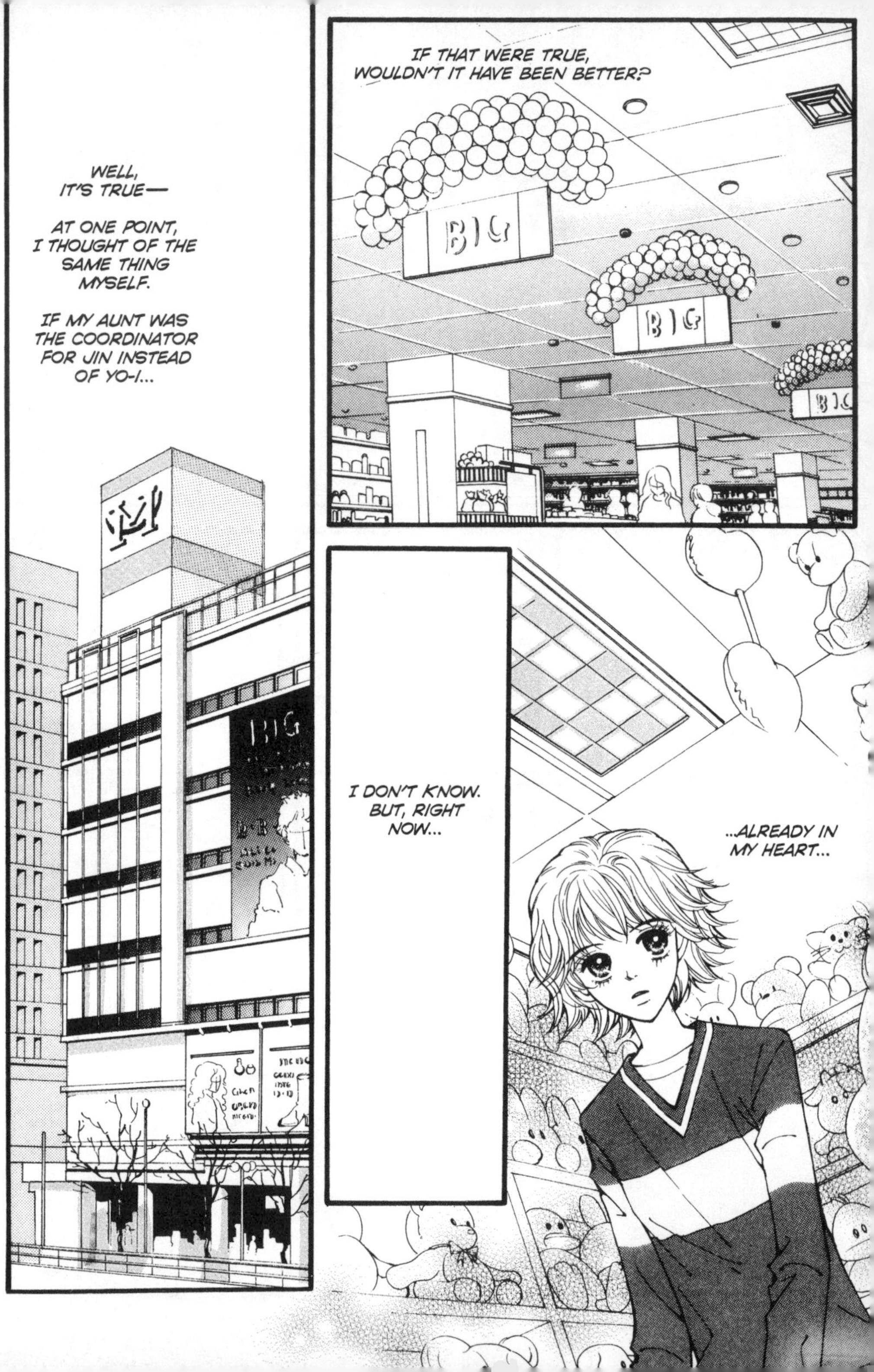
WELL, IT'S TRUE—
AT ONE POINT, I THOUGHT OF THE SAME THING MYSELF.
IF MY AUNT WAS THE COORDINATOR FOR JIN INSTEAD OF YO-I...
BIG
IF THAT WERE TRUE, WOULDN'T IT HAVE BEEN BETTER?
BIG
BIG
I DON'T KNOW. BUT, RIGHT NOW...
...ALREADY IN MY HEART...

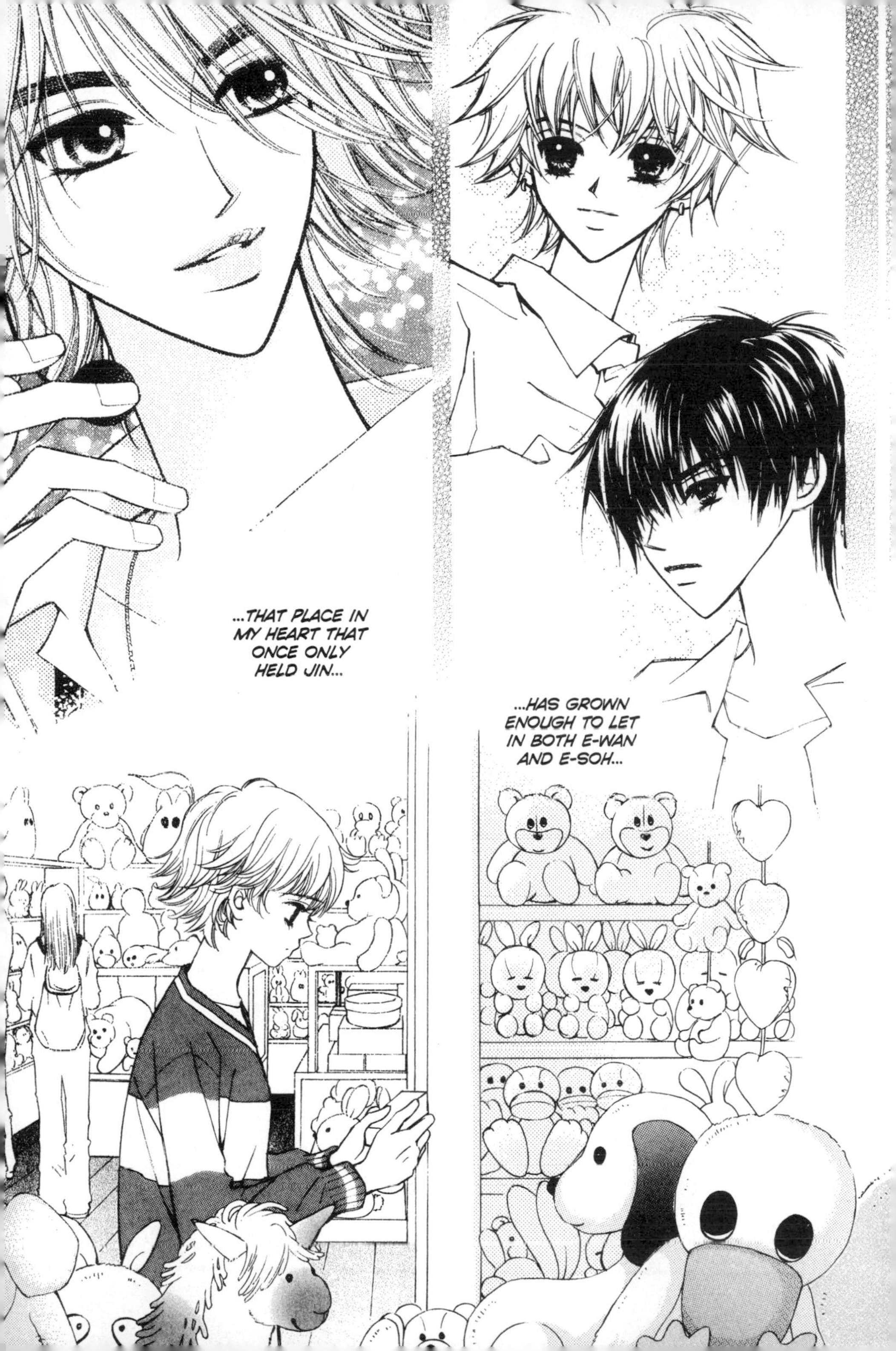
...THAT PLACE IN MY HEART THAT ONCE ONLY HELD JIN...
...HAS GROWN ENOUGH TO LET IN BOTH E-WAN AND E-SOH...

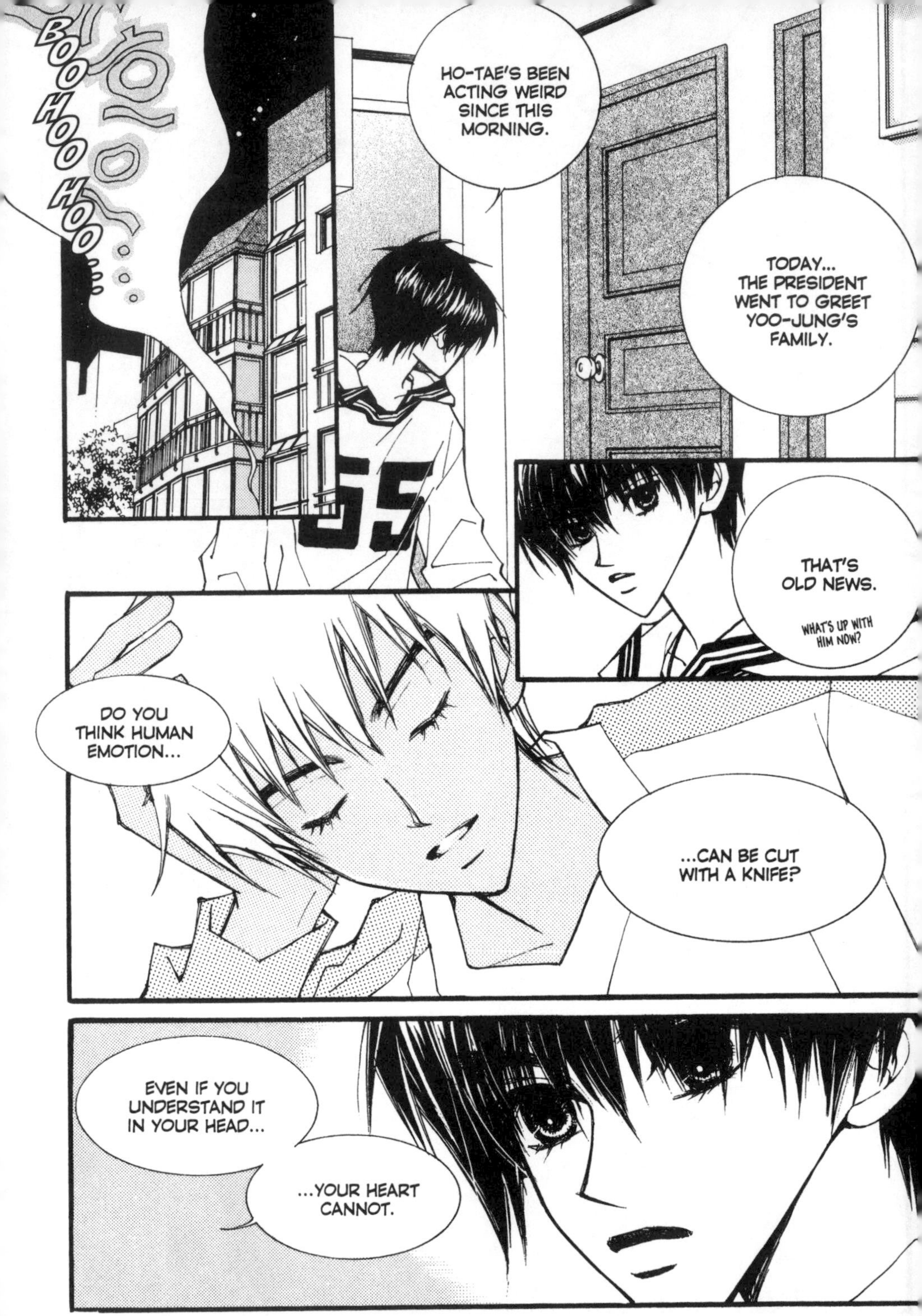
BOOHOOHOOHOO
HO-TAE'S BEEN ACTING WEIRD SINCE THIS MORNING.
TODAY... THE PRESIDENT WENT TO GREET YOO-JUNG'S FAMILY.
THAT'S OLD NEWS.
WHAT'S UP WITH HIM NOW?
DO YOU THINK HUMAN EMOTION...
...CAN BE CUT WITH A KNIFE?
EVEN IF YOU UNDERSTAND IT IN YOUR HEAD...
...YOUR HEART CANNOT.

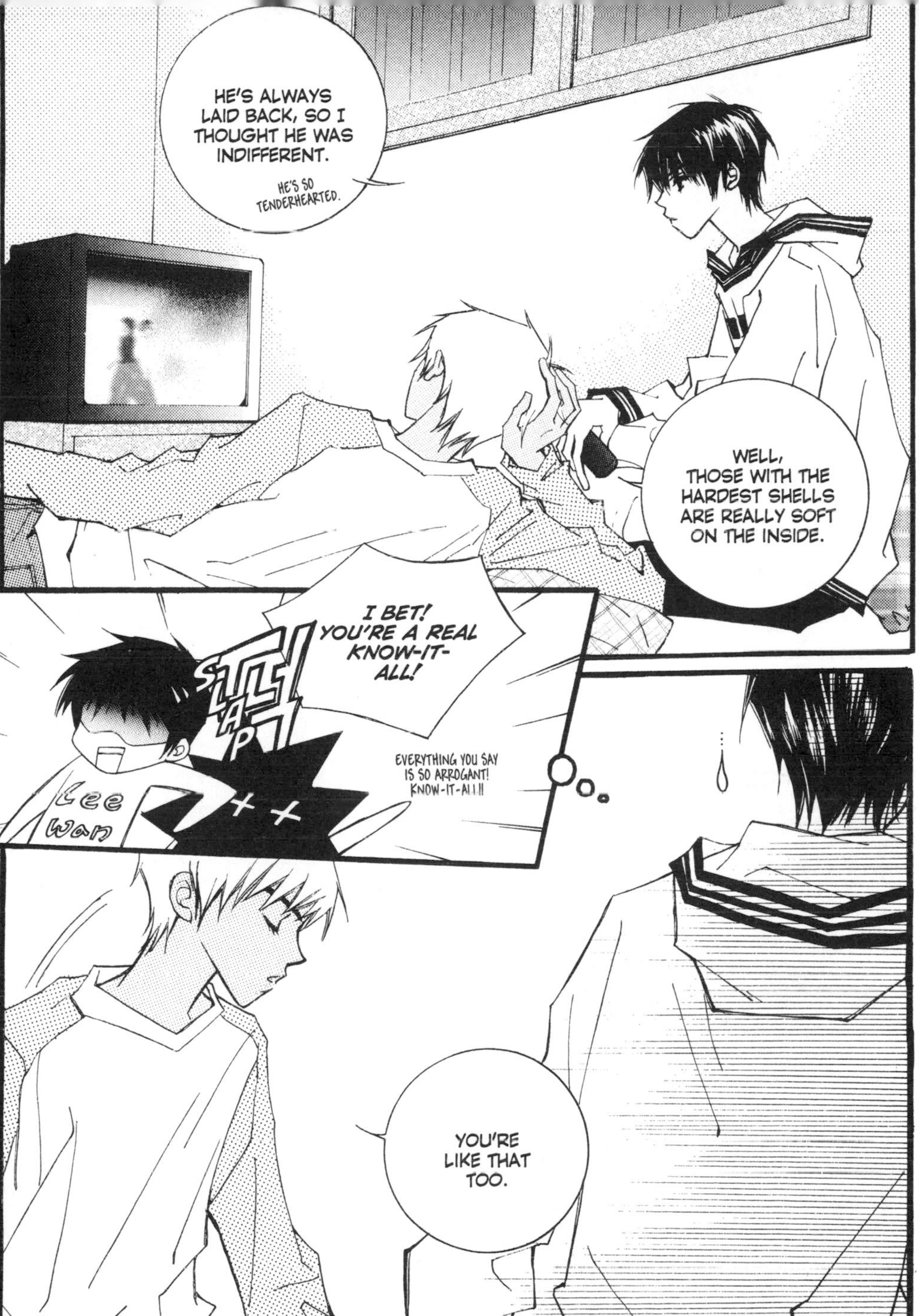
HE'S ALWAYS LAID BACK, SO I THOUGHT HE WAS INDIFFERENT.
HE'S SO TENDERHEARTED.
WELL, THOSE WITH THE HARDEST SHELLS ARE REALLY SOFT ON THE INSIDE.
Lee wan
SLAP
I BET! YOU'RE A REAL KNOW-IT-ALL!
EVERYTHING YOU SAY IS SO ARROGANT! KNOW-IT-ALL!!
YOU'RE LIKE THAT TOO.

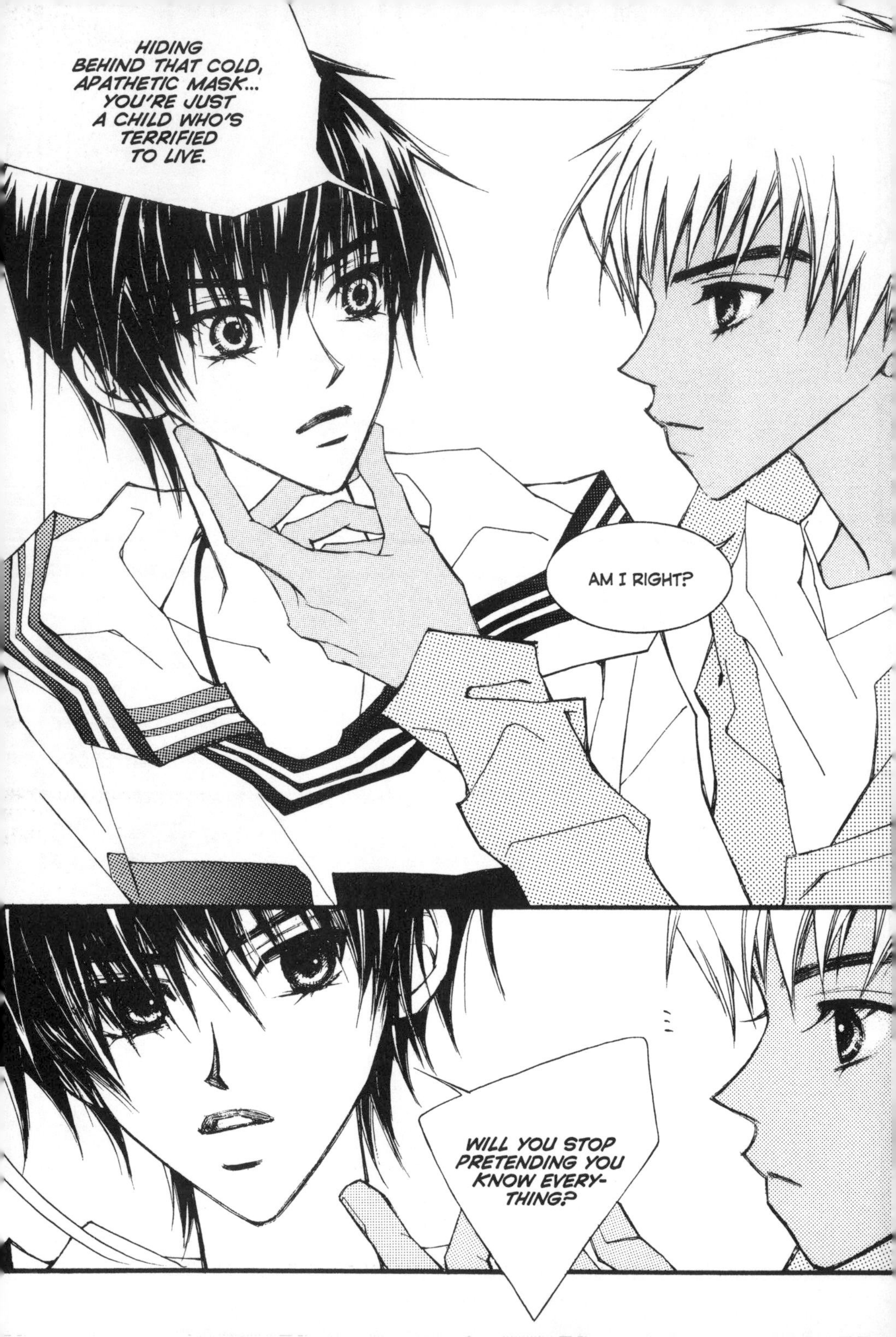
HIDING BEHIND THAT COLD, APATHETIC MASK... YOU'RE JUST A CHILD WHO'S TERRIFIED TO LIVE.
AM I RIGHT?
WILL YOU STOP PRETENDING YOU KNOW EVERY-THING?

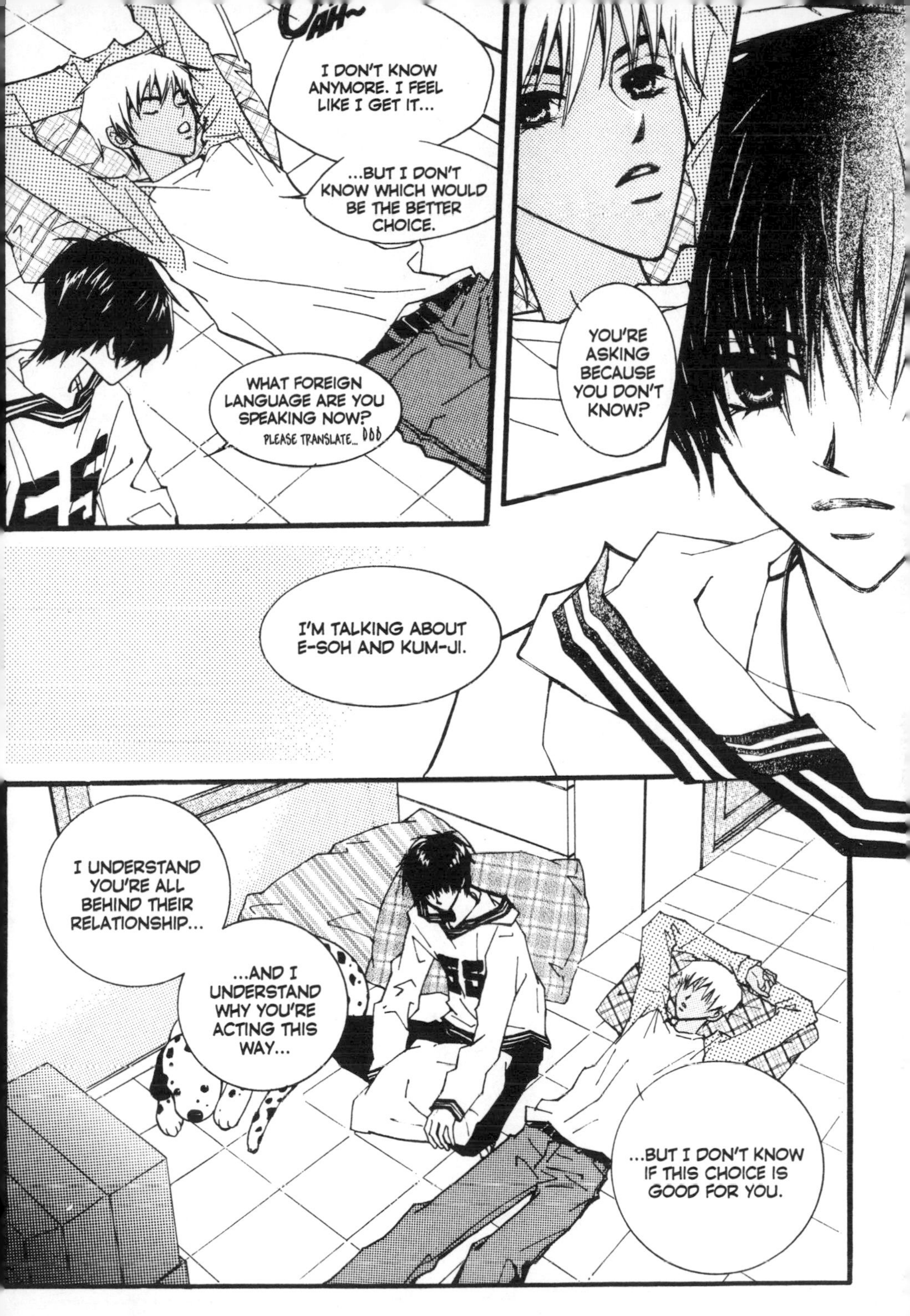
UAH~
I DON'T KNOW ANYMORE. I FEEL LIKE I GET IT...
...BUT I DON'T KNOW WHICH WOULD BE THE BETTER CHOICE.
WHAT FOREIGN LANGUAGE ARE YOU SPEAKING NOW?
PLEASE TRANSLATE...
YOU'RE ASKING BECAUSE YOU DON'T KNOW?
I'M TALKING ABOUT E-SOH AND KUM-JI.
I UNDERSTAND YOU'RE ALL BEHIND THEIR RELATIONSHIP...
...AND I UNDERSTAND WHY YOU'RE ACTING THIS WAY...
...BUT I DON'T KNOW IF THIS CHOICE IS GOOD FOR YOU.

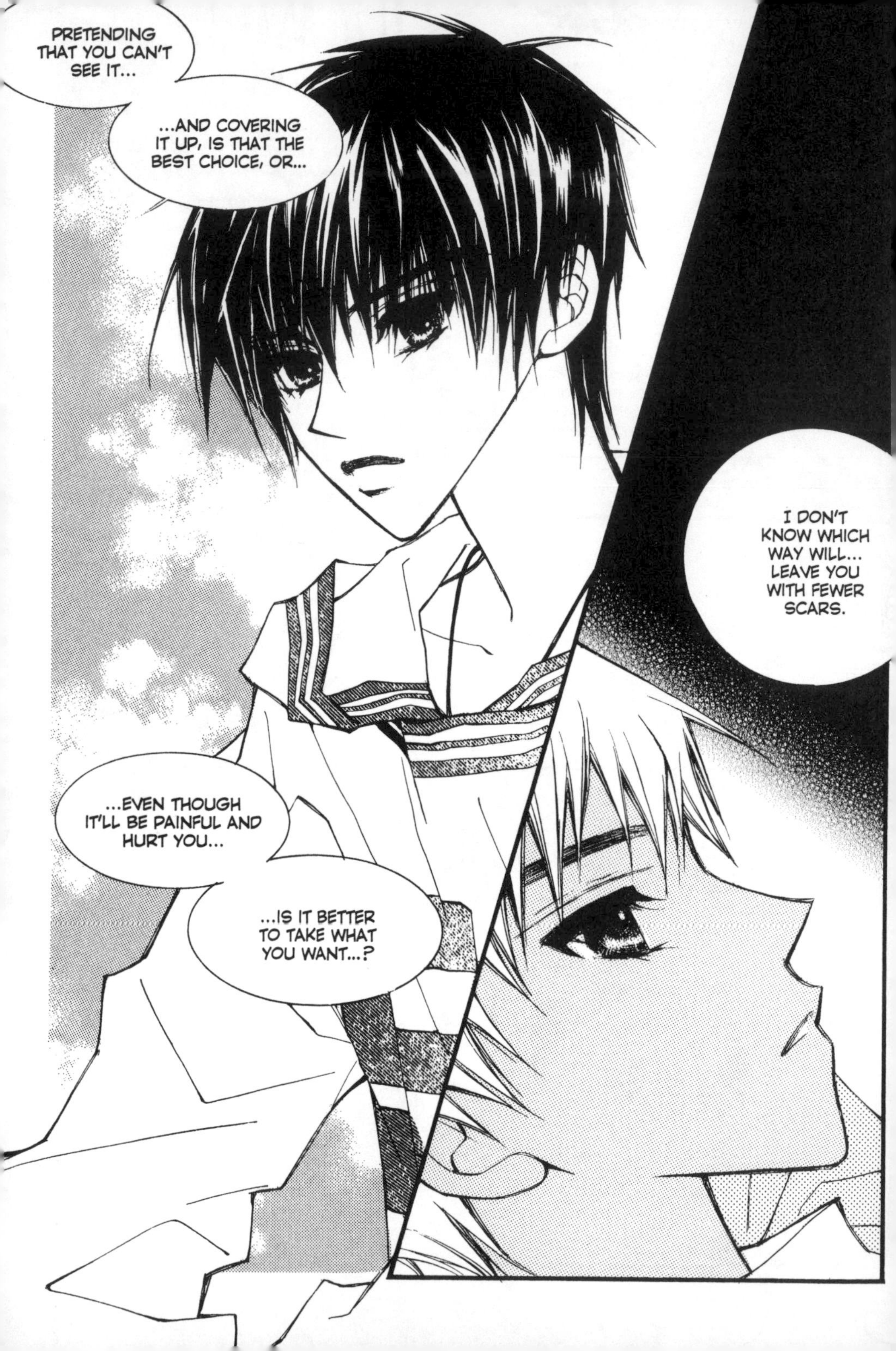
PRETENDING THAT YOU CAN'T SEE IT...
...AND COVERING IT UP, IS THAT THE BEST CHOICE, OR...
...EVEN THOUGH IT'LL BE PAINFUL AND HURT YOU...
...IS IT BETTER TO TAKE WHAT YOU WANT...?
I DON'T KNOW WHICH WAY WILL... LEAVE YOU WITH FEWER SCARS.

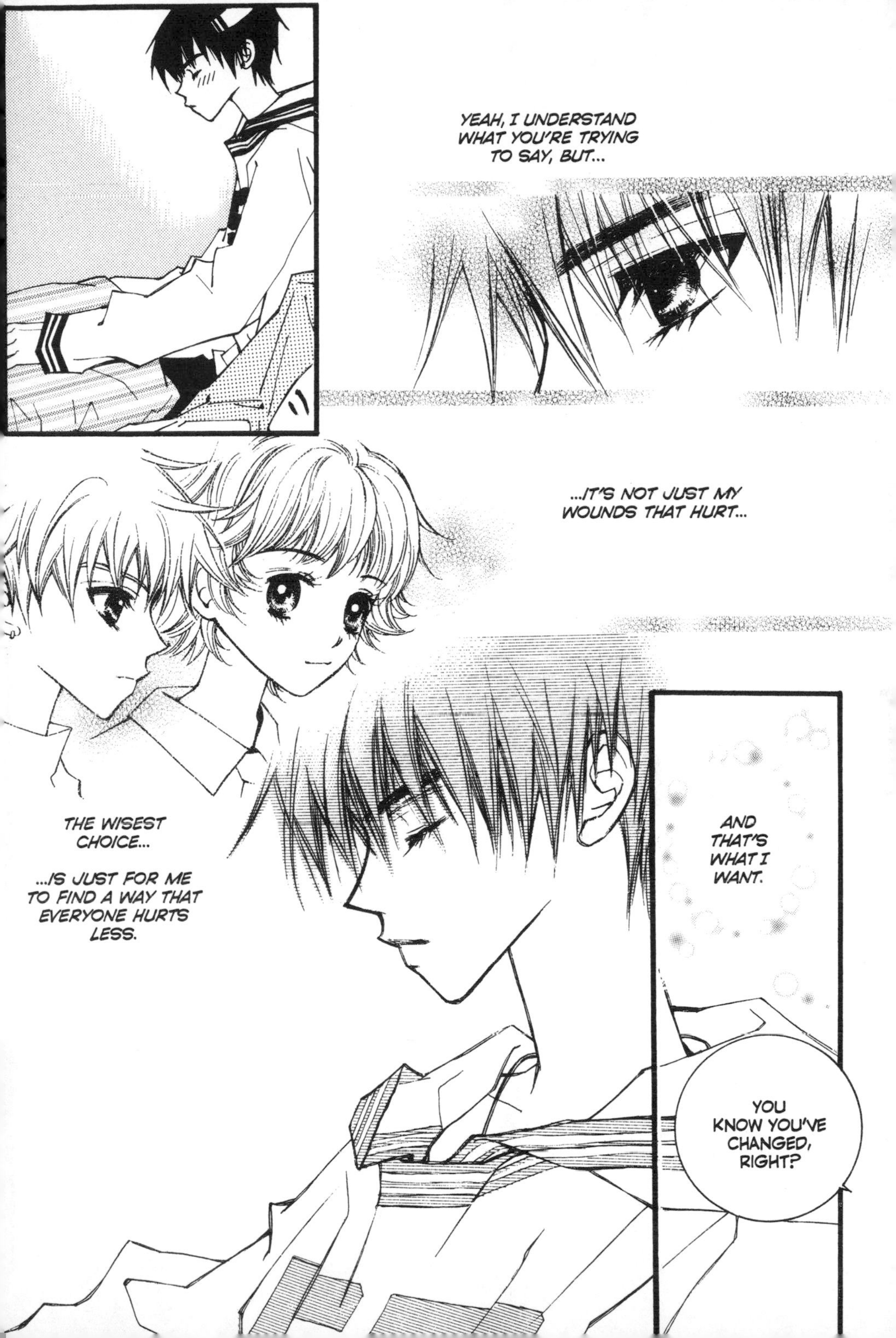
YEAH, I UNDERSTAND WHAT YOU'RE TRYING TO SAY, BUT...
...IT'S NOT JUST MY WOUNDS THAT HURT...
THE WISEST CHOICE...
...IS JUST FOR ME TO FIND A WAY THAT EVERYONE HURTS LESS.
AND THAT'S WHAT I WANT.
YOU KNOW YOU'VE CHANGED, RIGHT?

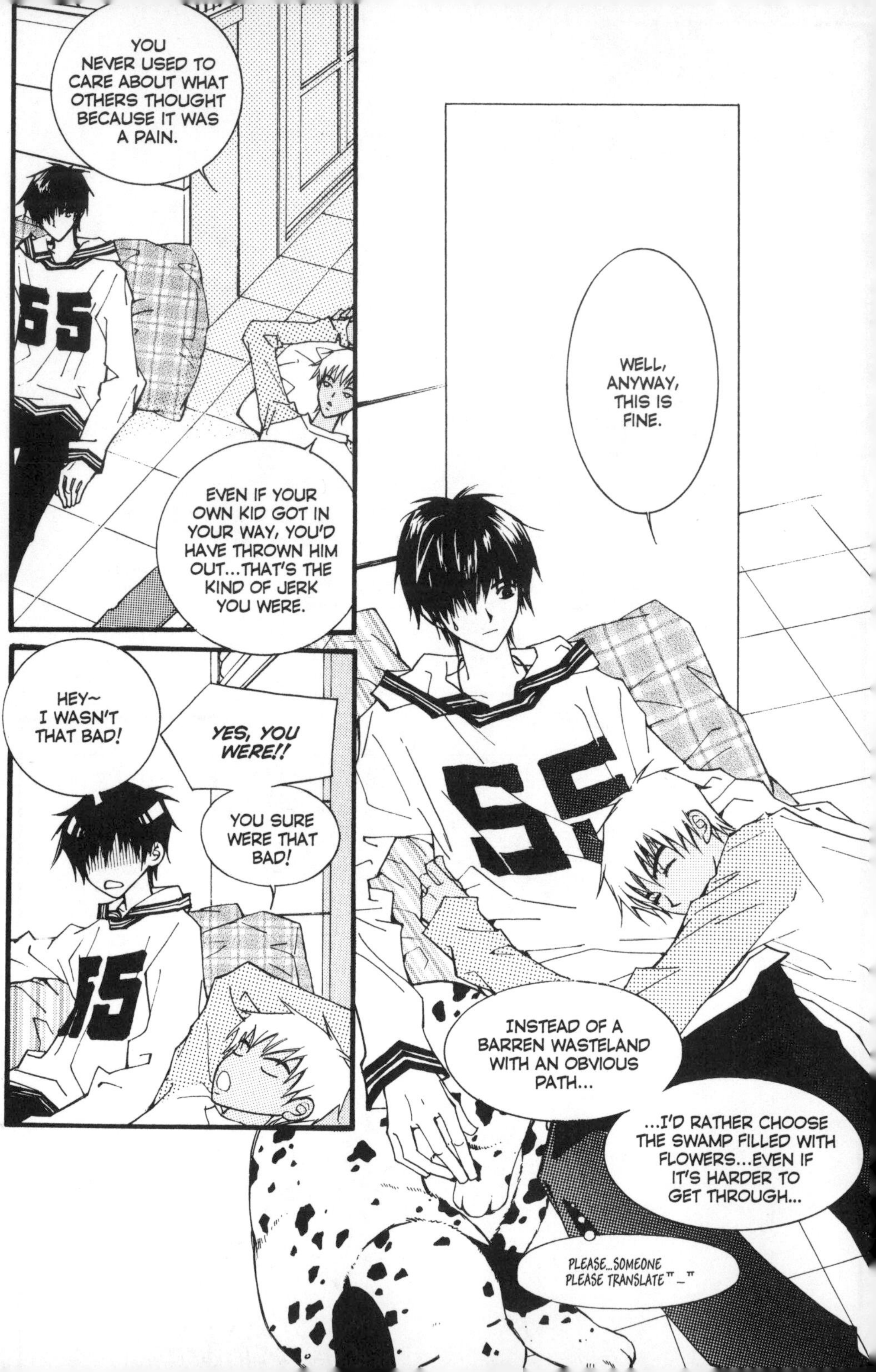
YOU NEVER USED TO CARE ABOUT WHAT OTHERS THOUGHT BECAUSE IT WAS A PAIN.
EVEN IF YOUR OWN KID GOT IN YOUR WAY, YOU'D HAVE THROWN HIM OUT...THAT'S THE KIND OF JERK YOU WERE.
HEY~ I WASN'T THAT BAD!
YES, YOU WERE!!
YOU SURE WERE THAT BAD!
WELL, ANYWAY, THIS IS FINE.
INSTEAD OF A BARREN WASTELAND WITH AN OBVIOUS PATH...
...I'D RATHER CHOOSE THE SWAMP FILLED WITH FLOWERS...EVEN IF IT'S HARDER TO GET THROUGH...
PLEASE...SOMEONE PLEASE TRANSLATE T_T

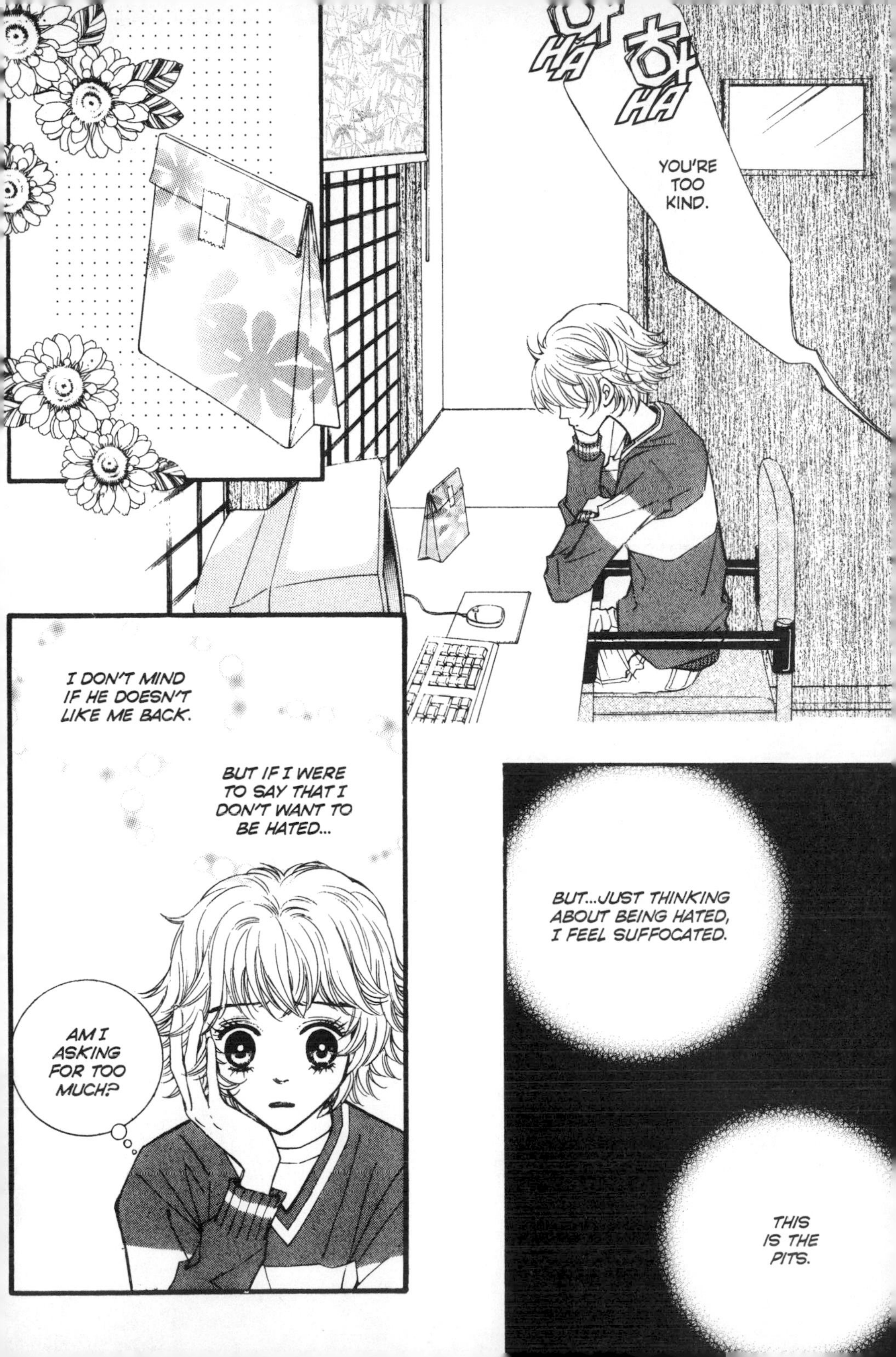
HA
하 HA
YOU'RE TOO KIND.
I DON'T MIND IF HE DOESN'T LIKE ME BACK.
BUT IF I WERE TO SAY THAT I DON'T WANT TO BE HATED...
AM I ASKING FOR TOO MUCH?
BUT...JUST THINKING ABOUT BEING HATED, I FEEL SUFFOCATED.
THIS IS THE PITS.

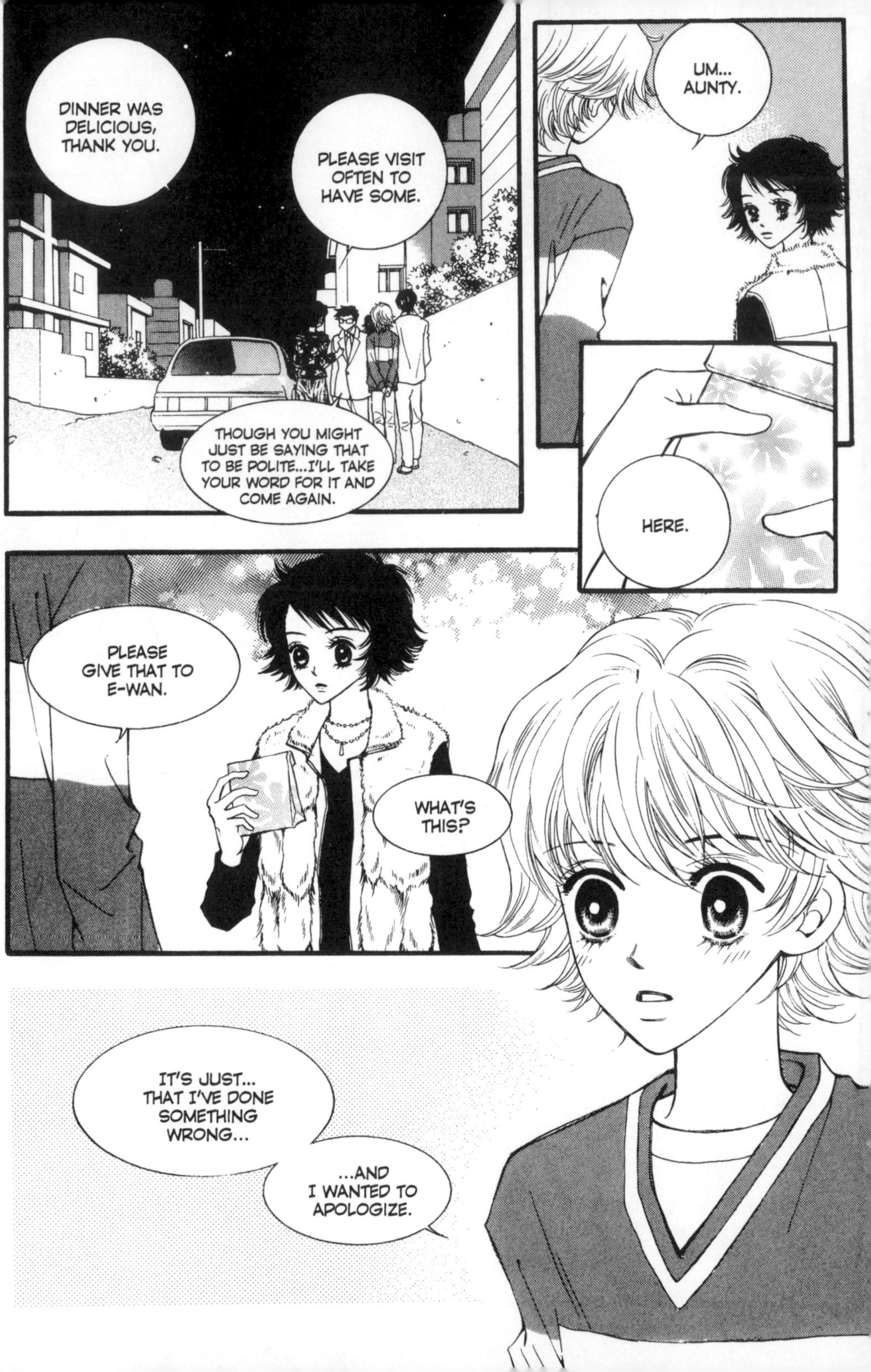
DINNER WAS DELICIOUS, THANK YOU.
PLEASE VISIT OFTEN TO HAVE SOME.
THOUGH YOU MIGHT JUST BE SAYING THAT TO BE POLITE...I'LL TAKE YOUR WORD FOR IT AND COME AGAIN.
UM... AUNTY.
HERE.
PLEASE GIVE THAT TO E-WAN.
WHAT'S THIS?
IT'S JUST... THAT I'VE DONE SOMETHING WRONG...
...AND I WANTED TO APOLOGIZE.

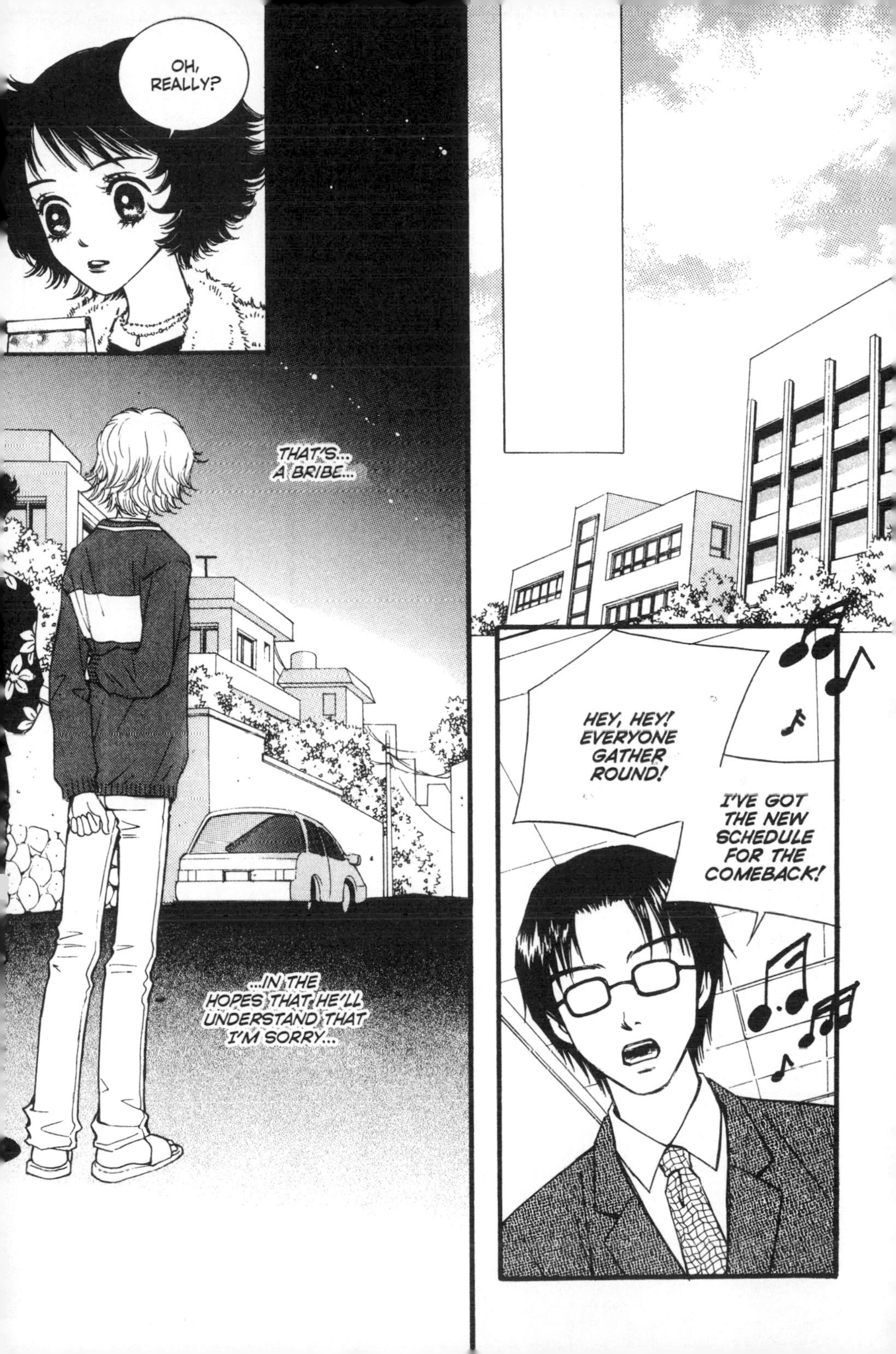
OH, REALLY?
THAT'S... A BRIBE...
...IN THE HOPES THAT HE'LL UNDERSTAND THAT I'M SORRY...
HEY, HEY! EVERYONE GATHER ROUND!
I'VE GOT THE NEW SCHEDULE FOR THE COMEBACK!

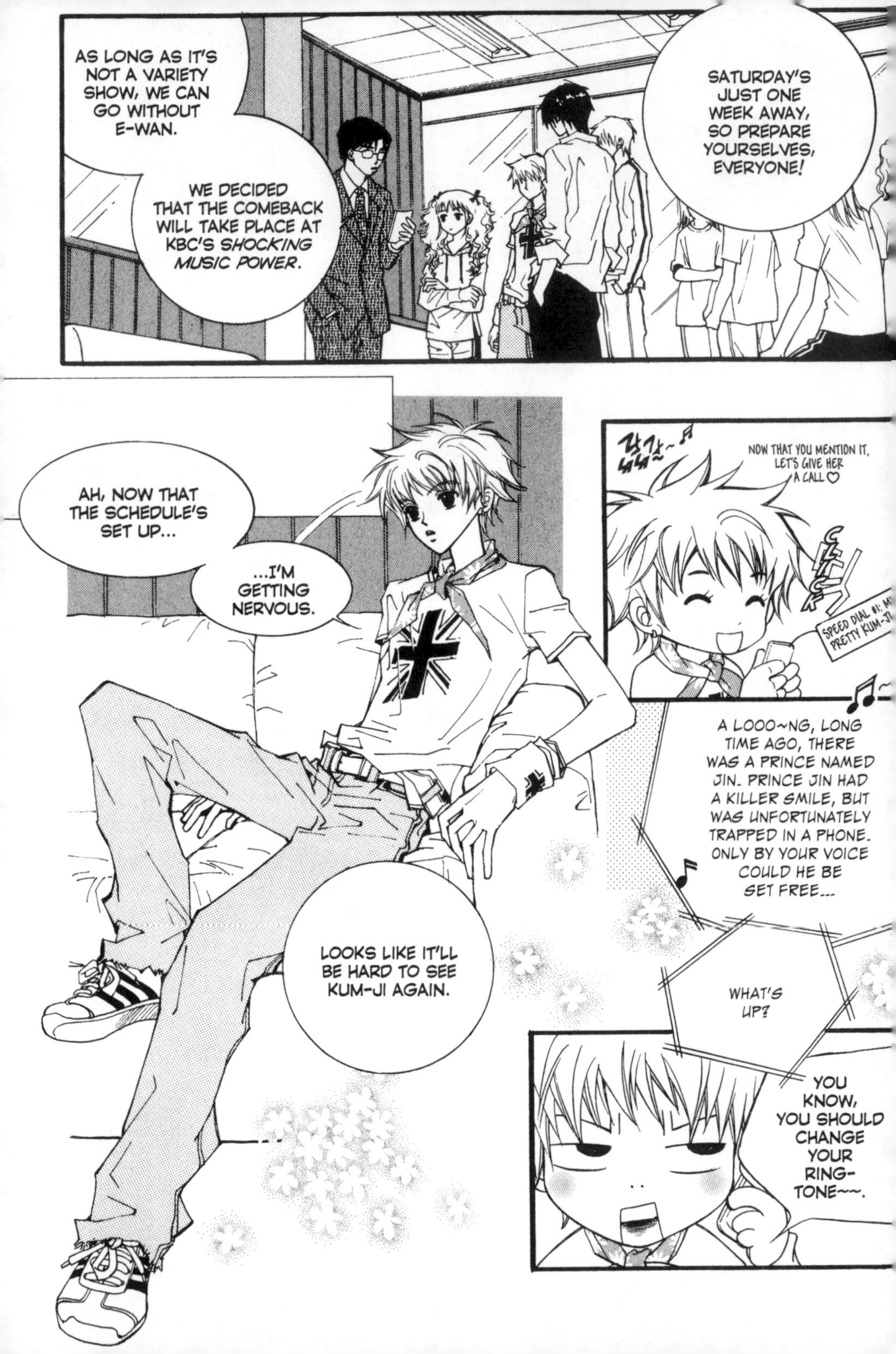
AS LONG AS IT'S NOT A VARIETY SHOW, WE CAN GO WITHOUT E-WAN.
WE DECIDED THAT THE COMEBACK WILL TAKE PLACE AT KBC'S *SHOCKING MUSIC POWER*.
SATURDAY'S JUST ONE WEEK AWAY, SO PREPARE YOURSELVES, EVERYONE!
AH, NOW THAT THE SCHEDULE'S SET UP...
...I'M GETTING NERVOUS.
LOOKS LIKE IT'LL BE HARD TO SEE KUM-JI AGAIN.
NOW THAT YOU MENTION IT, LET'S GIVE HER A CALL ♡
CLICK
SPEED DIAL #1: M
PRETTY KUM-J
A LOOO~NG, LONG TIME AGO, THERE WAS A PRINCE NAMED JIN. PRINCE JIN HAD A KILLER SMILE, BUT WAS UNFORTUNATELY TRAPPED IN A PHONE. ONLY BY YOUR VOICE COULD HE BE SET FREE...
WHAT'S UP?
YOU KNOW, YOU SHOULD CHANGE YOUR RING-TONE~~.

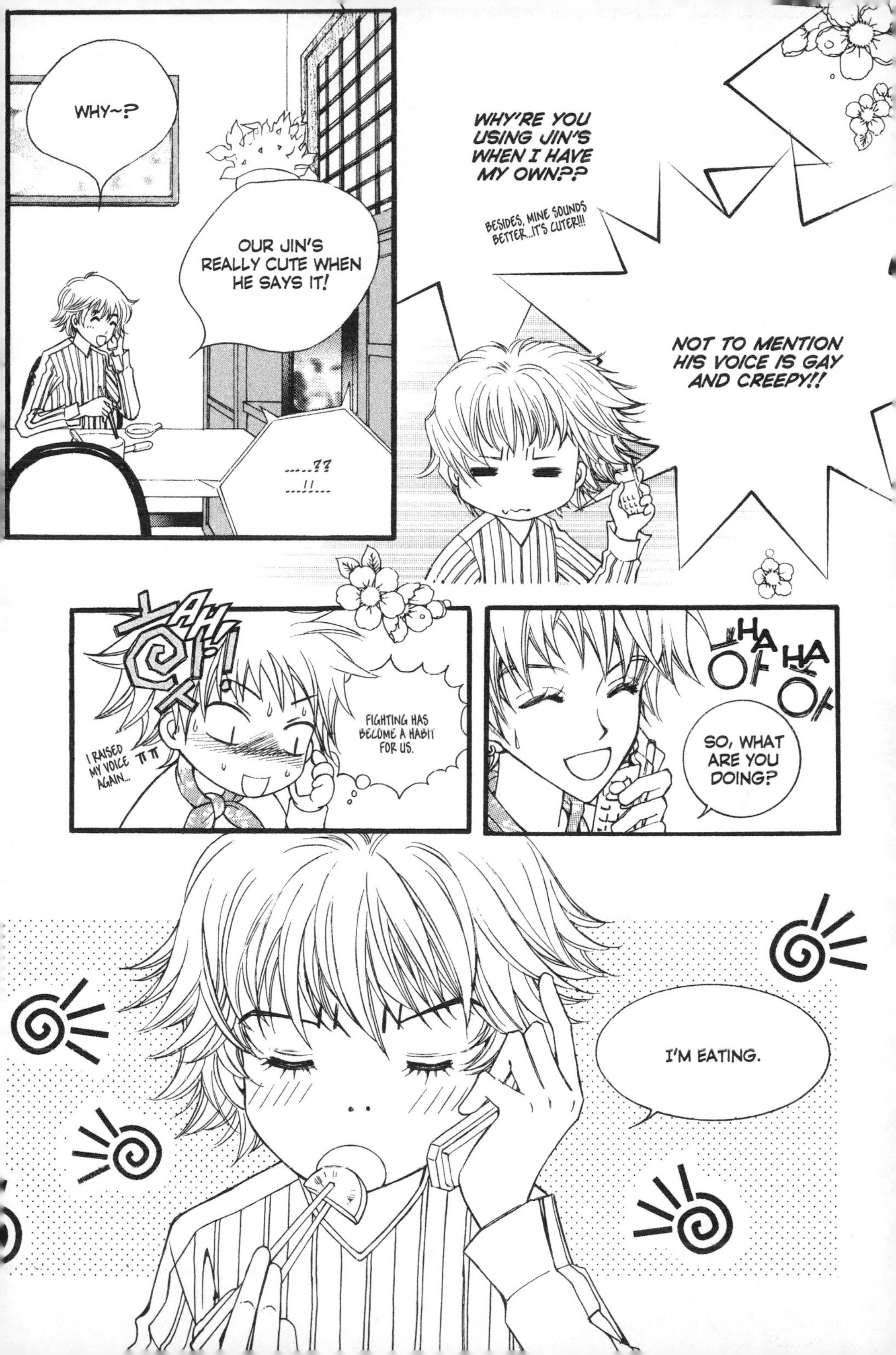
WHY~?
OUR JIN'S REALLY CUTE WHEN HE SAYS IT!
-----??
---!!----
WHY'RE YOU USING JIN'S WHEN I HAVE MY OWN??
BESIDES, MINE SOUNDS BETTER...IT'S CUTER!!!
NOT TO MENTION HIS VOICE IS GAY AND CREEPY!!
AH!
I RAISED MY VOICE AGAIN... TT TT
FIGHTING HAS BECOME A HABIT FOR US.
HA HA
SO, WHAT ARE YOU DOING?
I'M EATING.

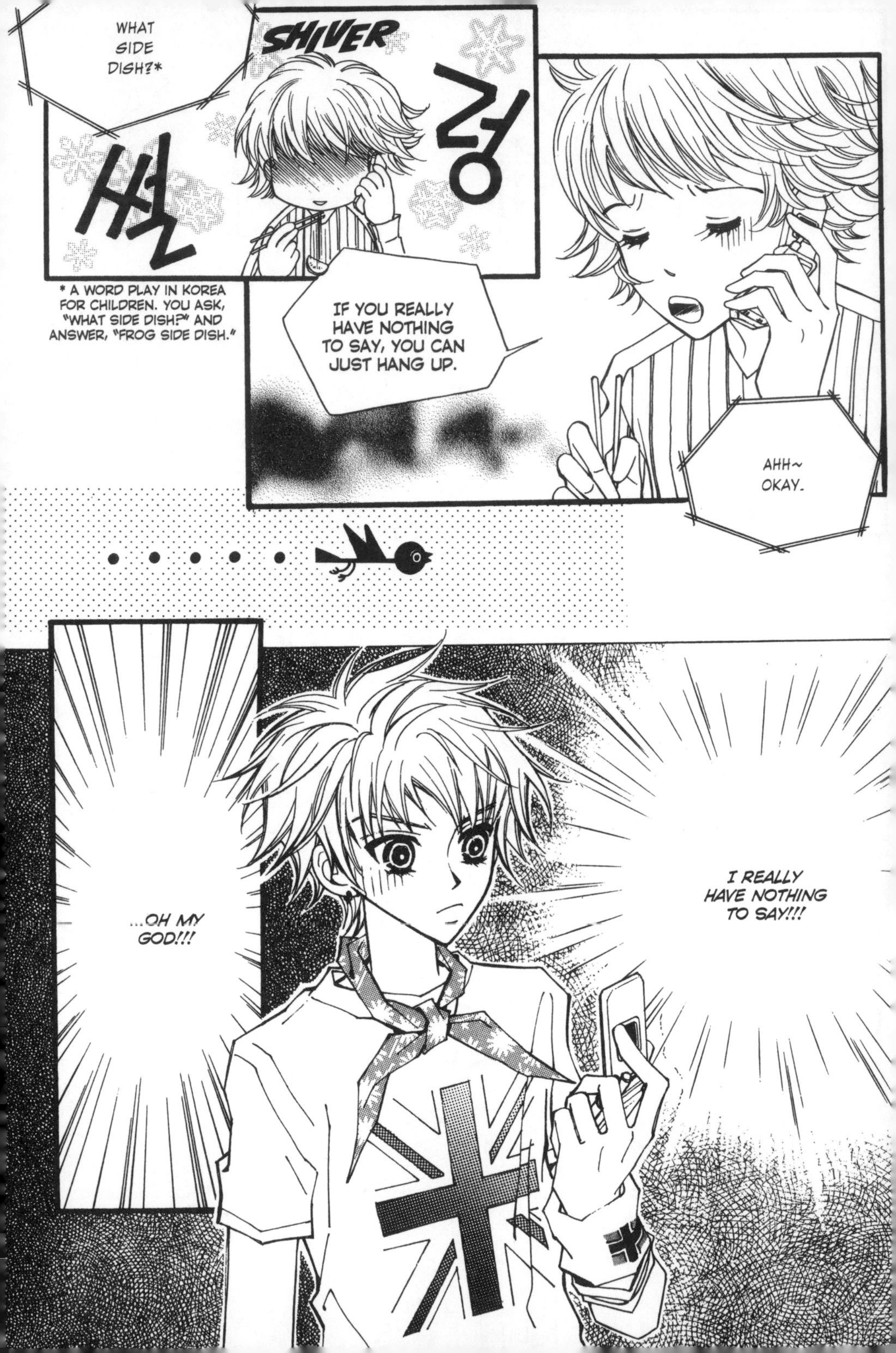
WHAT SIDE DISH?*
SHIVER
* A WORD PLAY IN KOREA FOR CHILDREN. YOU ASK, "WHAT SIDE DISH?" AND ANSWER, "FROG SIDE DISH."
IF YOU REALLY HAVE NOTHING TO SAY, YOU CAN JUST HANG UP.
AHH~ OKAY.
...OH MY GOD!!!
I REALLY HAVE NOTHING TO SAY!!!

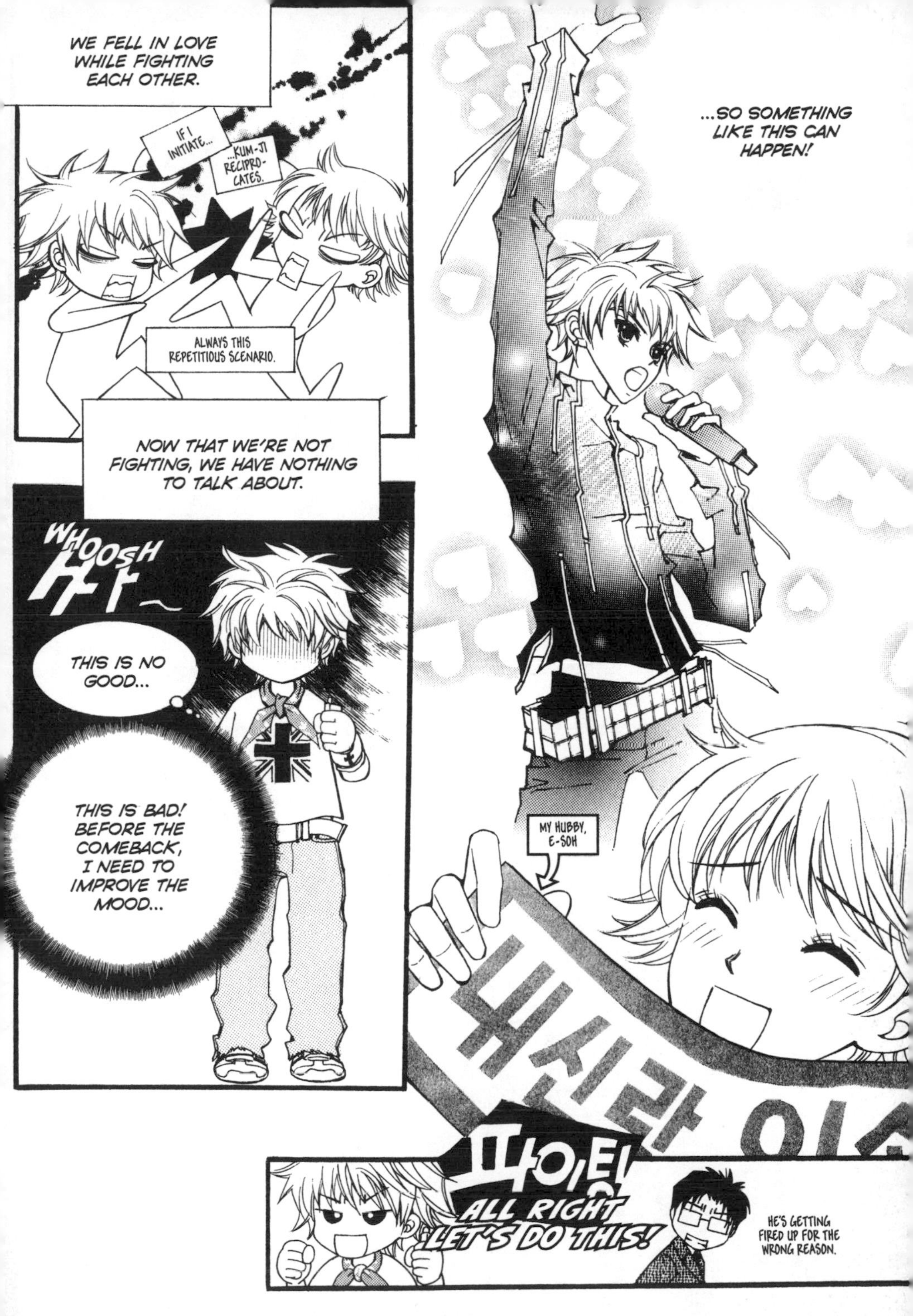
WE FELL IN LOVE WHILE FIGHTING EACH OTHER.
IF I INITIATE...
...KUM-JI RECIPRO-CATES.
ALWAYS THIS REPETITIOUS SCENARIO.
NOW THAT WE'RE NOT FIGHTING, WE HAVE NOTHING TO TALK ABOUT.
WHOOSH
THIS IS NO GOOD...
THIS IS BAD! BEFORE THE COMEBACK, I NEED TO IMPROVE THE MOOD...
...SO SOMETHING LIKE THIS CAN HAPPEN!
MY HUBBY, E-SOH
파이팅
ALL RIGHT LET'S DO THIS!
HE'S GETTING FIRED UP FOR THE WRONG REASON.

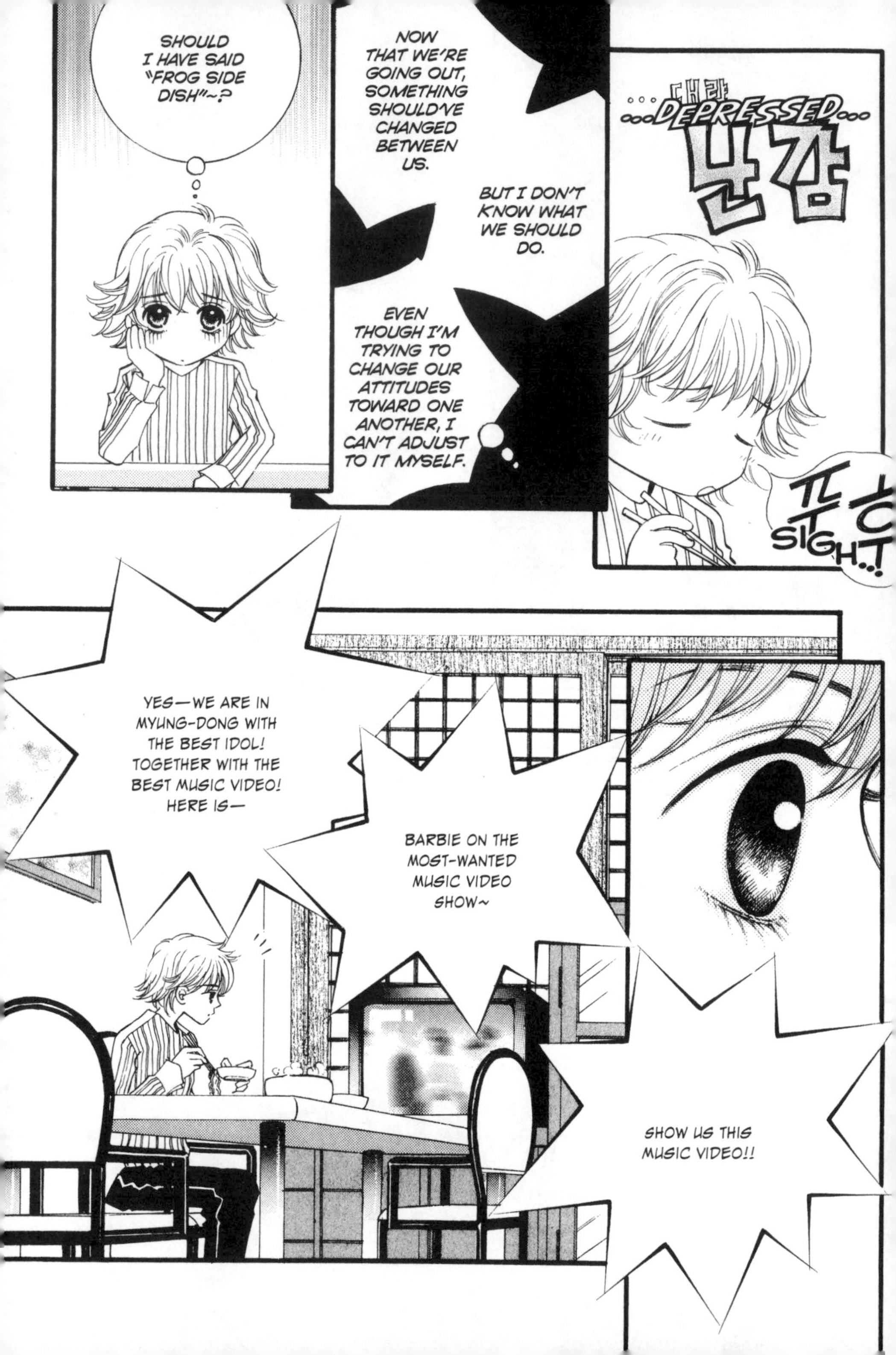
SHOULD I HAVE SAID "FROG SIDE DISH"~?
NOW THAT WE'RE GOING OUT, SOMETHING SHOULD'VE CHANGED BETWEEN US.
BUT I DON'T KNOW WHAT WE SHOULD DO.
EVEN THOUGH I'M TRYING TO CHANGE OUR ATTITUDES TOWARD ONE ANOTHER, I CAN'T ADJUST TO IT MYSELF.
...DEPRESSED...
난감
SIGH..!
YES—WE ARE IN MYUNG-DONG WITH THE BEST IDOL! TOGETHER WITH THE BEST MUSIC VIDEO! HERE IS—
BARBIE ON THE MOST-WANTED MUSIC VIDEO SHOW~
SHOW US THIS MUSIC VIDEO!!

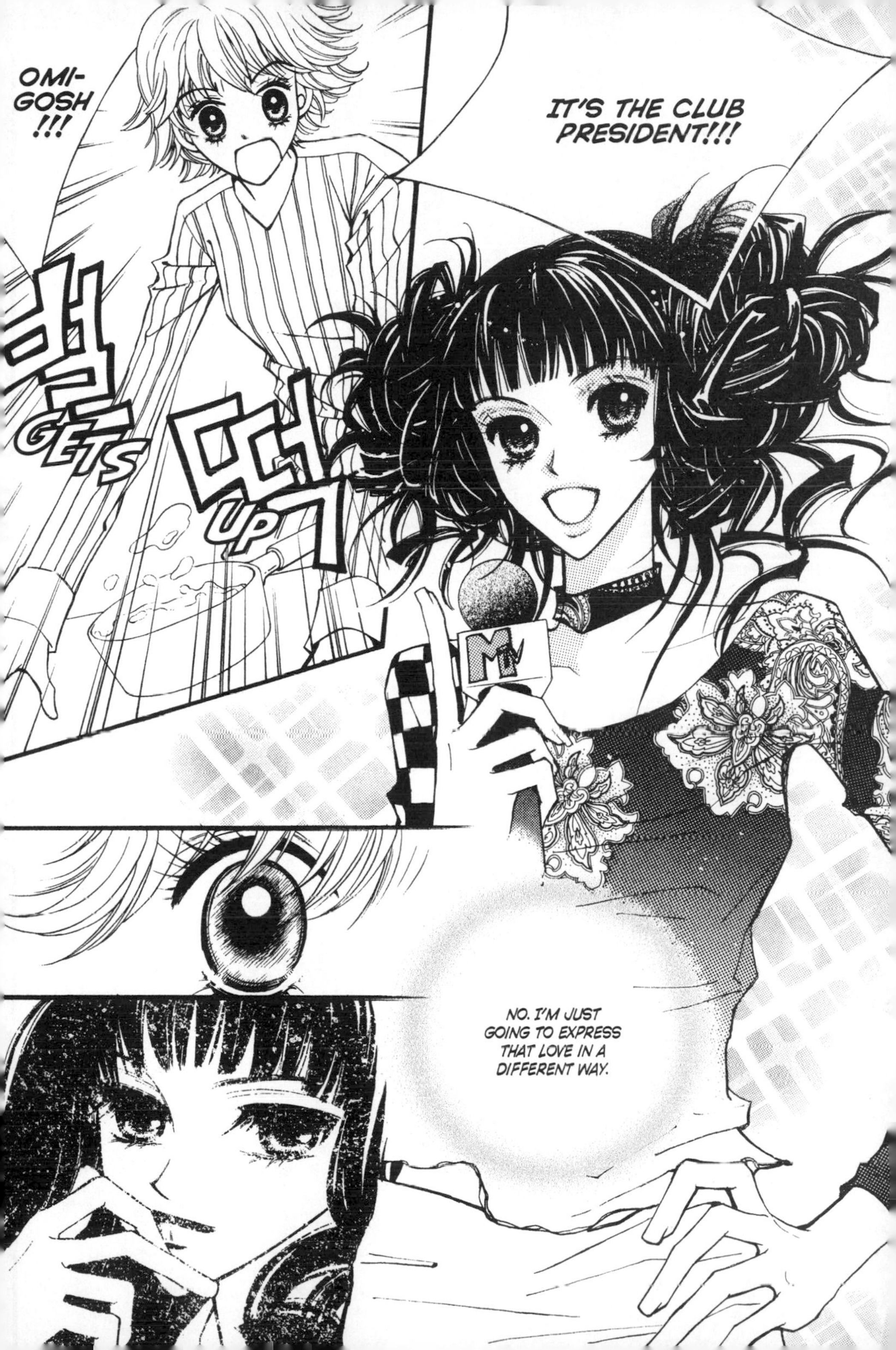
OMI-GOSH!!!
GETS UP
IT'S THE CLUB PRESIDENT!!!
NO. I'M JUST GOING TO EXPRESS THAT LOVE IN A DIFFERENT WAY.

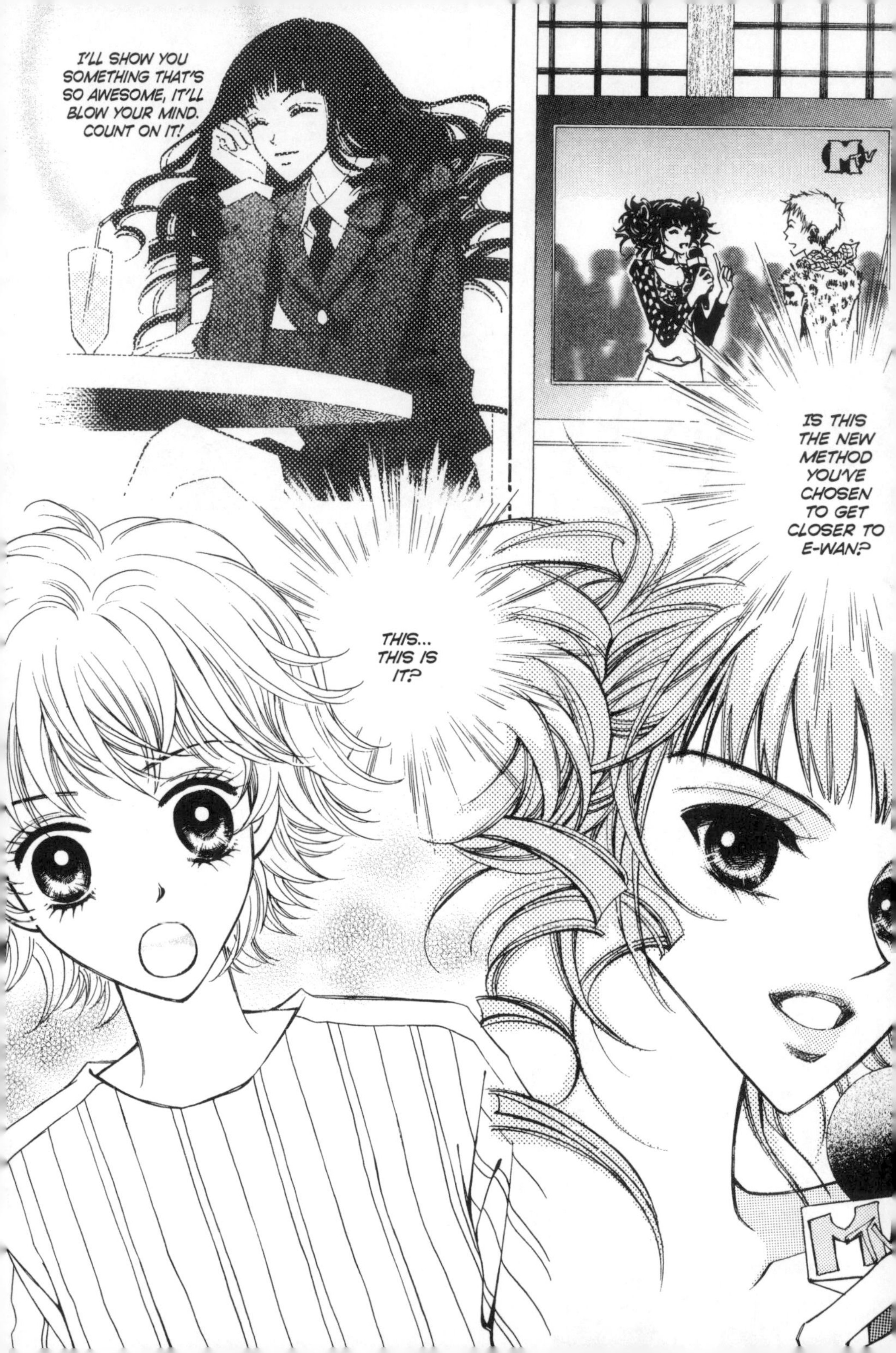
I'LL SHOW YOU SOMETHING THAT'S SO AWESOME, IT'LL BLOW YOUR MIND. COUNT ON IT!
IS THIS THE NEW METHOD YOU'VE CHOSEN TO GET CLOSER TO E-WAN?
THIS... THIS IS IT?

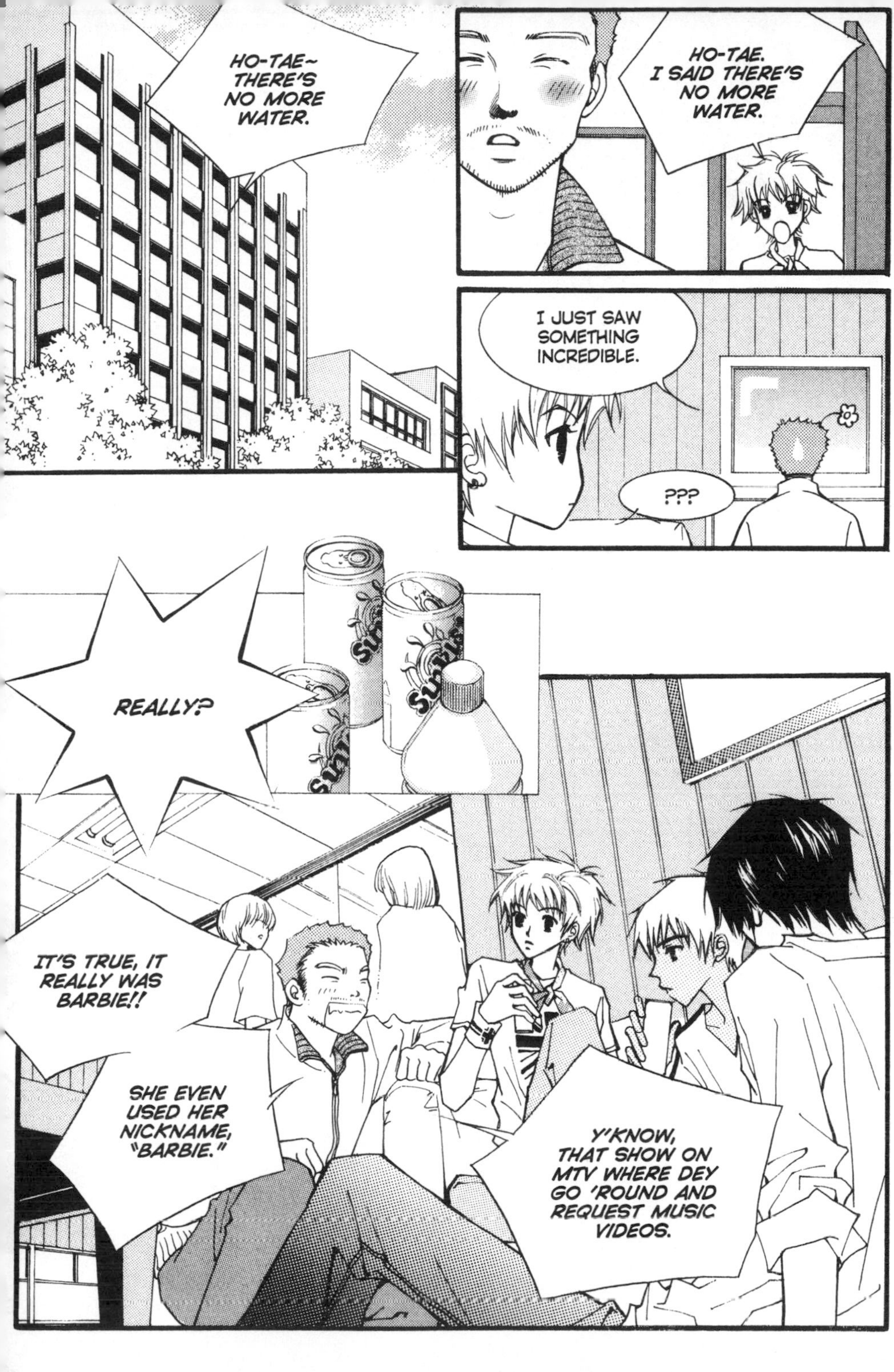
HO-TAE~ THERE'S NO MORE WATER.
HO-TAE. I SAID THERE'S NO MORE WATER.
I JUST SAW SOMETHING INCREDIBLE.
???
REALLY?
IT'S TRUE, IT REALLY WAS BARBIE!!
SHE EVEN USED HER NICKNAME, "BARBIE."
Y'KNOW, THAT SHOW ON MTV WHERE DEY GO 'ROUND AND REQUEST MUSIC VIDEOS.

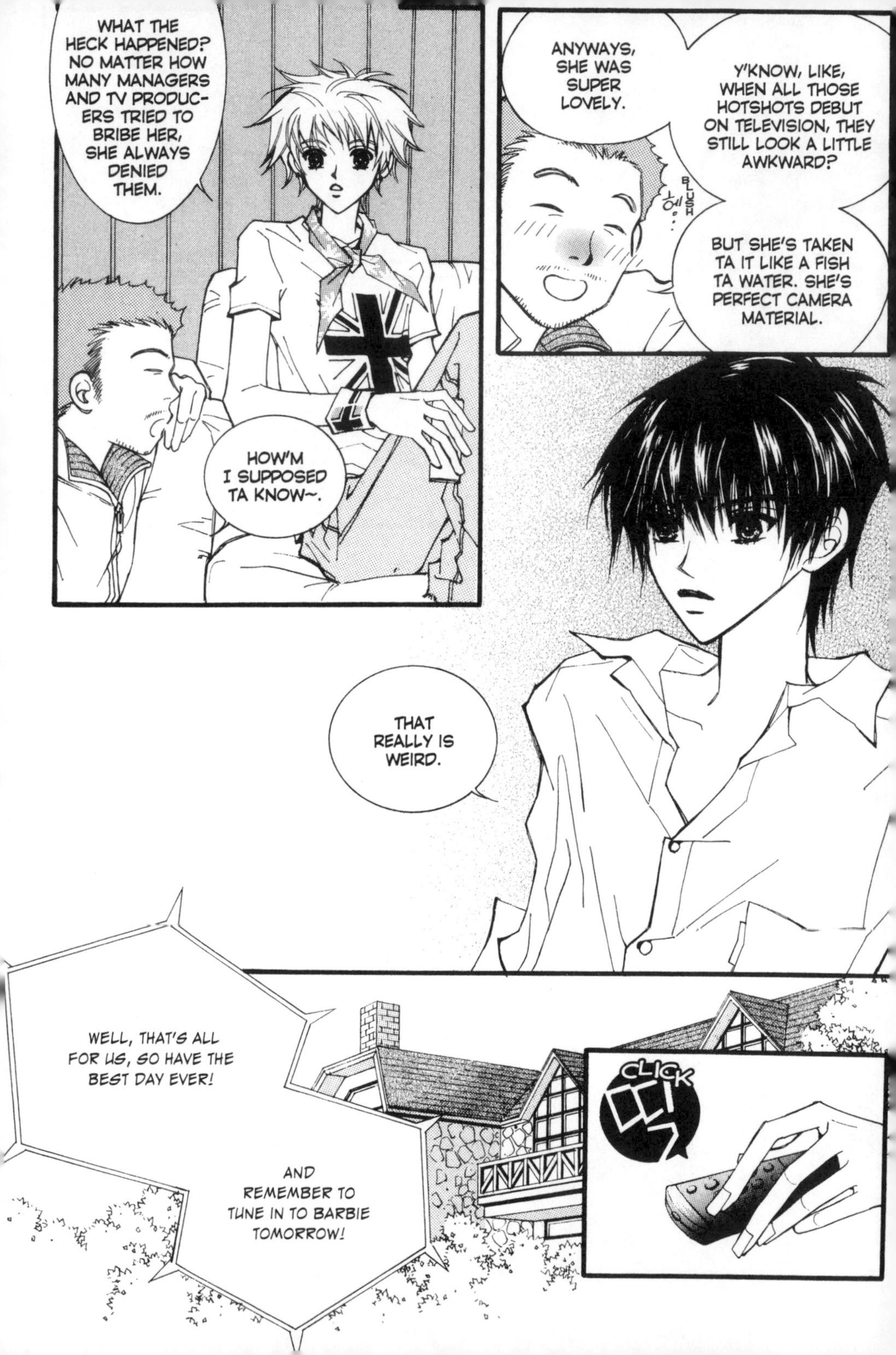
WHAT THE HECK HAPPENED? NO MATTER HOW MANY MANAGERS AND TV PRODUCERS TRIED TO BRIBE HER, SHE ALWAYS DENIED THEM.
HOW'M I SUPPOSED TA KNOW~.
ANYWAYS, SHE WAS SUPER LOVELY.
Y'KNOW, LIKE, WHEN ALL THOSE HOTSHOTS DEBUT ON TELEVISION, THEY STILL LOOK A LITTLE AWKWARD?
BLUSH
BUT SHE'S TAKEN TA IT LIKE A FISH TA WATER. SHE'S PERFECT CAMERA MATERIAL.
THAT REALLY IS WEIRD.
WELL, THAT'S ALL FOR US, SO HAVE THE BEST DAY EVER!
AND REMEMBER TO TUNE IN TO BARBIE TOMORROW!
CLICK

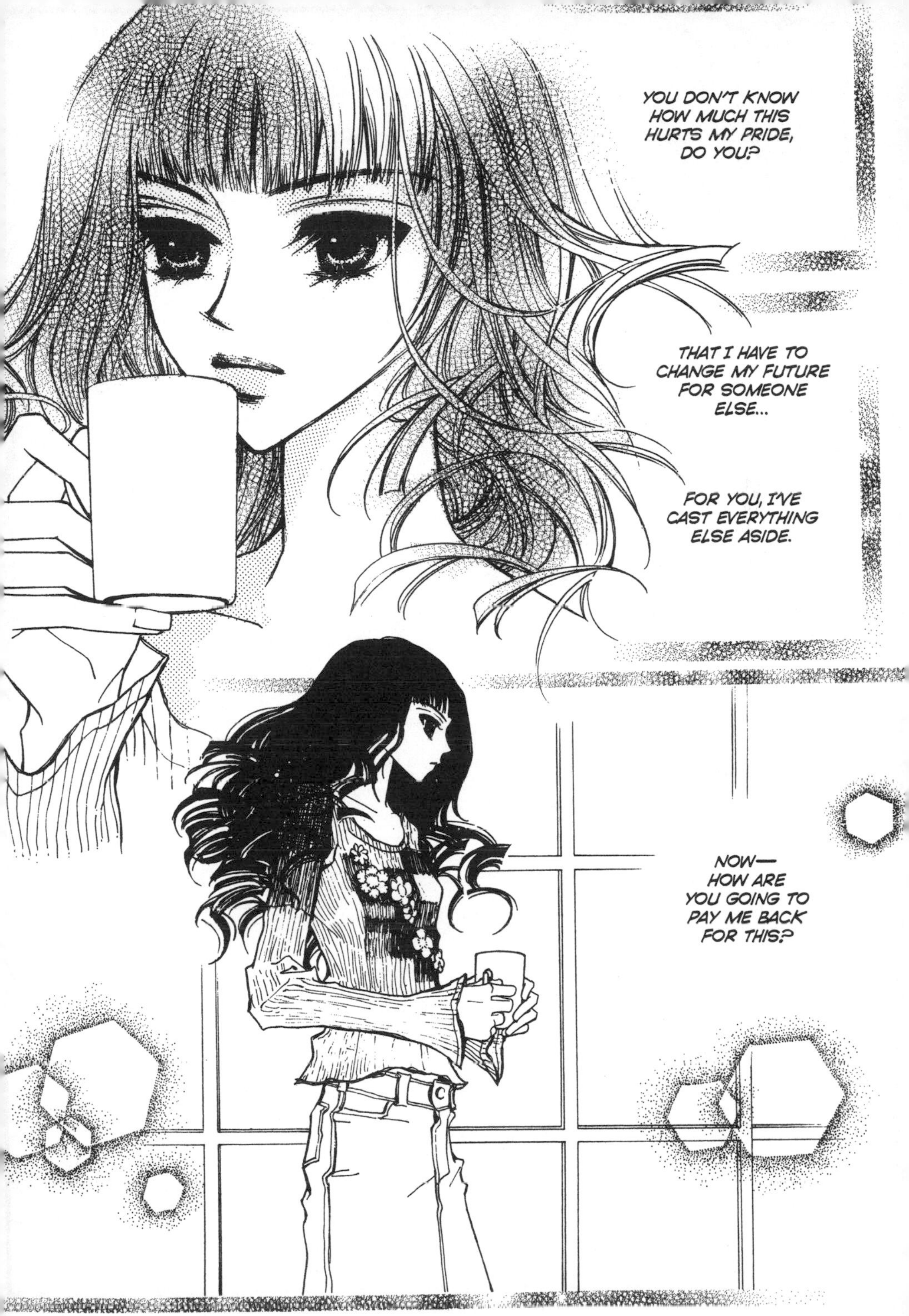
YOU DON'T KNOW HOW MUCH THIS HURTS MY PRIDE, DO YOU?
THAT I HAVE TO CHANGE MY FUTURE FOR SOMEONE ELSE...
FOR YOU, I'VE CAST EVERYTHING ELSE ASIDE.
NOW— HOW ARE YOU GOING TO PAY ME BACK FOR THIS?

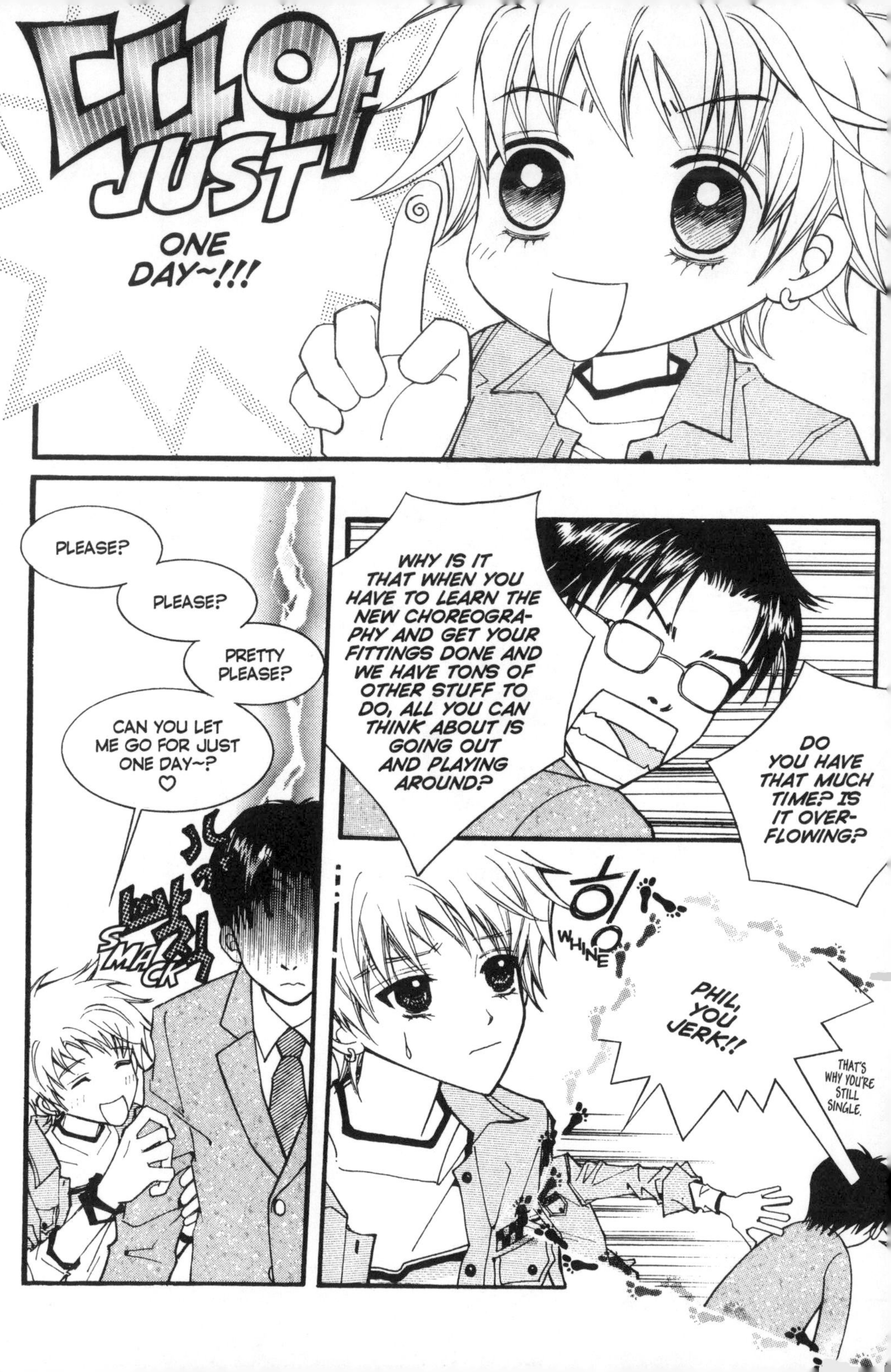
JUST
ONE DAY~!!!
PLEASE?
PLEASE?
PRETTY PLEASE?
CAN YOU LET ME GO FOR JUST ONE DAY~? ♡
SMACK
WHY IS IT THAT WHEN YOU HAVE TO LEARN THE NEW CHOREOGRAPHY AND GET YOUR FITTINGS DONE AND WE HAVE TONS OF OTHER STUFF TO DO, ALL YOU CAN THINK ABOUT IS GOING OUT AND PLAYING AROUND?
DO YOU HAVE THAT MUCH TIME? IS IT OVERFLOWING?
WHINE
PHIL, YOU JERK!!
THAT'S WHY YOU'RE STILL SINGLE.

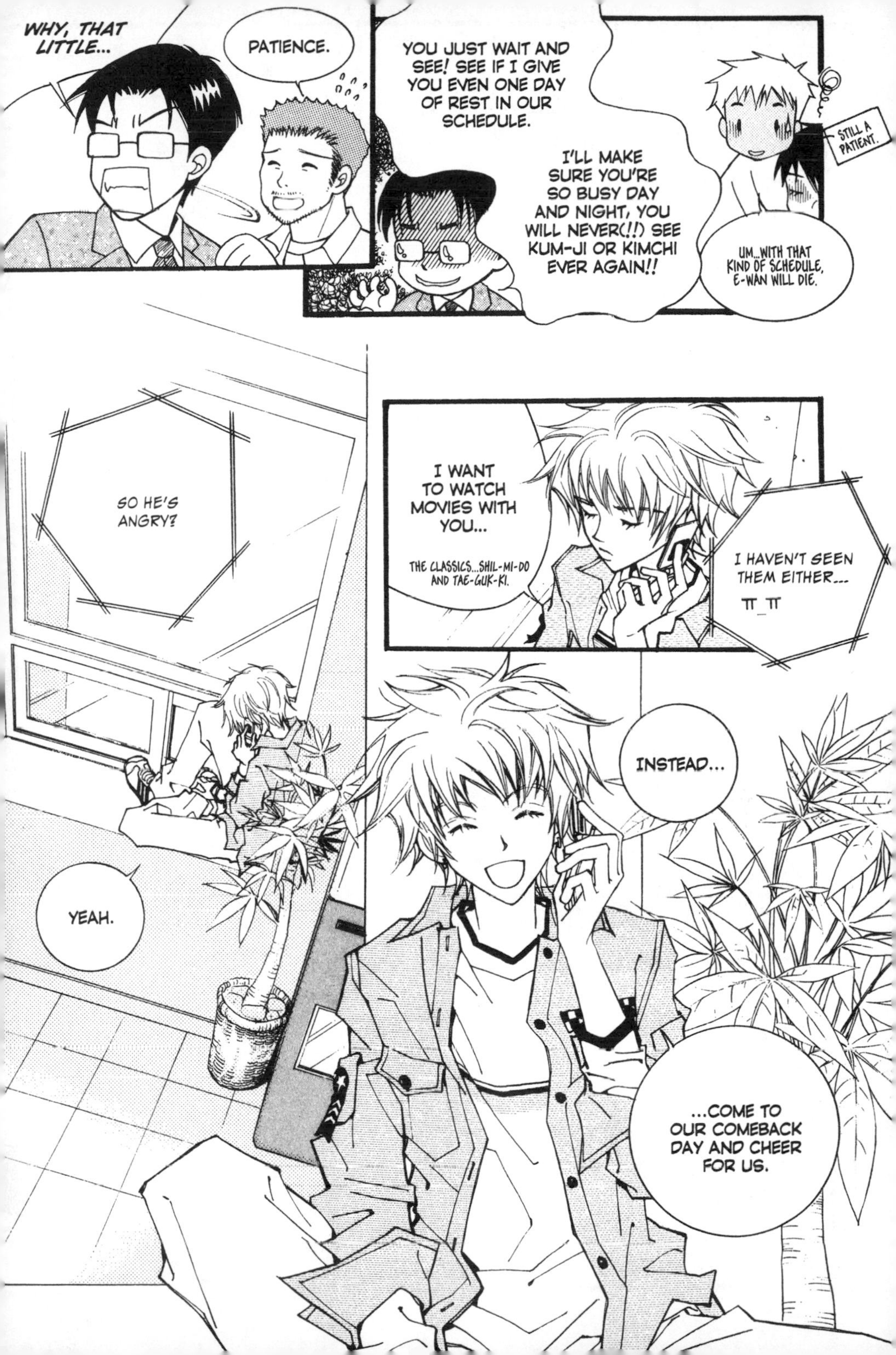
WHY, THAT LITTLE...
PATIENCE.
YOU JUST WAIT AND SEE! SEE IF I GIVE YOU EVEN ONE DAY OF REST IN OUR SCHEDULE.
I'LL MAKE SURE YOU'RE SO BUSY DAY AND NIGHT, YOU WILL NEVER(!!) SEE KUM-JI OR KIMCHI EVER AGAIN!!
STILL A PATIENT.
UM...WITH THAT KIND OF SCHEDULE, E-WAN WILL DIE.
SO HE'S ANGRY?
YEAH.
I WANT TO WATCH MOVIES WITH YOU...
THE CLASSICS...SHIL-MI-DO AND TAE-GUK-KI.
I HAVEN'T SEEN THEM EITHER...
π_π
INSTEAD...
...COME TO OUR COMEBACK DAY AND CHEER FOR US.

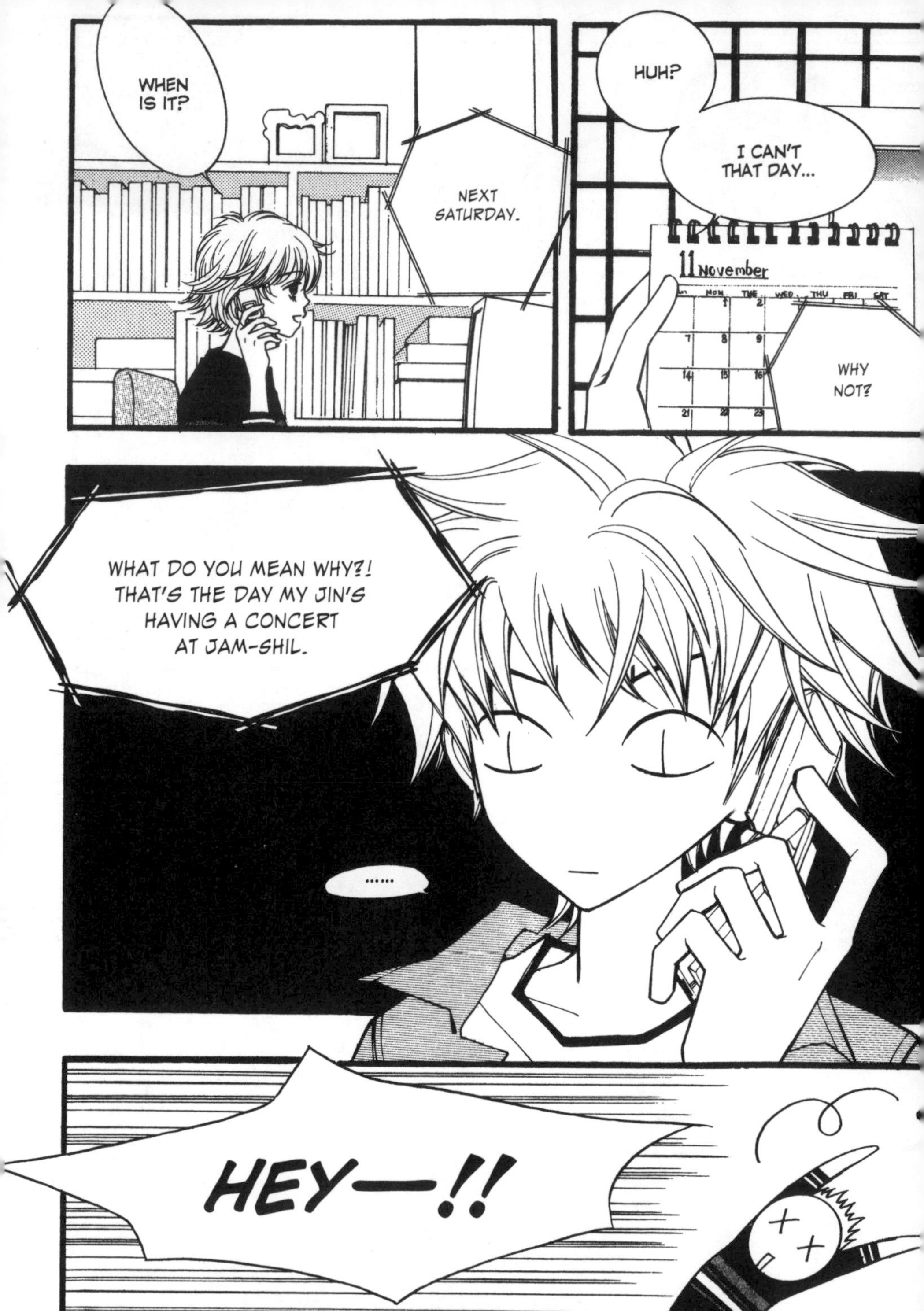
WHEN IS IT?
NEXT SATURDAY.
HUH?
I CAN'T THAT DAY...
11 November
WHY NOT?
WHAT DO YOU MEAN WHY?! THAT'S THE DAY MY JIN'S HAVING A CONCERT AT JAM-SHIL.
......
HEY—!!

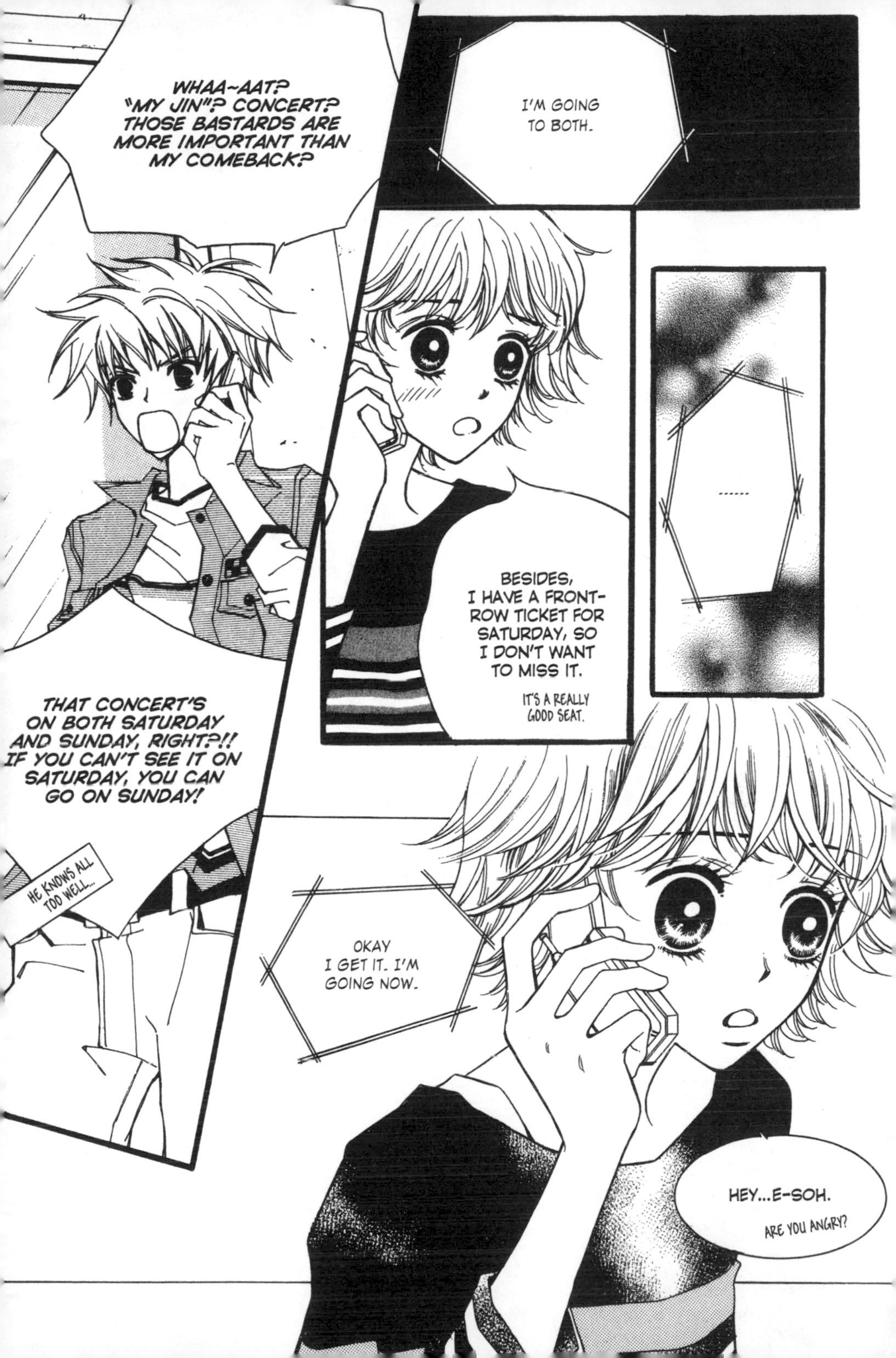
WHAA~AAT? "MY JIN"? CONCERT? THOSE BASTARDS ARE MORE IMPORTANT THAN MY COMEBACK?
I'M GOING TO BOTH.
BESIDES, I HAVE A FRONT-ROW TICKET FOR SATURDAY, SO I DON'T WANT TO MISS IT.
IT'S A REALLY GOOD SEAT.
......
THAT CONCERT'S ON BOTH SATURDAY AND SUNDAY, RIGHT?!! IF YOU CAN'T SEE IT ON SATURDAY, YOU CAN GO ON SUNDAY!
HE KNOWS ALL TOO WELL...
OKAY I GET IT. I'M GOING NOW.
HEY...E-SOH.
ARE YOU ANGRY?

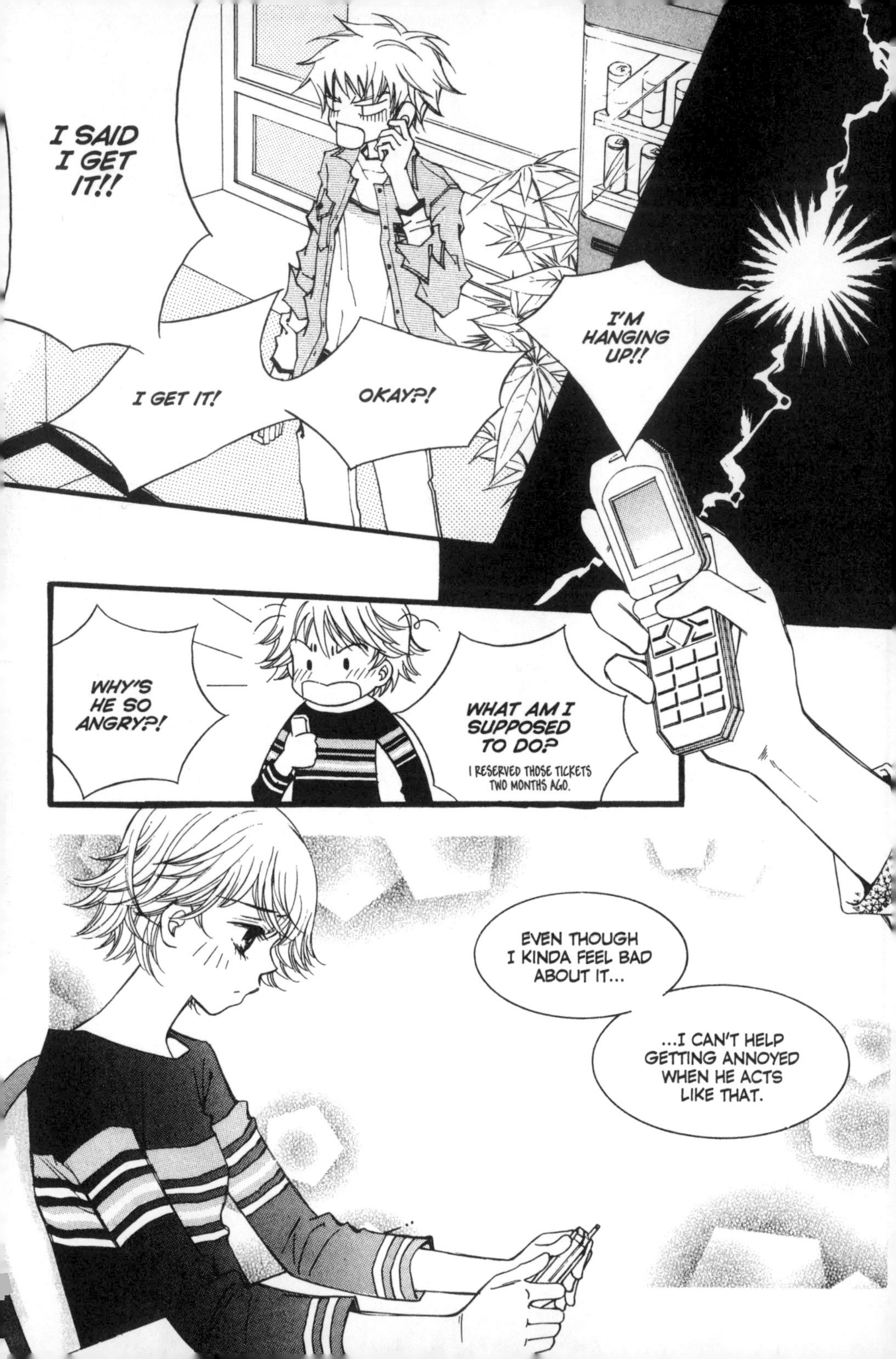
I SAID I GET IT!!
I GET IT!
OKAY?!
I'M HANGING UP!!
WHY'S HE SO ANGRY?!
WHAT AM I SUPPOSED TO DO?
I RESERVED THOSE TICKETS TWO MONTHS AGO.
EVEN THOUGH I KINDA FEEL BAD ABOUT IT...
...I CAN'T HELP GETTING ANNOYED WHEN HE ACTS LIKE THAT.

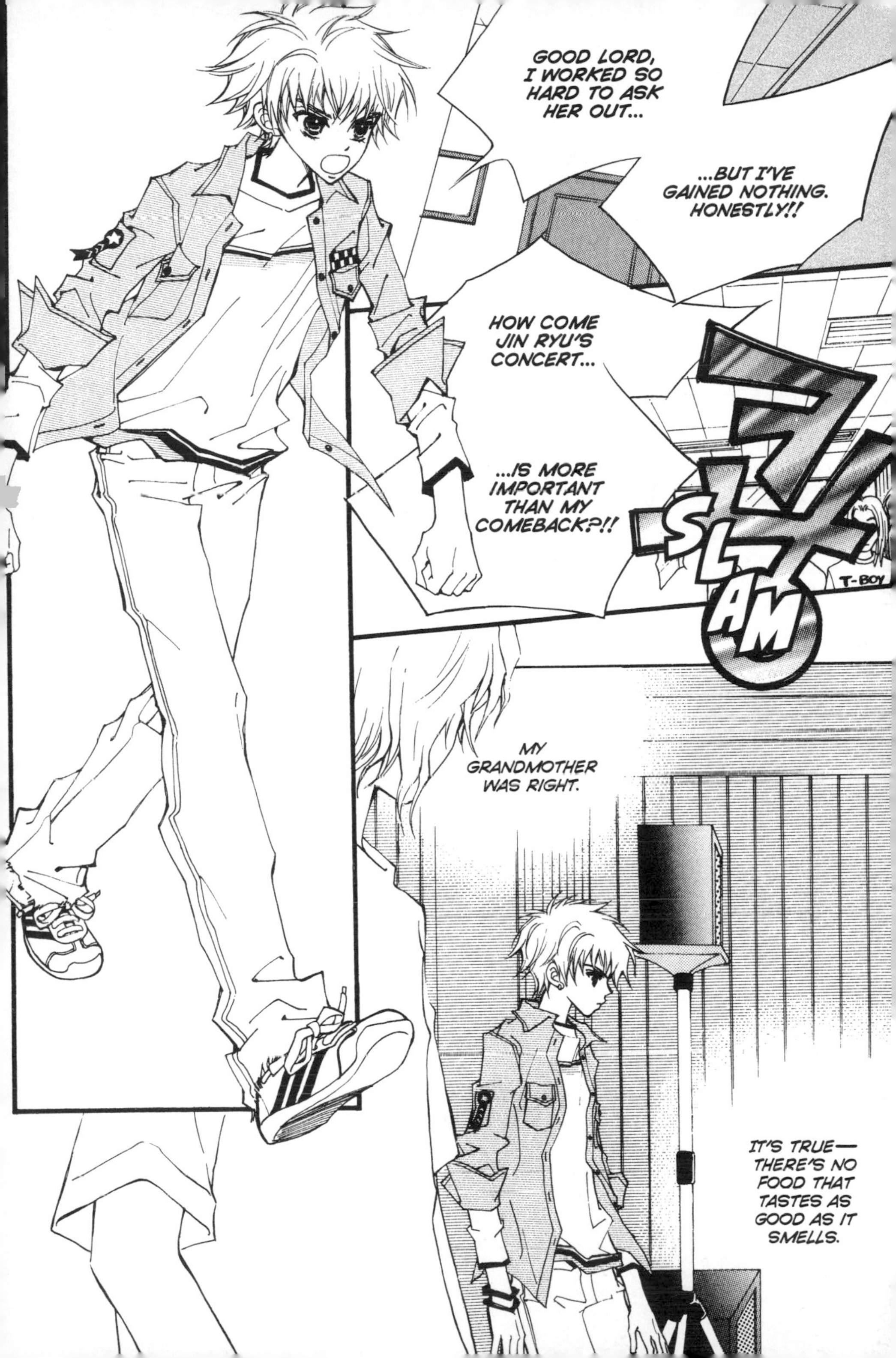
GOOD LORD, I WORKED SO HARD TO ASK HER OUT...
...BUT I'VE GAINED NOTHING. HONESTLY!!
HOW COME JIN RYU'S CONCERT...
...IS MORE IMPORTANT THAN MY COMEBACK?!!
SLAM
T-BOY
MY GRANDMOTHER WAS RIGHT.
IT'S TRUE—THERE'S NO FOOD THAT TASTES AS GOOD AS IT SMELLS.

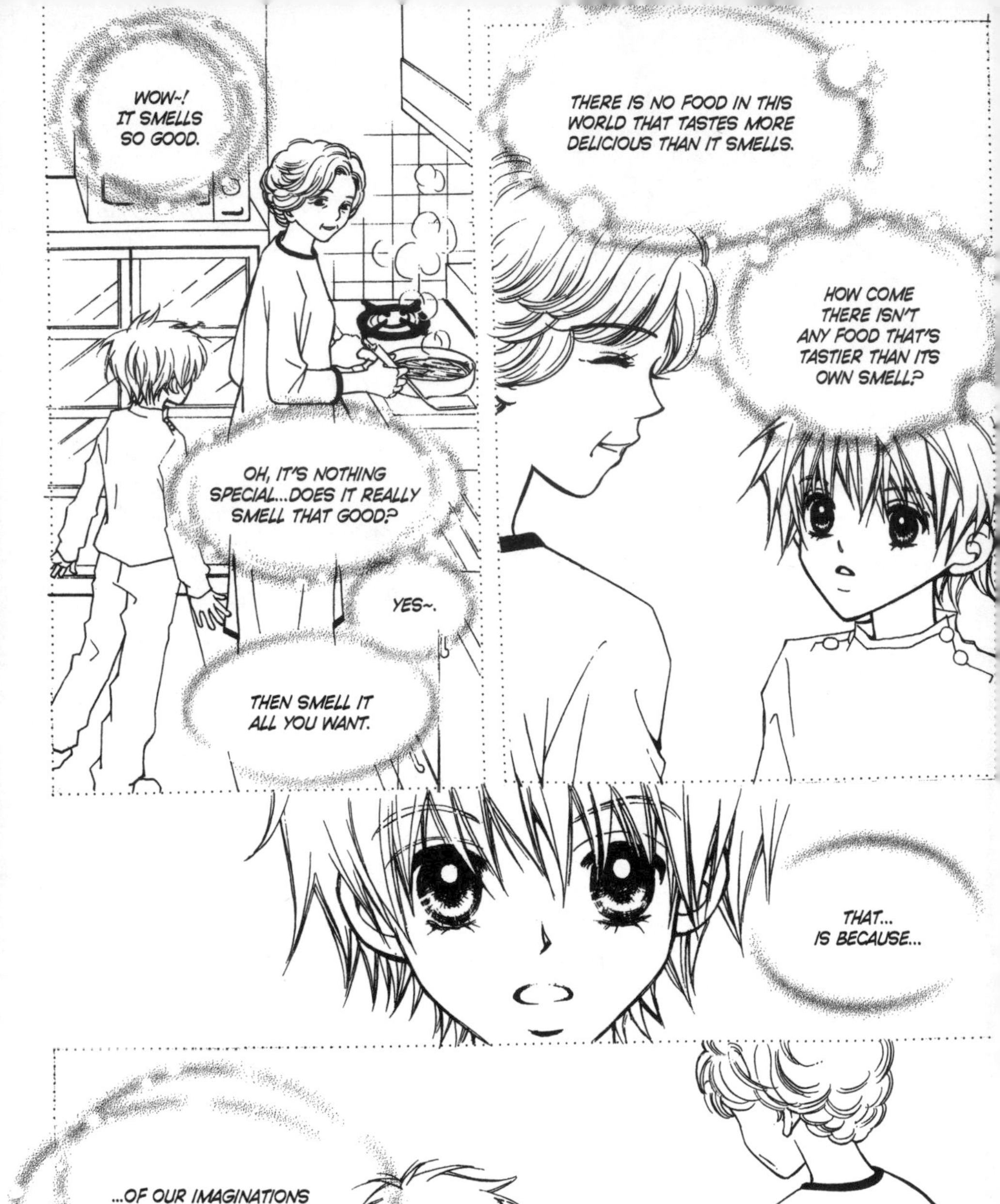
WOW~! IT SMELLS SO GOOD.
OH, IT'S NOTHING SPECIAL...DOES IT REALLY SMELL THAT GOOD?
YES~.
THEN SMELL IT ALL YOU WANT.
THERE IS NO FOOD IN THIS WORLD THAT TASTES MORE DELICIOUS THAN IT SMELLS.
HOW COME THERE ISN'T ANY FOOD THAT'S TASTIER THAN ITS OWN SMELL?
THAT... IS BECAUSE...
...OF OUR IMAGINATIONS AND OUR EXPECTATIONS, I SUPPOSE?

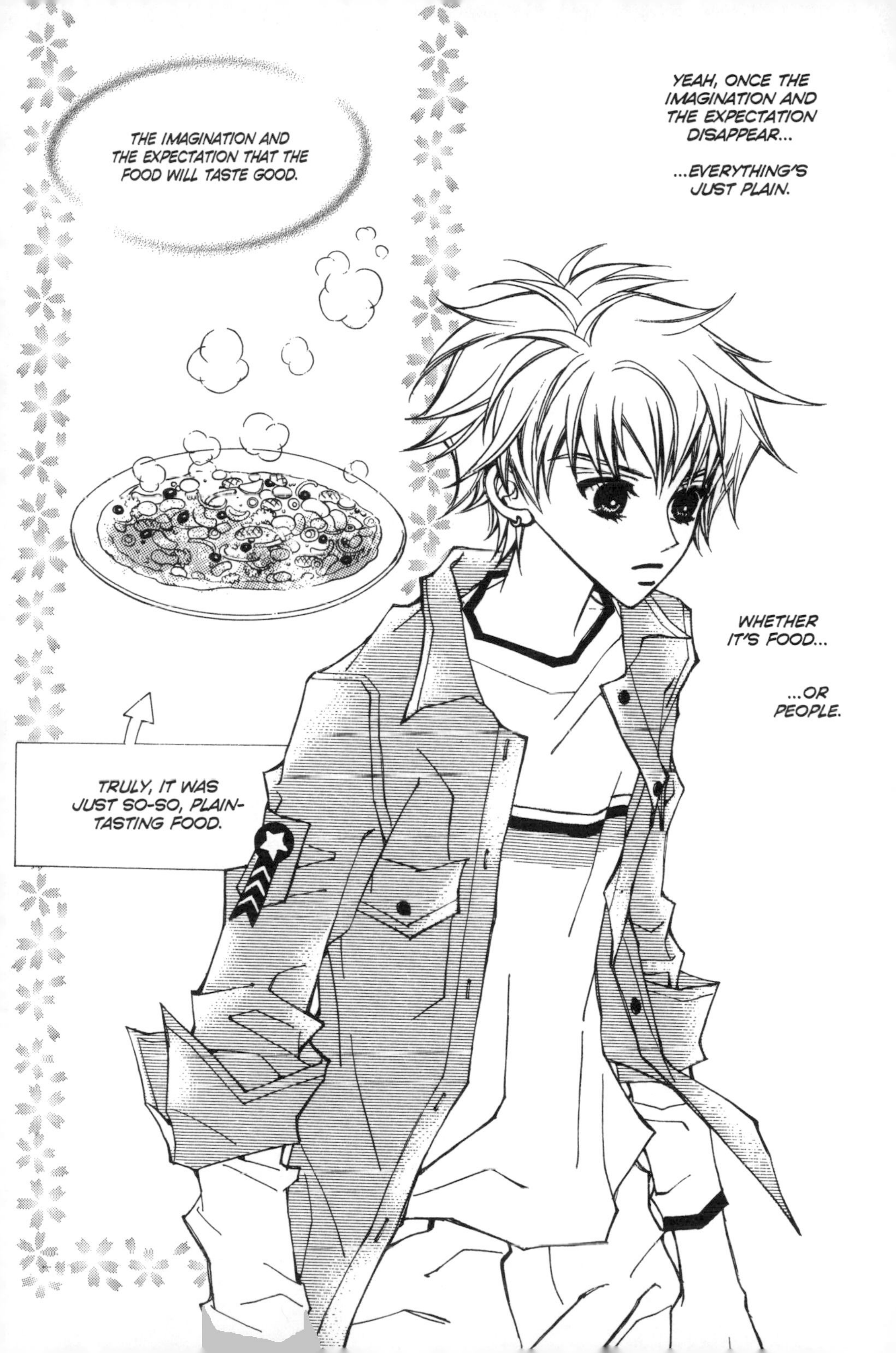
THE IMAGINATION AND THE EXPECTATION THAT THE FOOD WILL TASTE GOOD.
TRULY, IT WAS JUST SO-SO, PLAIN-TASTING FOOD.
YEAH, ONCE THE IMAGINATION AND THE EXPECTATION DISAPPEAR...
...EVERYTHING'S JUST PLAIN.
WHETHER IT'S FOOD...
...OR PEOPLE.

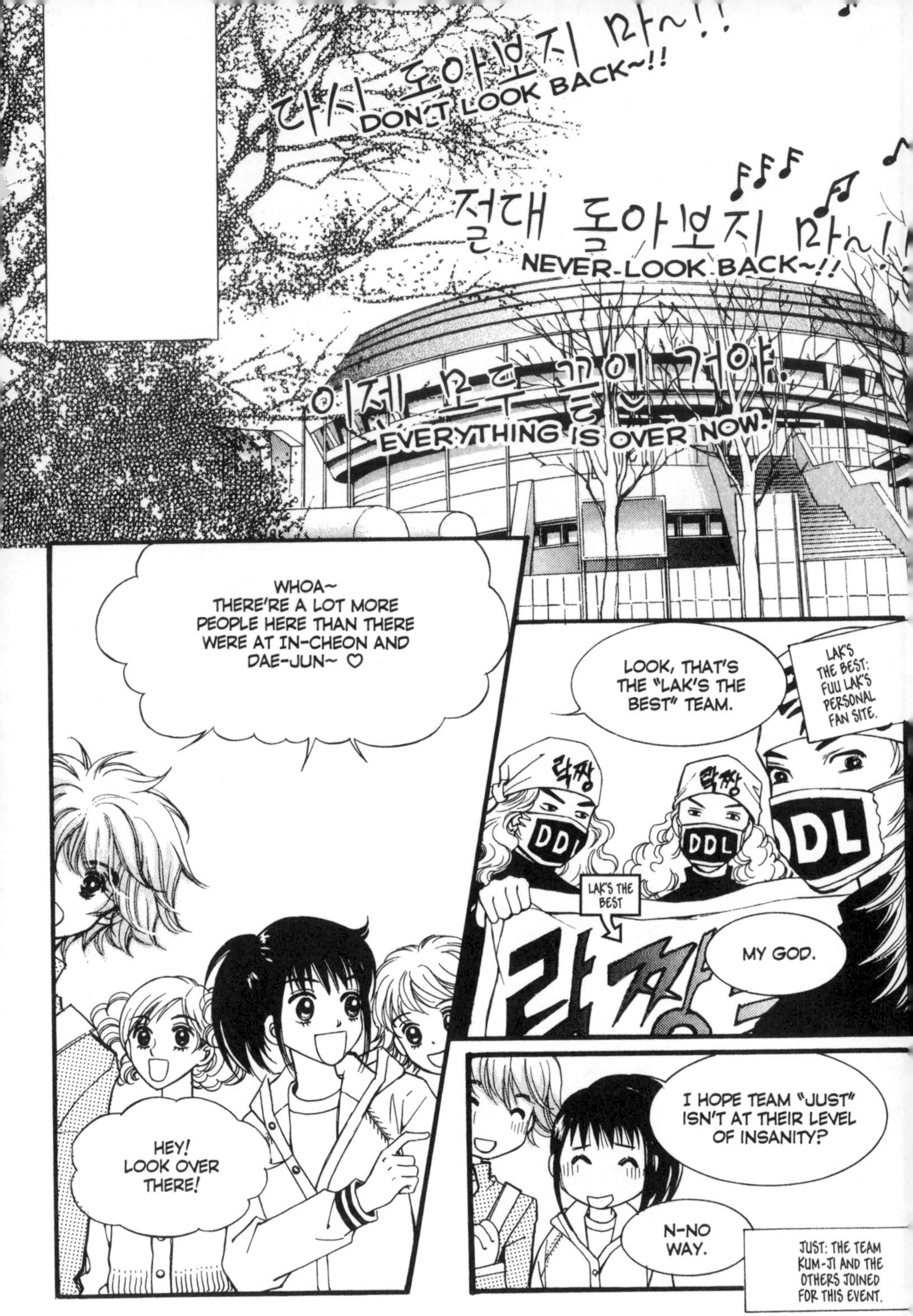

다시 돌아보지 마~!!
DON'T LOOK BACK~!!
절대 돌아보지 마~!!
NEVER LOOK BACK~!!
이제 모두 끝인 거야.
EVERYTHING IS OVER NOW.
WHOA~ THERE'RE A LOT MORE PEOPLE HERE THAN THERE WERE AT IN-CHEON AND DAE-JUN~ ♡
HEY! LOOK OVER THERE!
LOOK, THAT'S THE "LAK'S THE BEST" TEAM.
LAK'S THE BEST: FUU LAK'S PERSONAL FAN SITE.
락짱
DDL
LAK'S THE BEST
MY GOD.
I HOPE TEAM "JUST" ISN'T AT THEIR LEVEL OF INSANITY?
N-NO WAY.
JUST: THE TEAM KUM-JI AND THE OTHERS JOINED FOR THIS EVENT.

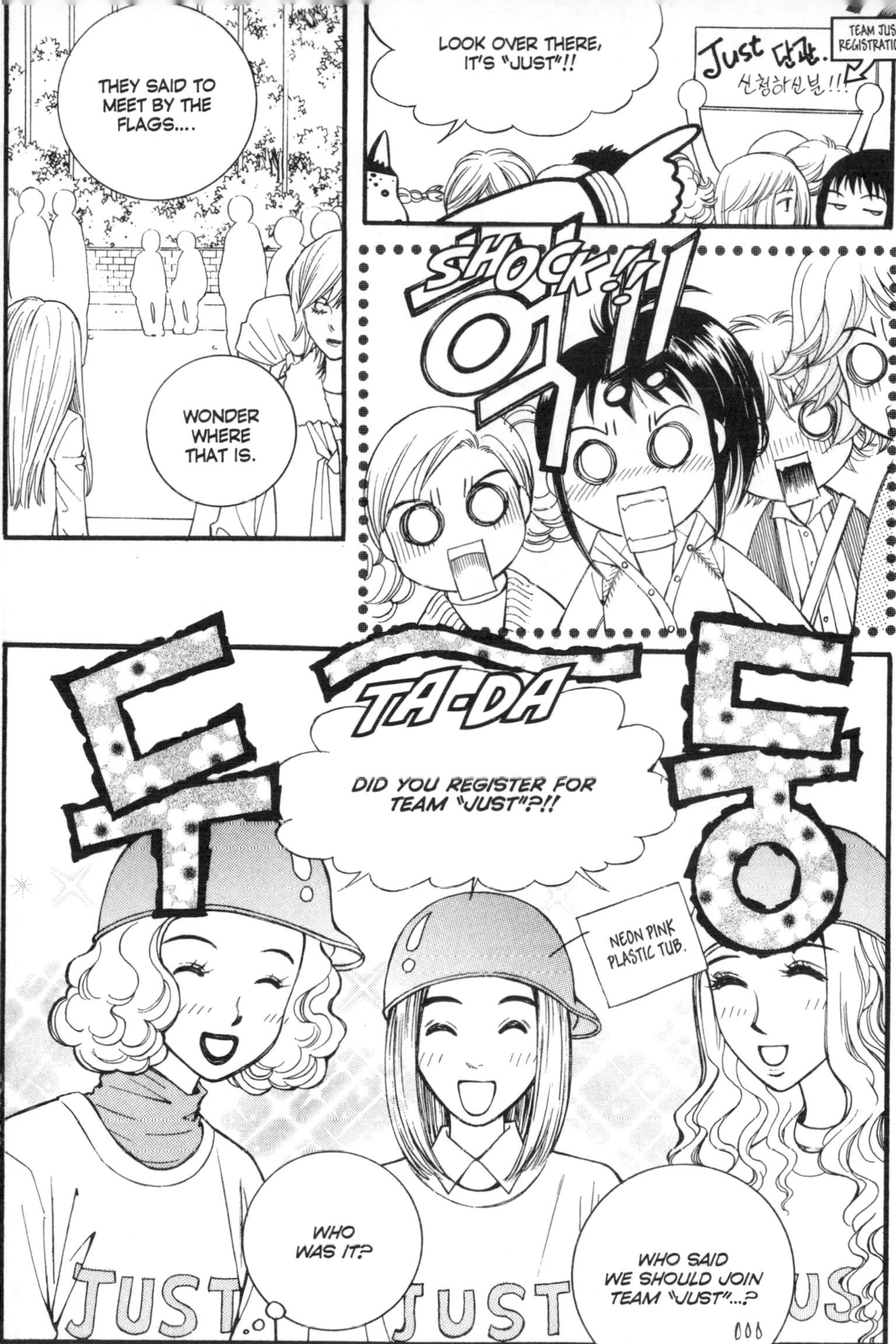
THEY SAID TO MEET BY THE FLAGS....
WONDER WHERE THAT IS.
LOOK OVER THERE, IT'S "JUST"!!
Just 단관..
신청하신분!!!
TEAM JUST. REGISTRATION!!!
SHOCK!!!
두둥
TA-DA
DID YOU REGISTER FOR TEAM "JUST"?!!
NEON PINK PLASTIC TUB.
JUST
JUST
WHO WAS IT?
WHO SAID WE SHOULD JOIN TEAM "JUST"...?

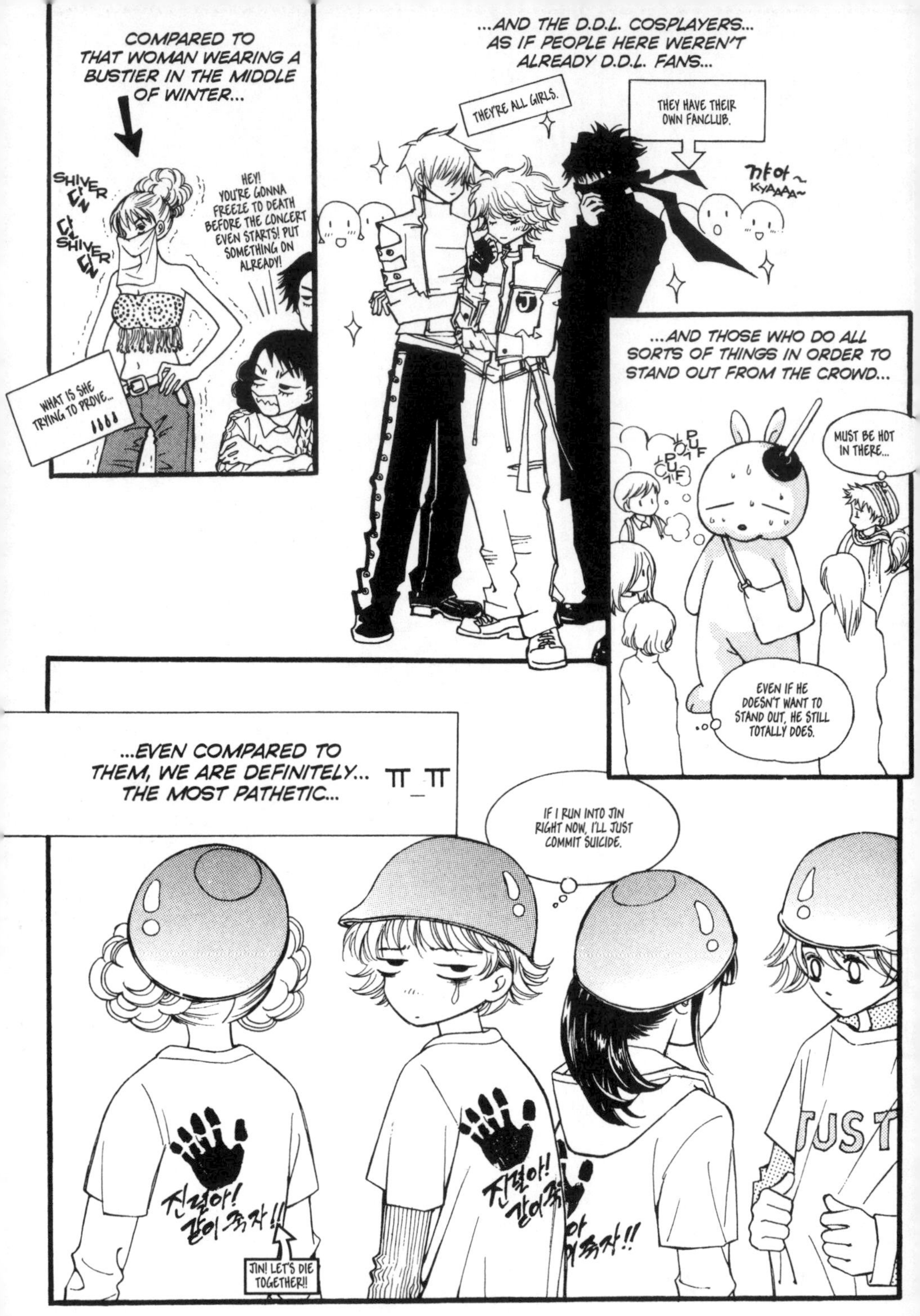
COMPARED TO THAT WOMAN WEARING A BUSTIER IN THE MIDDLE OF WINTER...
SHIVER SHIVER
HEY! YOU'RE GONNA FREEZE TO DEATH BEFORE THE CONCERT EVEN STARTS! PUT SOMETHING ON ALREADY!
WHAT IS SHE TRYING TO PROVE...
...AND THE D.D.L. COSPLAYERS... AS IF PEOPLE HERE WEREN'T ALREADY D.D.L. FANS...
THEY'RE ALL GIRLS.
THEY HAVE THEIR OWN FANCLUB.
꺄아~ KYAAAA~
...AND THOSE WHO DO ALL SORTS OF THINGS IN ORDER TO STAND OUT FROM THE CROWD...
PUF PUF
MUST BE HOT IN THERE...
EVEN IF HE DOESN'T WANT TO STAND OUT, HE STILL TOTALLY DOES.
...EVEN COMPARED TO THEM, WE ARE DEFINITELY... THE MOST PATHETIC... TT_TT
IF I RUN INTO JIN RIGHT NOW, I'LL JUST COMMIT SUICIDE.
진결아! 같이 죽자!!
JIN! LET'S DIE TOGETHER!!

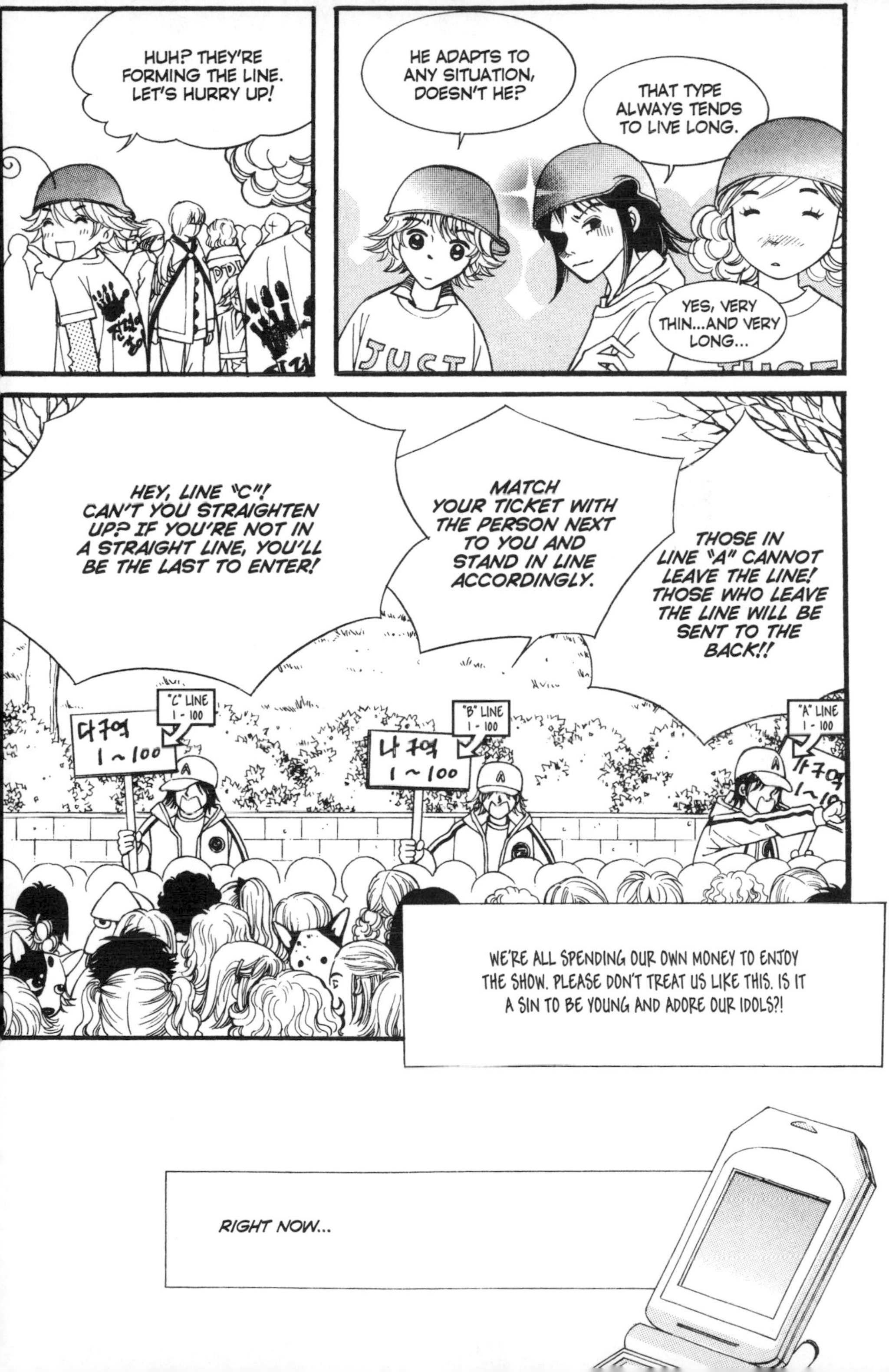
HUH? THEY'RE FORMING THE LINE. LET'S HURRY UP!
HE ADAPTS TO ANY SITUATION, DOESN'T HE?
THAT TYPE ALWAYS TENDS TO LIVE LONG.
YES, VERY THIN...AND VERY LONG...
HEY, LINE "C"! CAN'T YOU STRAIGHTEN UP? IF YOU'RE NOT IN A STRAIGHT LINE, YOU'LL BE THE LAST TO ENTER!
MATCH YOUR TICKET WITH THE PERSON NEXT TO YOU AND STAND IN LINE ACCORDINGLY.
THOSE IN LINE "A" CANNOT LEAVE THE LINE! THOSE WHO LEAVE THE LINE WILL BE SENT TO THE BACK!!
"C" LINE 1 - 100
"B" LINE 1 - 100
"A" LINE 1 - 100
WE'RE ALL SPENDING OUR OWN MONEY TO ENJOY THE SHOW. PLEASE DON'T TREAT US LIKE THIS. IS IT A SIN TO BE YOUNG AND ADORE OUR IDOLS?!
RIGHT NOW...

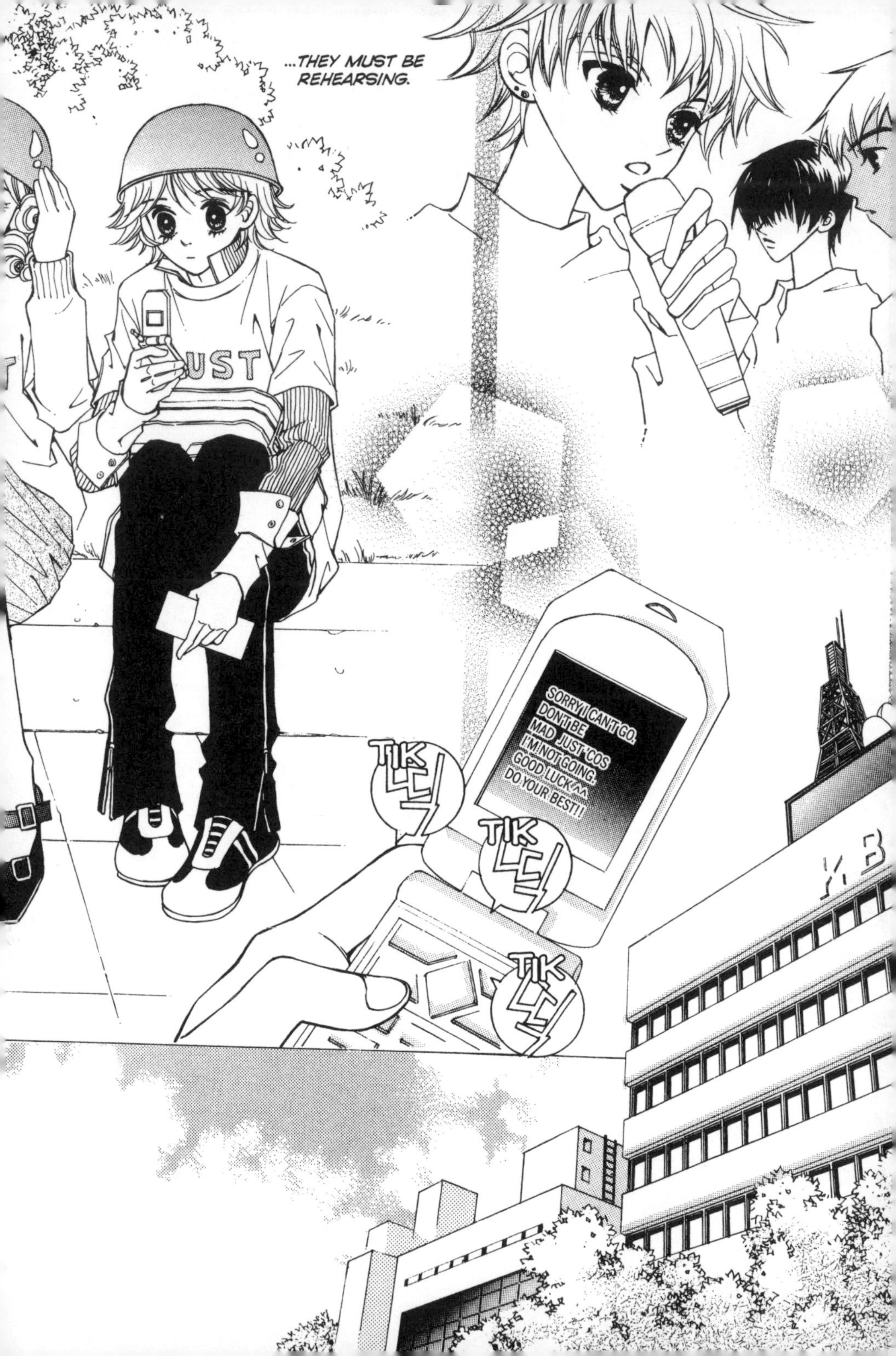
...THEY MUST BE REHEARSING.
SORRY I CAN'T GO.
DON'T BE
MAD JUST 'COS
I'M NOT GOING.
GOOD LUCK ^^
DO YOUR BEST!
TIK
TIK
TIK

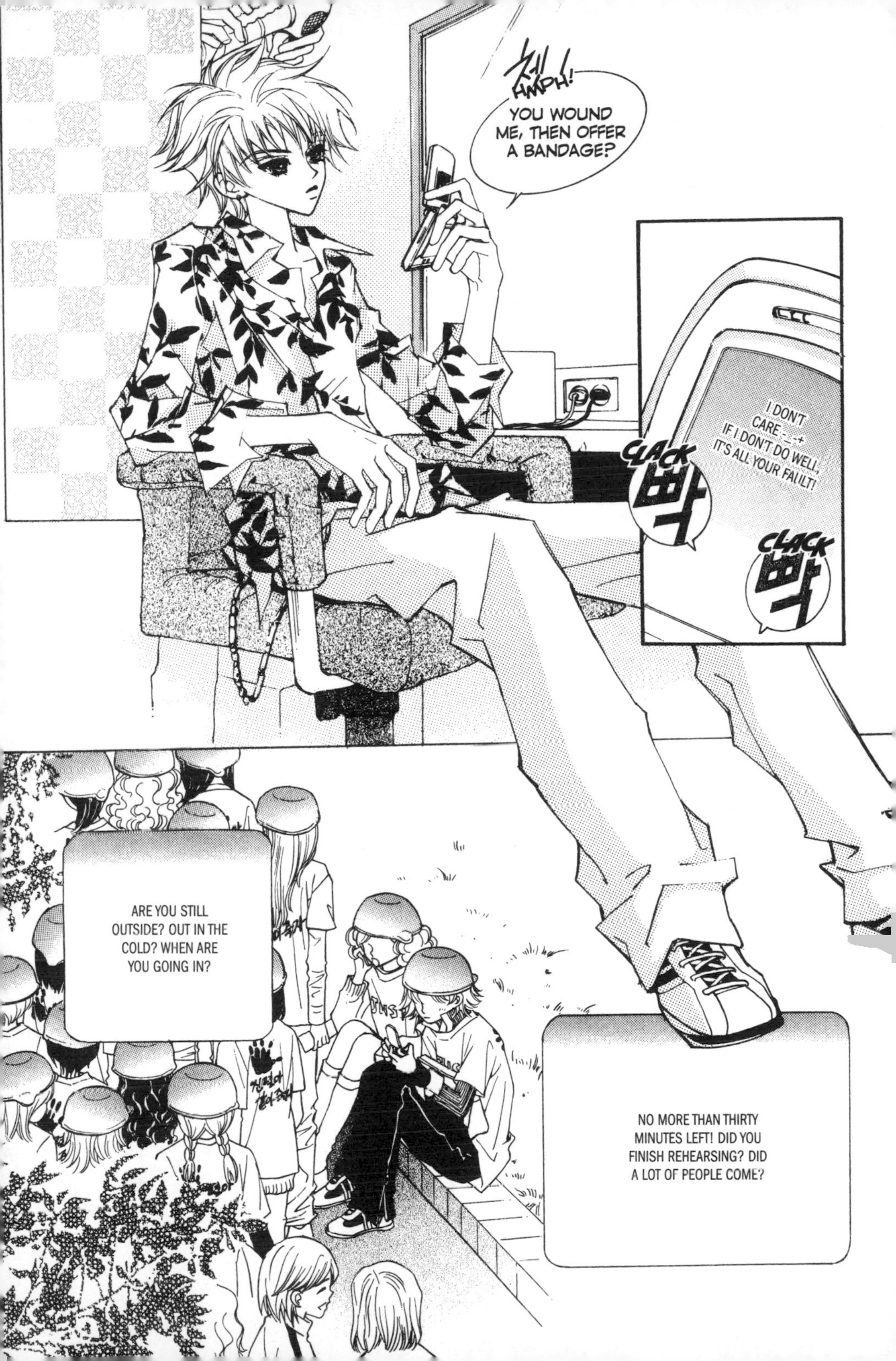
HMPH!
YOU WOUND ME, THEN OFFER A BANDAGE?
I DON'T CARE -_-+ IF I DON'T DO WELL, IT'S ALL YOUR FAULT!
CLACK
CLACK
ARE YOU STILL OUTSIDE? OUT IN THE COLD? WHEN ARE YOU GOING IN?
NO MORE THAN THIRTY MINUTES LEFT! DID YOU FINISH REHEARSING? DID A LOT OF PEOPLE COME?

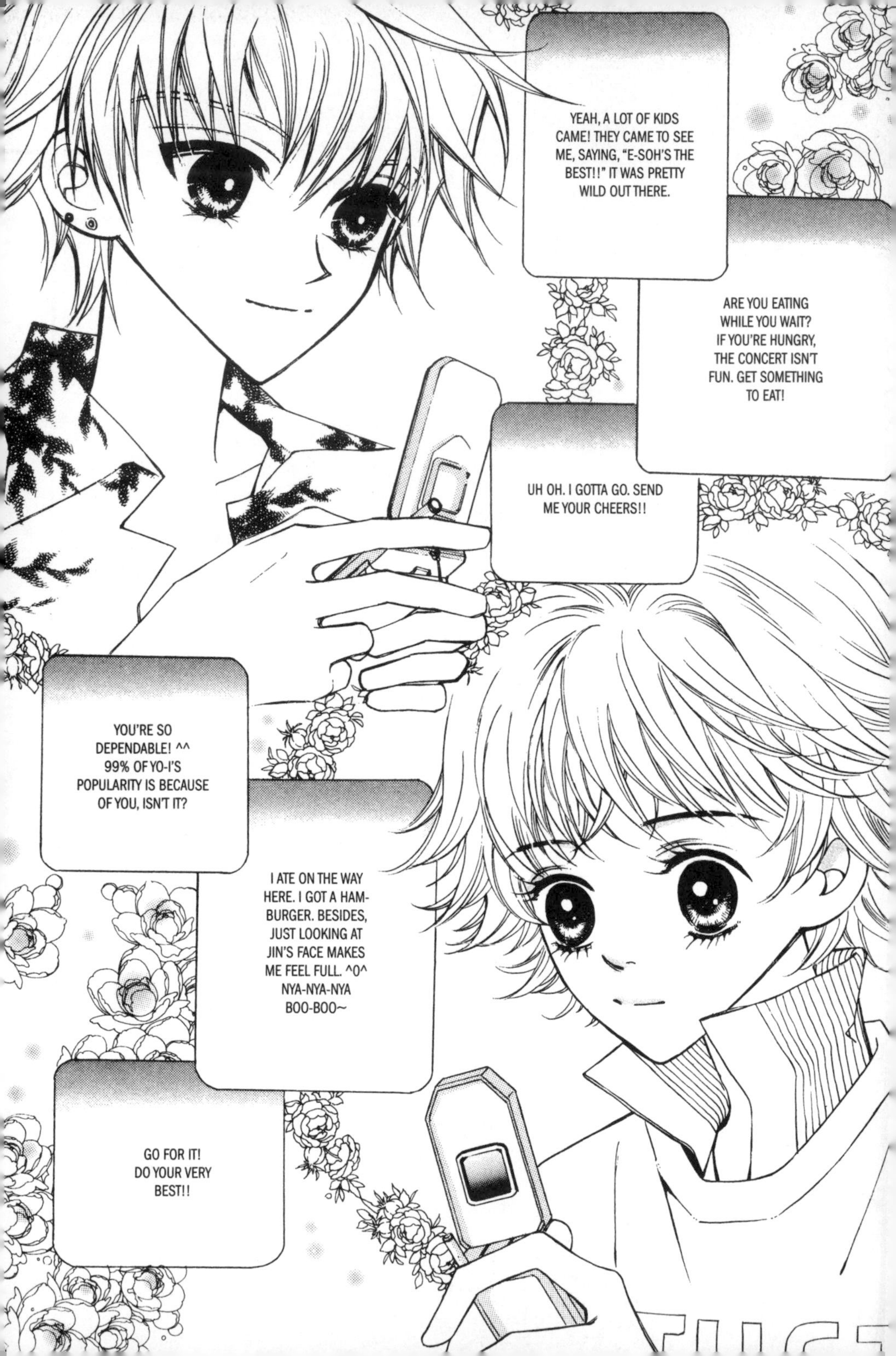
YEAH, A LOT OF KIDS CAME! THEY CAME TO SEE ME, SAYING, "E-SOH'S THE BEST!!" IT WAS PRETTY WILD OUT THERE.
ARE YOU EATING WHILE YOU WAIT? IF YOU'RE HUNGRY, THE CONCERT ISN'T FUN. GET SOMETHING TO EAT!
UH OH. I GOTTA GO. SEND ME YOUR CHEERS!!
YOU'RE SO DEPENDABLE! ^^ 99% OF YO-I'S POPULARITY IS BECAUSE OF YOU, ISN'T IT?
I ATE ON THE WAY HERE. I GOT A HAM-BURGER. BESIDES, JUST LOOKING AT JIN'S FACE MAKES ME FEEL FULL. ^0^ NYA-NYA-NYA BOO-BOO~
GO FOR IT! DO YOUR VERY BEST!!

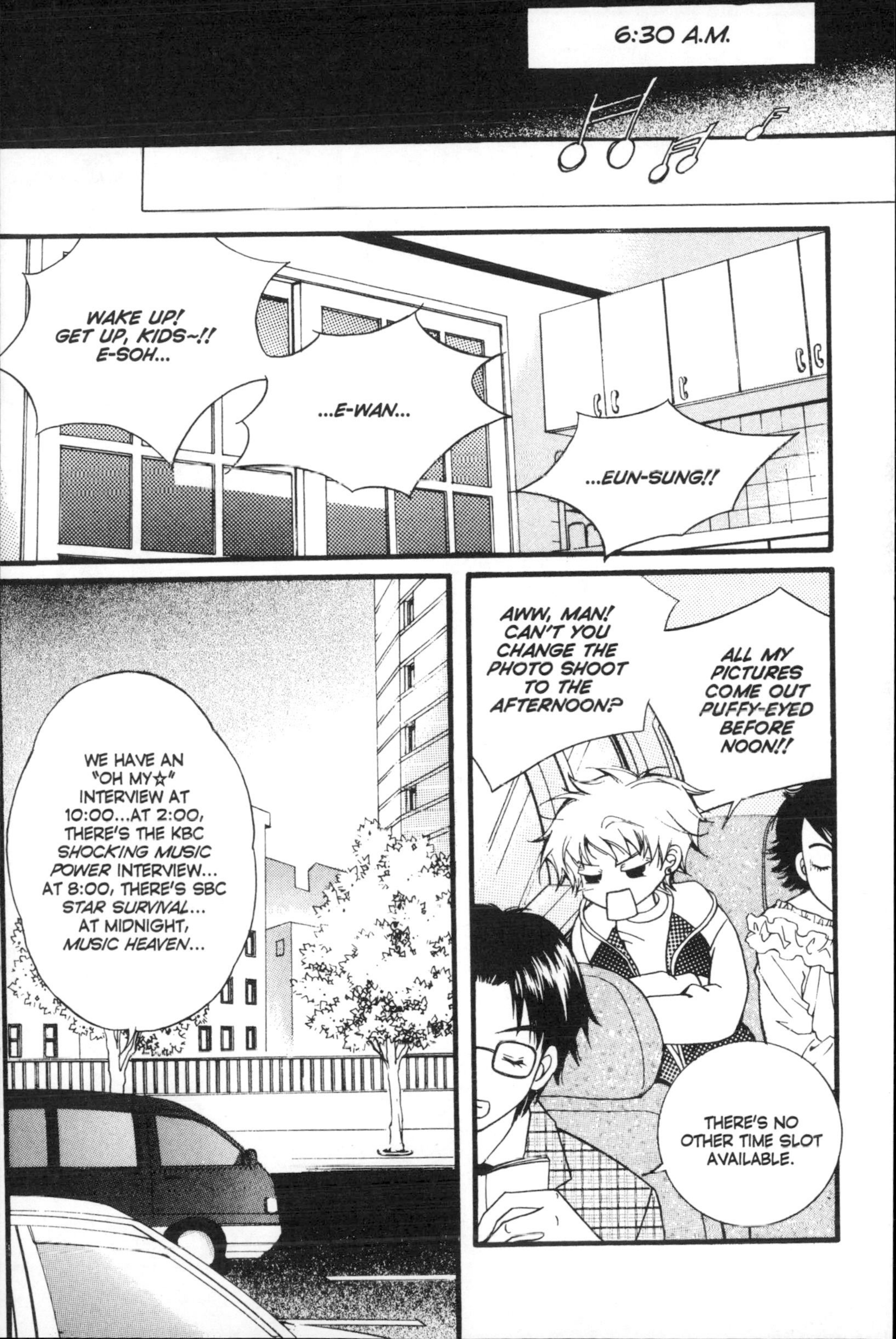
6:30 A.M.
WAKE UP! GET UP, KIDS~!! E-SOH...
...E-WAN...
...EUN-SUNG!!
WE HAVE AN "OH MY☆" INTERVIEW AT 10:00...AT 2:00, THERE'S THE KBC *SHOCKING MUSIC POWER* INTERVIEW... AT 8:00, THERE'S SBC *STAR SURVIVAL*... AT MIDNIGHT, *MUSIC HEAVEN*...
AWW, MAN! CAN'T YOU CHANGE THE PHOTO SHOOT TO THE AFTERNOON?
ALL MY PICTURES COME OUT PUFFY-EYED BEFORE NOON!!
THERE'S NO OTHER TIME SLOT AVAILABLE.

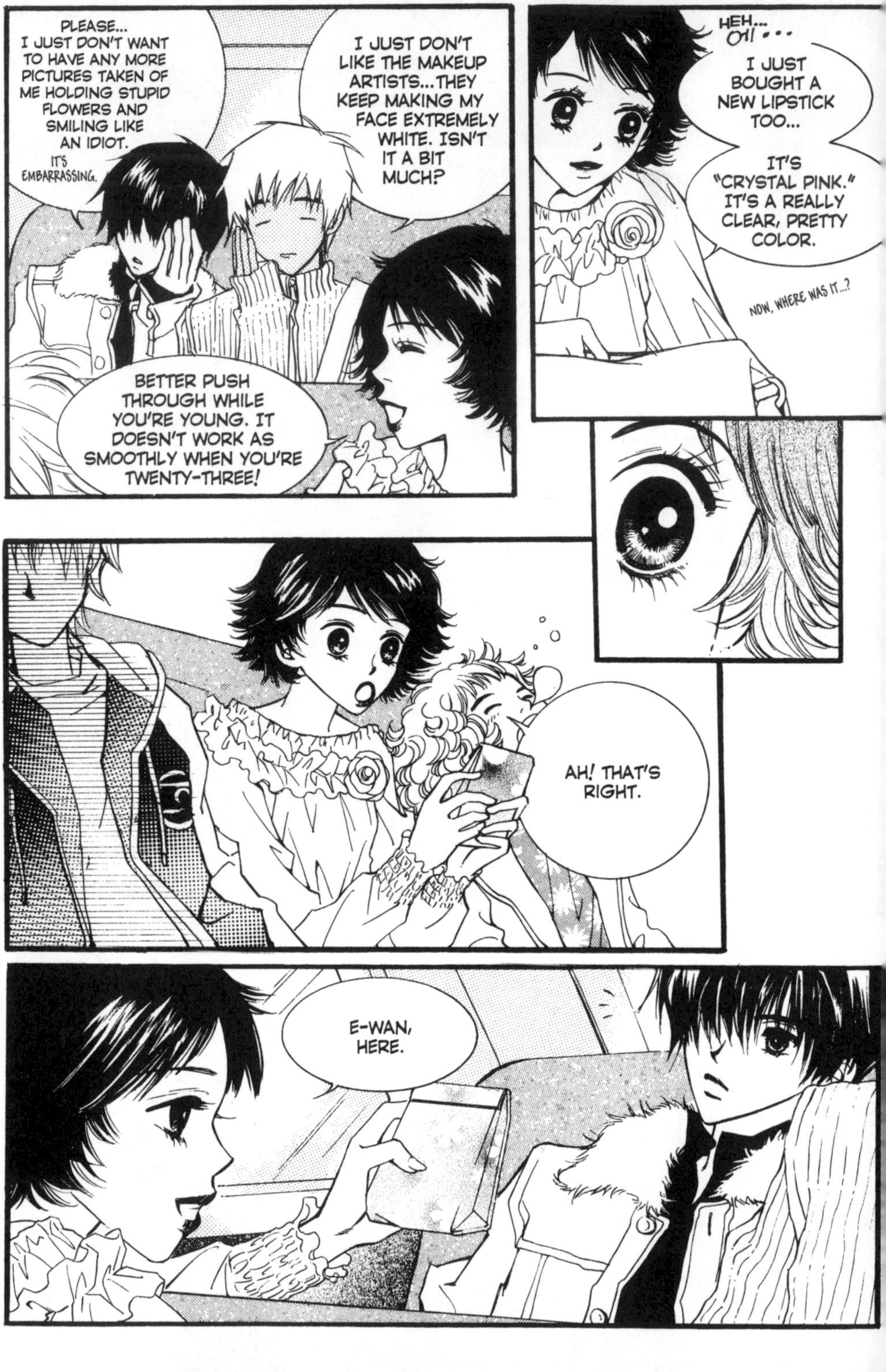
PLEASE... I JUST DON'T WANT TO HAVE ANY MORE PICTURES TAKEN OF ME HOLDING STUPID FLOWERS AND SMILING LIKE AN IDIOT.
IT'S EMBARRASSING.
I JUST DON'T LIKE THE MAKEUP ARTISTS...THEY KEEP MAKING MY FACE EXTREMELY WHITE. ISN'T IT A BIT MUCH?
BETTER PUSH THROUGH WHILE YOU'RE YOUNG. IT DOESN'T WORK AS SMOOTHLY WHEN YOU'RE TWENTY-THREE!
HEH...
I JUST BOUGHT A NEW LIPSTICK TOO...
IT'S "CRYSTAL PINK." IT'S A REALLY CLEAR, PRETTY COLOR.
NOW, WHERE WAS IT...?
AH! THAT'S RIGHT.
E-WAN, HERE.

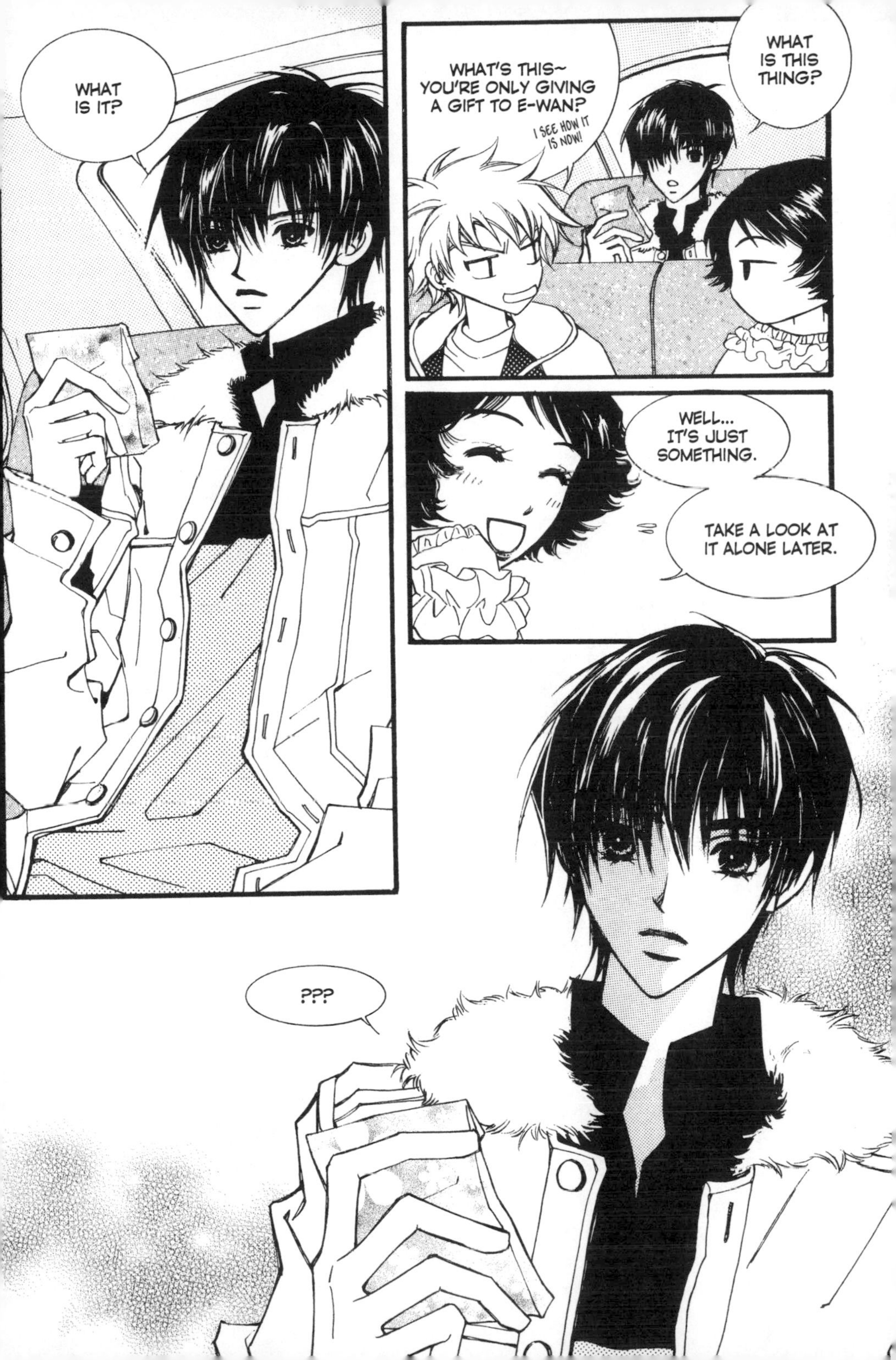
WHAT IS IT?
WHAT'S THIS~ YOU'RE ONLY GIVING A GIFT TO E-WAN?
I SEE HOW IT IS NOW!
WHAT IS THIS THING?
WELL... IT'S JUST SOMETHING.
TAKE A LOOK AT IT ALONE LATER.
???

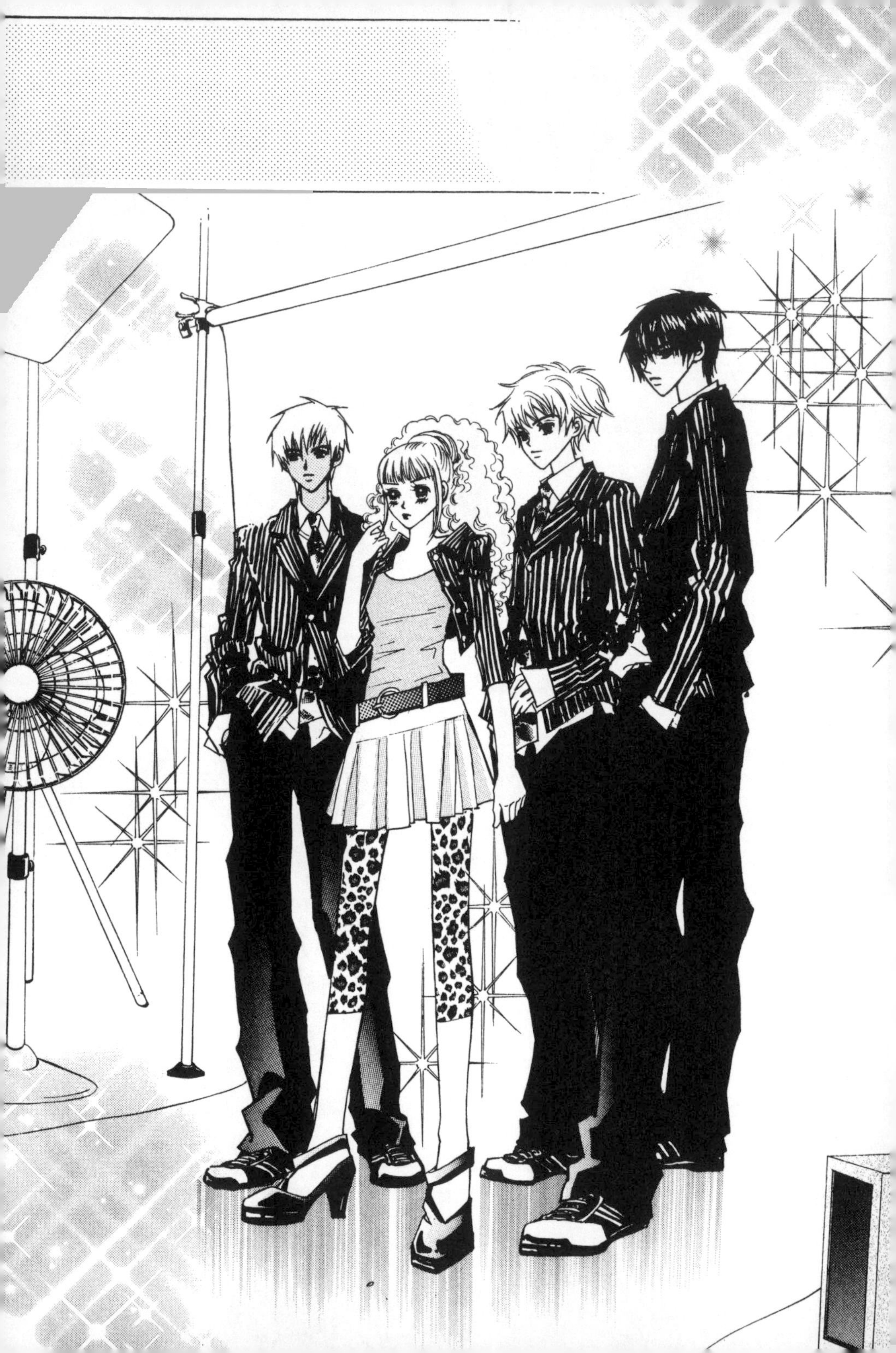

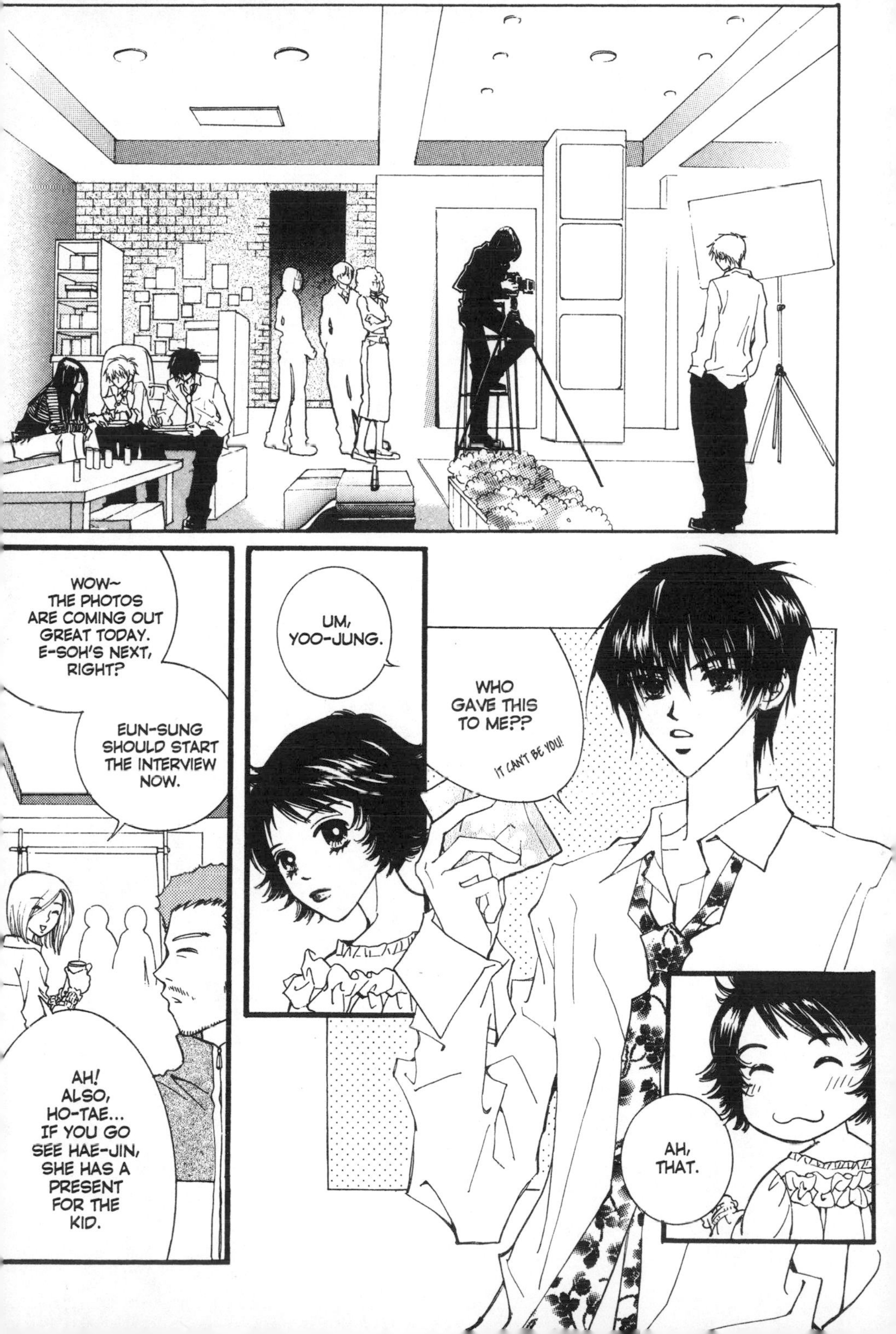
WOW~ THE PHOTOS ARE COMING OUT GREAT TODAY. E-SOH'S NEXT, RIGHT?
EUN-SUNG SHOULD START THE INTERVIEW NOW.
AH! ALSO, HO-TAE... IF YOU GO SEE HAE-JIN, SHE HAS A PRESENT FOR THE KID.
UM, YOO-JUNG.
WHO GAVE THIS TO ME??
IT CAN'T BE YOU!
AH, THAT.

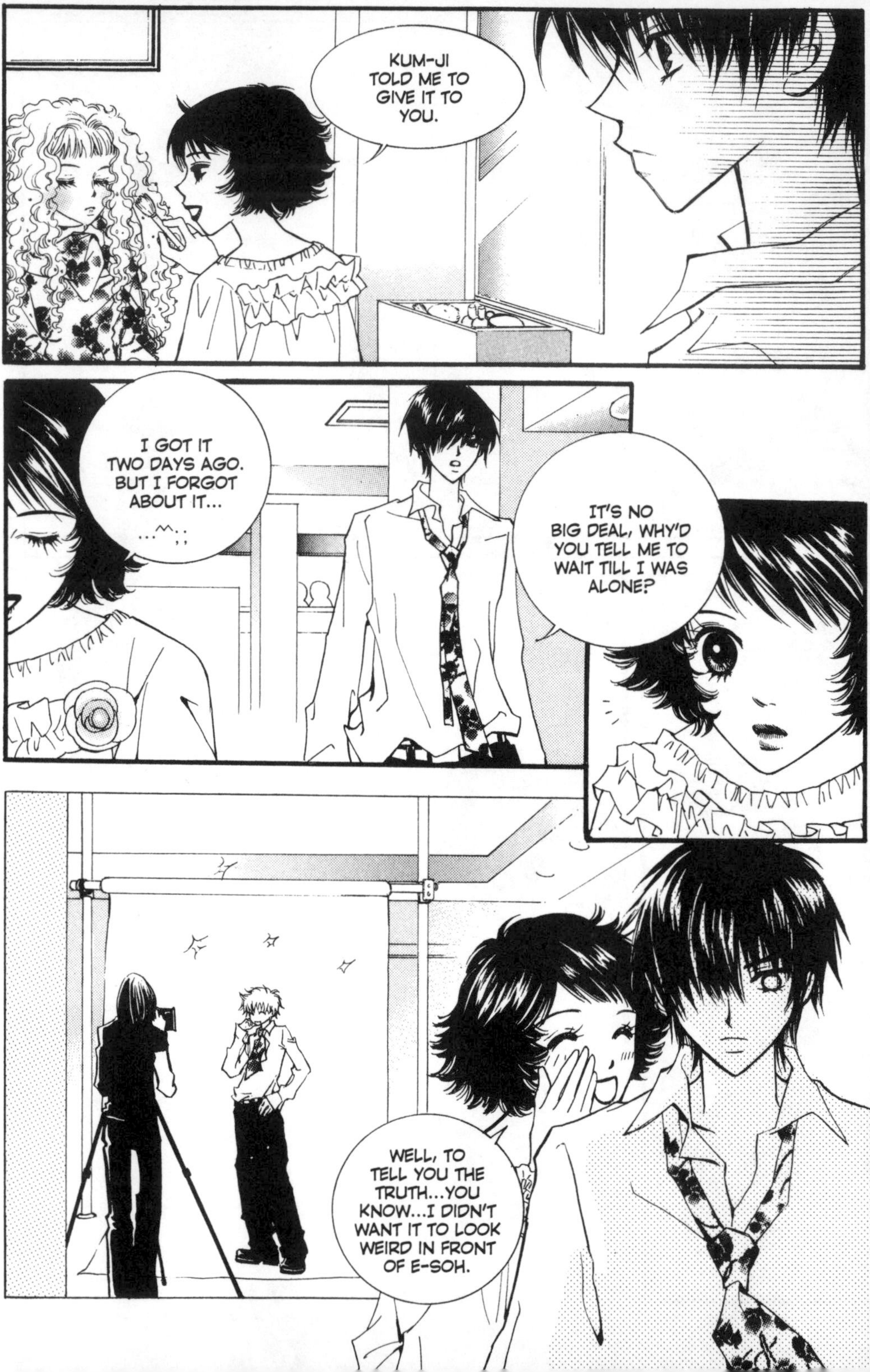
KUM-JI TOLD ME TO GIVE IT TO YOU.
I GOT IT TWO DAYS AGO. BUT I FORGOT ABOUT IT... ...^;;
IT'S NO BIG DEAL, WHY'D YOU TELL ME TO WAIT TILL I WAS ALONE?
WELL, TO TELL YOU THE TRUTH...YOU KNOW...I DIDN'T WANT IT TO LOOK WEIRD IN FRONT OF E-SOH.

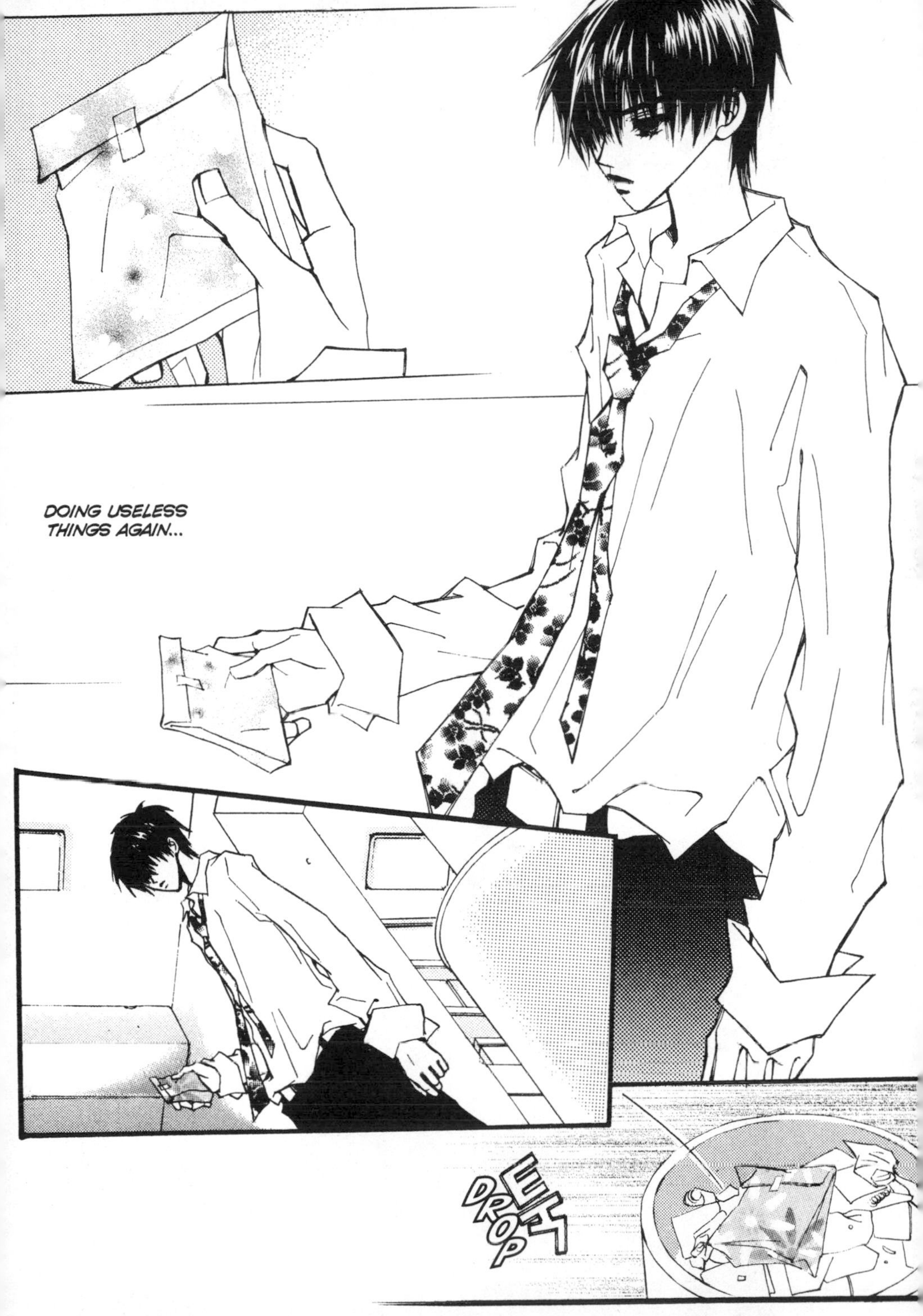
DOING USELESS THINGS AGAIN...
DROP

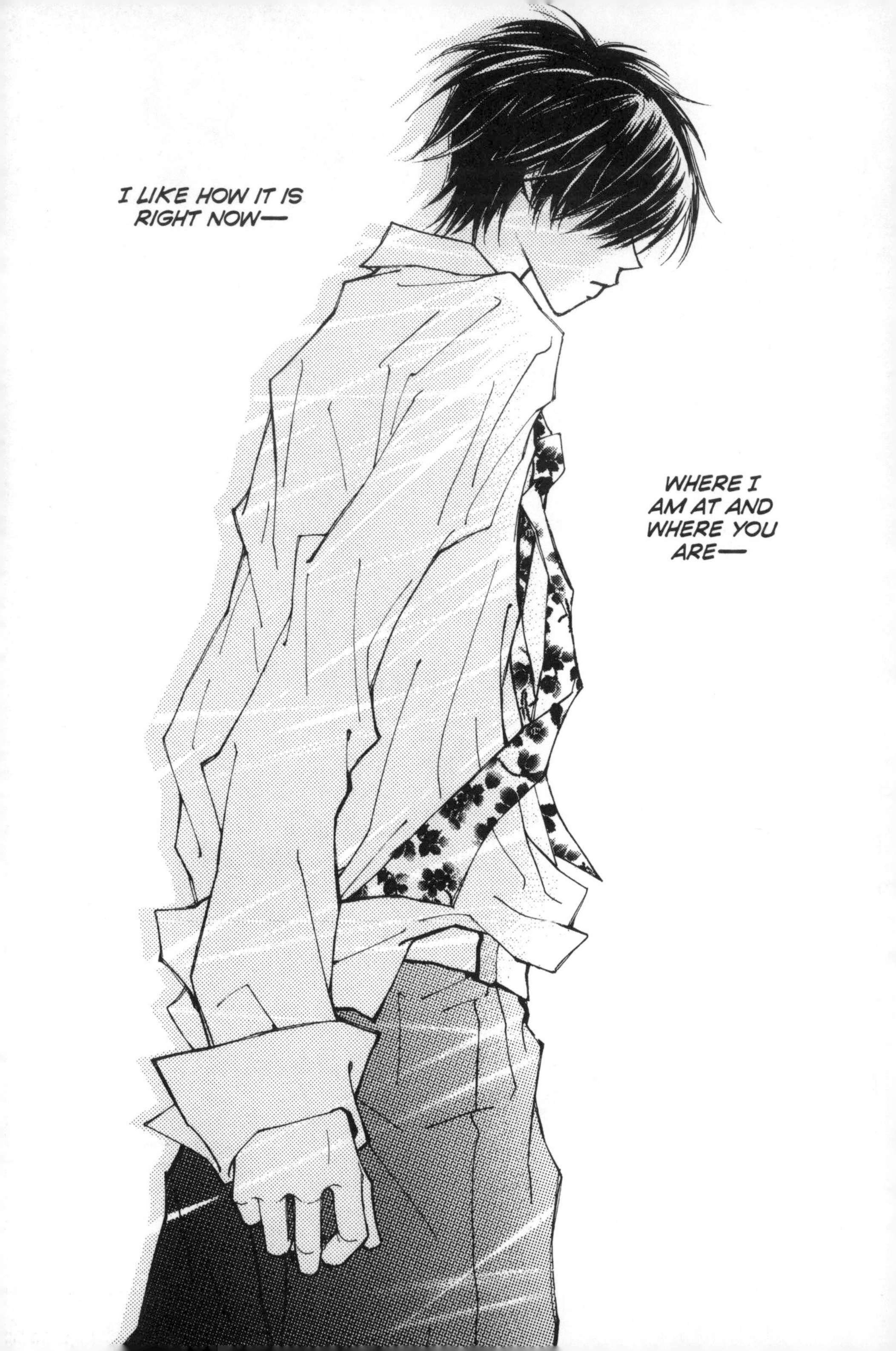
I LIKE HOW IT IS RIGHT NOW—
WHERE I AM AT AND WHERE YOU ARE—

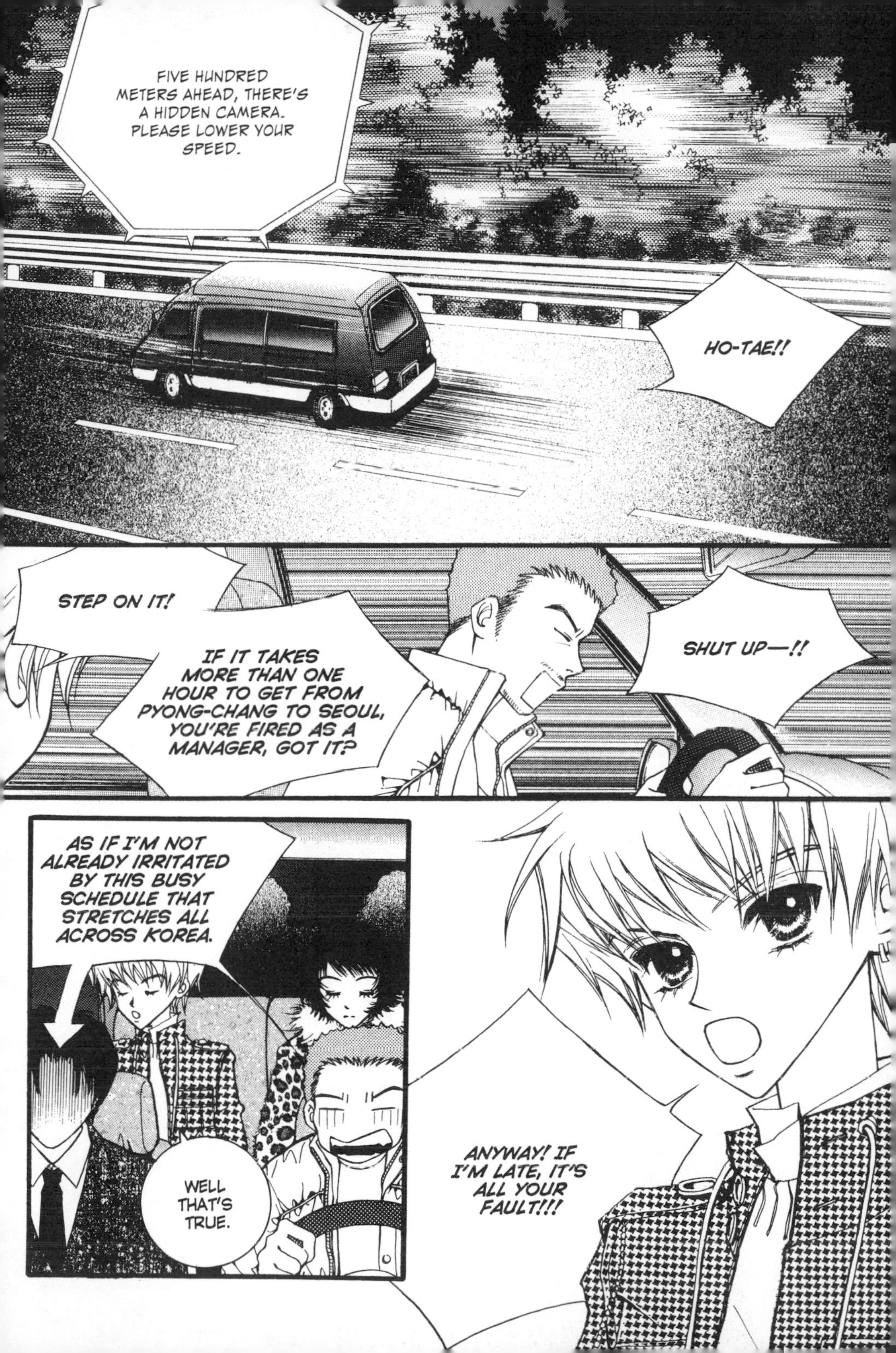
FIVE HUNDRED METERS AHEAD, THERE'S A HIDDEN CAMERA. PLEASE LOWER YOUR SPEED.
HO-TAE!!
STEP ON IT!
IF IT TAKES MORE THAN ONE HOUR TO GET FROM PYONG-CHANG TO SEOUL, YOU'RE FIRED AS A MANAGER, GOT IT?
SHUT UP—!!
AS IF I'M NOT ALREADY IRRITATED BY THIS BUSY SCHEDULE THAT STRETCHES ALL ACROSS KOREA.
WELL THAT'S TRUE.
ANYWAY! IF I'M LATE, IT'S ALL YOUR FAULT!!!

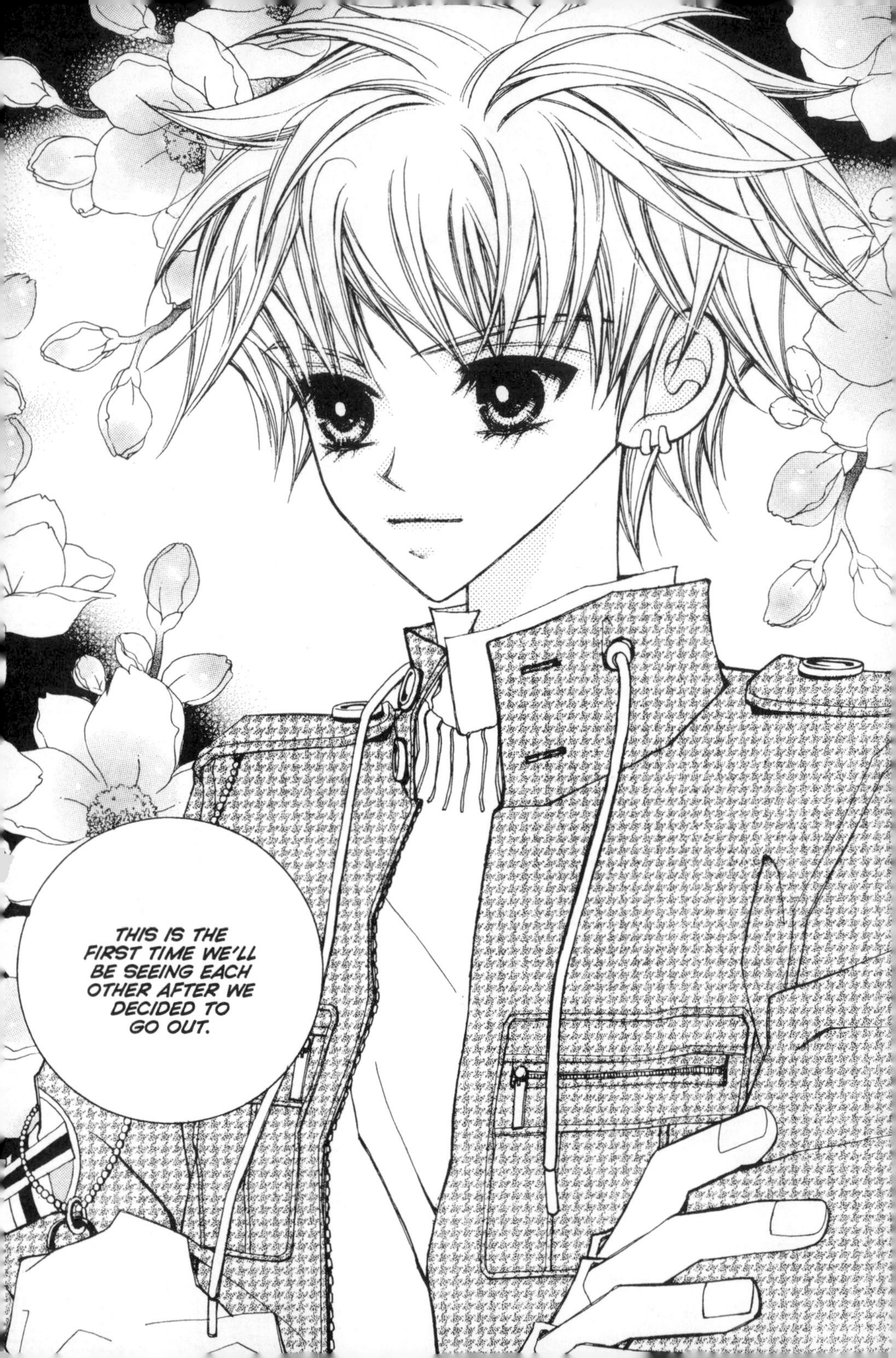
THIS IS THE FIRST TIME WE'LL BE SEEING EACH OTHER AFTER WE DECIDED TO GO OUT.

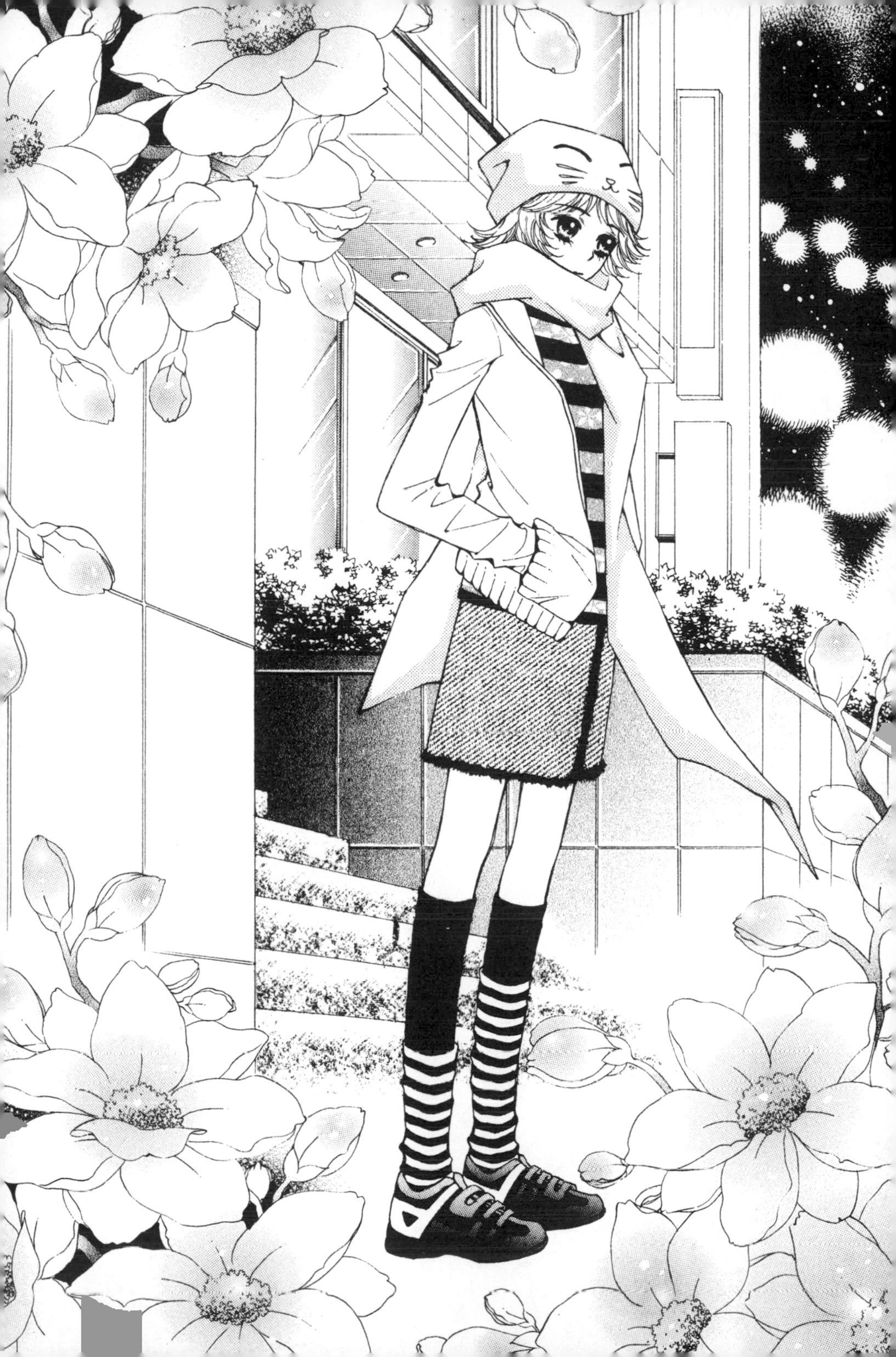

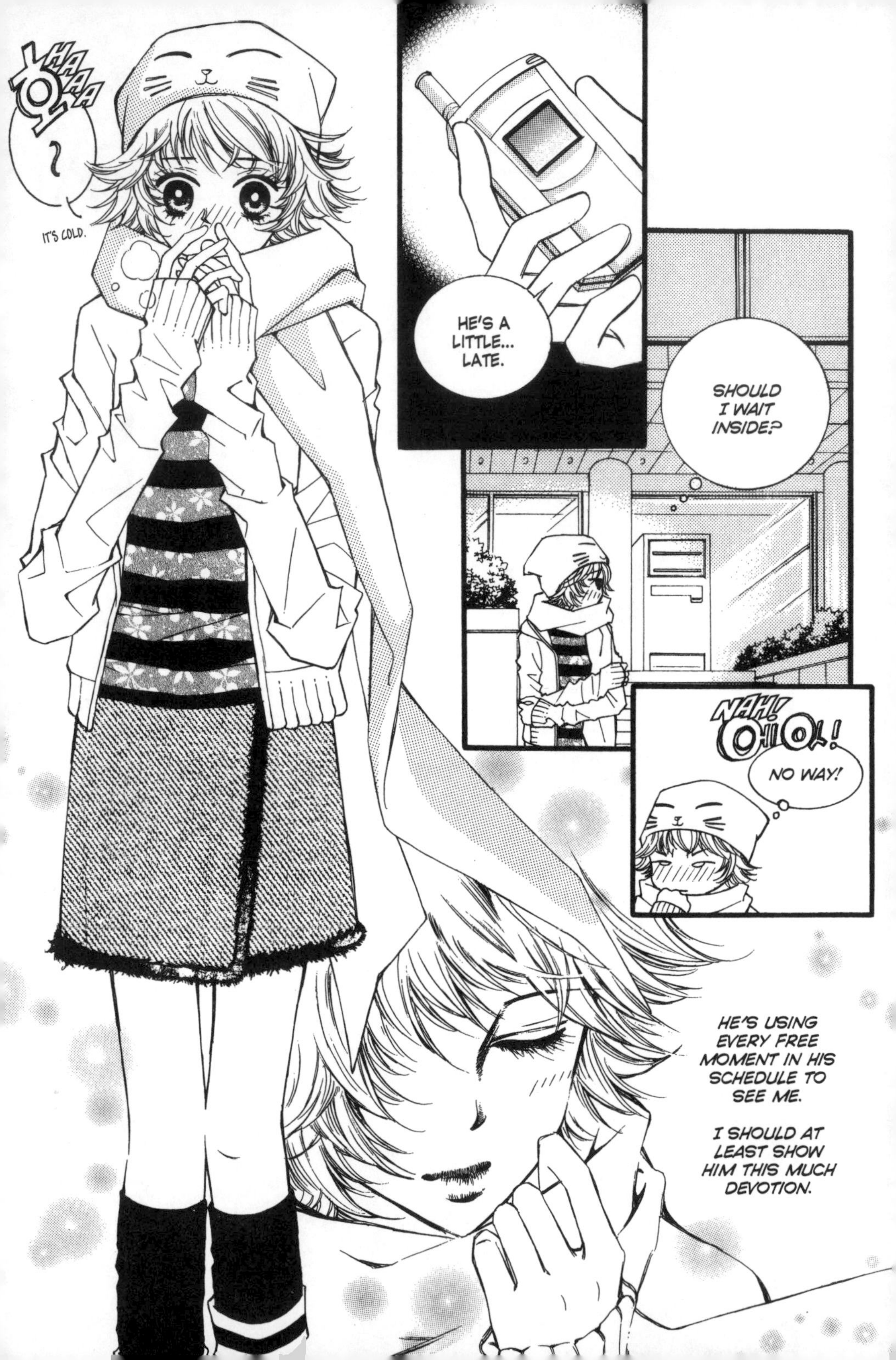
HAAA
~
IT'S COLD.
HE'S A LITTLE... LATE.
SHOULD I WAIT INSIDE?
NAH!
NO WAY!
HE'S USING EVERY FREE MOMENT IN HIS SCHEDULE TO SEE ME.
I SHOULD AT LEAST SHOW HIM THIS MUCH DEVOTION.

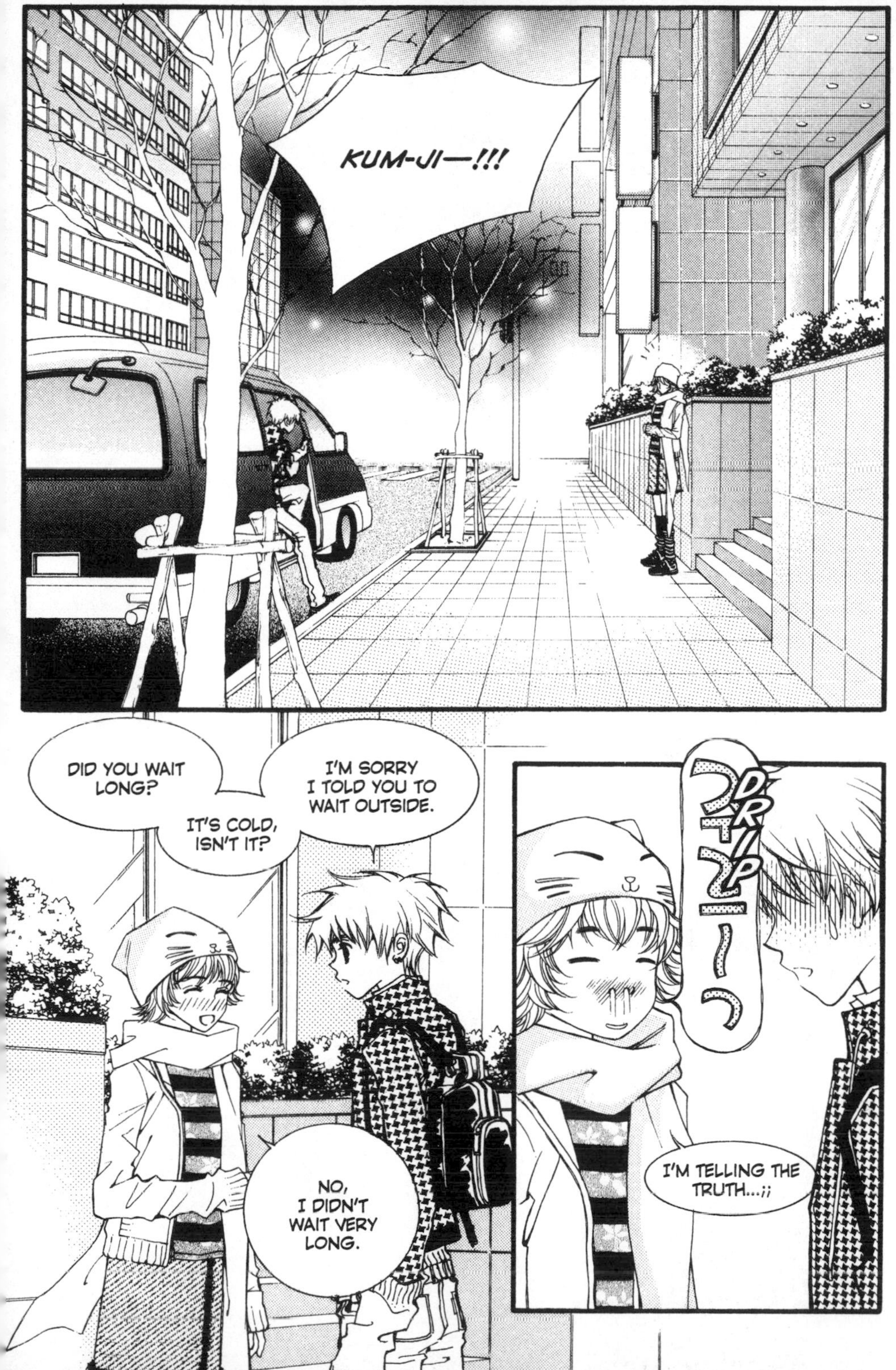
KUM-JI—!!!
DID YOU WAIT LONG?
IT'S COLD, ISN'T IT?
I'M SORRY I TOLD YOU TO WAIT OUTSIDE.
NO, I DIDN'T WAIT VERY LONG.
DRIP
I'M TELLING THE TRUTH...;;

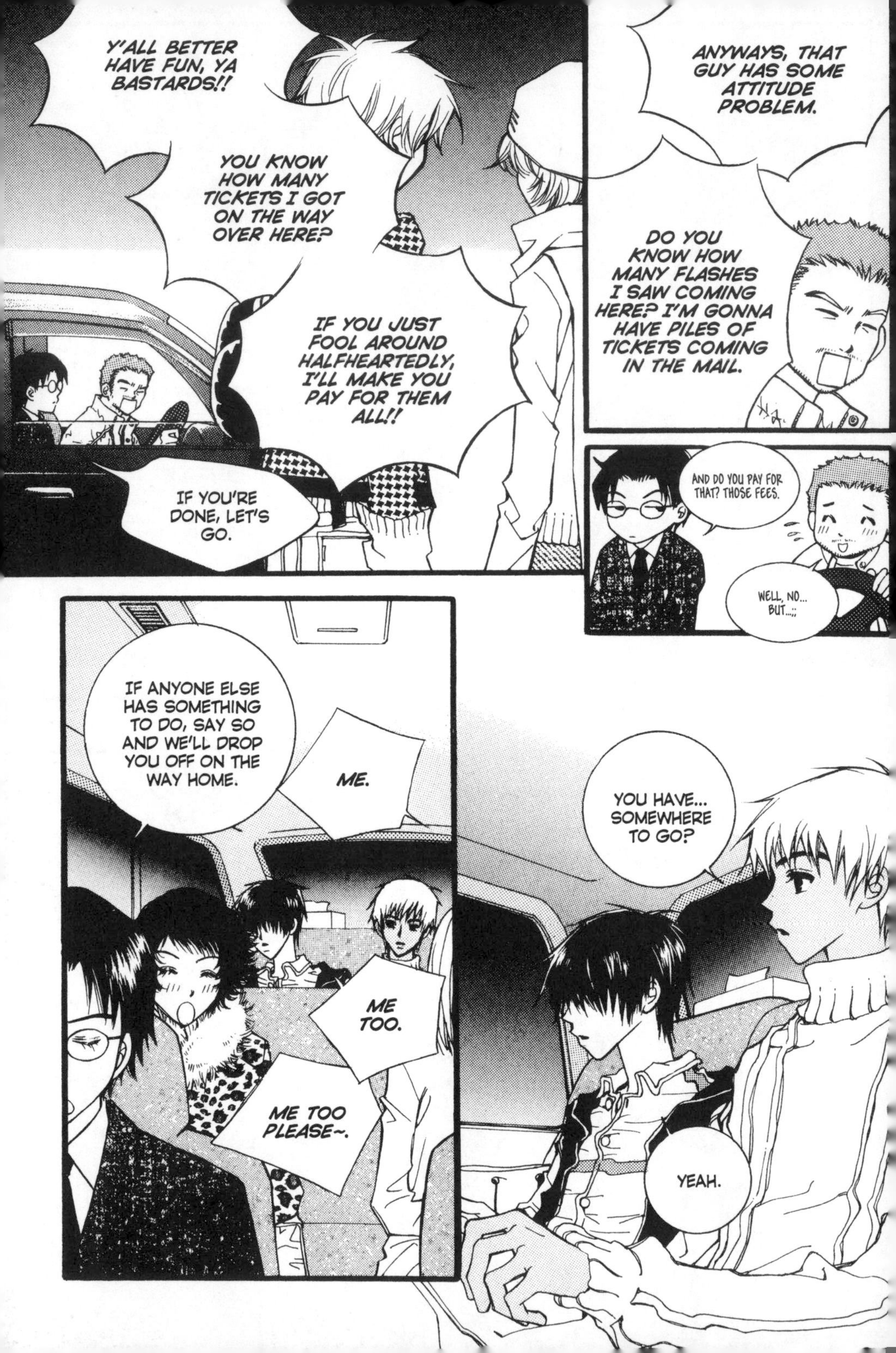
Y'ALL BETTER HAVE FUN, YA BASTARDS!!
YOU KNOW HOW MANY TICKETS I GOT ON THE WAY OVER HERE?
IF YOU JUST FOOL AROUND HALFHEARTEDLY, I'LL MAKE YOU PAY FOR THEM ALL!!
IF YOU'RE DONE, LET'S GO.
ANYWAYS, THAT GUY HAS SOME ATTITUDE PROBLEM.
DO YOU KNOW HOW MANY FLASHES I SAW COMING HERE? I'M GONNA HAVE PILES OF TICKETS COMING IN THE MAIL.
AND DO YOU PAY FOR THAT? THOSE FEES.
WELL, NO... BUT...;;
IF ANYONE ELSE HAS SOMETHING TO DO, SAY SO AND WE'LL DROP YOU OFF ON THE WAY HOME.
ME.
ME TOO.
ME TOO PLEASE~.
YOU HAVE... SOMEWHERE TO GO?
YEAH.

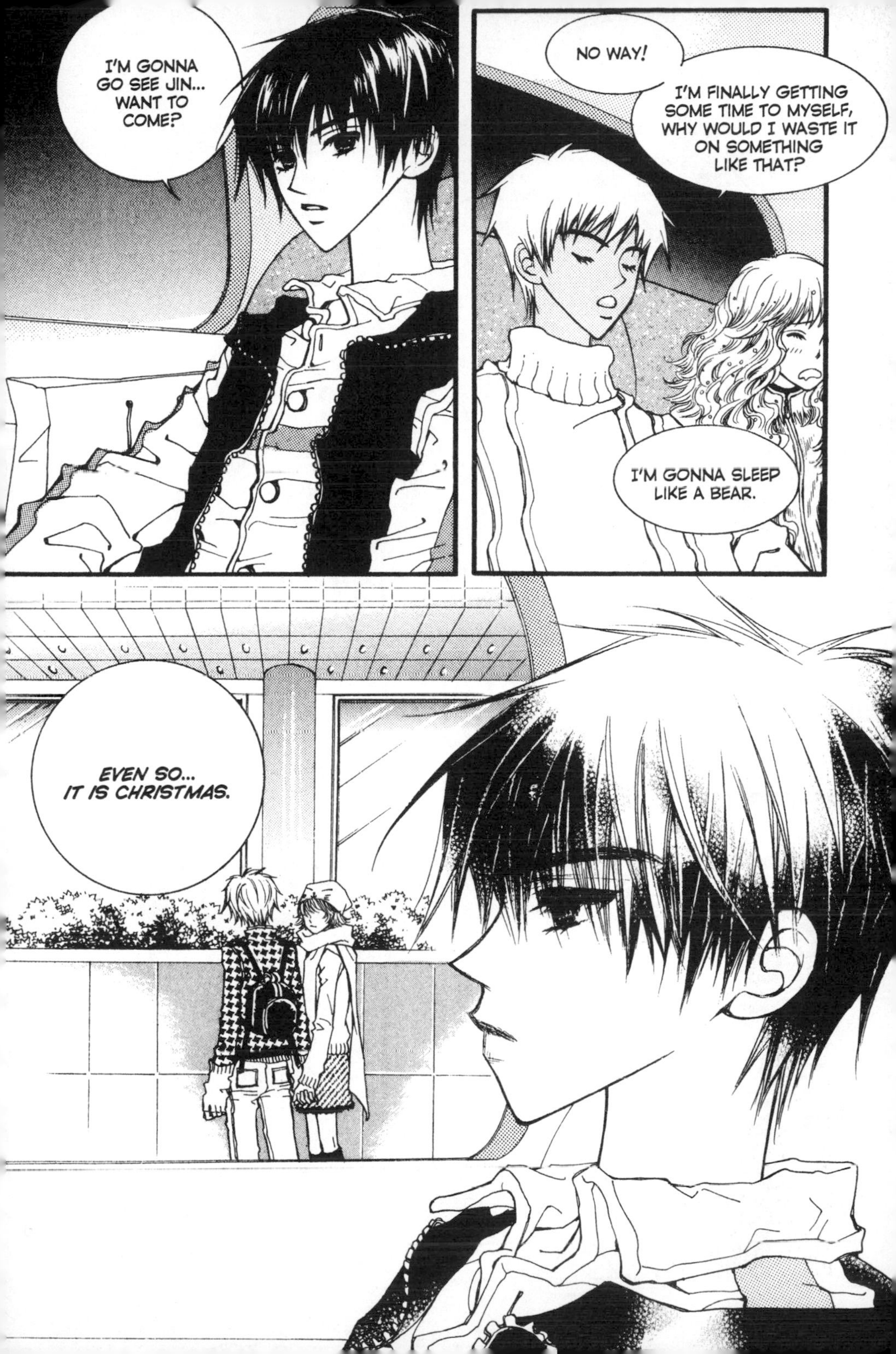
I'M GONNA GO SEE JIN... WANT TO COME?
NO WAY!
I'M FINALLY GETTING SOME TIME TO MYSELF, WHY WOULD I WASTE IT ON SOMETHING LIKE THAT?
I'M GONNA SLEEP LIKE A BEAR.
EVEN SO... IT IS CHRISTMAS.

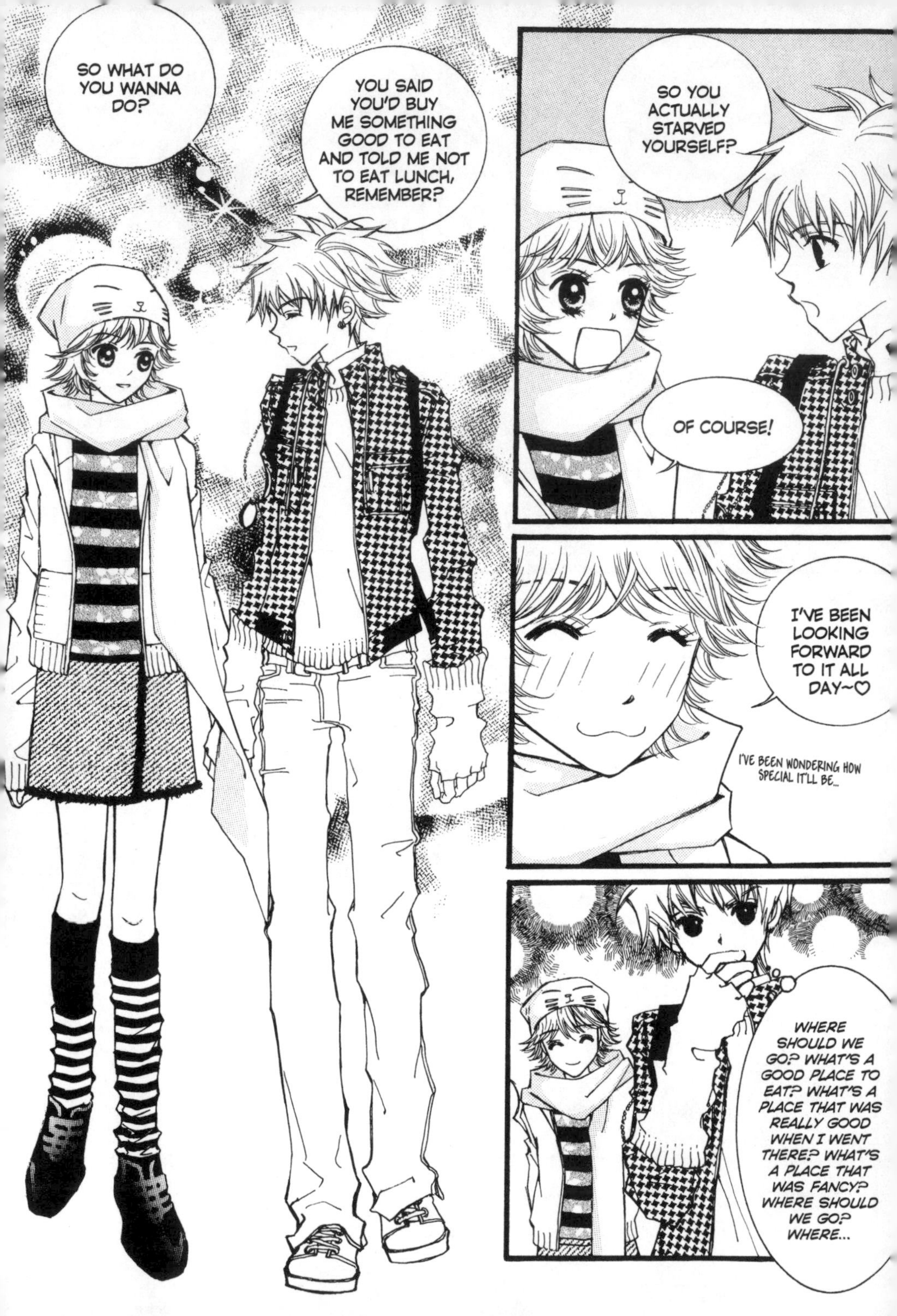
SO WHAT DO YOU WANNA DO?
YOU SAID YOU'D BUY ME SOMETHING GOOD TO EAT AND TOLD ME NOT TO EAT LUNCH, REMEMBER?
SO YOU ACTUALLY STARVED YOURSELF?
OF COURSE!
I'VE BEEN LOOKING FORWARD TO IT ALL DAY~♡
I'VE BEEN WONDERING HOW SPECIAL IT'LL BE...
WHERE SHOULD WE GO? WHAT'S A GOOD PLACE TO EAT? WHAT'S A PLACE THAT WAS REALLY GOOD WHEN I WENT THERE? WHAT'S A PLACE THAT WAS FANCY? WHERE SHOULD WE GO? WHERE...

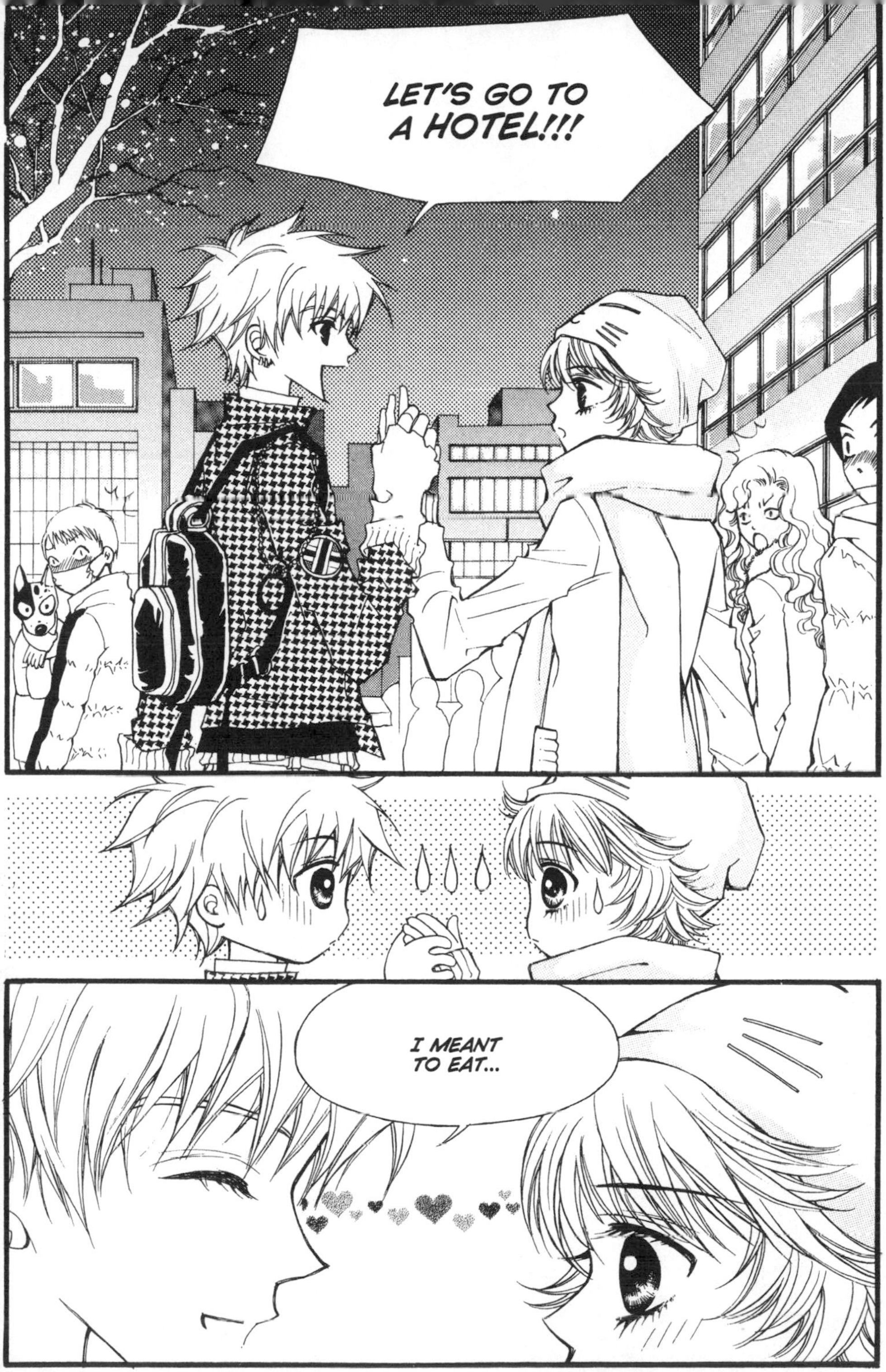
LET'S GO TO
A HOTEL!!!
I MEANT
TO EAT...

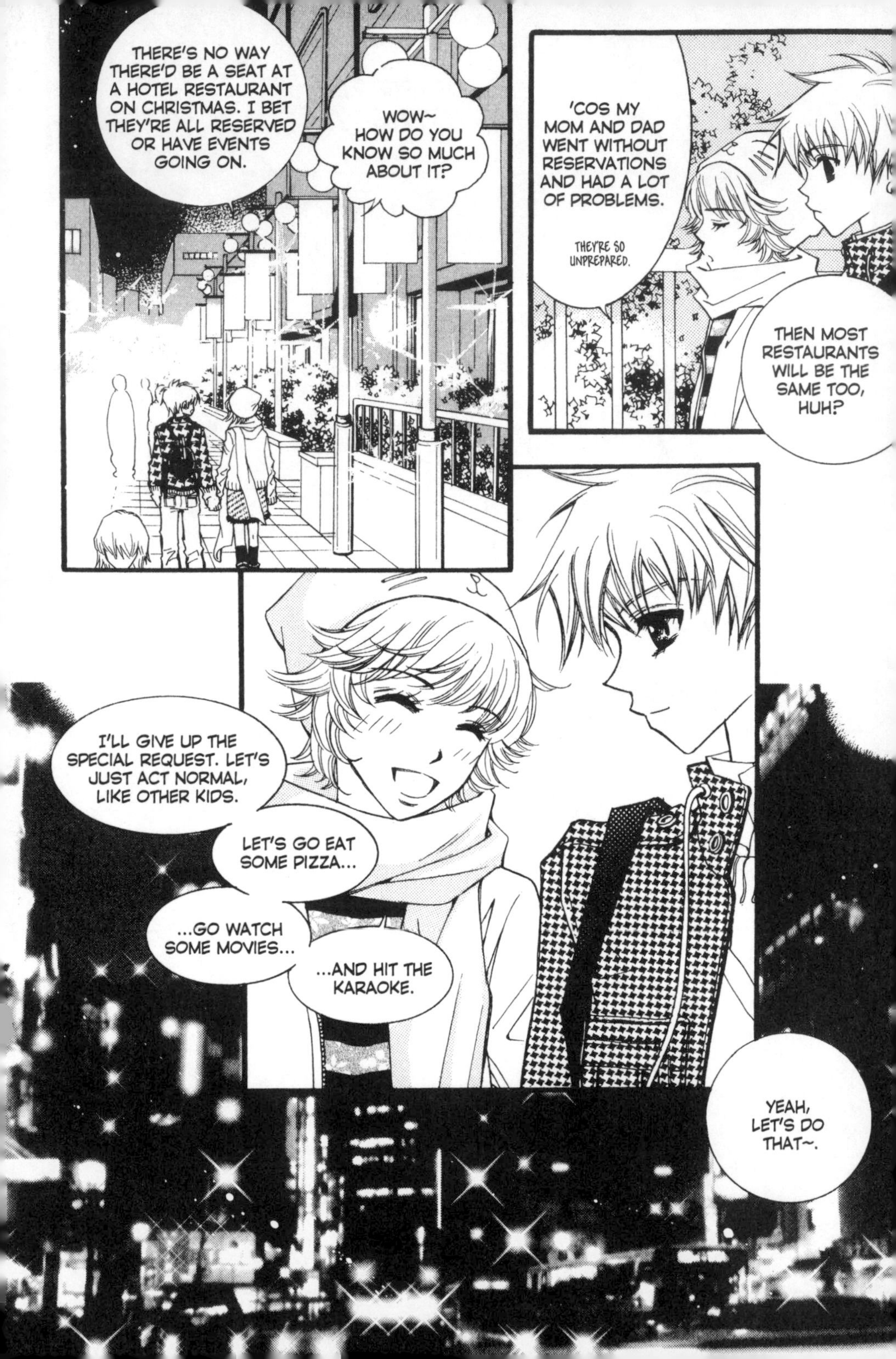
THERE'S NO WAY THERE'D BE A SEAT AT A HOTEL RESTAURANT ON CHRISTMAS. I BET THEY'RE ALL RESERVED OR HAVE EVENTS GOING ON.
WOW~ HOW DO YOU KNOW SO MUCH ABOUT IT?
'COS MY MOM AND DAD WENT WITHOUT RESERVATIONS AND HAD A LOT OF PROBLEMS.
THEY'RE SO UNPREPARED.
THEN MOST RESTAURANTS WILL BE THE SAME TOO, HUH?
I'LL GIVE UP THE SPECIAL REQUEST. LET'S JUST ACT NORMAL, LIKE OTHER KIDS.
LET'S GO EAT SOME PIZZA...
...GO WATCH SOME MOVIES...
...AND HIT THE KARAOKE.
YEAH, LET'S DO THAT~.

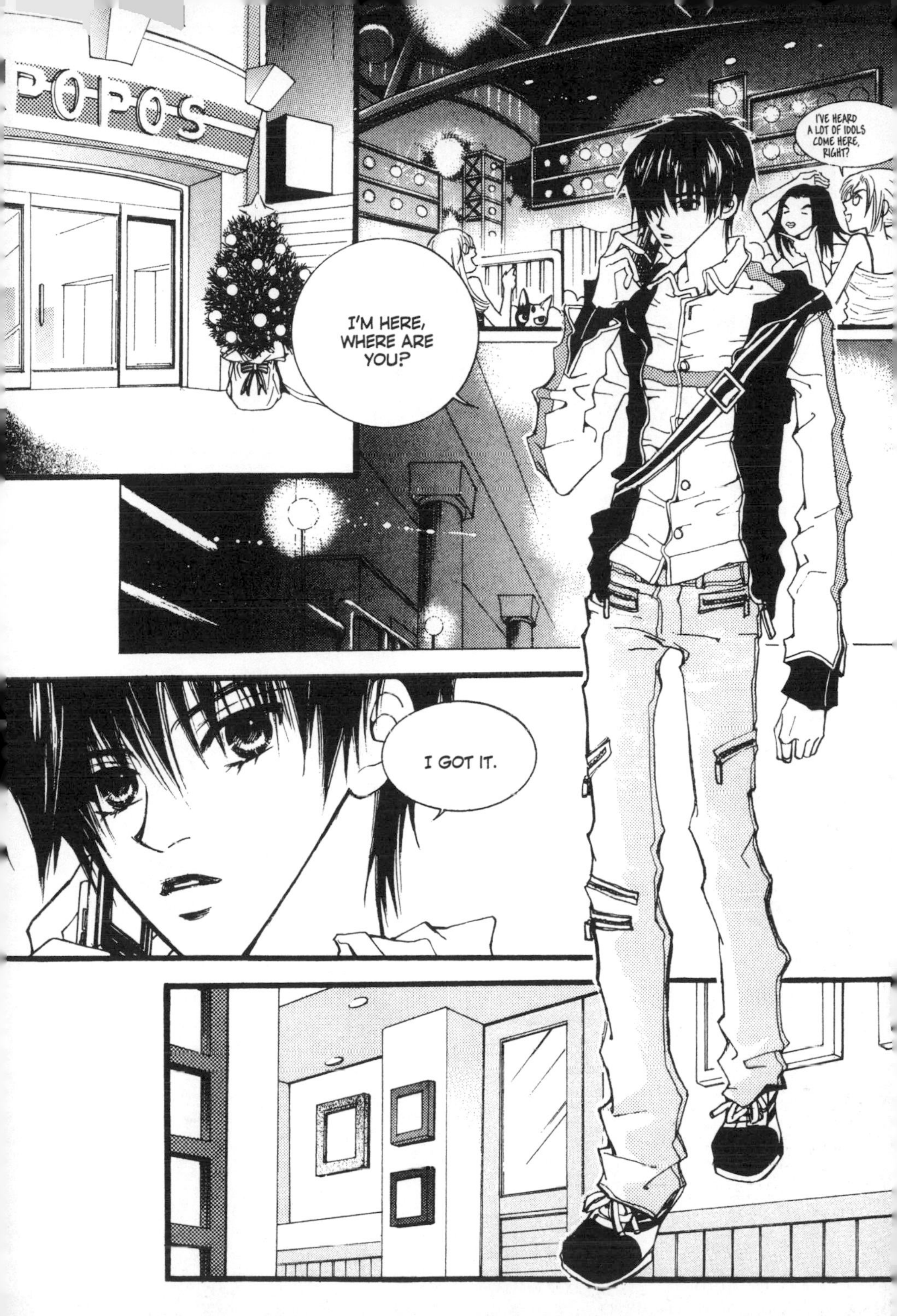
POPOS
I'M HERE, WHERE ARE YOU?
I'VE HEARD A LOT OF IDOLS COME HERE, RIGHT?
I GOT IT.

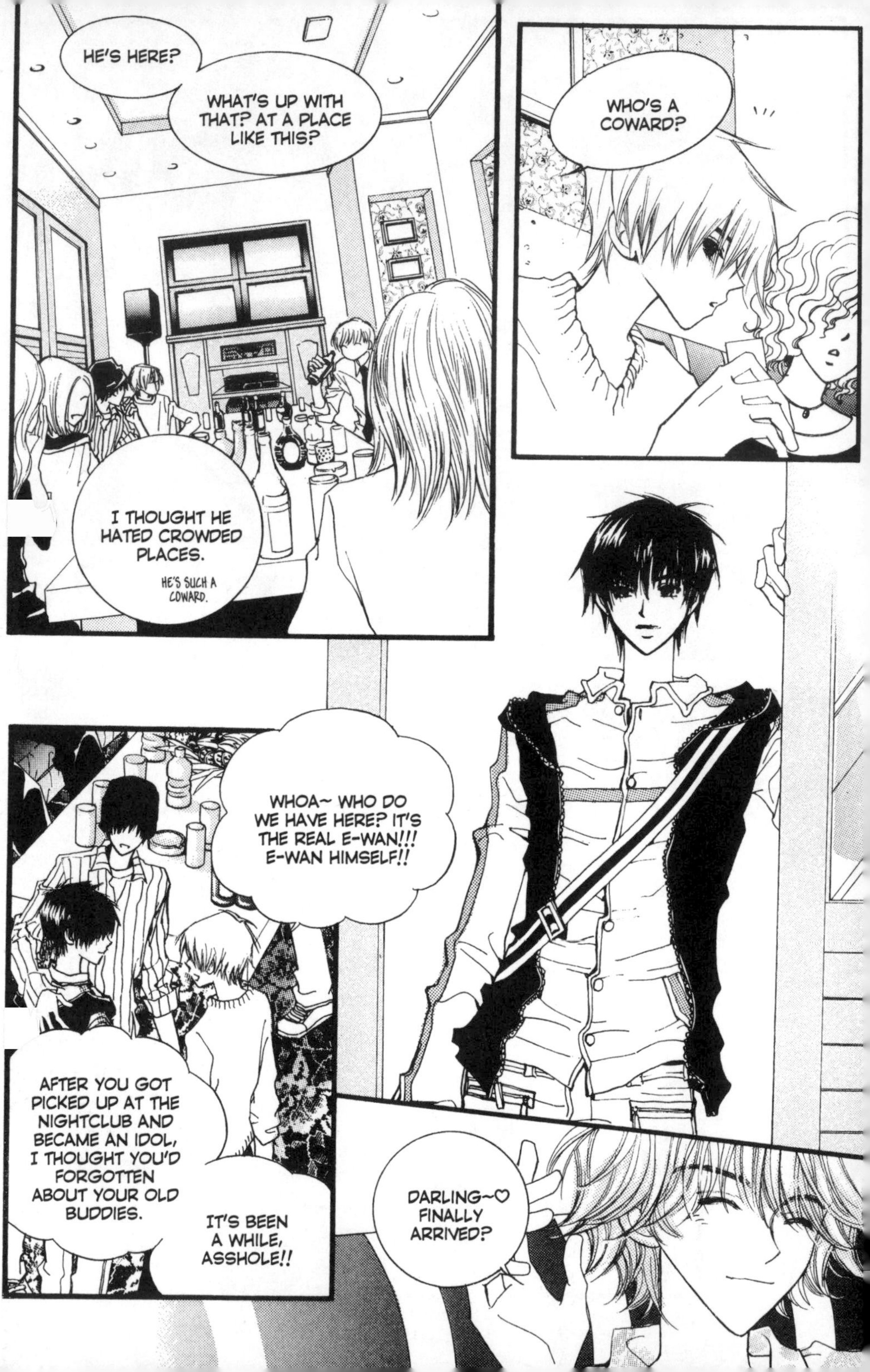
HE'S HERE?
WHAT'S UP WITH THAT? AT A PLACE LIKE THIS?
I THOUGHT HE HATED CROWDED PLACES.
HE'S SUCH A COWARD.
WHO'S A COWARD?
WHOA~ WHO DO WE HAVE HERE? IT'S THE REAL E-WAN!!! E-WAN HIMSELF!!
AFTER YOU GOT PICKED UP AT THE NIGHTCLUB AND BECAME AN IDOL, I THOUGHT YOU'D FORGOTTEN ABOUT YOUR OLD BUDDIES.
IT'S BEEN A WHILE, ASSHOLE!!
DARLING~♡ FINALLY ARRIVED?

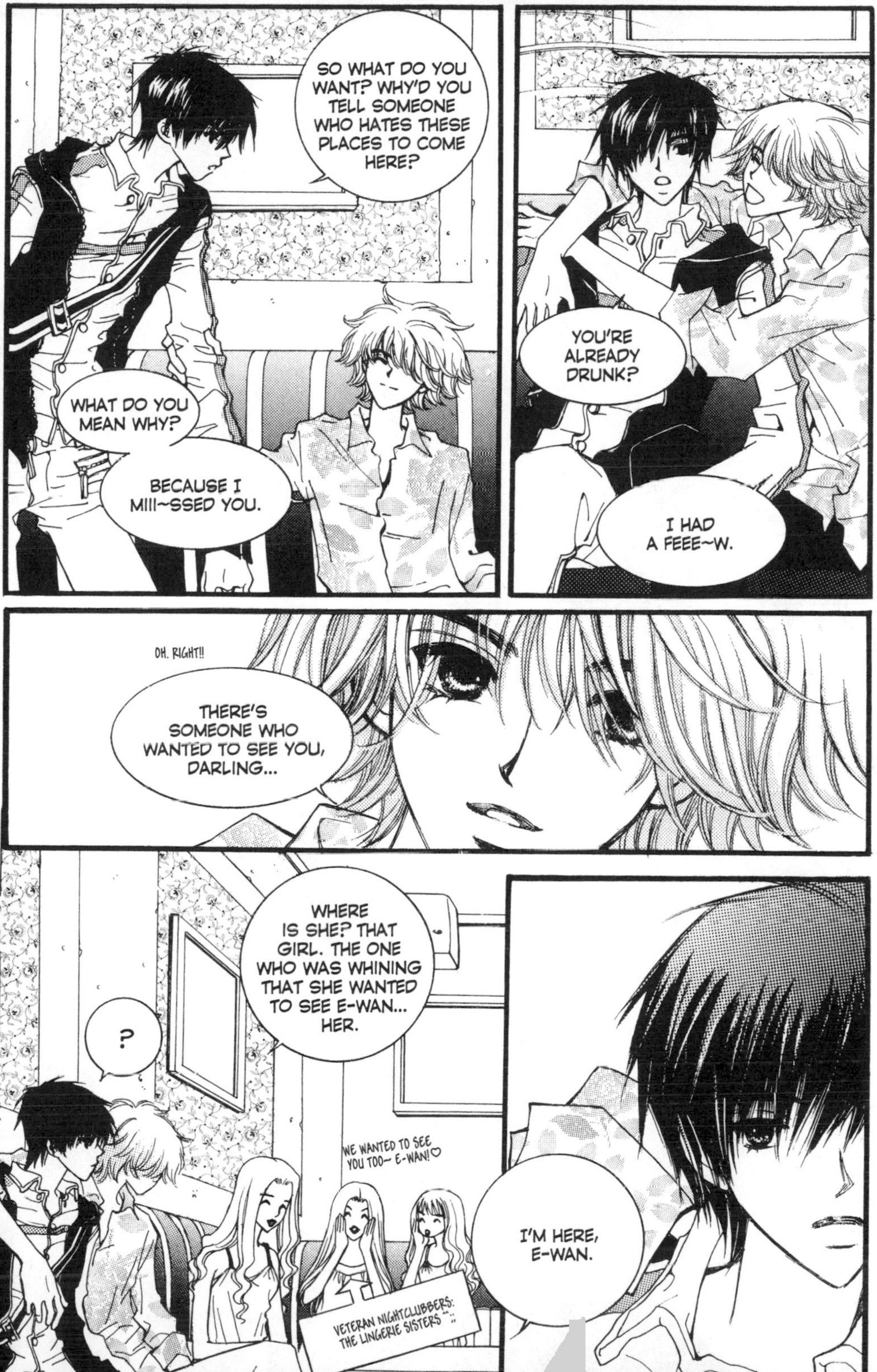
SO WHAT DO YOU WANT? WHY'D YOU TELL SOMEONE WHO HATES THESE PLACES TO COME HERE?
WHAT DO YOU MEAN WHY?
BECAUSE I MIII~SSED YOU.
YOU'RE ALREADY DRUNK?
I HAD A FEEE~W.
OH. RIGHT!!
THERE'S SOMEONE WHO WANTED TO SEE YOU, DARLING...
?
WHERE IS SHE? THAT GIRL. THE ONE WHO WAS WHINING THAT SHE WANTED TO SEE E-WAN... HER.
WE WANTED TO SEE YOU TOO~ E-WAN!♡
VETERAN NIGHTCLUBBERS: THE LINGERIE SISTERS ^^;;
I'M HERE, E-WAN.

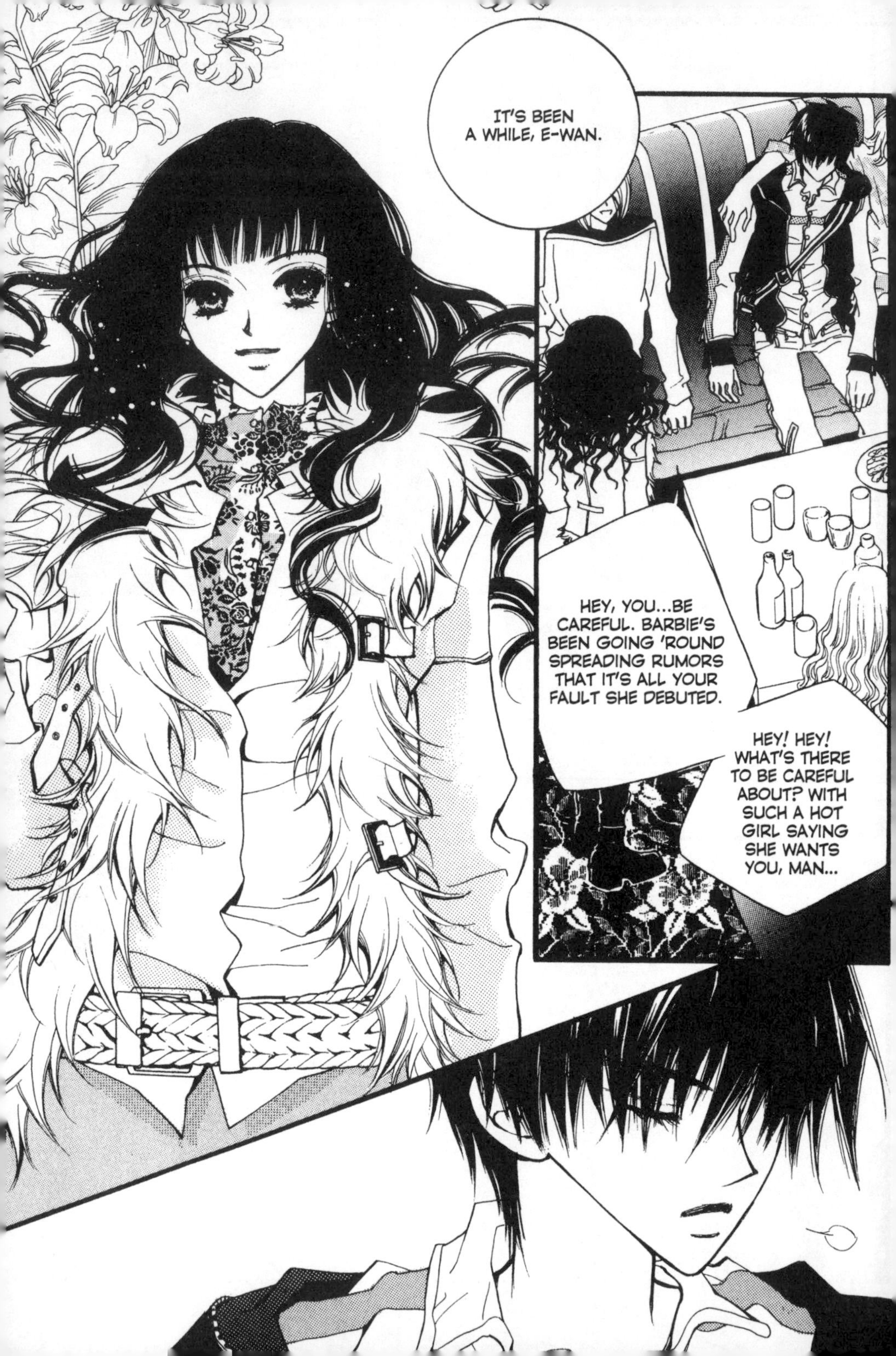
IT'S BEEN A WHILE, E-WAN.
HEY, YOU...BE CAREFUL. BARBIE'S BEEN GOING 'ROUND SPREADING RUMORS THAT IT'S ALL YOUR FAULT SHE DEBUTED.
HEY! HEY! WHAT'S THERE TO BE CAREFUL ABOUT? WITH SUCH A HOT GIRL SAYING SHE WANTS YOU, MAN...

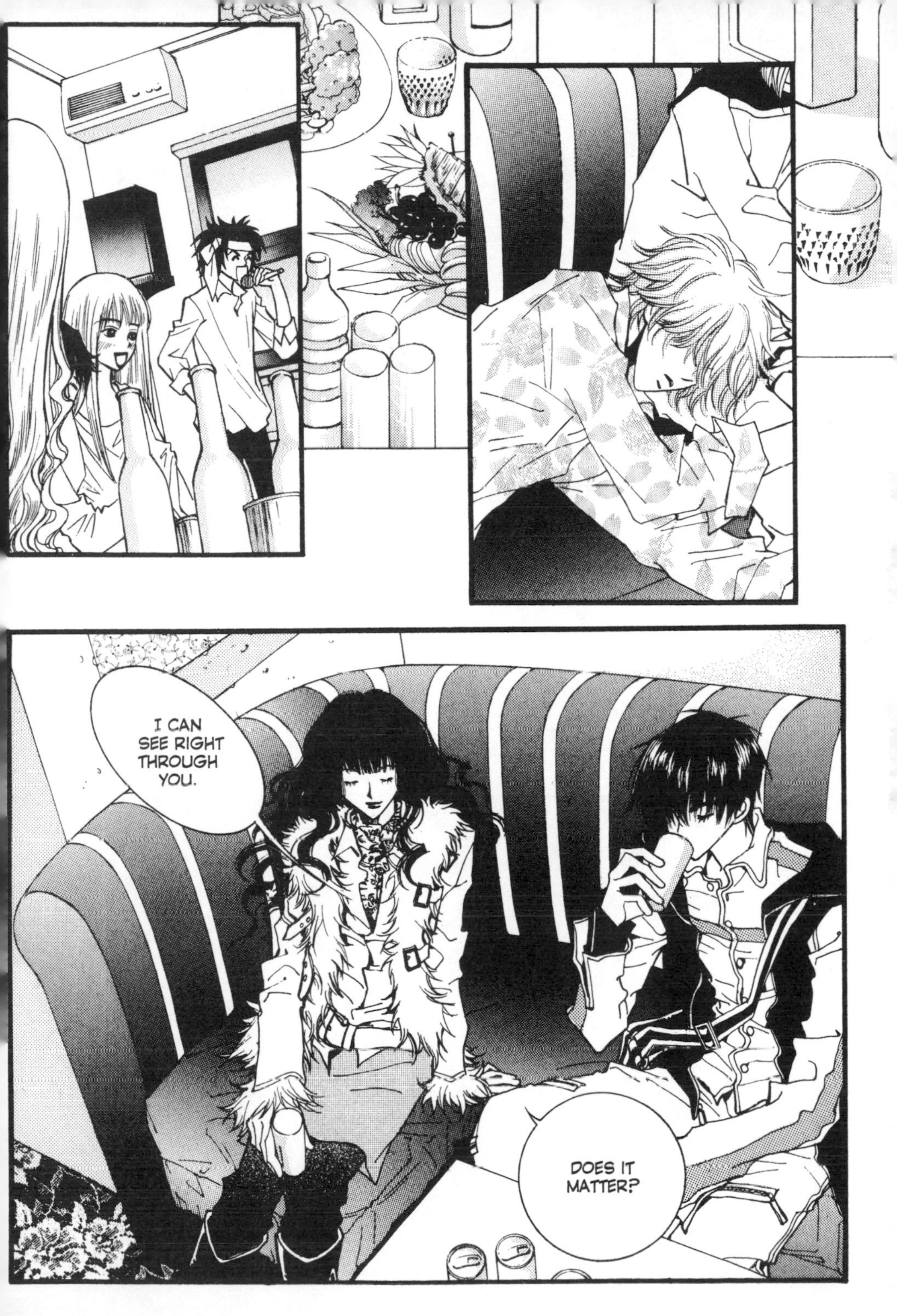
I CAN SEE RIGHT THROUGH YOU.
DOES IT MATTER?

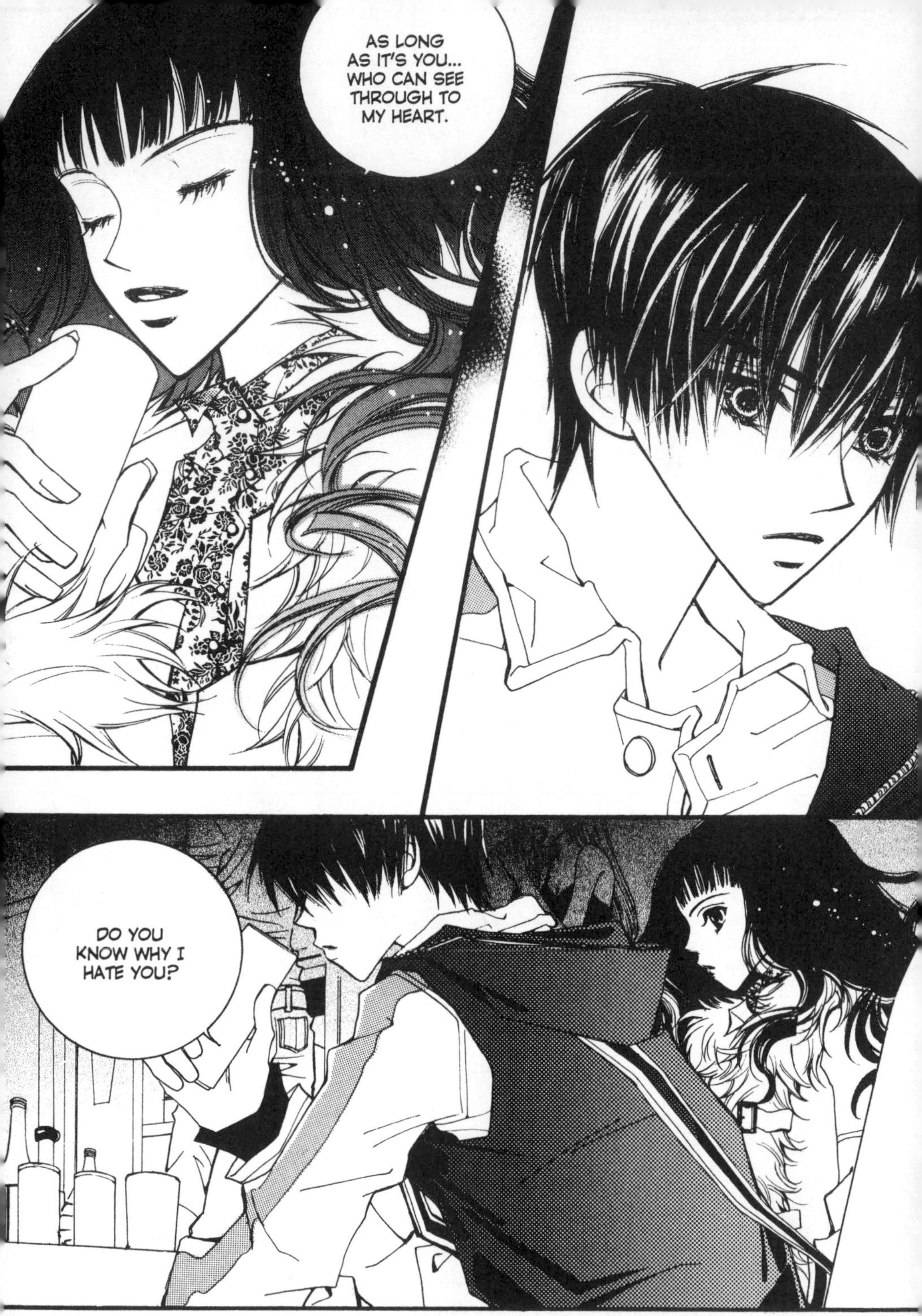
AS LONG AS IT'S YOU... WHO CAN SEE THROUGH TO MY HEART.
DO YOU KNOW WHY I HATE YOU?

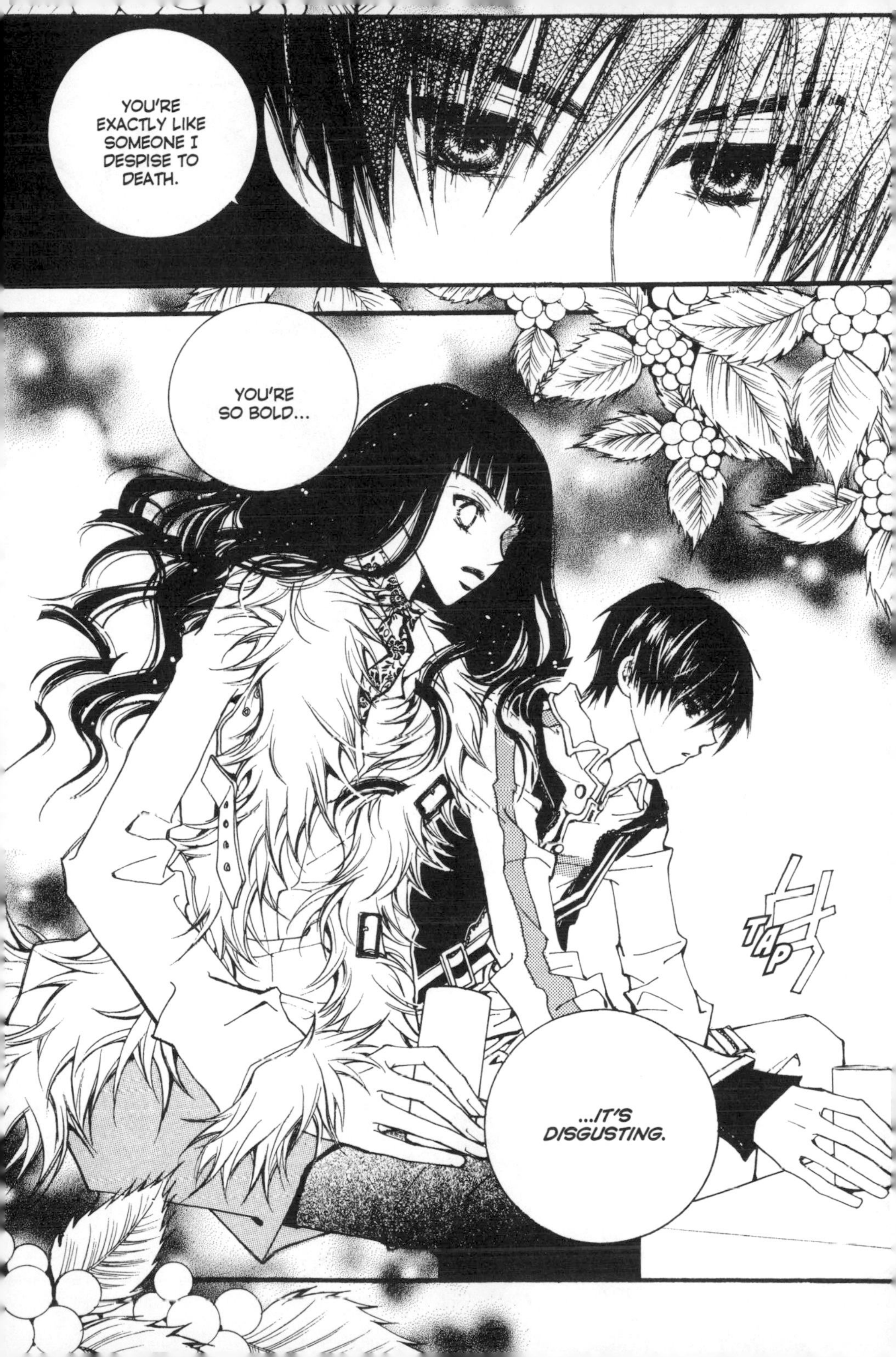
YOU'RE EXACTLY LIKE SOMEONE I DESPISE TO DEATH.
YOU'RE SO BOLD...
TAP
...IT'S DISGUSTING.

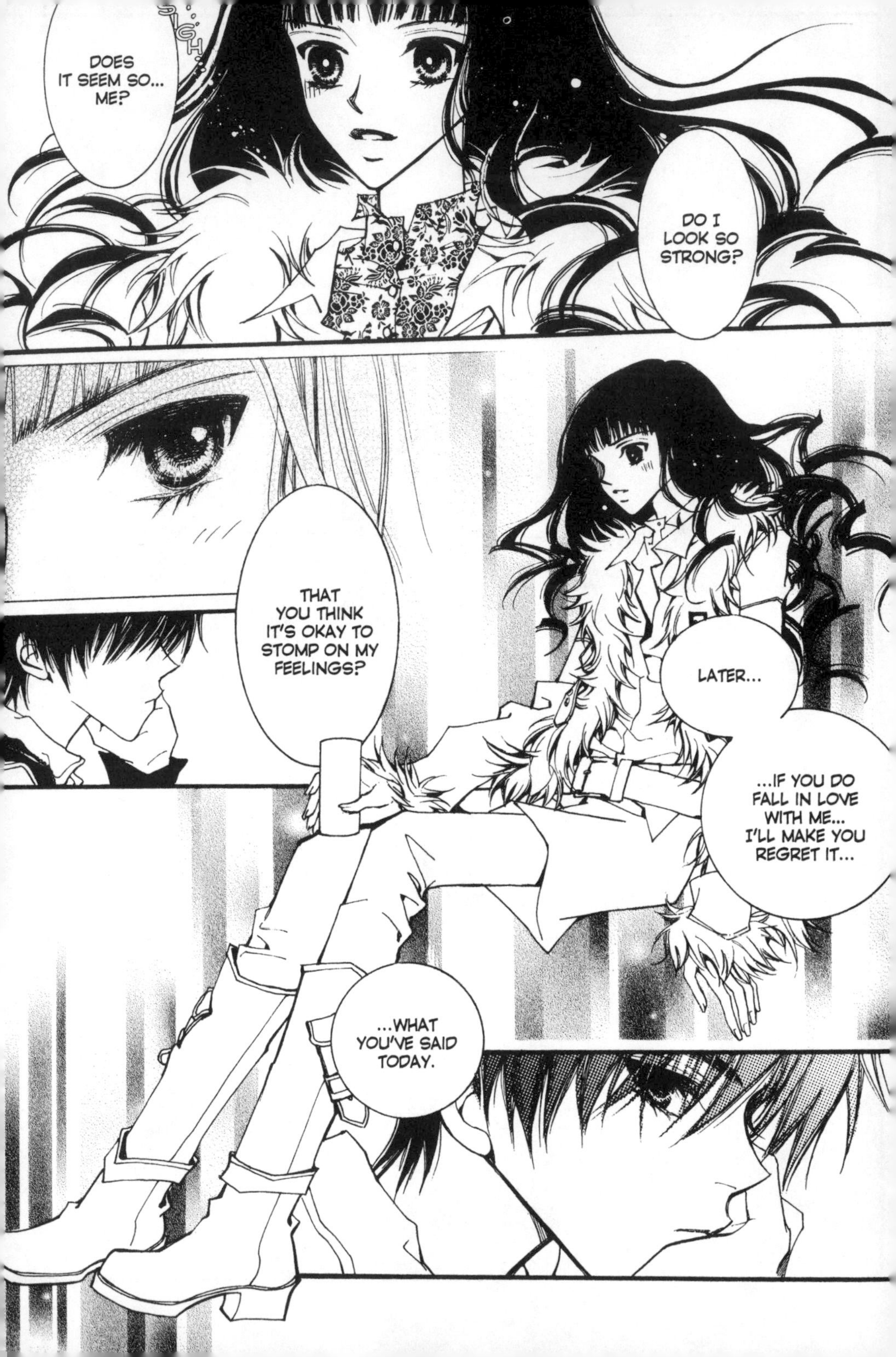
SIGH
DOES IT SEEM SO... ME?
DO I LOOK SO STRONG?
THAT YOU THINK IT'S OKAY TO STOMP ON MY FEELINGS?
LATER...
...IF YOU DO FALL IN LOVE WITH ME... I'LL MAKE YOU REGRET IT...
...WHAT YOU'VE SAID TODAY.

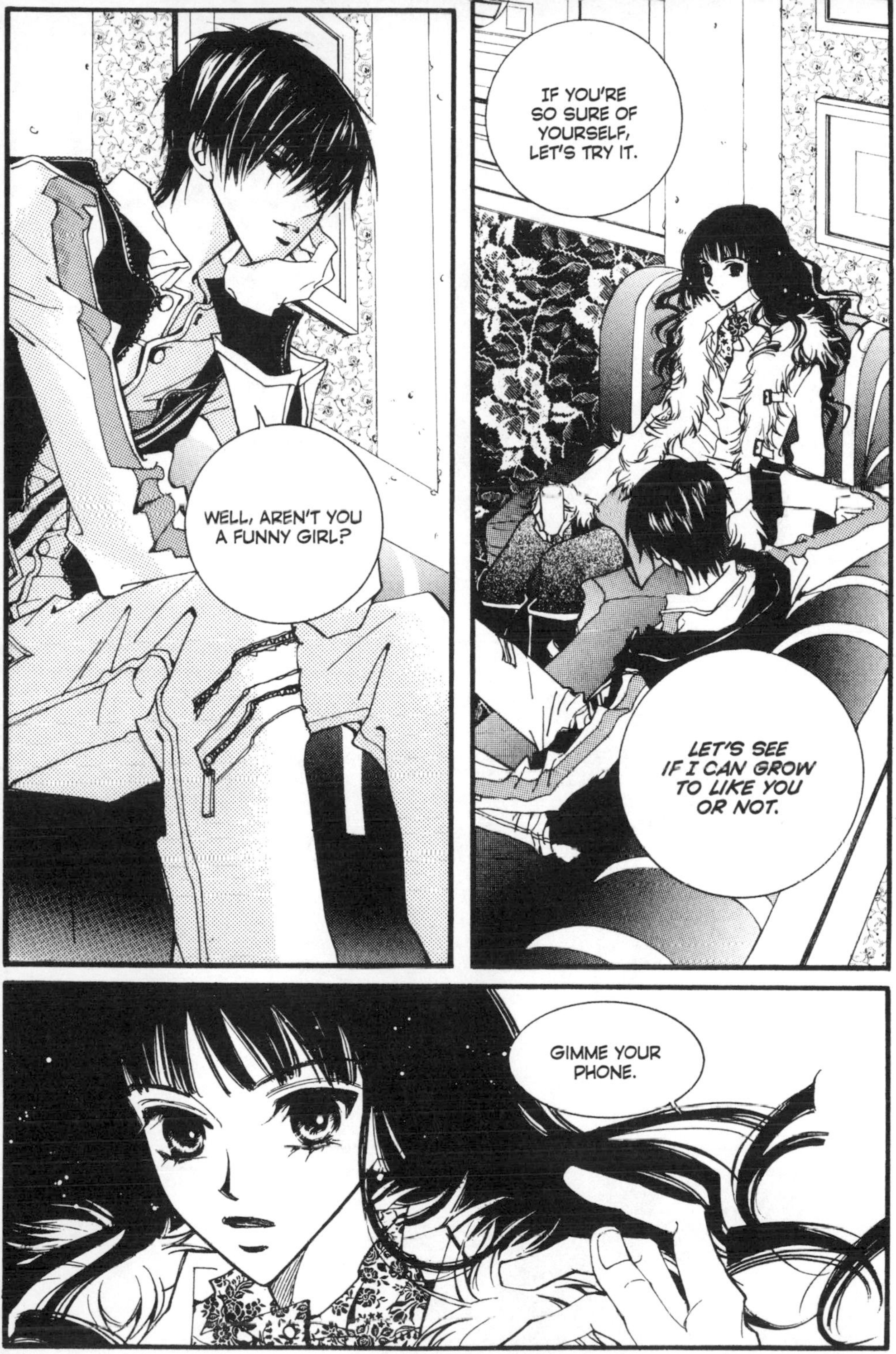
WELL, AREN'T YOU A FUNNY GIRL?
IF YOU'RE SO SURE OF YOURSELF, LET'S TRY IT.
LET'S SEE IF I CAN GROW TO LIKE YOU OR NOT.
GIMME YOUR PHONE.

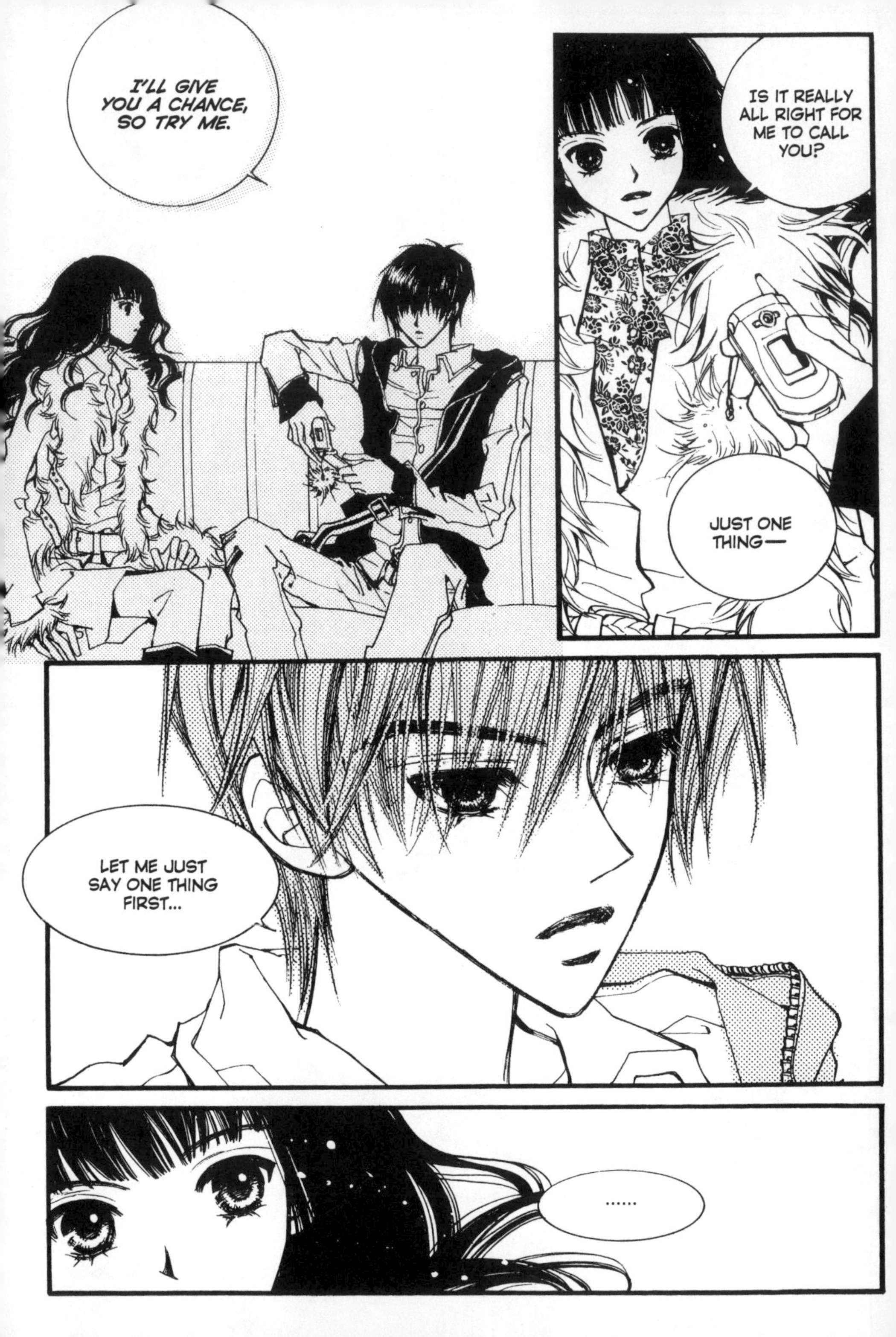
I'LL GIVE YOU A CHANCE, SO TRY ME.
IS IT REALLY ALL RIGHT FOR ME TO CALL YOU?
JUST ONE THING—
LET ME JUST SAY ONE THING FIRST...
......

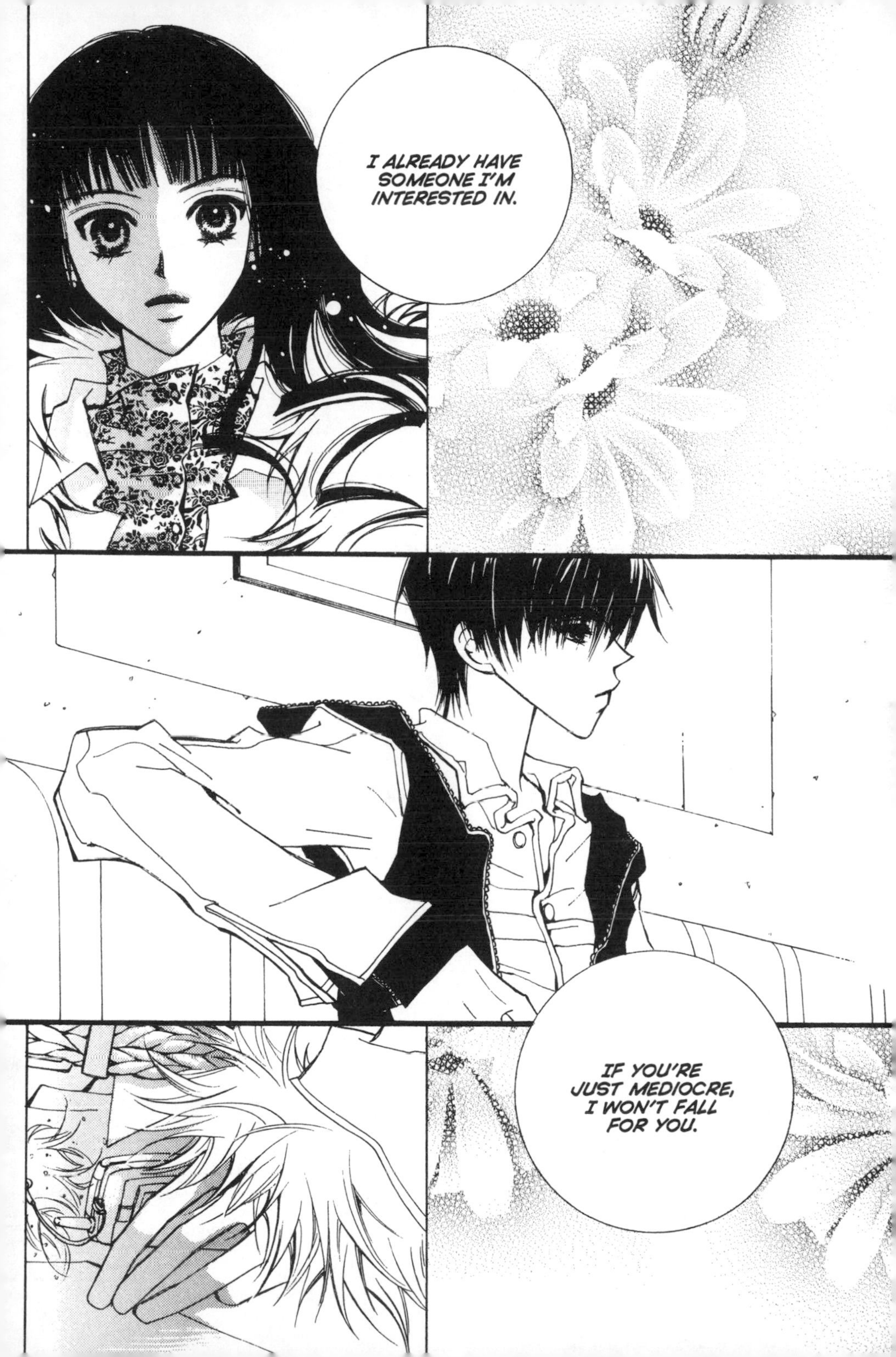
I ALREADY HAVE SOMEONE I'M INTERESTED IN.
IF YOU'RE JUST MEDIOCRE, I WON'T FALL FOR YOU.

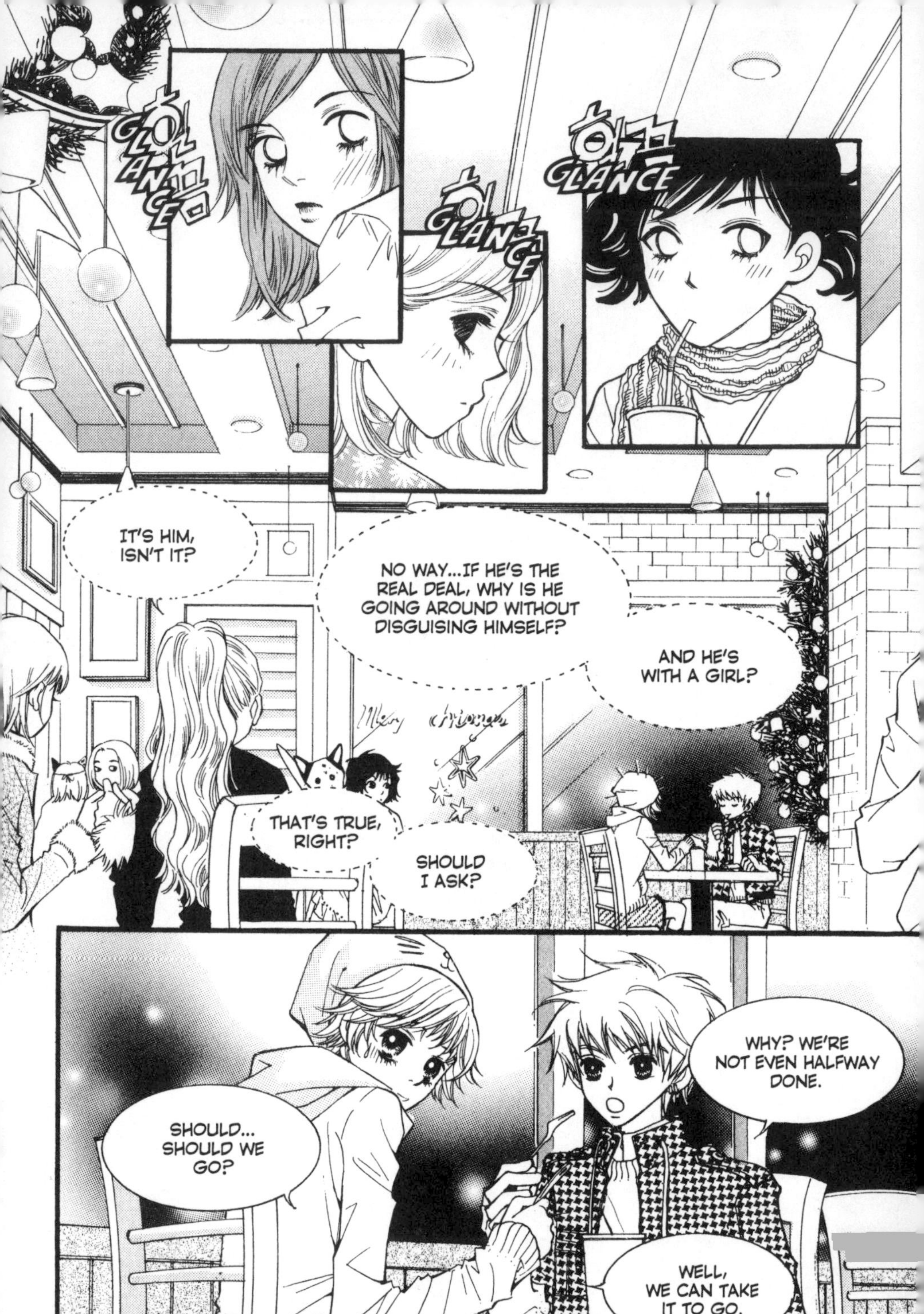
GLANCE
GLANCE
GLANCE
IT'S HIM, ISN'T IT?
NO WAY...IF HE'S THE REAL DEAL, WHY IS HE GOING AROUND WITHOUT DISGUISING HIMSELF?
AND HE'S WITH A GIRL?
THAT'S TRUE, RIGHT?
SHOULD I ASK?
SHOULD... SHOULD WE GO?
WHY? WE'RE NOT EVEN HALFWAY DONE.
WELL, WE CAN TAKE IT TO GO.

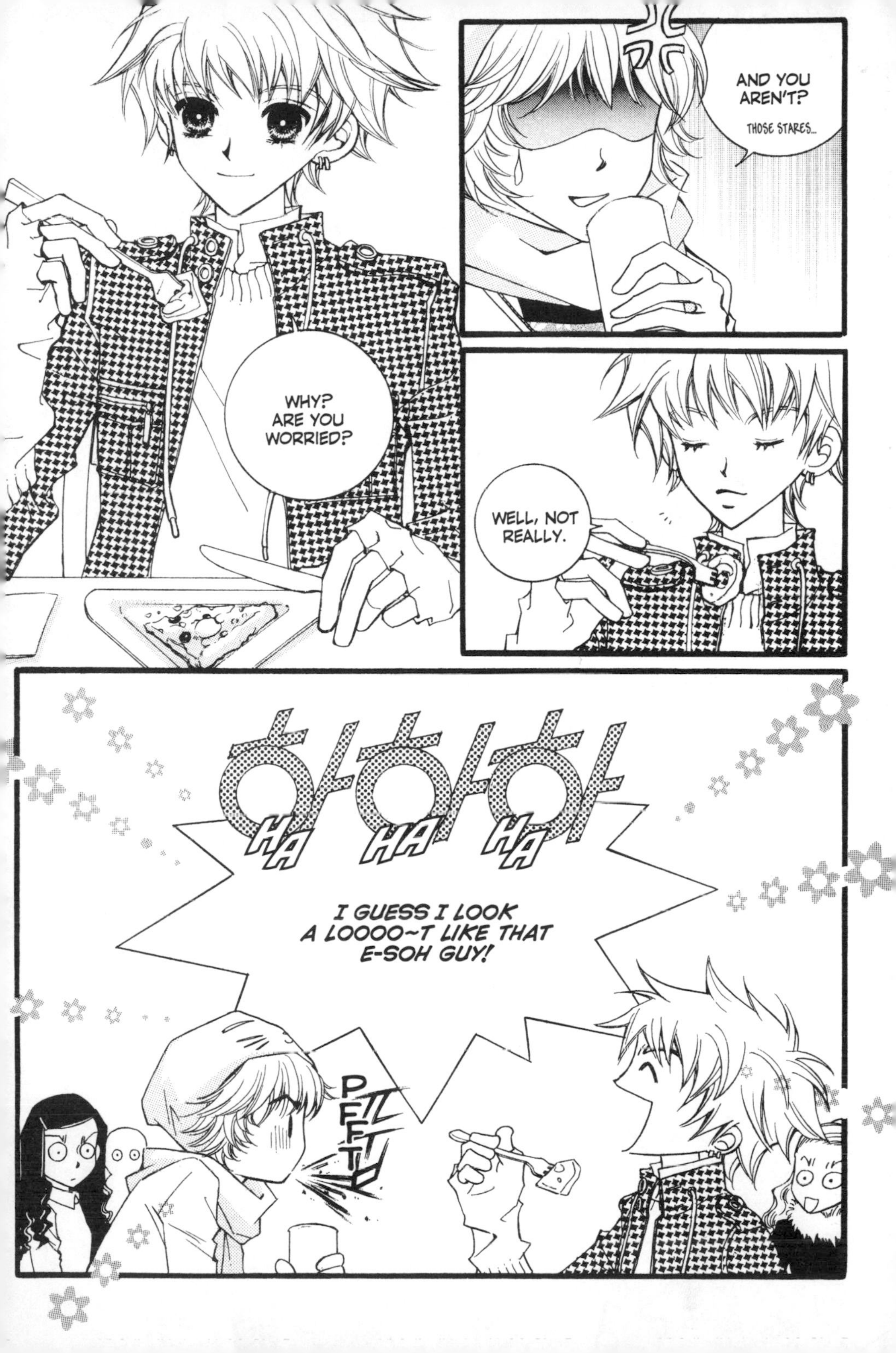
AND YOU AREN'T?
THOSE STARES...
WHY? ARE YOU WORRIED?
WELL, NOT REALLY.
하하하
HA HA HA
I GUESS I LOOK A LOOOO~T LIKE THAT E-SOH GUY!
PFFT!

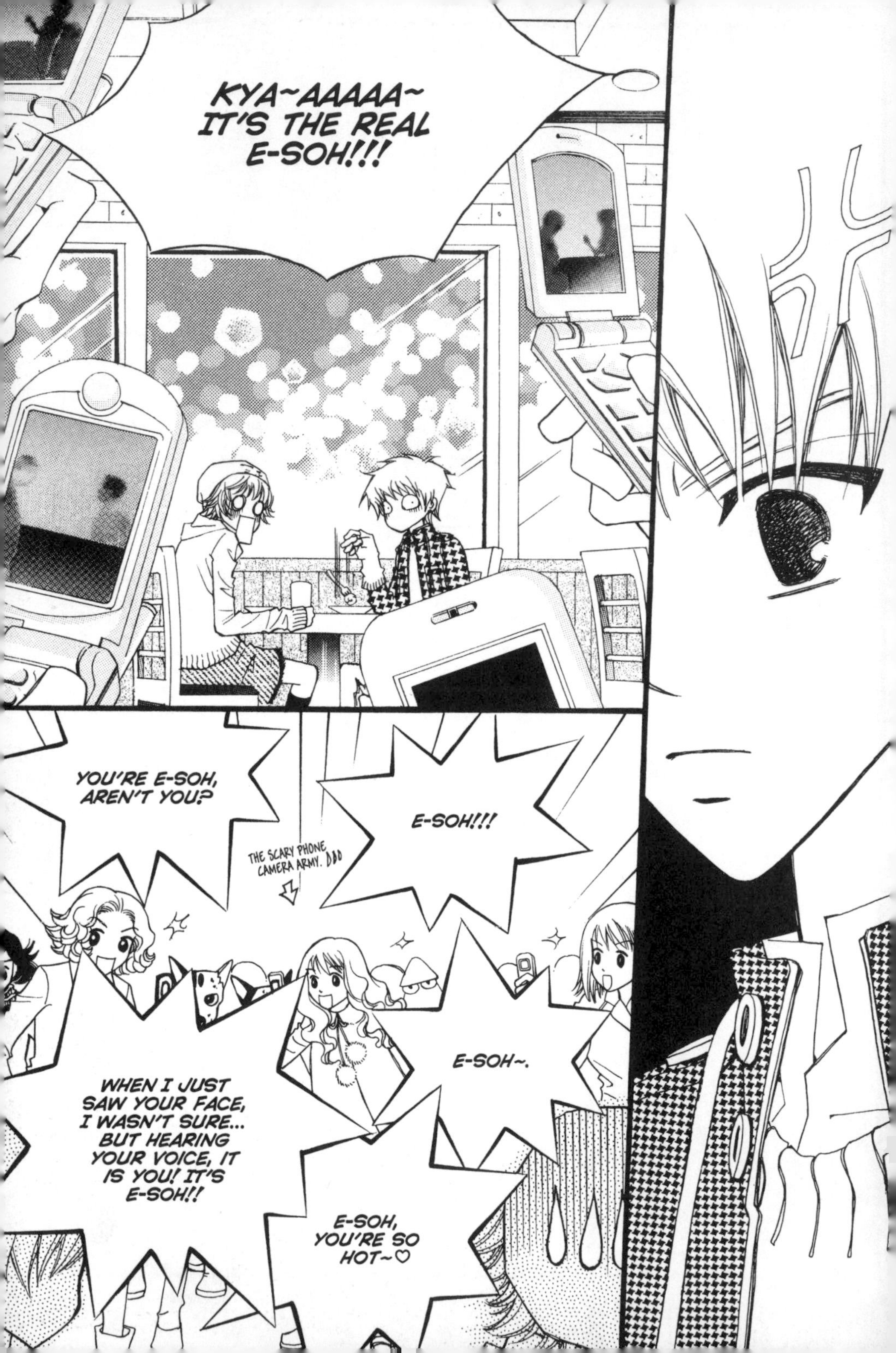
KYA~AAAAA~ IT'S THE REAL E-SOH!!!
YOU'RE E-SOH, AREN'T YOU?
THE SCARY PHONE CAMERA ARMY. ΔΔΔ
E-SOH!!!
E-SOH~.
WHEN I JUST SAW YOUR FACE, I WASN'T SURE... BUT HEARING YOUR VOICE, IT IS YOU! IT'S E-SOH!!
E-SOH, YOU'RE SO HOT~♡

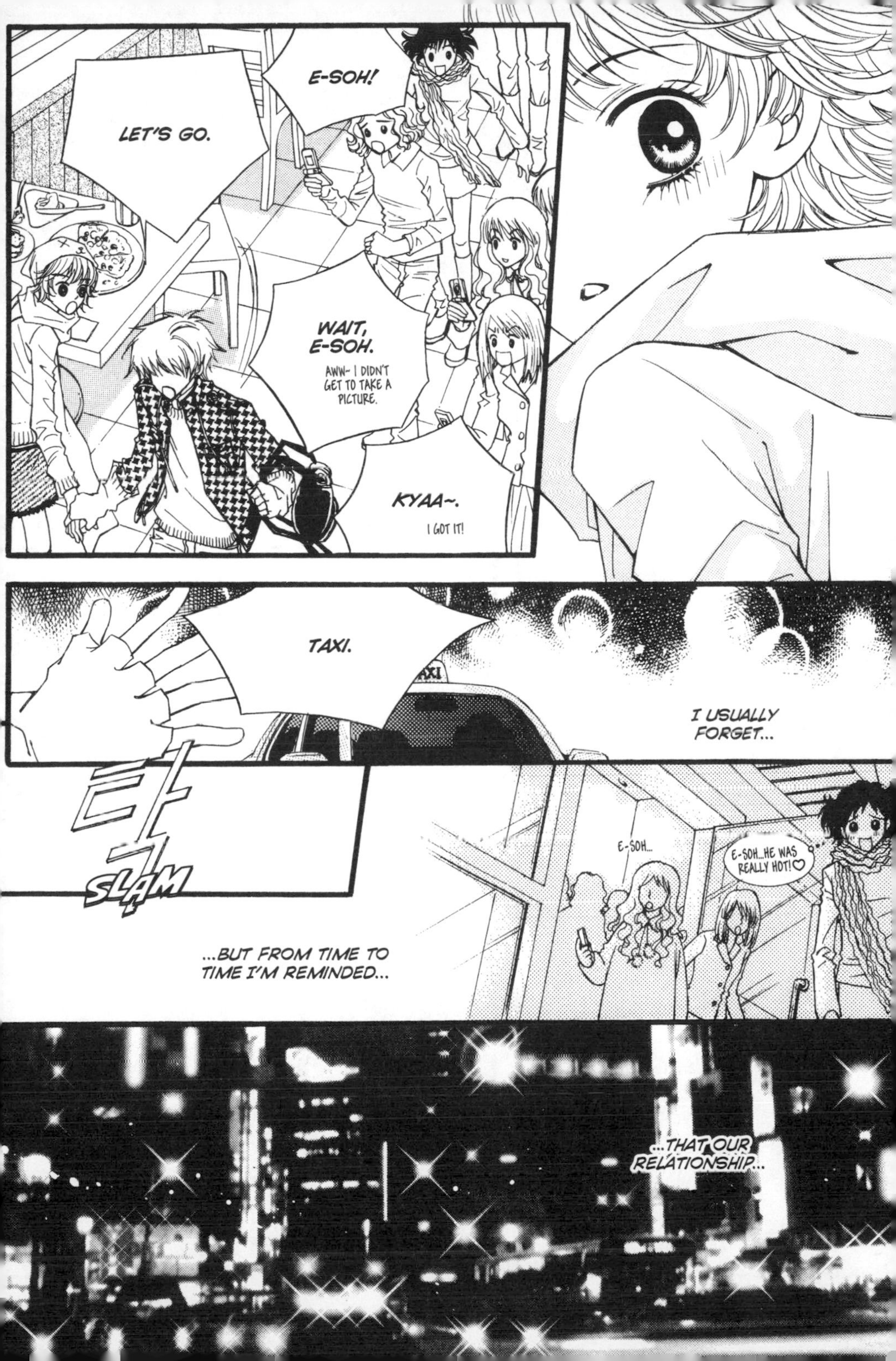
LET'S GO.
E-SOH!
WAIT, E-SOH.
AWW~ I DIDN'T GET TO TAKE A PICTURE.
KYAA~.
I GOT IT!
TAXI.
I USUALLY FORGET...
탁
SLAM
...BUT FROM TIME TO TIME I'M REMINDED...
E-SOH...
E-SOH...HE WAS REALLY HOT!♡
...THAT OUR RELATIONSHIP...

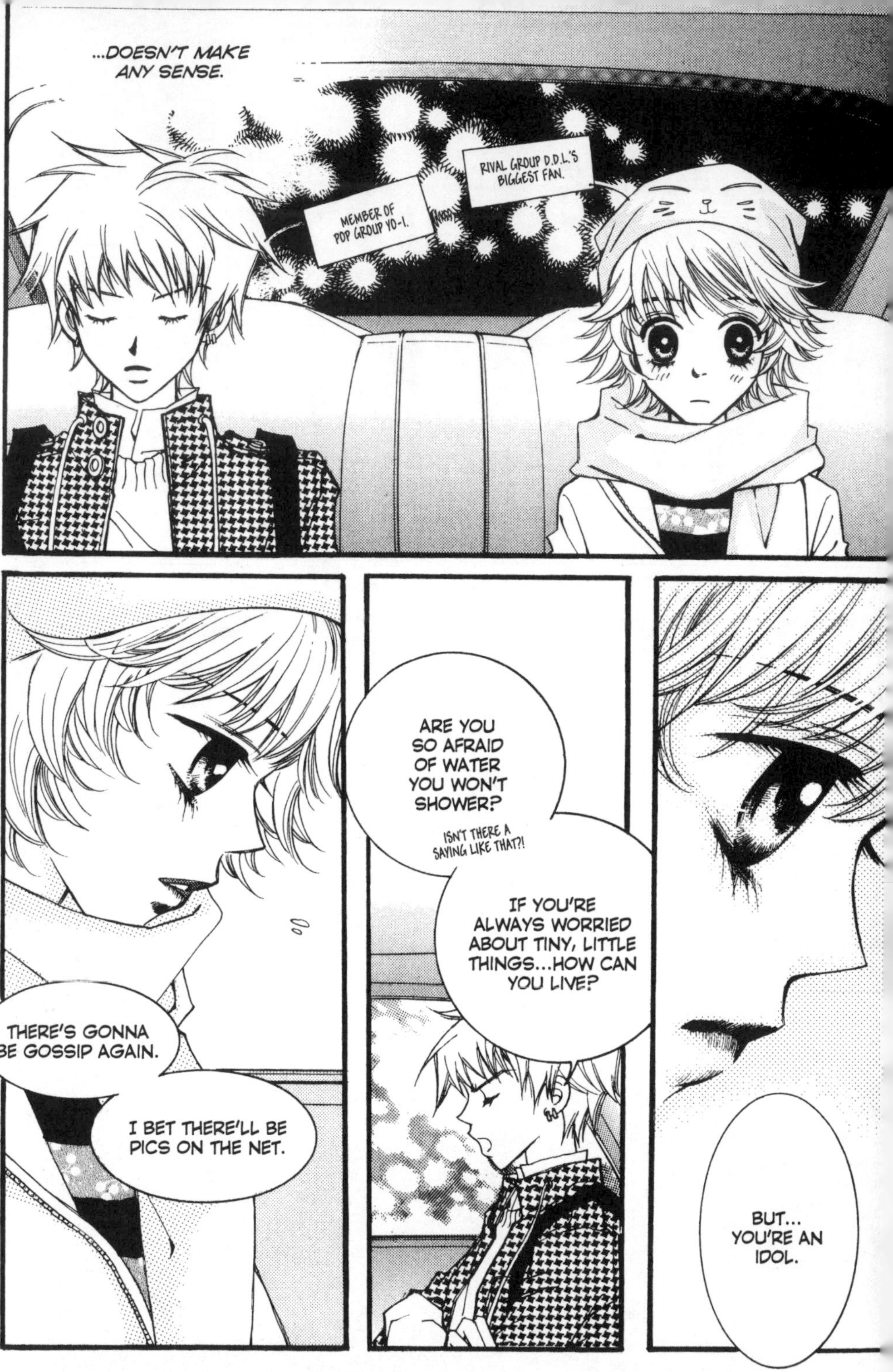
...DOESN'T MAKE ANY SENSE.
MEMBER OF POP GROUP YO-1.
RIVAL GROUP D.D.L.'S BIGGEST FAN.
THERE'S GONNA BE GOSSIP AGAIN.
I BET THERE'LL BE PICS ON THE NET.
ARE YOU SO AFRAID OF WATER YOU WON'T SHOWER?
ISN'T THERE A SAYING LIKE THAT?!
IF YOU'RE ALWAYS WORRIED ABOUT TINY, LITTLE THINGS...HOW CAN YOU LIVE?
BUT... YOU'RE AN IDOL.

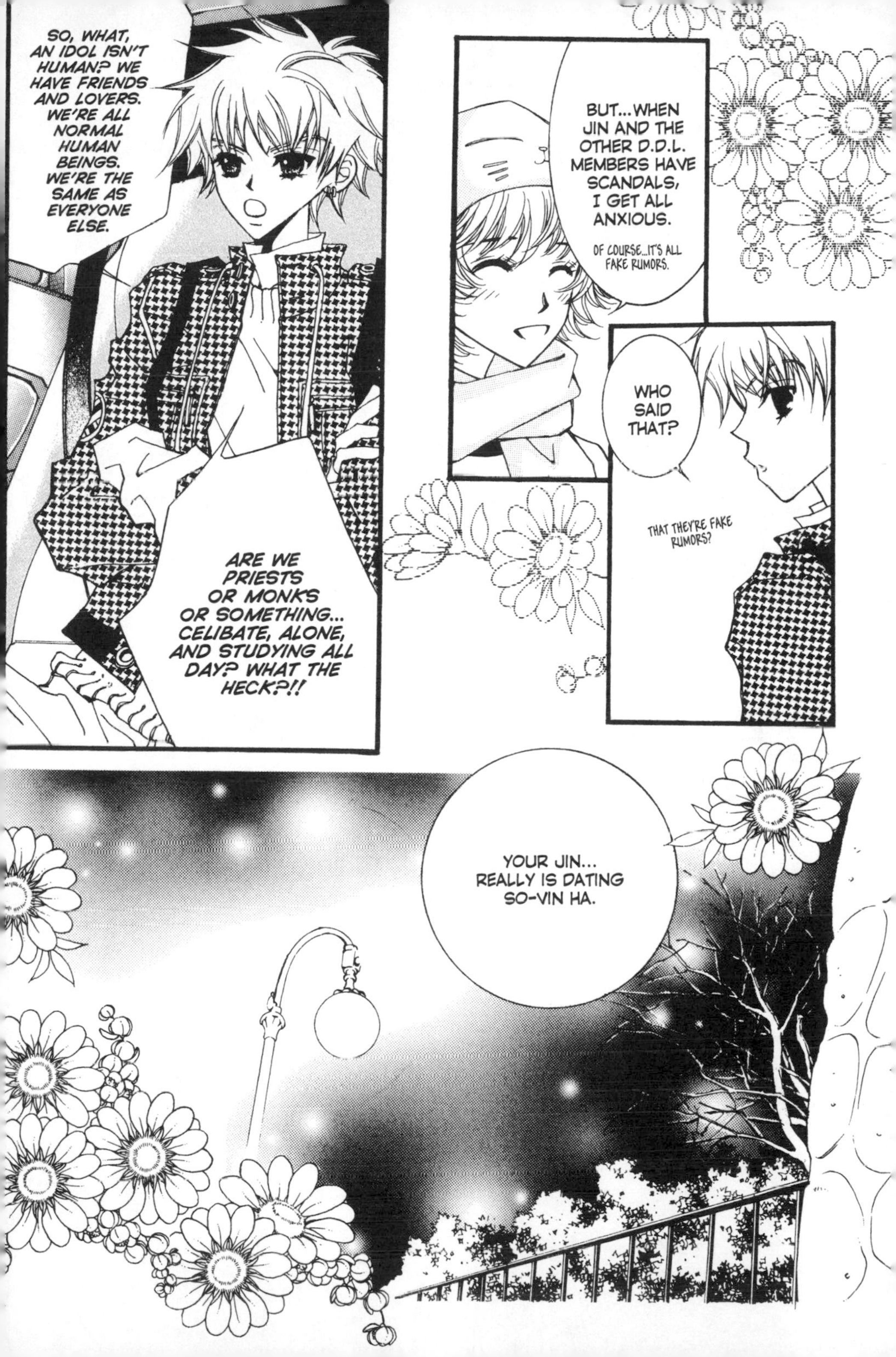
SO, WHAT, AN IDOL ISN'T HUMAN? WE HAVE FRIENDS AND LOVERS. WE'RE ALL NORMAL HUMAN BEINGS. WE'RE THE SAME AS EVERYONE ELSE.
ARE WE PRIESTS OR MONKS OR SOMETHING... CELIBATE, ALONE, AND STUDYING ALL DAY? WHAT THE HECK?!!
BUT...WHEN JIN AND THE OTHER D.D.L. MEMBERS HAVE SCANDALS, I GET ALL ANXIOUS.
OF COURSE...IT'S ALL FAKE RUMORS.
WHO SAID THAT?
THAT THEY'RE FAKE RUMORS?
YOUR JIN... REALLY IS DATING SO-VIN HA.

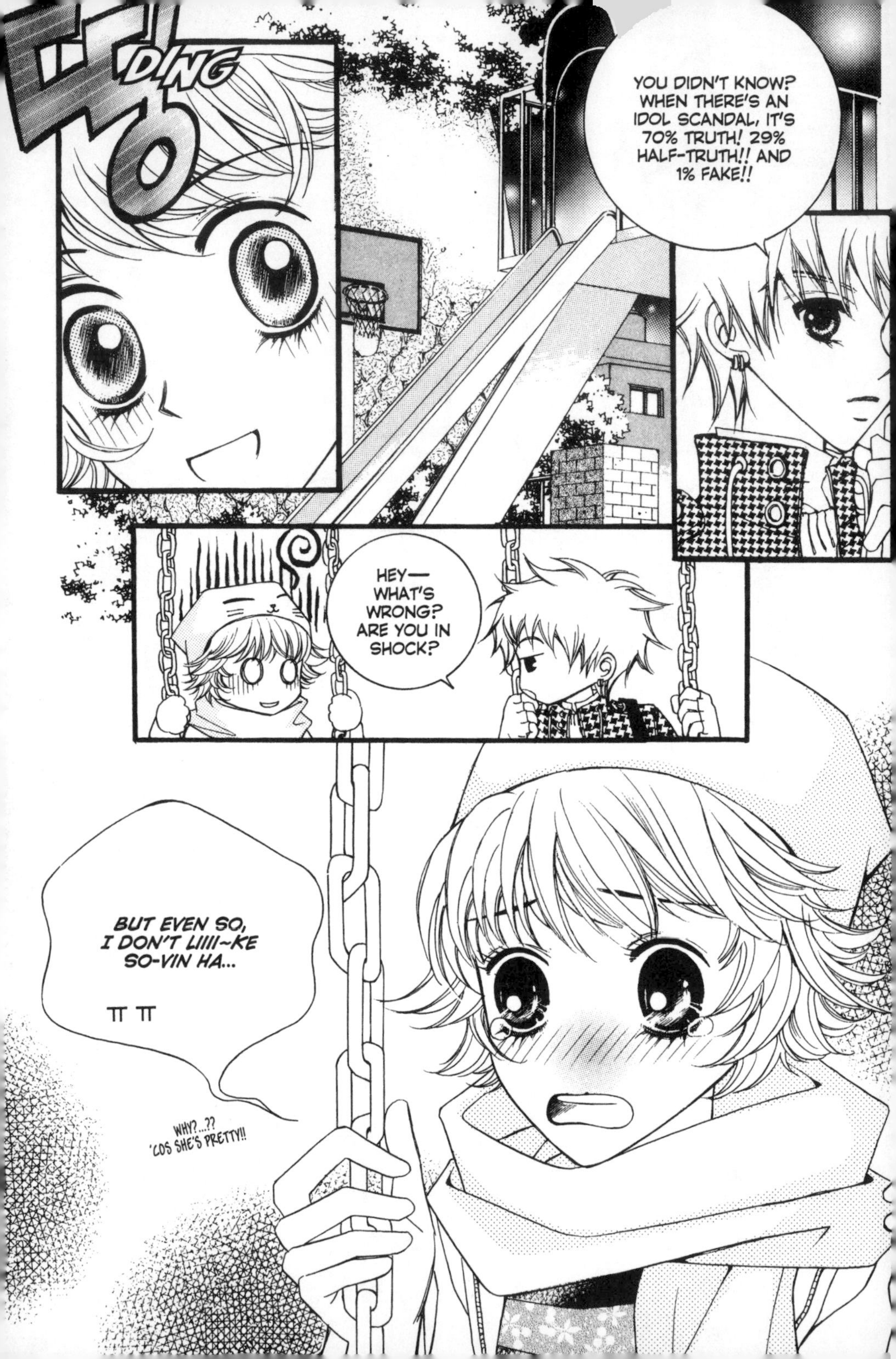
DING
YOU DIDN'T KNOW? WHEN THERE'S AN IDOL SCANDAL, IT'S 70% TRUTH! 29% HALF-TRUTH!! AND 1% FAKE!!
HEY— WHAT'S WRONG? ARE YOU IN SHOCK?
BUT EVEN SO, I DON'T LIIII~KE SO-VIN HA...
π π
WHY?...?? 'COS SHE'S PRETTY!!

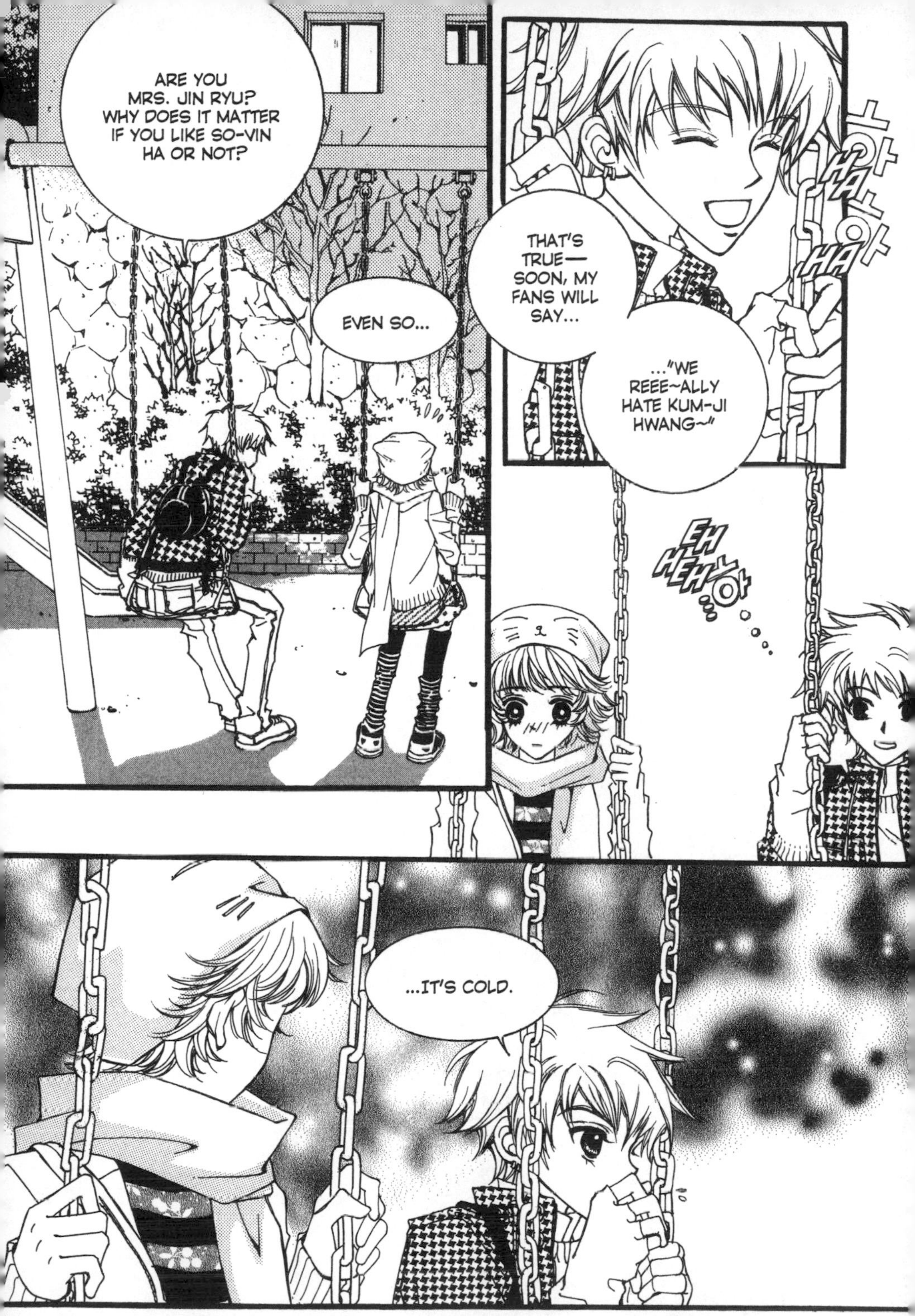
ARE YOU MRS. JIN RYU? WHY DOES IT MATTER IF YOU LIKE SO-VIN HA OR NOT?
EVEN SO...
THAT'S TRUE— SOON, MY FANS WILL SAY...
..."WE REEE~ALLY HATE KUM-JI HWANG~"
HA HA
EH HEH
...IT'S COLD.

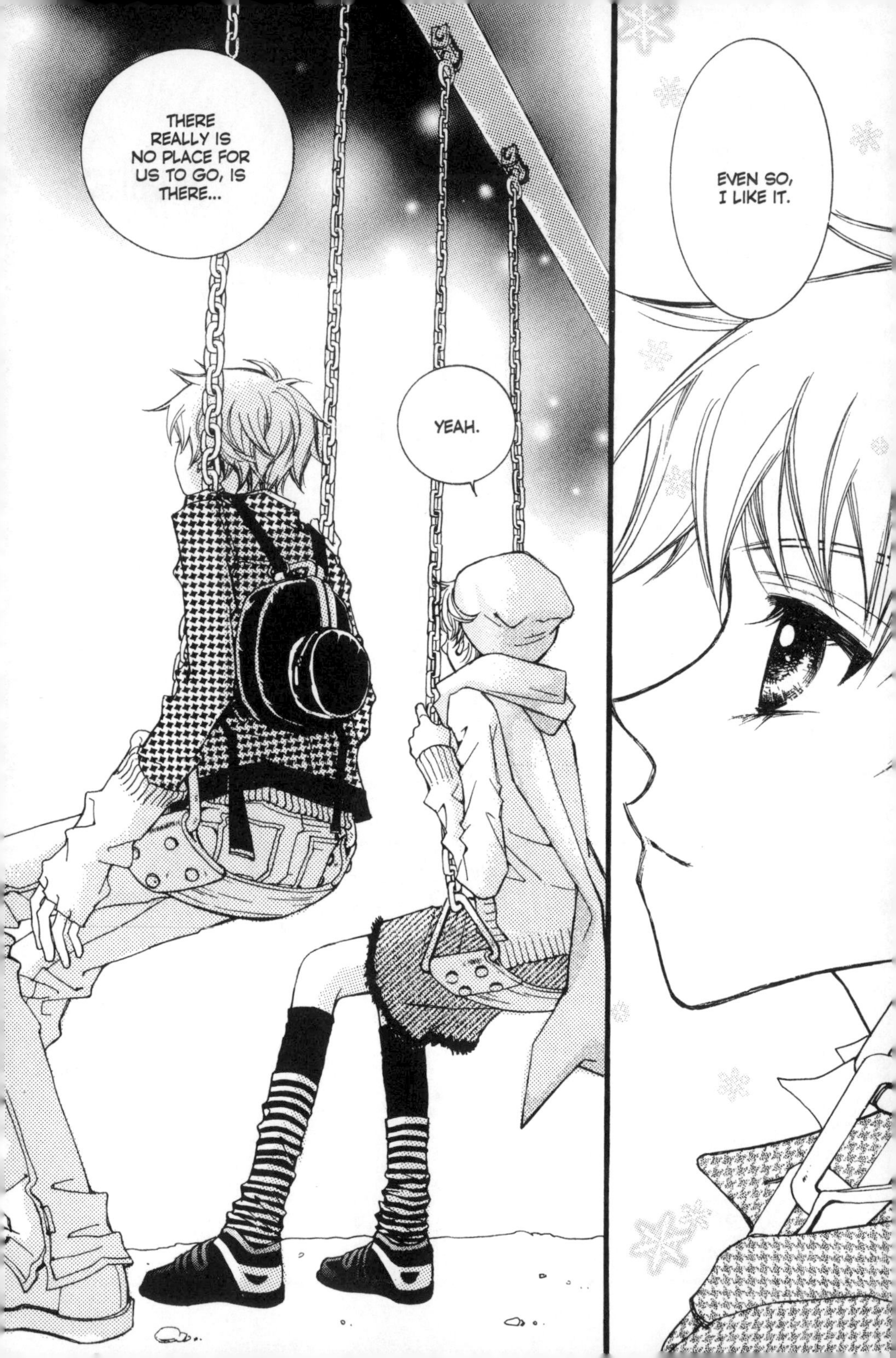
THERE REALLY IS NO PLACE FOR US TO GO, IS THERE...
YEAH.
EVEN SO, I LIKE IT.

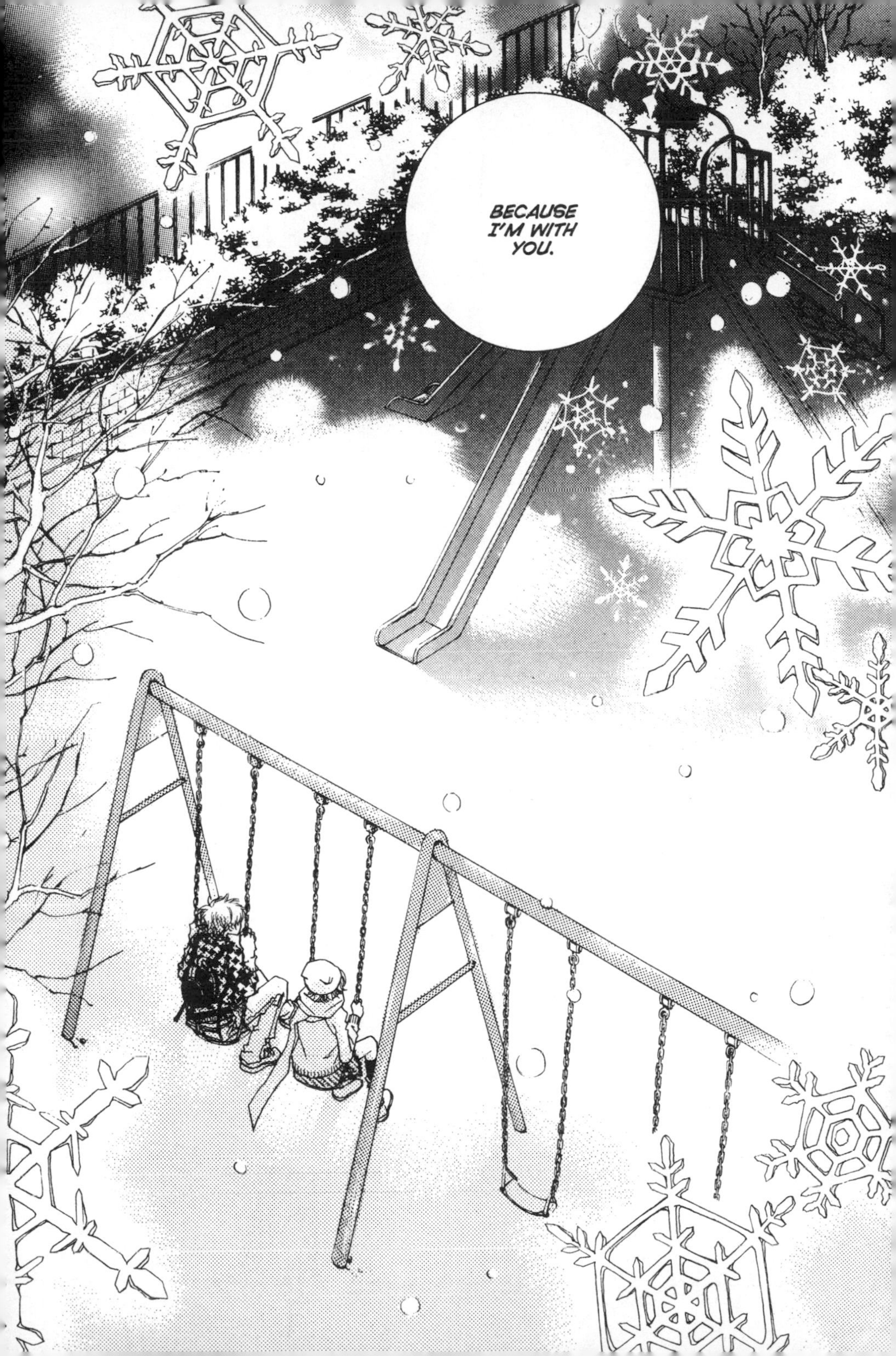
BECAUSE I'M WITH YOU.

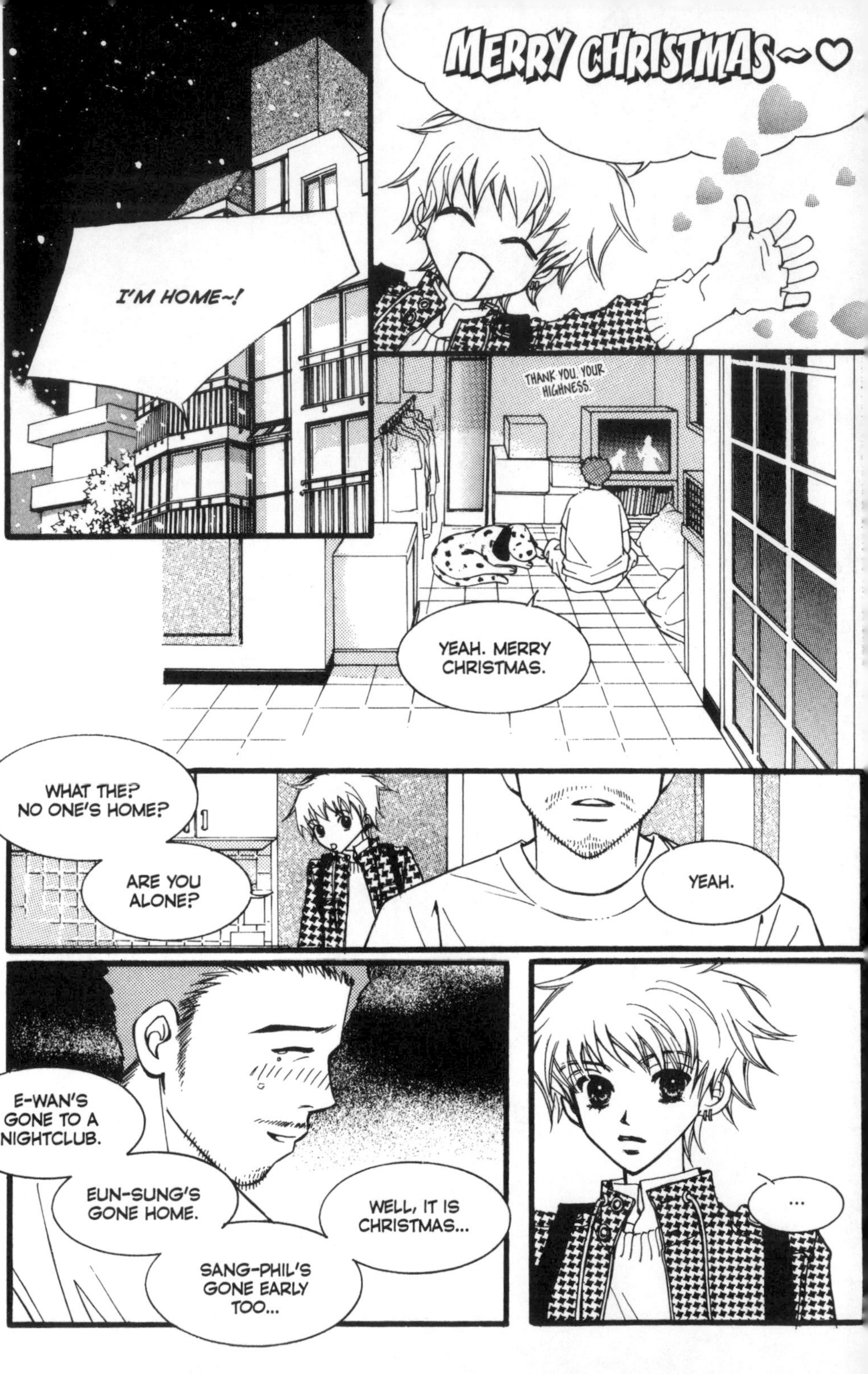
I'M HOME~!
MERRY CHRISTMAS~♡
THANK YOU, YOUR HIGHNESS.
YEAH. MERRY CHRISTMAS.
WHAT THE? NO ONE'S HOME?
ARE YOU ALONE?
YEAH.
E-WAN'S GONE TO A NIGHTCLUB.
EUN-SUNG'S GONE HOME.
WELL, IT IS CHRISTMAS...
SANG-PHIL'S GONE EARLY TOO...
...

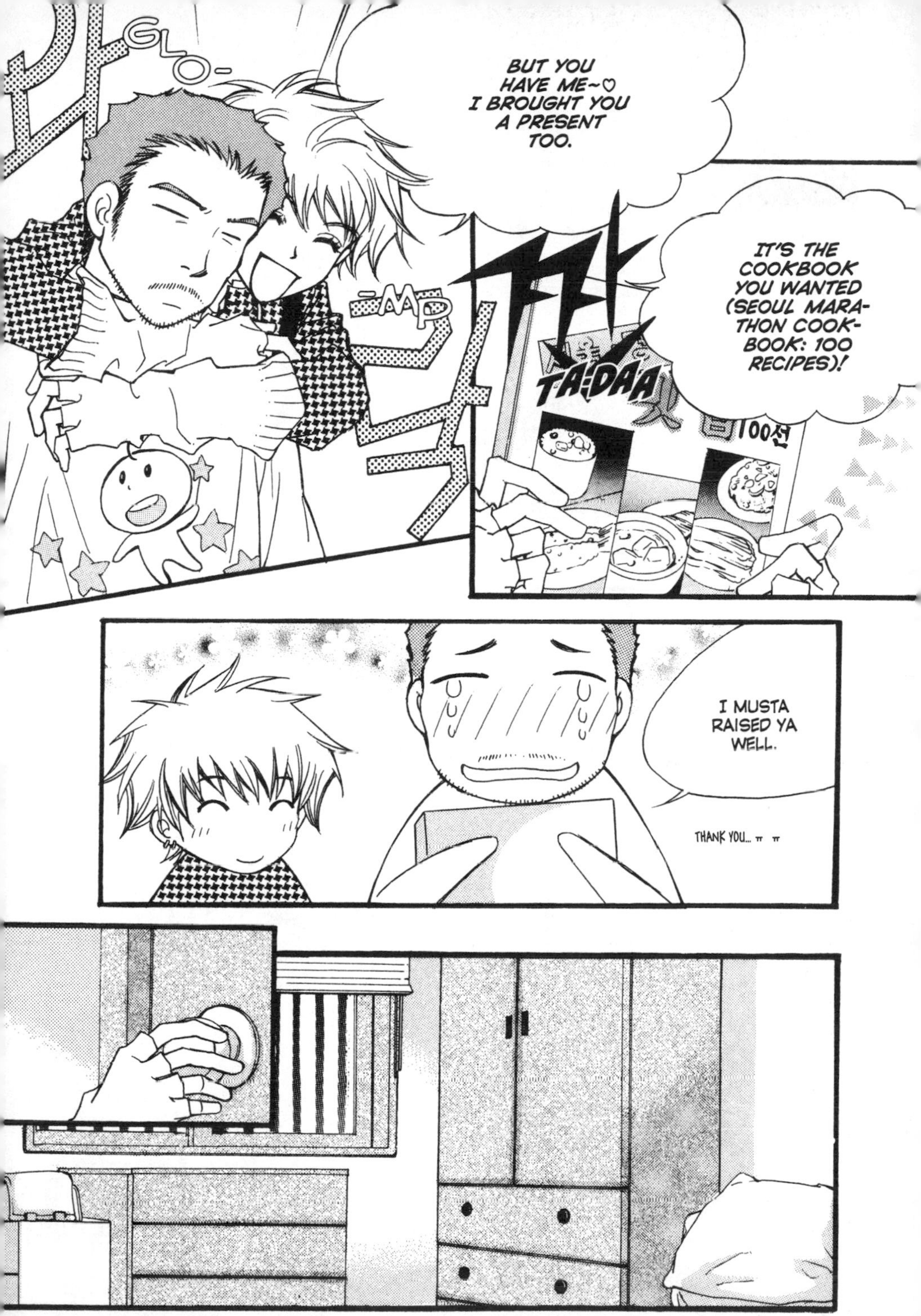
GLO-
BUT YOU HAVE ME~♡ I BROUGHT YOU A PRESENT TOO.
-MP
TA-DAA
IT'S THE COOKBOOK YOU WANTED (SEOUL MARA-THON COOK-BOOK: 100 RECIPES)!
100선
I MUSTA RAISED YA WELL.
THANK YOU... ㅠ ㅠ

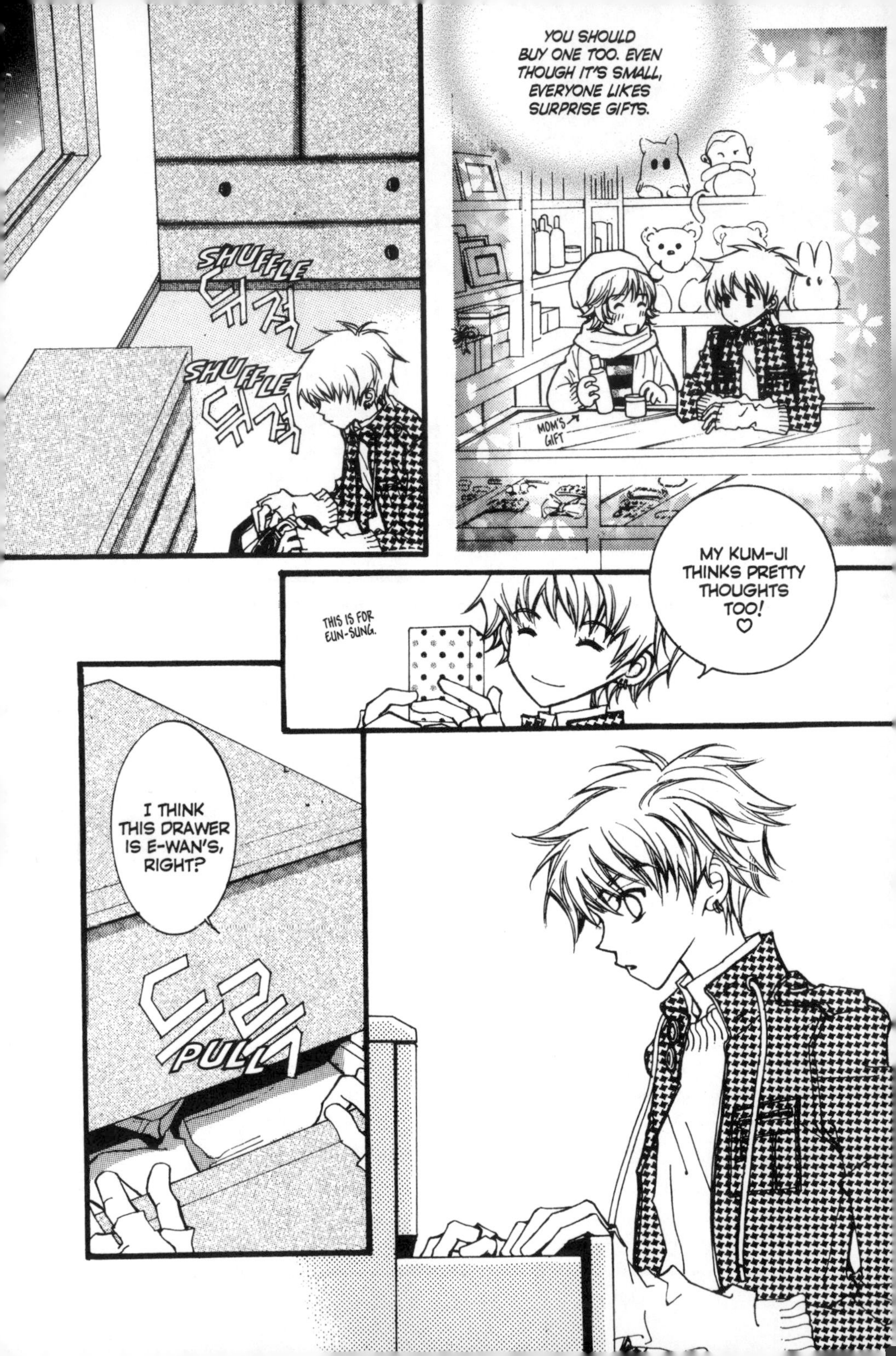
SHUFFLE
SHUFFLE
YOU SHOULD BUY ONE TOO. EVEN THOUGH IT'S SMALL, EVERYONE LIKES SURPRISE GIFTS.
MOM'S GIFT
THIS IS FOR EUN-SUNG.
MY KUM-JI THINKS PRETTY THOUGHTS TOO! ♡
I THINK THIS DRAWER IS E-WAN'S, RIGHT?
PULL

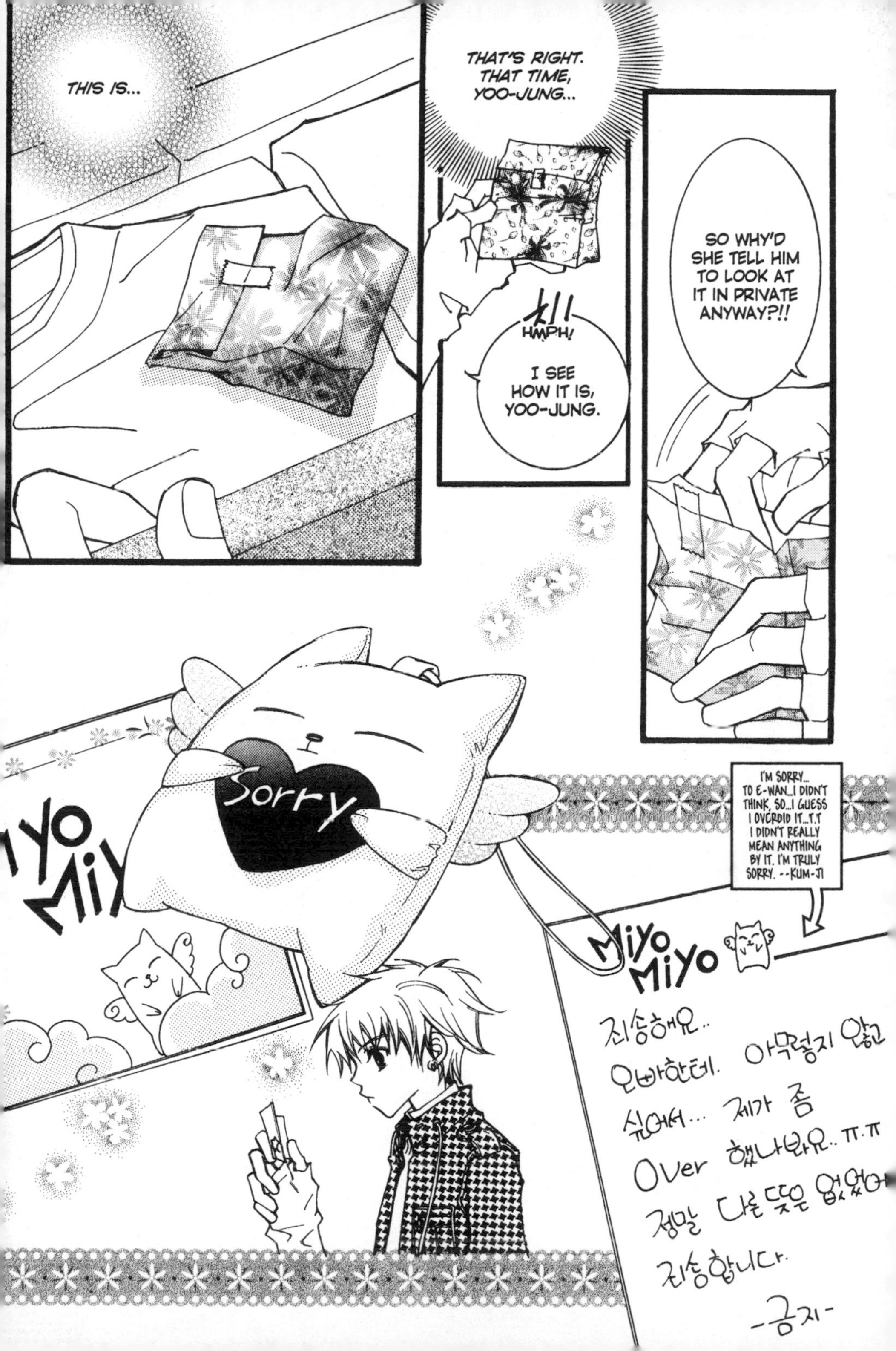
THIS IS...
THAT'S RIGHT. THAT TIME, YOO-JUNG...
칫! HMPH!
I SEE HOW IT IS, YOO-JUNG.
SO WHY'D SHE TELL HIM TO LOOK AT IT IN PRIVATE ANYWAY?!!
iYO MiY
Sorry
I'M SORRY... TO E-WAN...I DIDN'T THINK, SO...I GUESS I OVERDID IT...T.T I DIDN'T REALLY MEAN ANYTHING BY IT. I'M TRULY SORRY. --KUM-JI
MiYO MiYO
죄송해요..
오빠한테. 아무렇지 않고
싶어서... 제가 좀
Over 했나봐요.. ㅠ.ㅠ
정말 다른 뜻은 없었어
죄송합니다.
-금지-

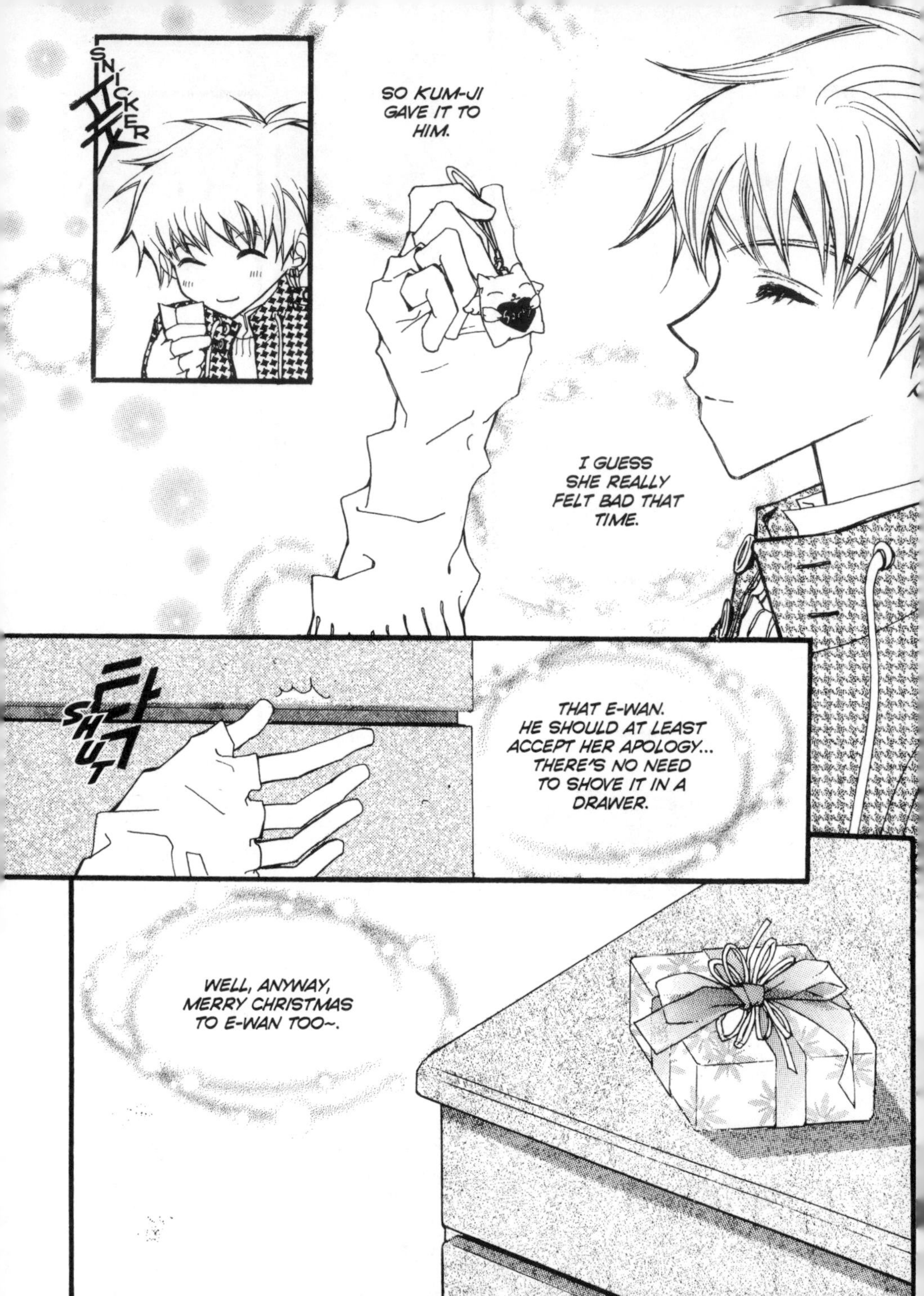
SNICKER
SO KUM-JI GAVE IT TO HIM.
I GUESS SHE REALLY FELT BAD THAT TIME.
SHUT
THAT E-WAN. HE SHOULD AT LEAST ACCEPT HER APOLOGY... THERE'S NO NEED TO SHOVE IT IN A DRAWER.
WELL, ANYWAY, MERRY CHRISTMAS TO E-WAN TOO~.

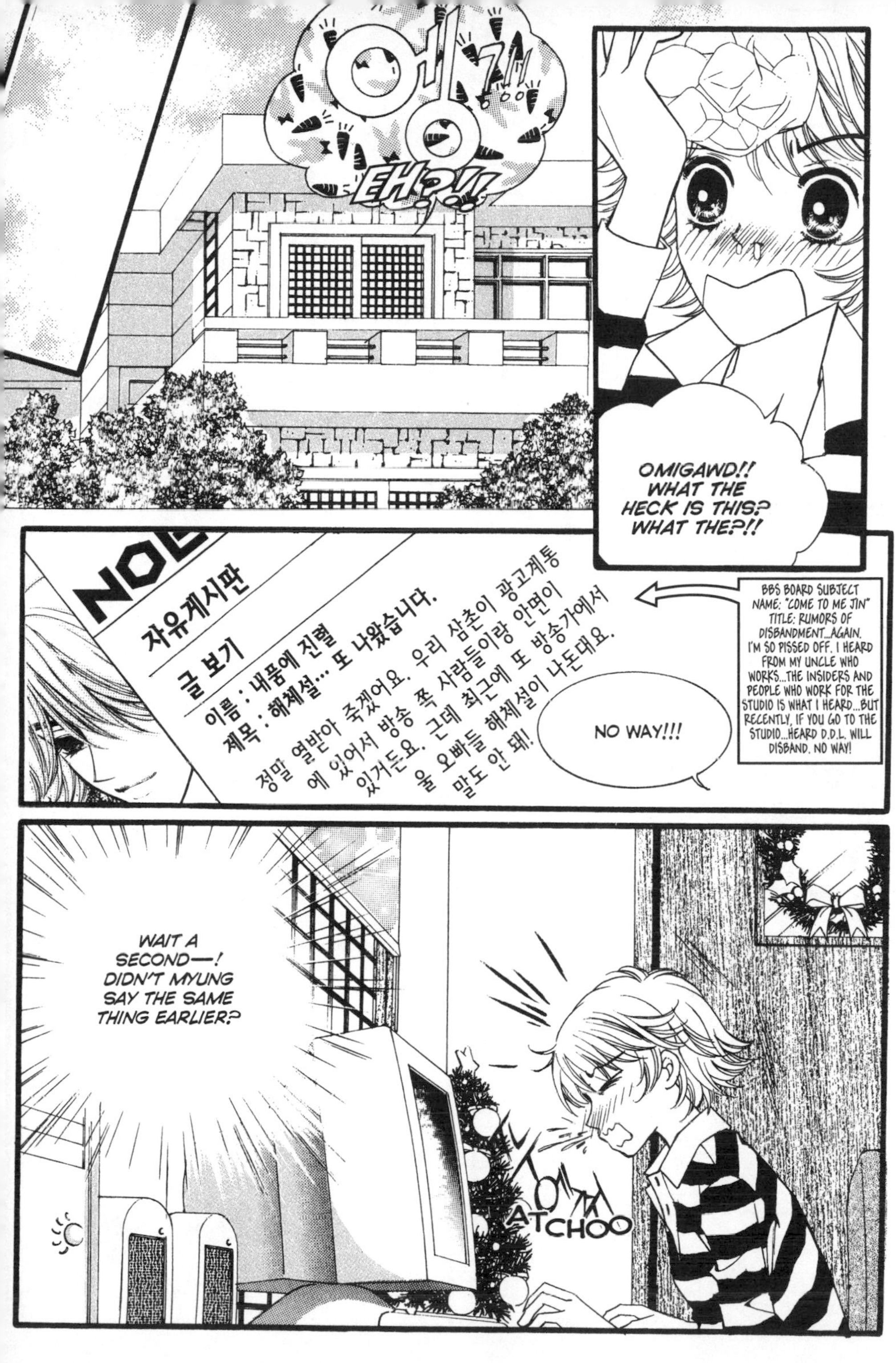
에엥
EH?!!
OMIGAWD!! WHAT THE HECK IS THIS? WHAT THE?!!
NO
자유게시판
글 보기
이름 : 내품에 진렬
제목 : 해체설... 또 나왔습니다.
정말 열받아 죽겠어요. 우리 삼촌이 광고계통에 있어서 방송 쪽 사람들이랑 안면이 있거든요. 근데 최근에 또 방송가에서 울 오빠들 해체설이 나돈대요. 말도 안 돼!
NO WAY!!!
BBS BOARD SUBJECT NAME: "COME TO ME JIN" TITLE: RUMORS OF DISBANDMENT...AGAIN. I'M SO PISSED OFF. I HEARD FROM MY UNCLE WHO WORKS...THE INSIDERS AND PEOPLE WHO WORK FOR THE STUDIO IS WHAT I HEARD...BUT RECENTLY, IF YOU GO TO THE STUDIO...HEARD D.D.L. WILL DISBAND. NO WAY!
WAIT A SECOND—! DIDN'T MYUNG SAY THE SAME THING EARLIER?
에취
ATCHOO

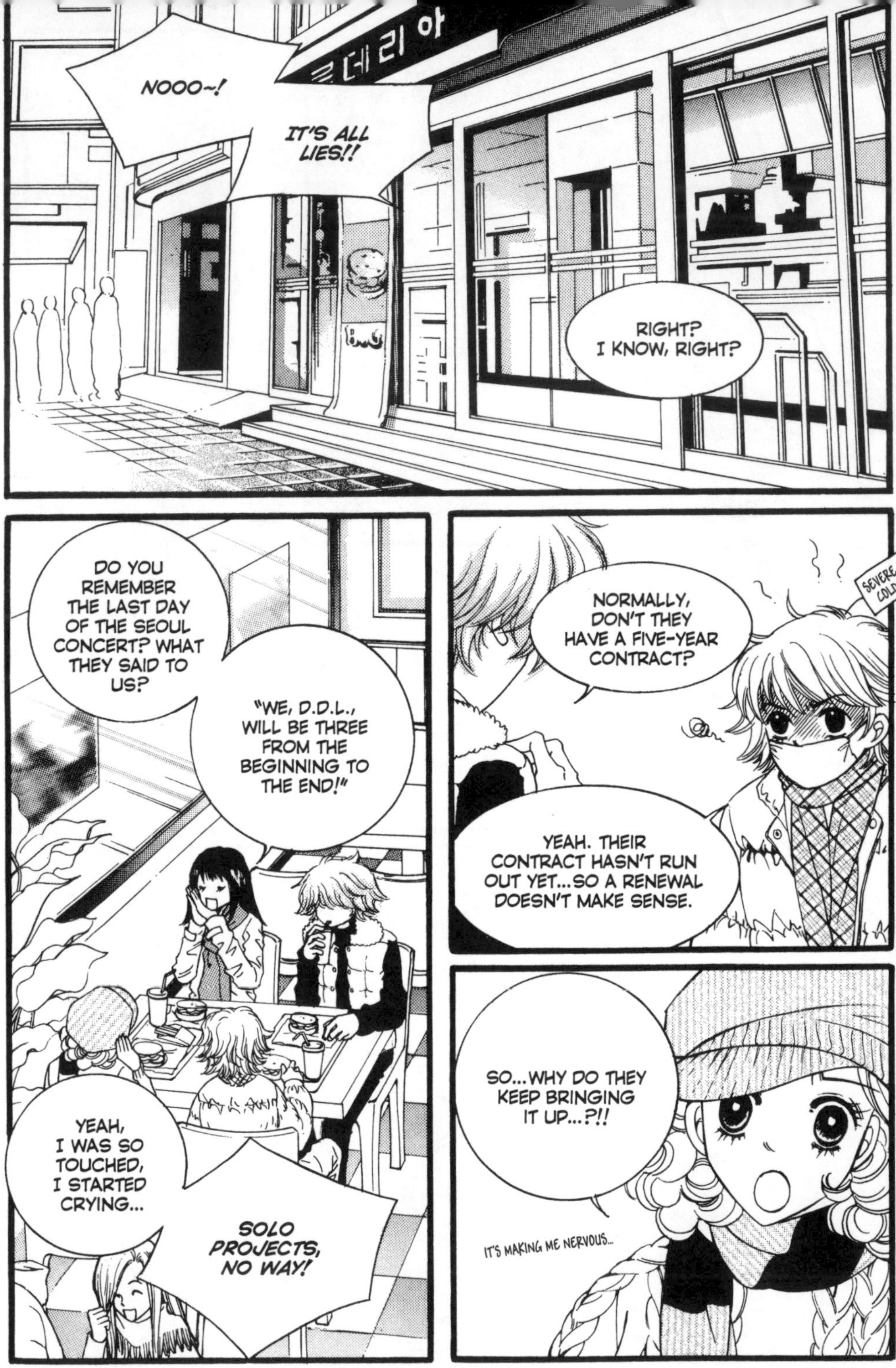

데리아
NOOO~!
IT'S ALL LIES!!
RIGHT? I KNOW, RIGHT?
DO YOU REMEMBER THE LAST DAY OF THE SEOUL CONCERT? WHAT THEY SAID TO US?
"WE, D.D.L., WILL BE THREE FROM THE BEGINNING TO THE END!"
YEAH, I WAS SO TOUCHED, I STARTED CRYING...
SOLO PROJECTS, NO WAY!
NORMALLY, DON'T THEY HAVE A FIVE-YEAR CONTRACT?
SEVERE COLD
YEAH. THEIR CONTRACT HASN'T RUN OUT YET...SO A RENEWAL DOESN'T MAKE SENSE.
SO...WHY DO THEY KEEP BRINGING IT UP...?!!
IT'S MAKING ME NERVOUS...

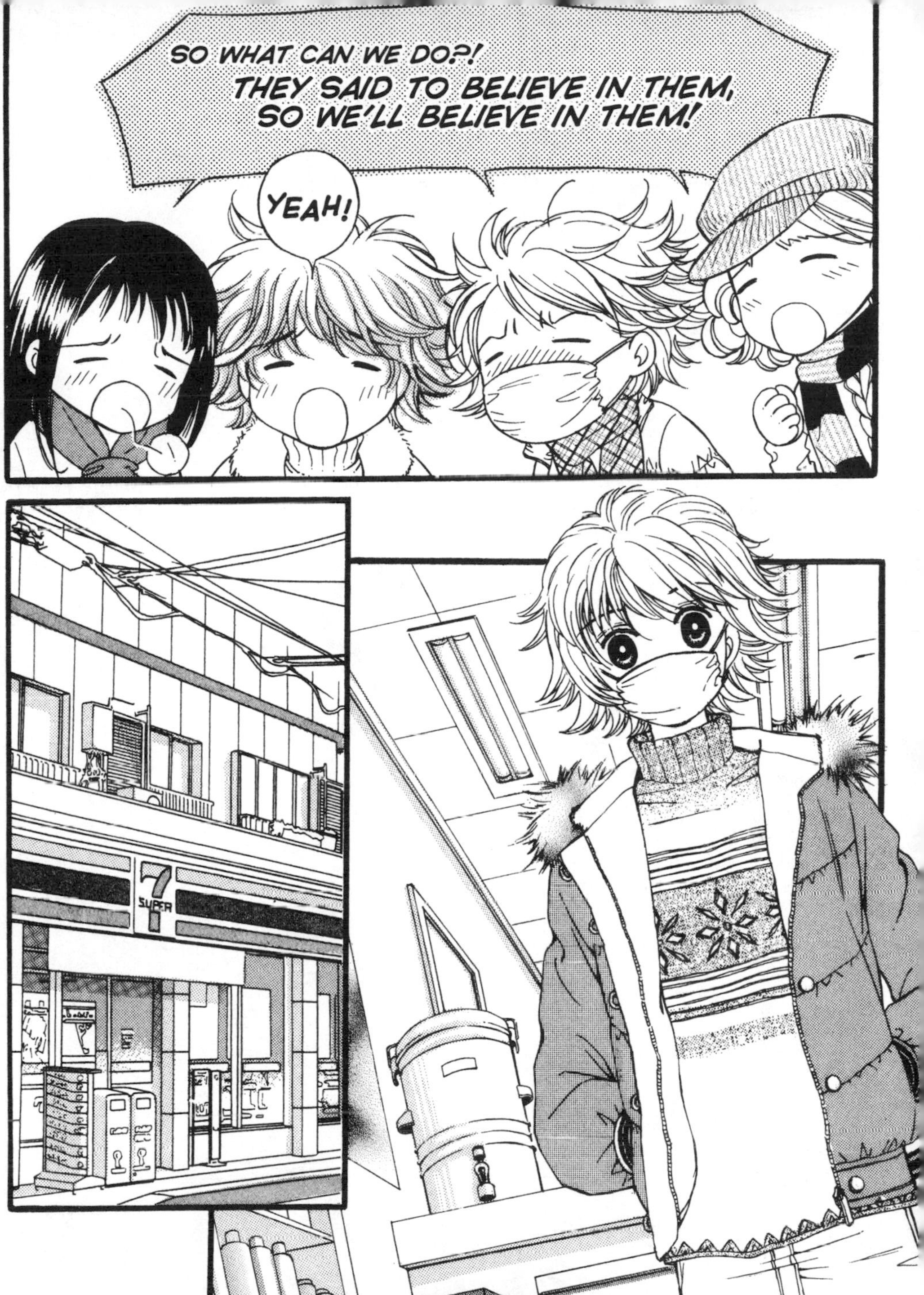
SO WHAT CAN WE DO?! THEY SAID TO BELIEVE IN THEM, SO WE'LL BELIEVE IN THEM!
YEAH!
일반쓰레기
TRASH

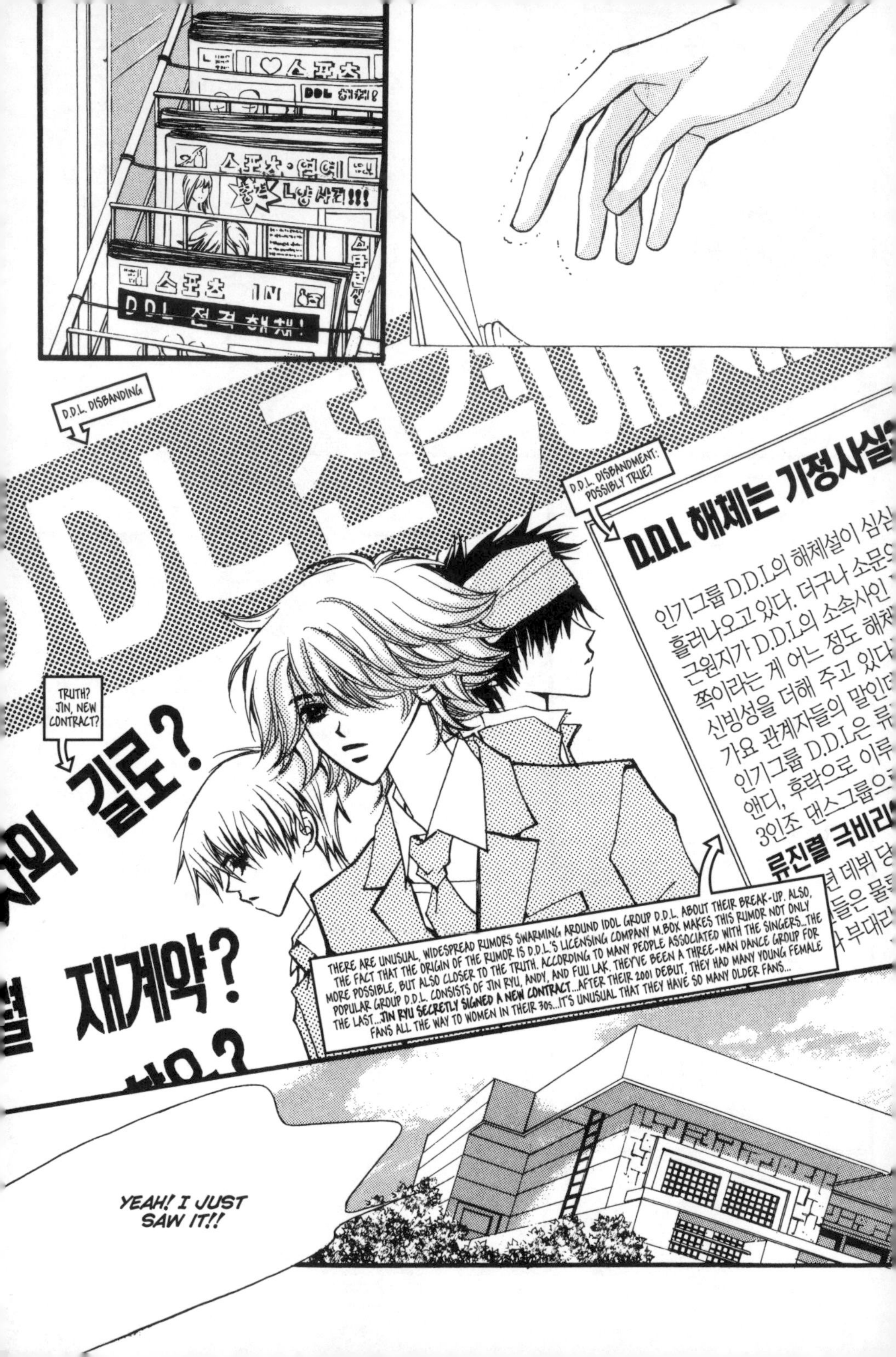
D.D.L 전격 해체!
D.D.L. DISBANDING
D.D.L. DISBANDMENT: POSSIBLY TRUE?
D.D.L 해체는 기정사실
TRUTH? JIN, NEW CONTRACT?
재계약?
THERE ARE UNUSUAL, WIDESPREAD RUMORS SWARMING AROUND IDOL GROUP D.D.L. ABOUT THEIR BREAK-UP. ALSO, THE FACT THAT THE ORIGIN OF THE RUMOR IS D.D.L.'S LICENSING COMPANY M.BOX MAKES THIS RUMOR NOT ONLY MORE POSSIBLE, BUT ALSO CLOSER TO THE TRUTH. ACCORDING TO MANY PEOPLE ASSOCIATED WITH THE SINGERS...THE POPULAR GROUP D.D.L. CONSISTS OF JIN RYU, ANDY, AND FUU LAK. THEY'VE BEEN A THREE-MAN DANCE GROUP FOR THE LAST... **JIN RYU SECRETLY SIGNED A NEW CONTRACT**...AFTER THEIR 2001 DEBUT, THEY HAD MANY YOUNG FEMALE FANS ALL THE WAY TO WOMEN IN THEIR 30S...IT'S UNUSUAL THAT THEY HAVE SO MANY OLDER FANS...
YEAH! I JUST SAW IT!!

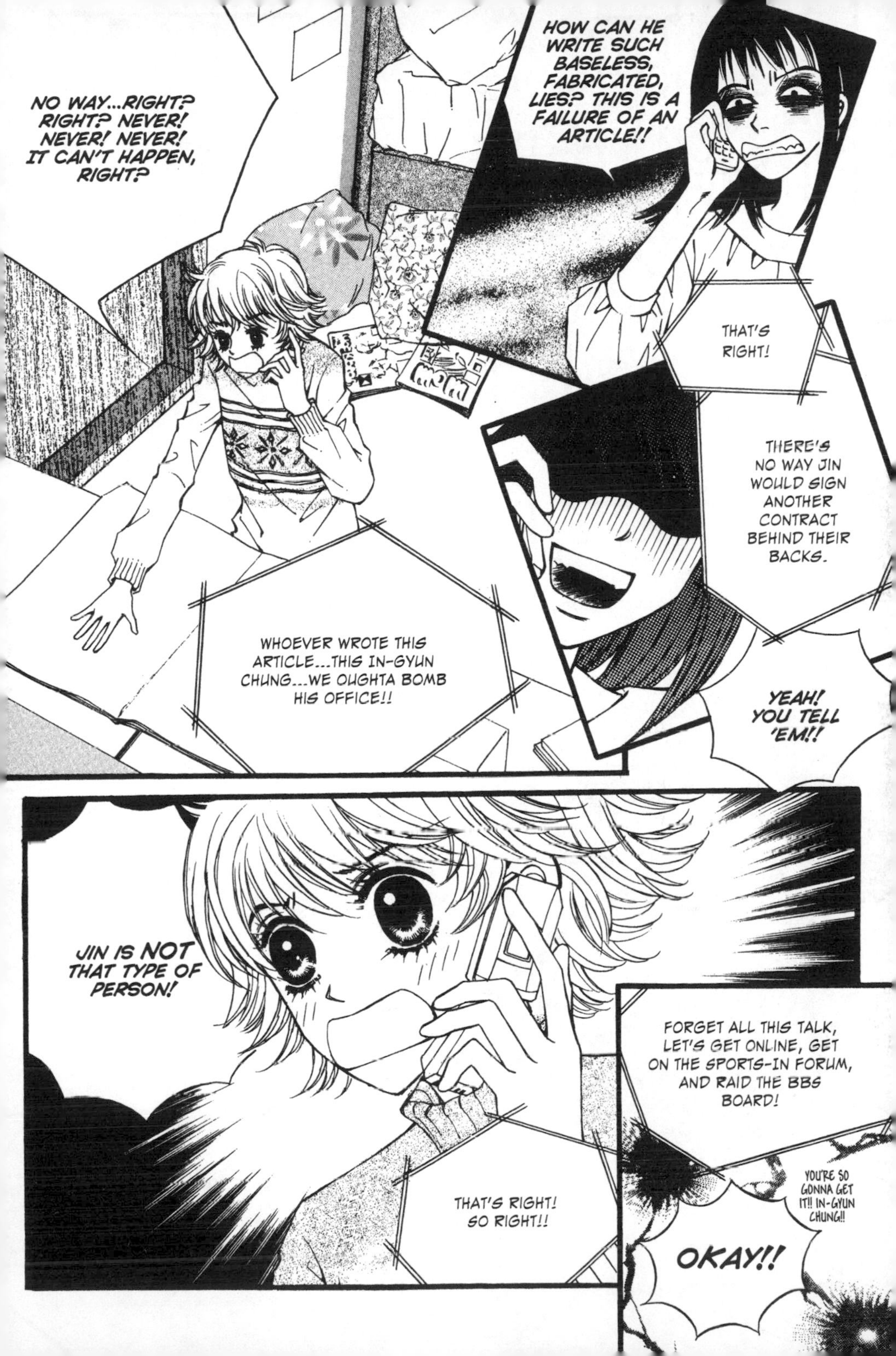
NO WAY...RIGHT? RIGHT? NEVER! NEVER! NEVER! IT CAN'T HAPPEN, RIGHT?
WHOEVER WROTE THIS ARTICLE...THIS IN-GYUN CHUNG...WE OUGHTA BOMB HIS OFFICE!!
HOW CAN HE WRITE SUCH BASELESS, FABRICATED, LIES? THIS IS A FAILURE OF AN ARTICLE!!
THAT'S RIGHT!
THERE'S NO WAY JIN WOULD SIGN ANOTHER CONTRACT BEHIND THEIR BACKS.
YEAH! YOU TELL 'EM!!
JIN IS NOT THAT TYPE OF PERSON!
THAT'S RIGHT! SO RIGHT!!
FORGET ALL THIS TALK, LET'S GET ONLINE, GET ON THE SPORTS-IN FORUM, AND RAID THE BBS BOARD!
YOU'RE SO GONNA GET IT!! IN-GYUN CHUNG!!
OKAY!!

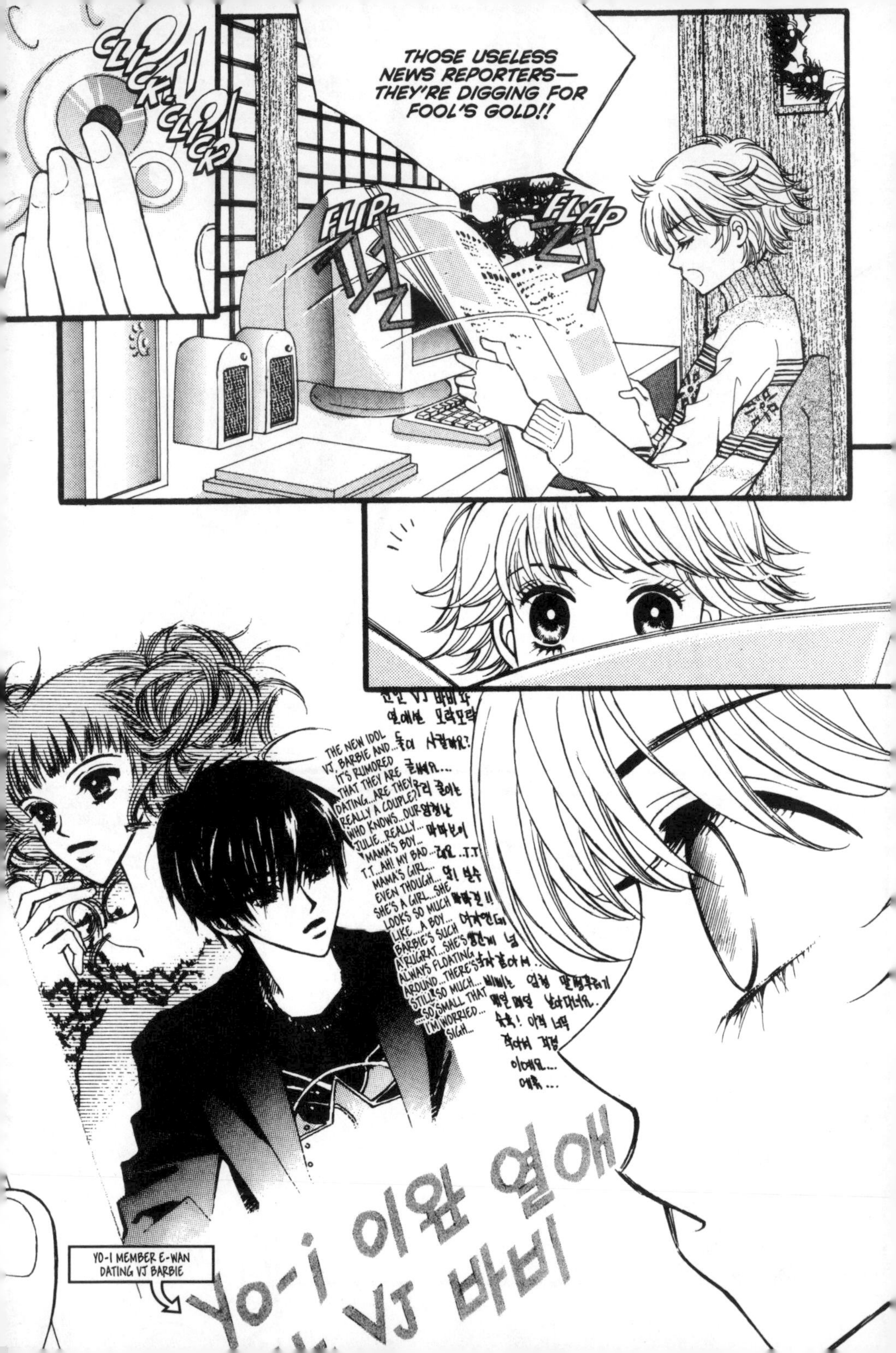
CLICK CLICK
THOSE USELESS NEWS REPORTERS—THEY'RE DIGGING FOR FOOL'S GOLD!!
FLIP-FLAP
THE NEW IDOL VJ, BARBIE AND... IT'S RUMORED THAT THEY ARE DATING...ARE THEY REALLY A COUPLE? WHO KNOWS...OUR JULIE...REALLY... MAMA'S BOY... T.T...AH! MY BAD... MAMA'S GIRL... EVEN THOUGH... SHE'S A GIRL...SHE LOOKS SO MUCH LIKE...A BOY... BARBIE'S SUCH A RUGRAT...SHE'S ALWAYS FLOATING AROUND...THERE'S STILL SO MUCH... SO SMALL THAT I'M WORRIED... SIGH...
Yo-i 이완 열애
VJ 바비
YO-I MEMBER E-WAN DATING VJ BARBIE

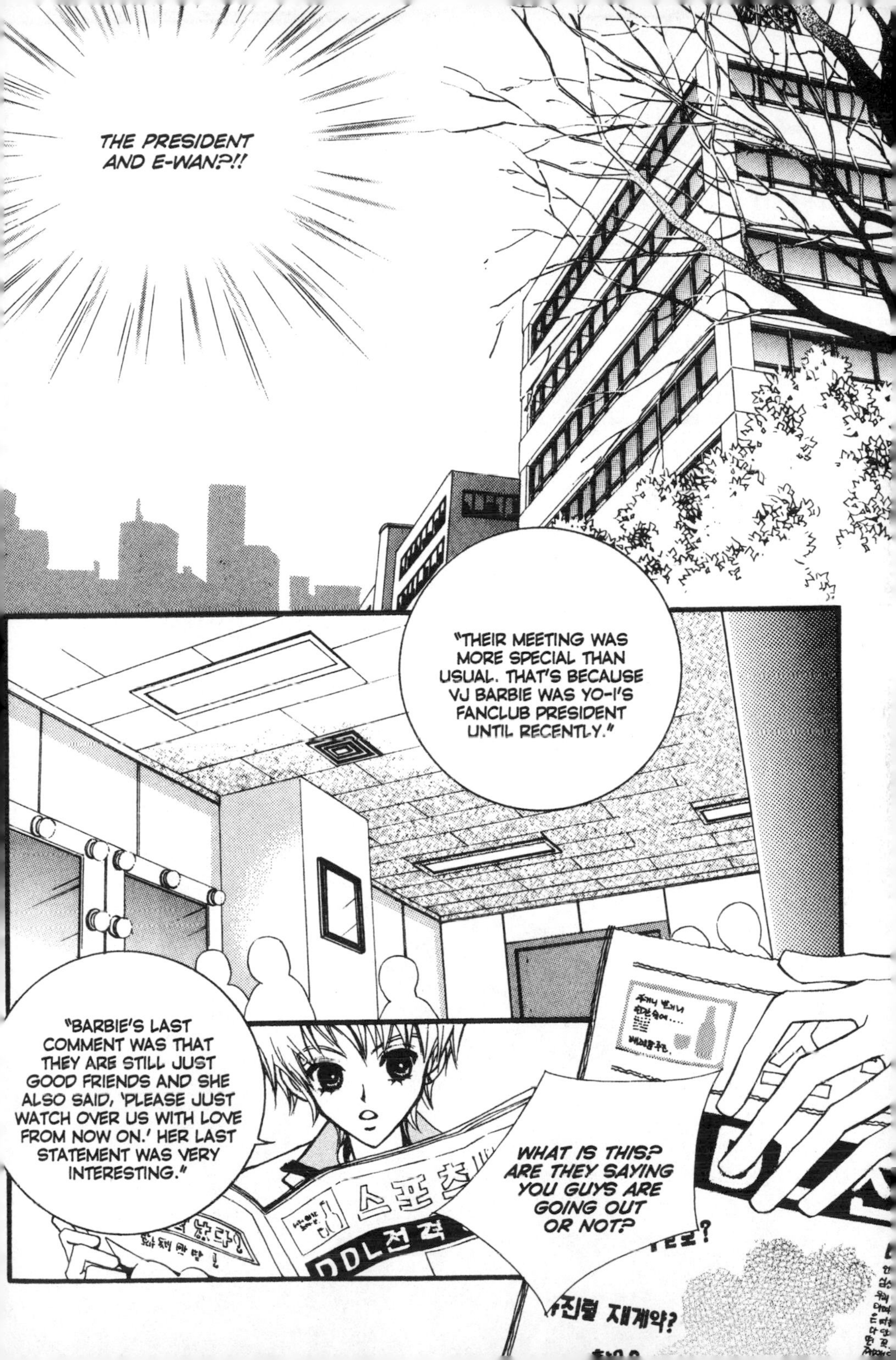
THE PRESIDENT AND E-WAN?!!
"THEIR MEETING WAS MORE SPECIAL THAN USUAL. THAT'S BECAUSE VJ BARBIE WAS YO-I'S FANCLUB PRESIDENT UNTIL RECENTLY."
"BARBIE'S LAST COMMENT WAS THAT THEY ARE STILL JUST GOOD FRIENDS AND SHE ALSO SAID, 'PLEASE JUST WATCH OVER US WITH LOVE FROM NOW ON.' HER LAST STATEMENT WAS VERY INTERESTING."
스포츠
WHAT IS THIS? ARE THEY SAYING YOU GUYS ARE GOING OUT OR NOT?

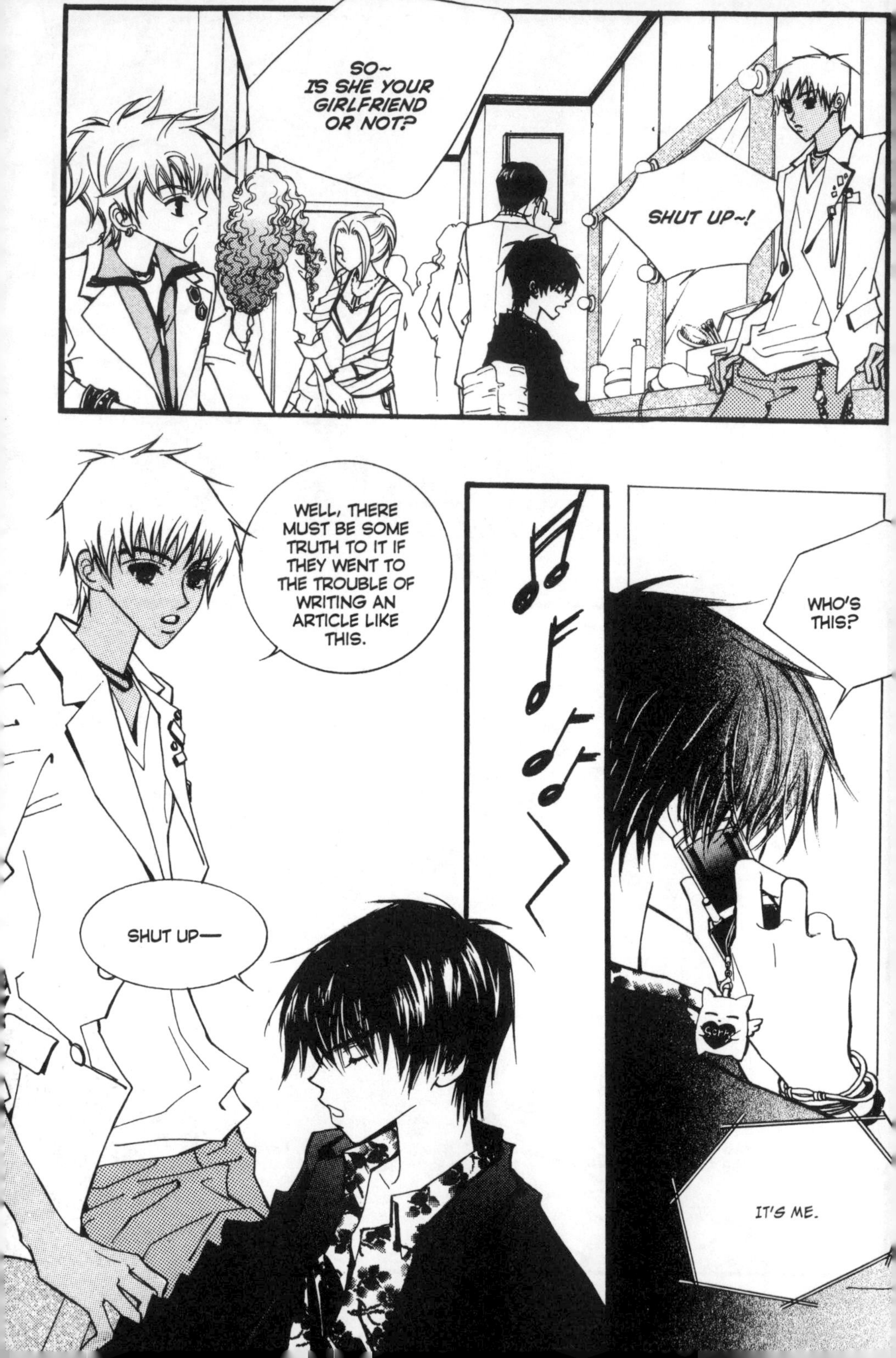
SO~ IS SHE YOUR GIRLFRIEND OR NOT?
SHUT UP~!
WELL, THERE MUST BE SOME TRUTH TO IT IF THEY WENT TO THE TROUBLE OF WRITING AN ARTICLE LIKE THIS.
SHUT UP—
WHO'S THIS?
IT'S ME.

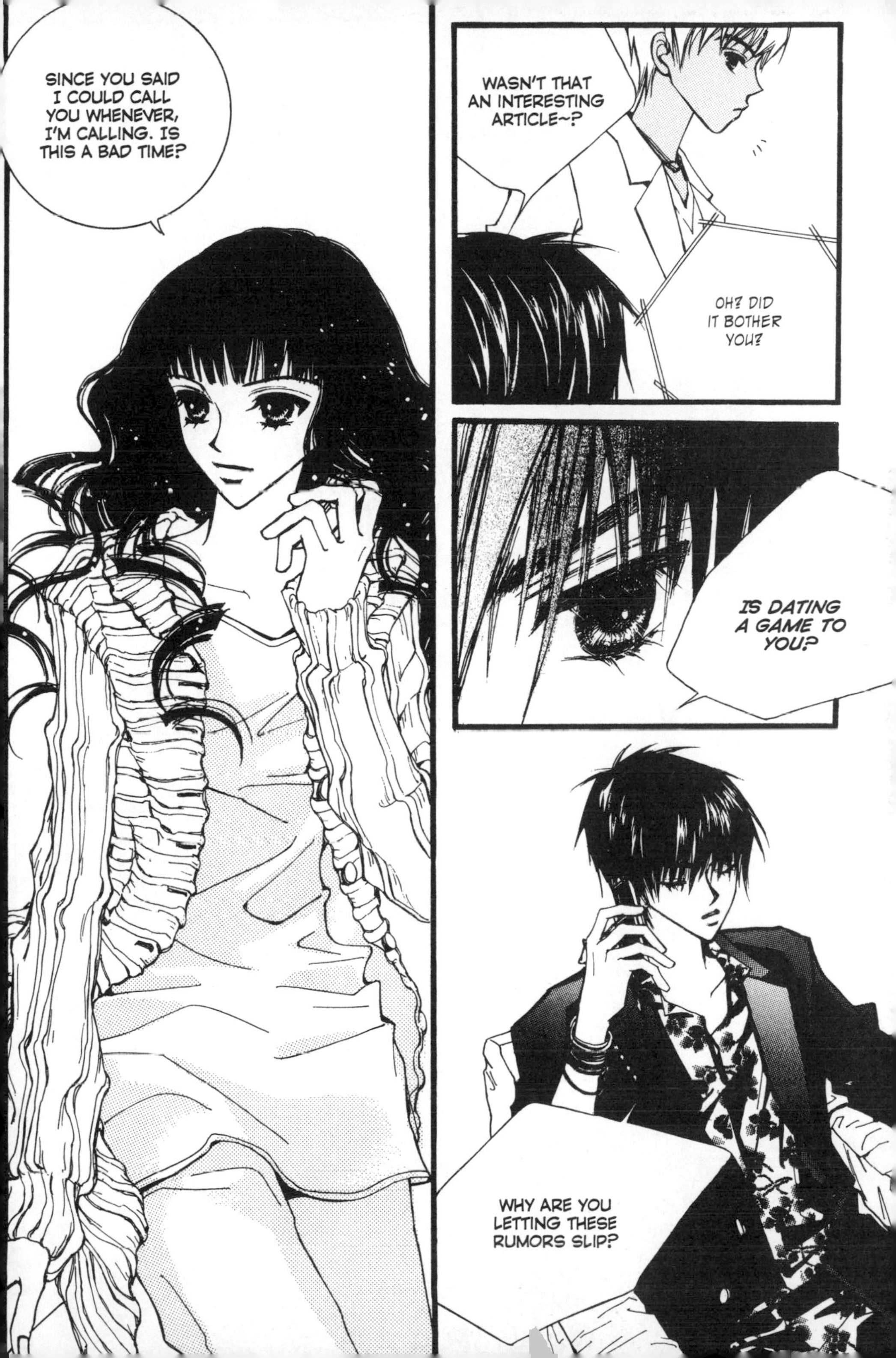
SINCE YOU SAID I COULD CALL YOU WHENEVER, I'M CALLING. IS THIS A BAD TIME?
WASN'T THAT AN INTERESTING ARTICLE~?
OH? DID IT BOTHER YOU?
IS DATING A GAME TO YOU?
WHY ARE YOU LETTING THESE RUMORS SLIP?

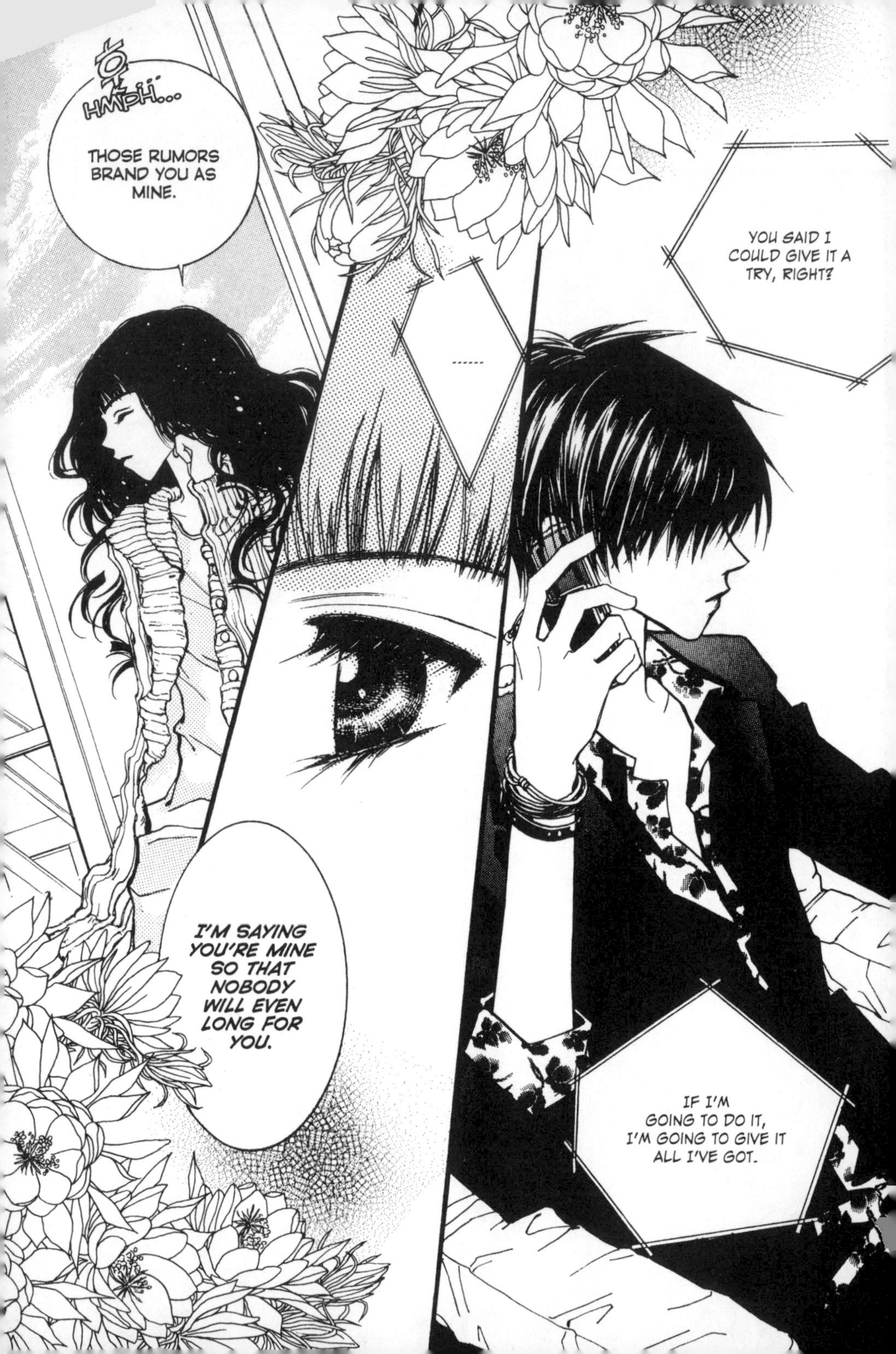
HMPH...
THOSE RUMORS BRAND YOU AS MINE.
I'M SAYING YOU'RE MINE SO THAT NOBODY WILL EVEN LONG FOR YOU.
......
YOU SAID I COULD GIVE IT A TRY, RIGHT?
IF I'M GOING TO DO IT, I'M GOING TO GIVE IT ALL I'VE GOT.

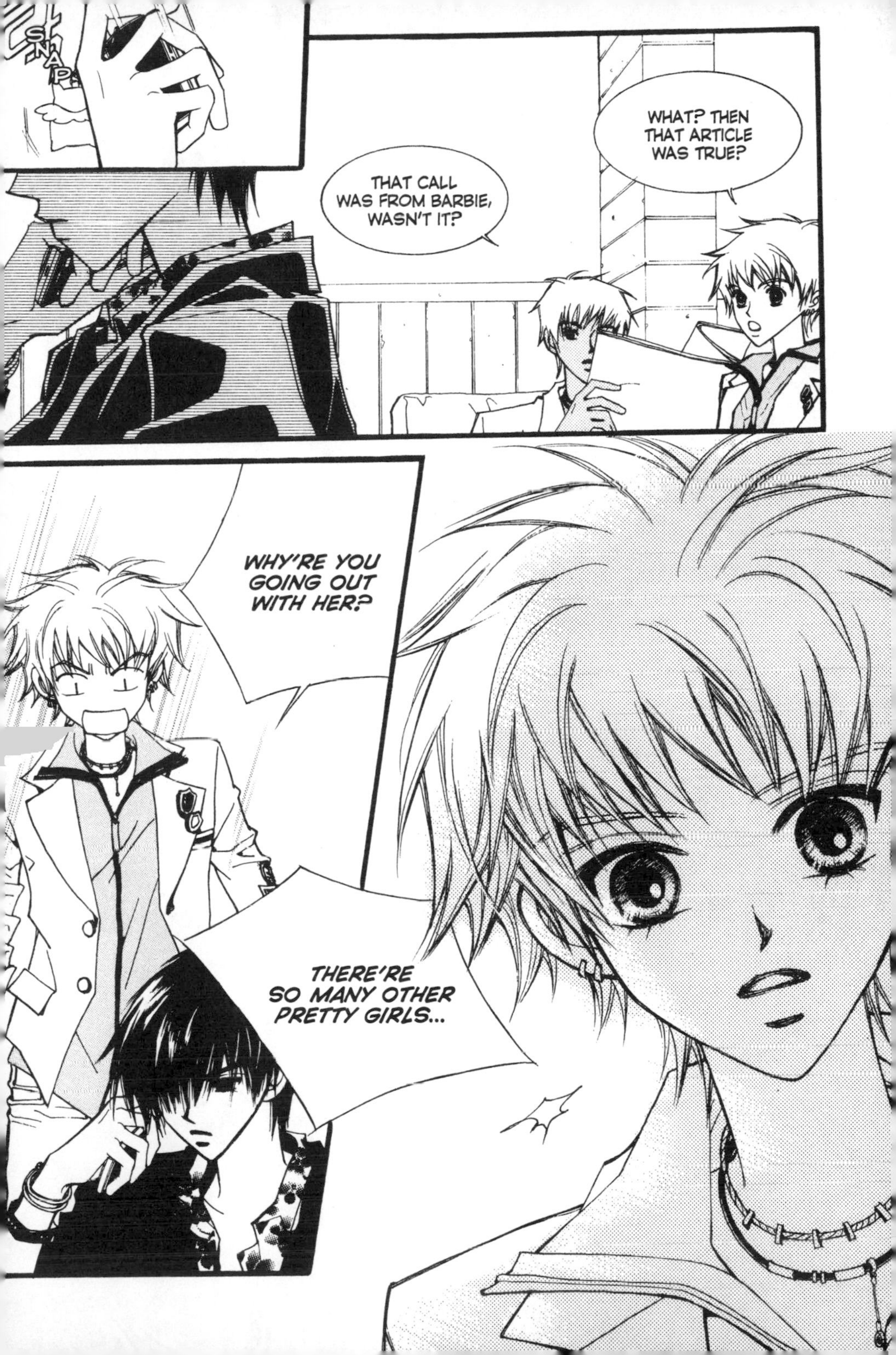
SNAP
THAT CALL WAS FROM BARBIE, WASN'T IT?
WHAT? THEN THAT ARTICLE WAS TRUE?
WHY'RE YOU GOING OUT WITH HER?
THERE'RE SO MANY OTHER PRETTY GIRLS...

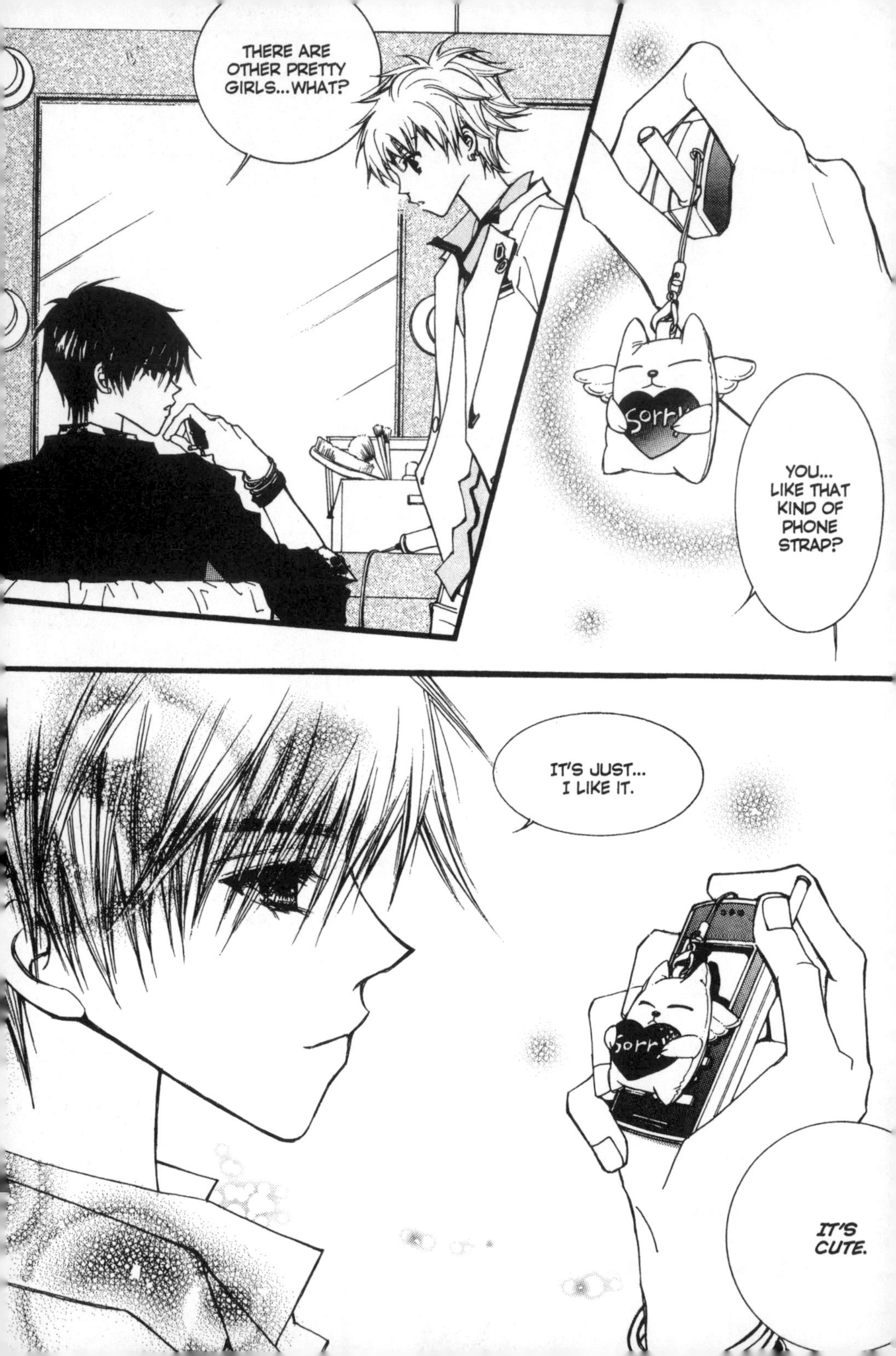
THERE ARE OTHER PRETTY GIRLS...WHAT?
YOU... LIKE THAT KIND OF PHONE STRAP?
IT'S JUST... I LIKE IT.
IT'S CUTE.

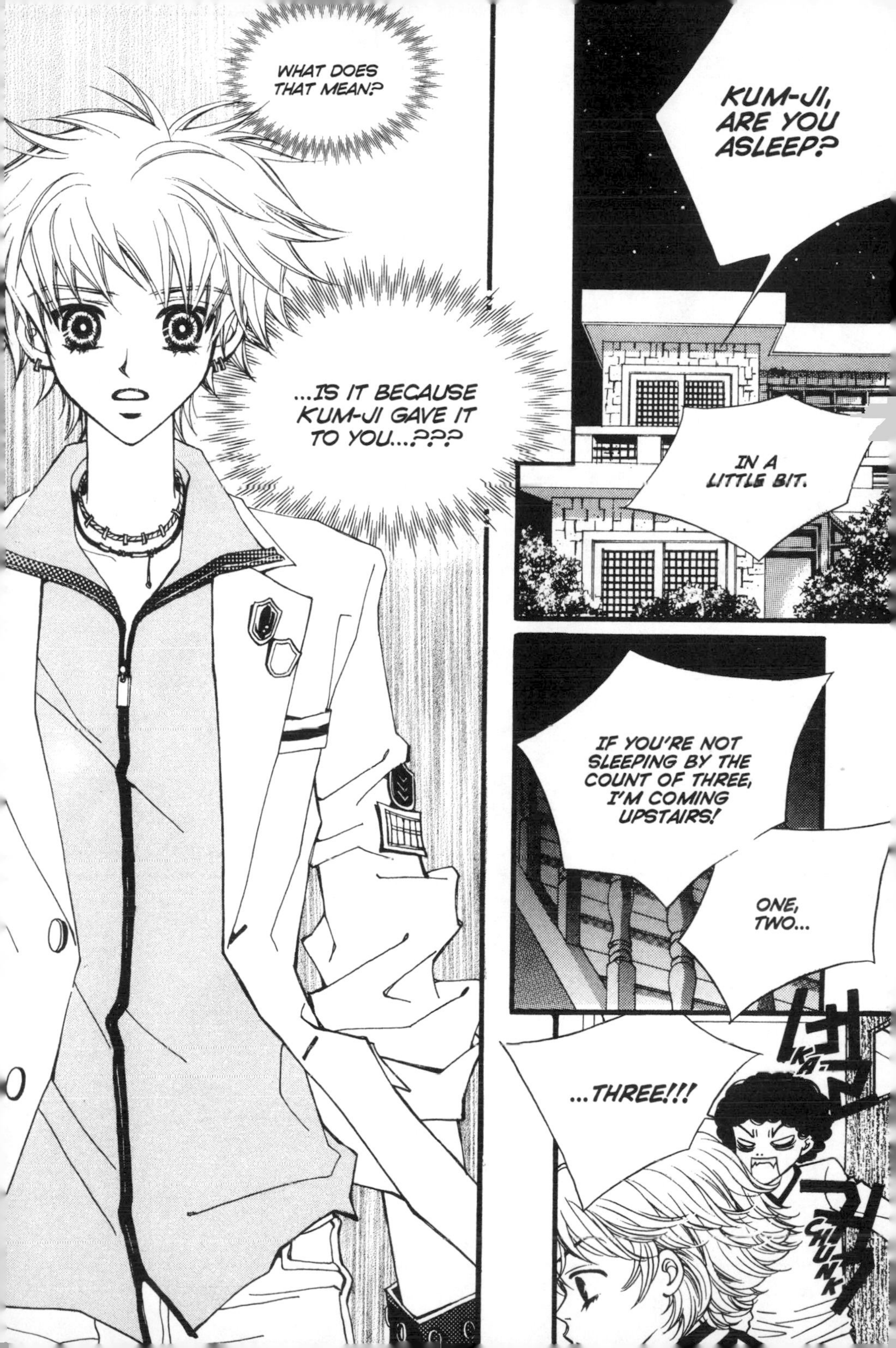
WHAT DOES THAT MEAN?
...IS IT BECAUSE KUM-JI GAVE IT TO YOU...???
KUM-JI, ARE YOU ASLEEP?
IN A LITTLE BIT.
IF YOU'RE NOT SLEEPING BY THE COUNT OF THREE, I'M COMING UPSTAIRS!
ONE, TWO...
...THREE!!!
KA-
CHUNK

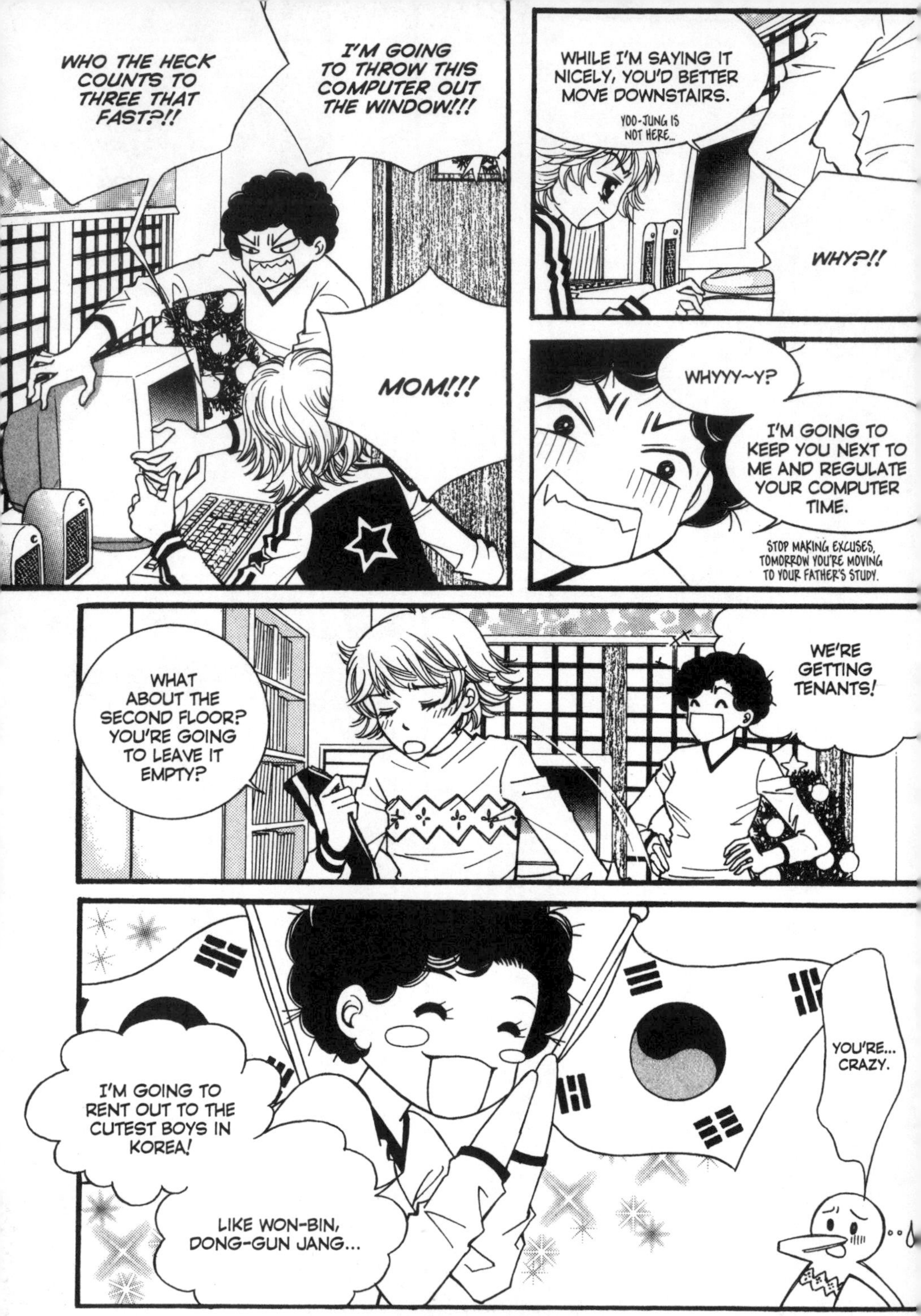
WHO THE HECK COUNTS TO THREE THAT FAST?!!
I'M GOING TO THROW THIS COMPUTER OUT THE WINDOW!!!
MOM!!!
WHILE I'M SAYING IT NICELY, YOU'D BETTER MOVE DOWNSTAIRS.
YOO-JUNG IS NOT HERE...
WHY?!!
WHYYY~Y?
I'M GOING TO KEEP YOU NEXT TO ME AND REGULATE YOUR COMPUTER TIME.
STOP MAKING EXCUSES, TOMORROW YOU'RE MOVING TO YOUR FATHER'S STUDY.
WHAT ABOUT THE SECOND FLOOR? YOU'RE GOING TO LEAVE IT EMPTY?
WE'RE GETTING TENANTS!
I'M GOING TO RENT OUT TO THE CUTEST BOYS IN KOREA!
LIKE WON-BIN, DONG-GUN JANG...
YOU'RE... CRAZY.

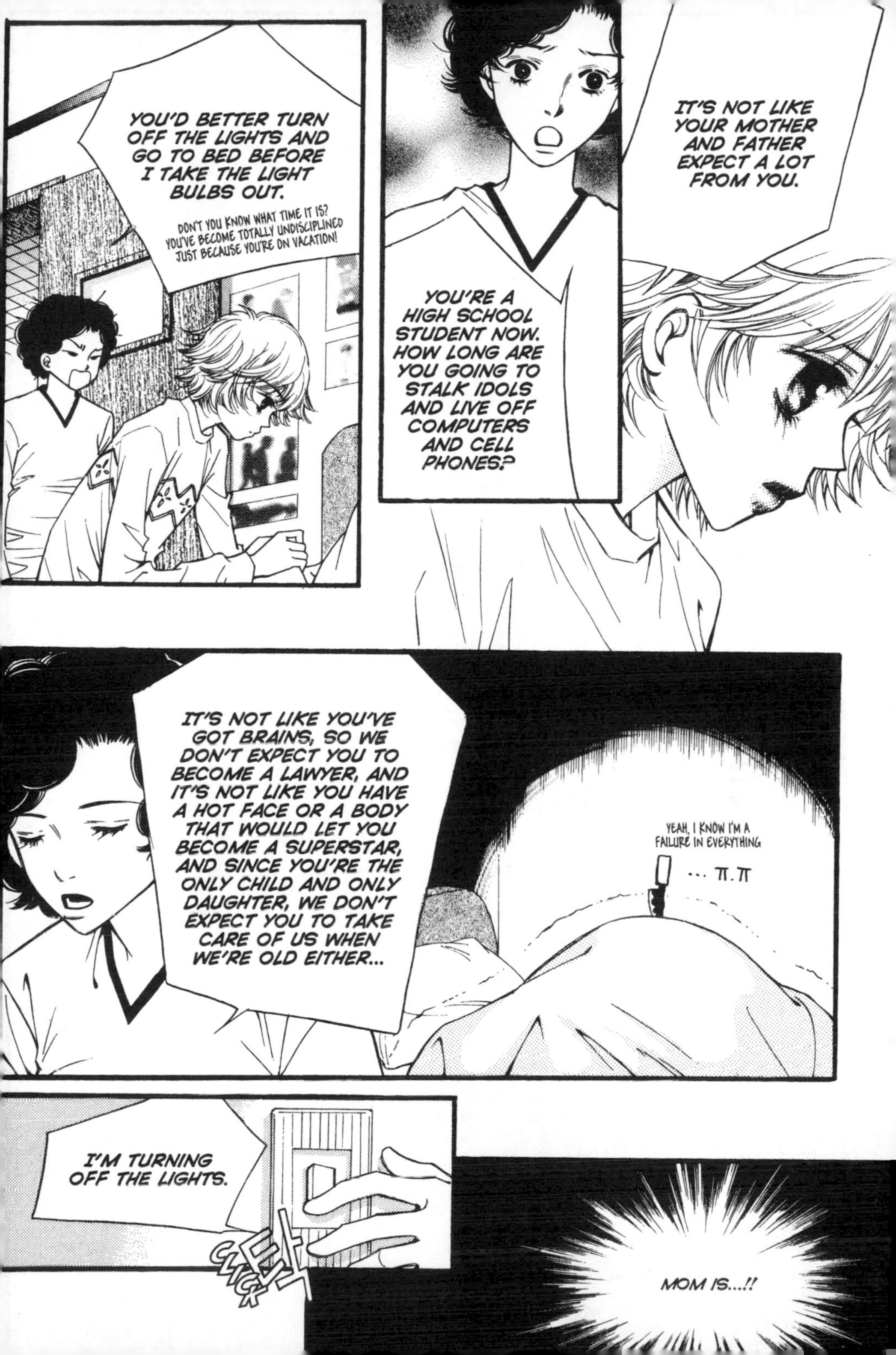
YOU'D BETTER TURN OFF THE LIGHTS AND GO TO BED BEFORE I TAKE THE LIGHT BULBS OUT.
DON'T YOU KNOW WHAT TIME IT IS? YOU'VE BECOME TOTALLY UNDISCIPLINED JUST BECAUSE YOU'RE ON VACATION!
YOU'RE A HIGH SCHOOL STUDENT NOW. HOW LONG ARE YOU GOING TO STALK IDOLS AND LIVE OFF COMPUTERS AND CELL PHONES?
IT'S NOT LIKE YOUR MOTHER AND FATHER EXPECT A LOT FROM YOU.
IT'S NOT LIKE YOU'VE GOT BRAINS, SO WE DON'T EXPECT YOU TO BECOME A LAWYER, AND IT'S NOT LIKE YOU HAVE A HOT FACE OR A BODY THAT WOULD LET YOU BECOME A SUPERSTAR, AND SINCE YOU'RE THE ONLY CHILD AND ONLY DAUGHTER, WE DON'T EXPECT YOU TO TAKE CARE OF US WHEN WE'RE OLD EITHER...
YEAH, I KNOW I'M A FAILURE IN EVERYTHING
... π.π
I'M TURNING OFF THE LIGHTS.
CLICK
MOM IS...!!

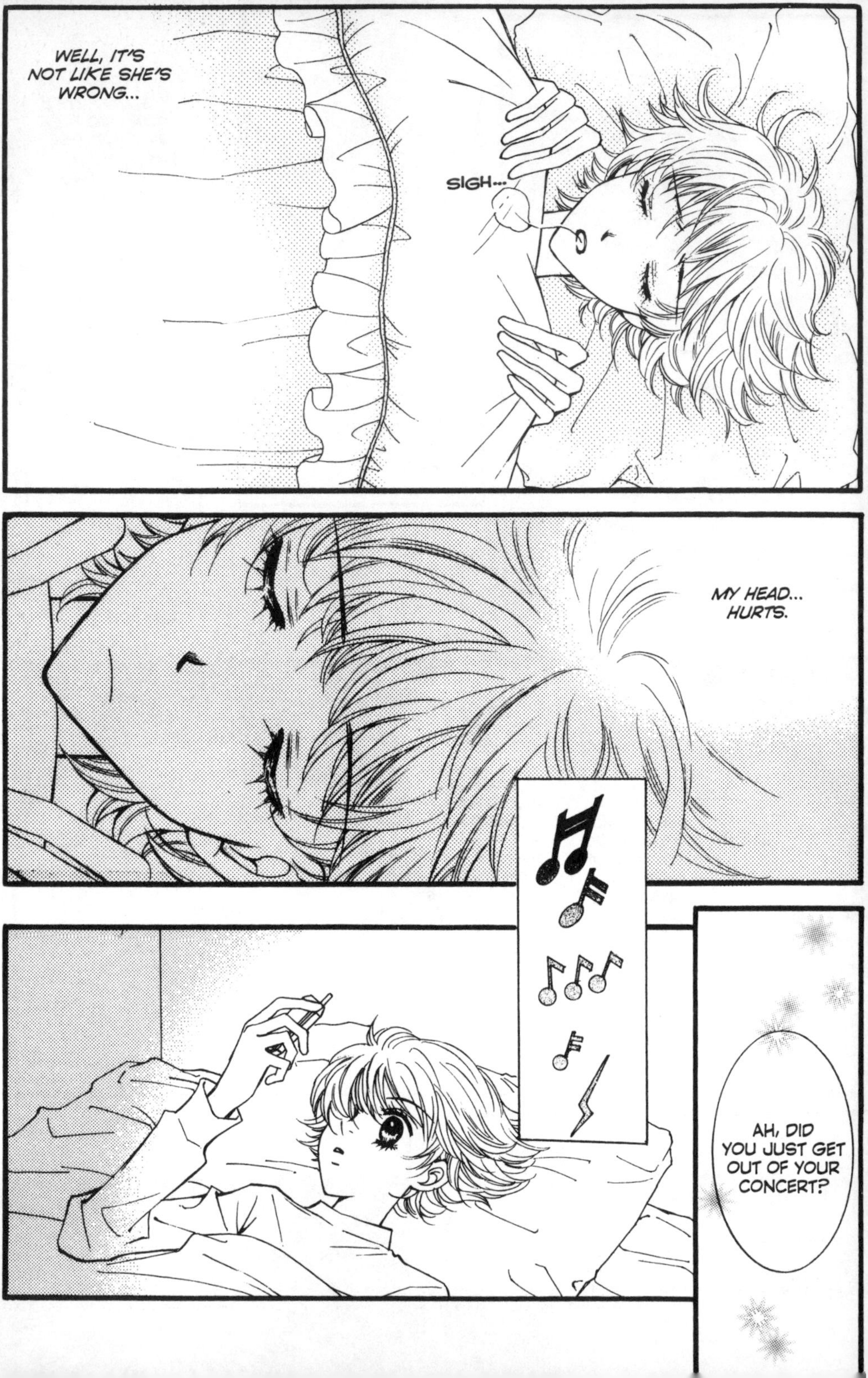
WELL, IT'S NOT LIKE SHE'S WRONG...
SIGH...
MY HEAD... HURTS.
AH, DID YOU JUST GET OUT OF YOUR CONCERT?

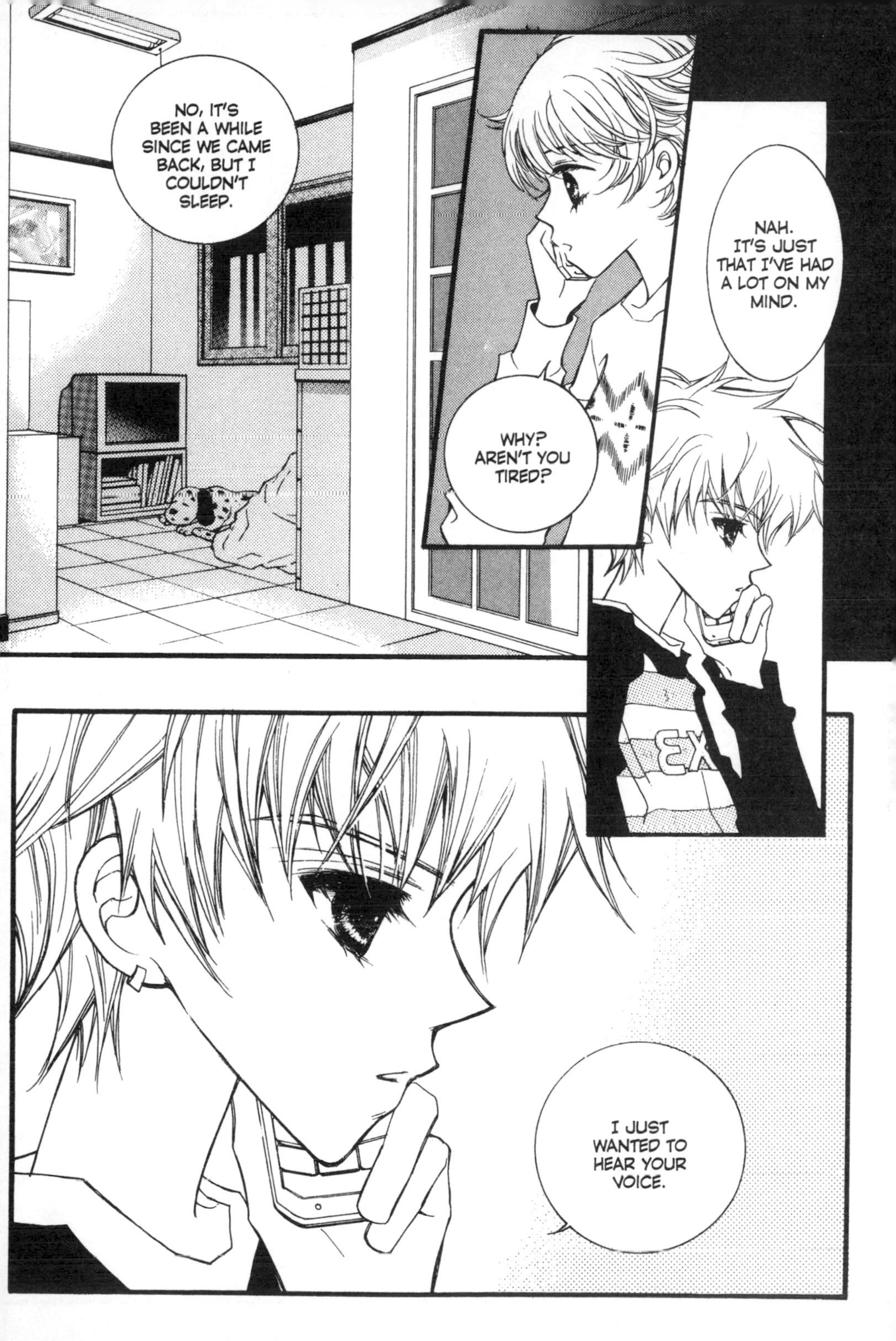
NO, IT'S BEEN A WHILE SINCE WE CAME BACK, BUT I COULDN'T SLEEP.
WHY? AREN'T YOU TIRED?
NAH. IT'S JUST THAT I'VE HAD A LOT ON MY MIND.
I JUST WANTED TO HEAR YOUR VOICE.

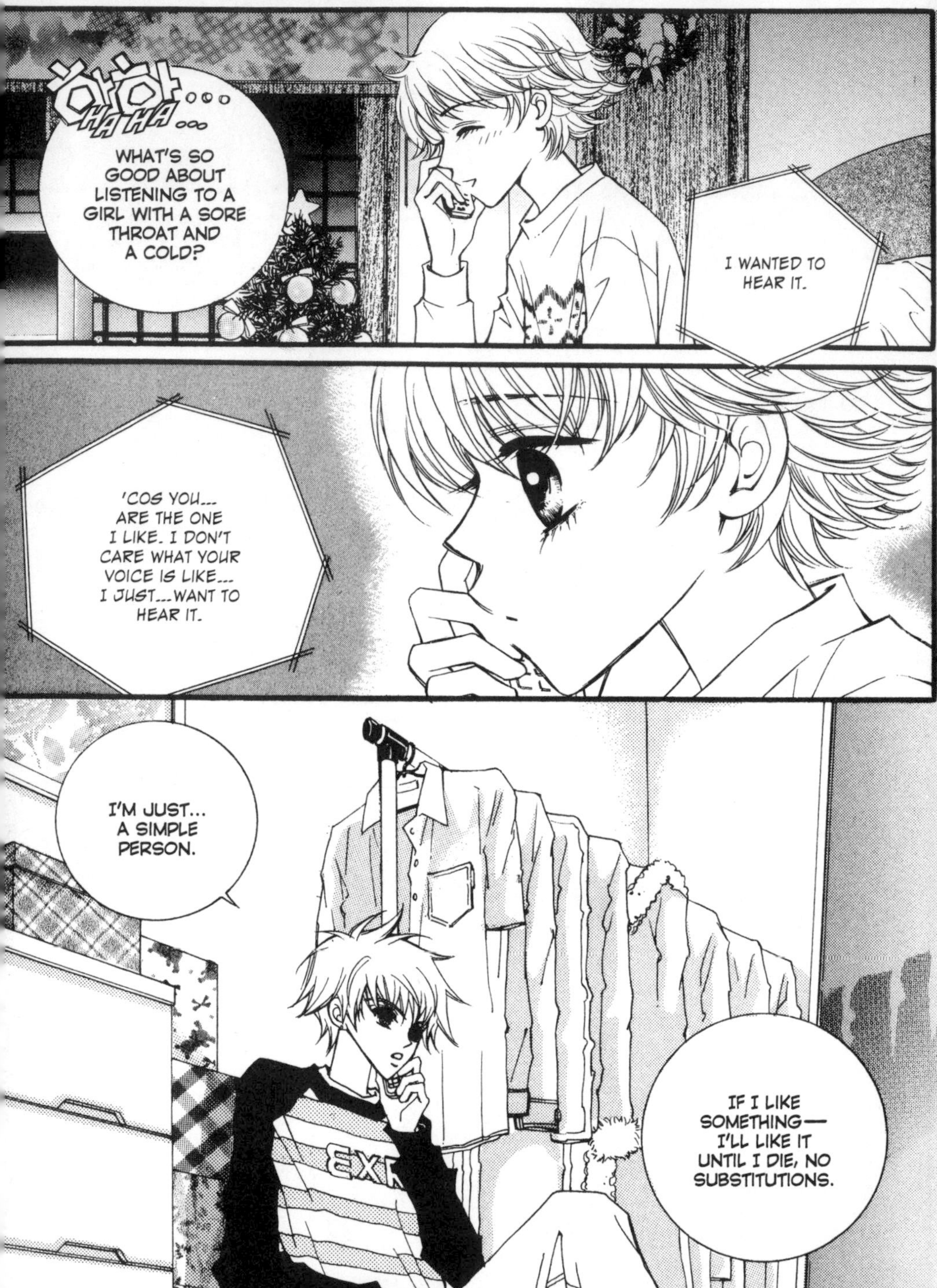
하하...
HA HA...
WHAT'S SO GOOD ABOUT LISTENING TO A GIRL WITH A SORE THROAT AND A COLD?
I WANTED TO HEAR IT.
'COS YOU... ARE THE ONE I LIKE. I DON'T CARE WHAT YOUR VOICE IS LIKE... I JUST...WANT TO HEAR IT.
I'M JUST... A SIMPLE PERSON.
IF I LIKE SOMETHING— I'LL LIKE IT UNTIL I DIE, NO SUBSTITUTIONS.

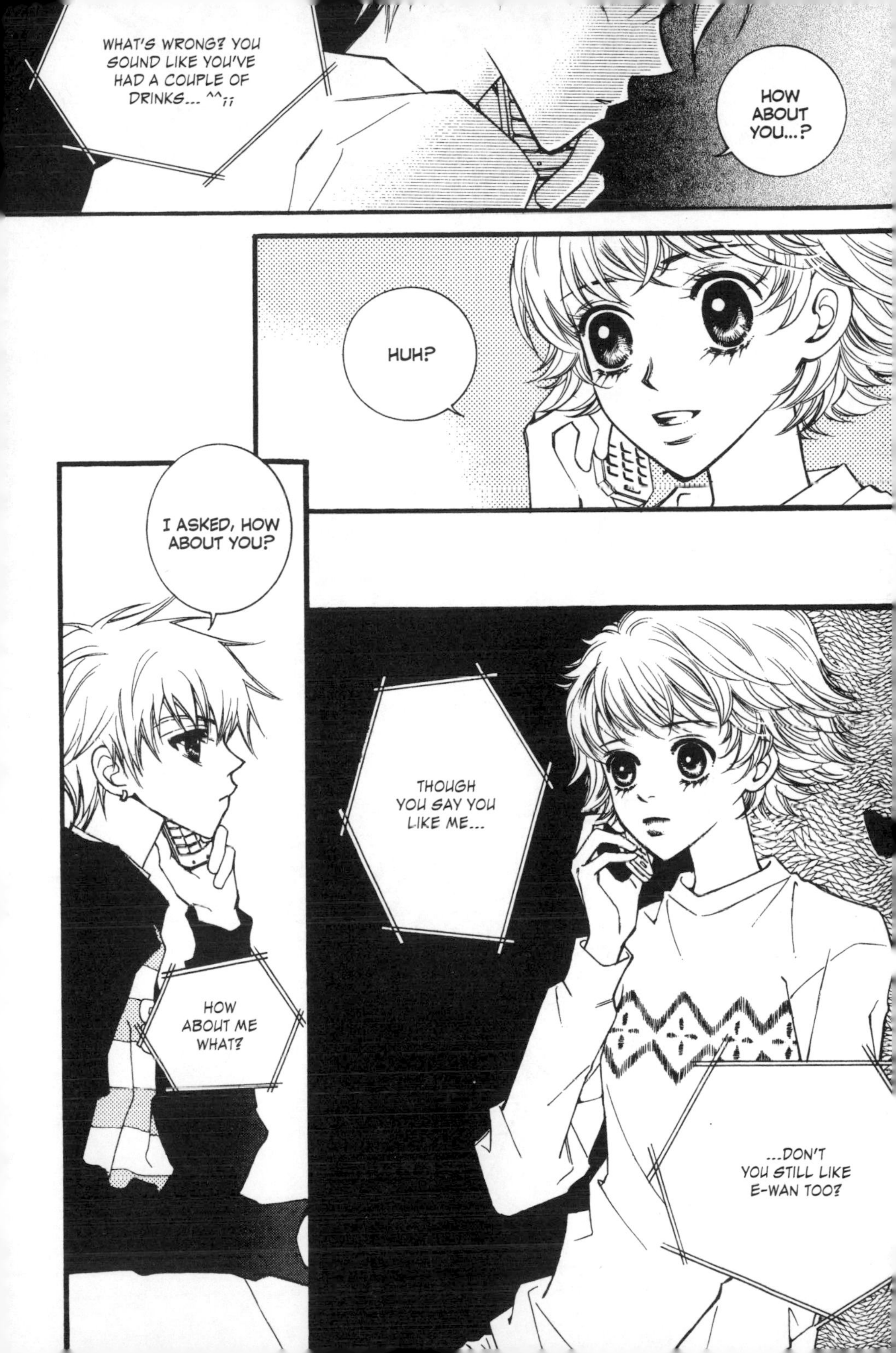
WHAT'S WRONG? YOU SOUND LIKE YOU'VE HAD A COUPLE OF DRINKS... ^^;;
HOW ABOUT YOU...?
HUH?
I ASKED, HOW ABOUT YOU?
HOW ABOUT ME WHAT?
THOUGH YOU SAY YOU LIKE ME...
...DON'T YOU STILL LIKE E-WAN TOO?

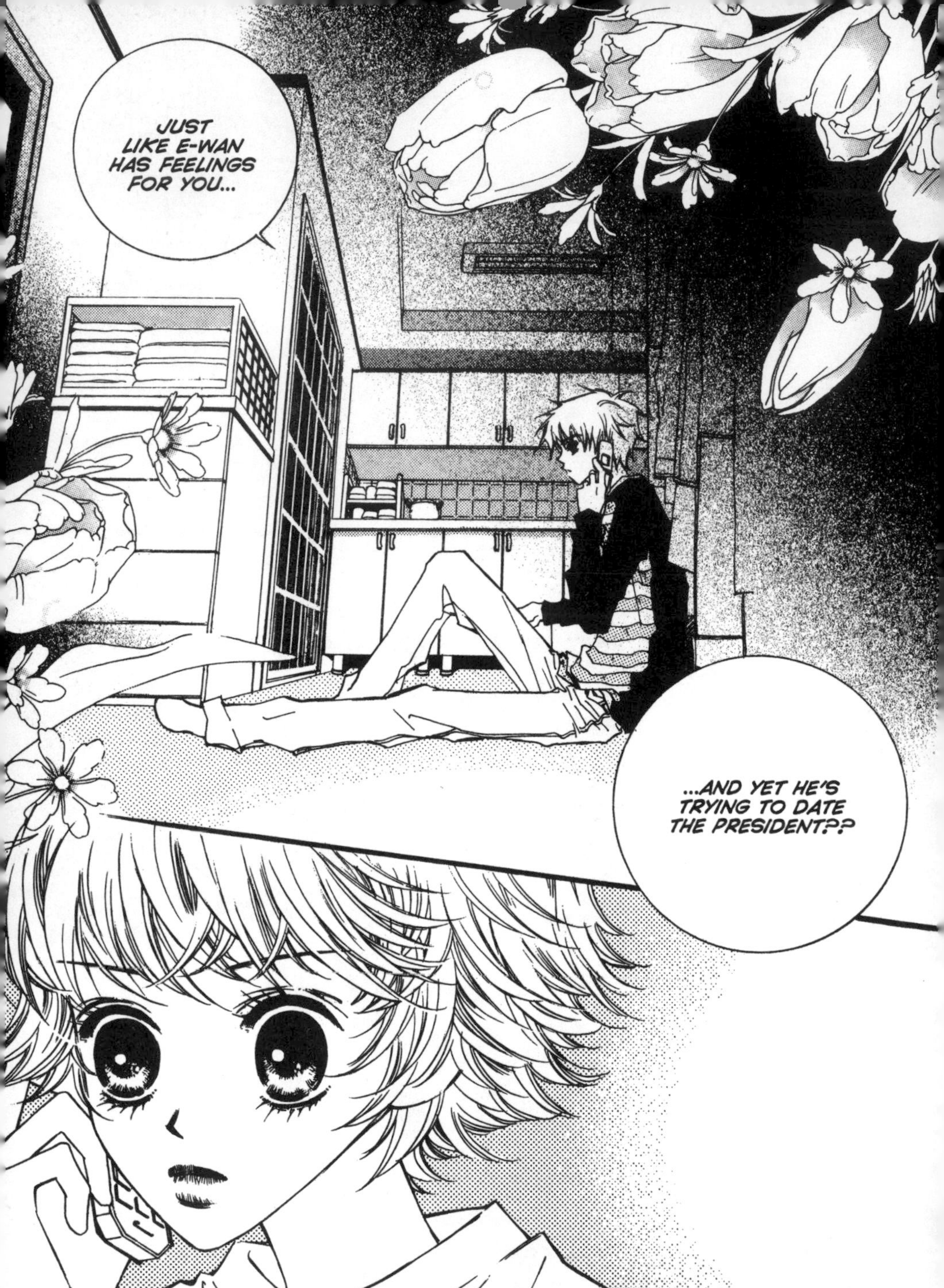
JUST LIKE E-WAN HAS FEELINGS FOR YOU...
...AND YET HE'S TRYING TO DATE THE PRESIDENT?

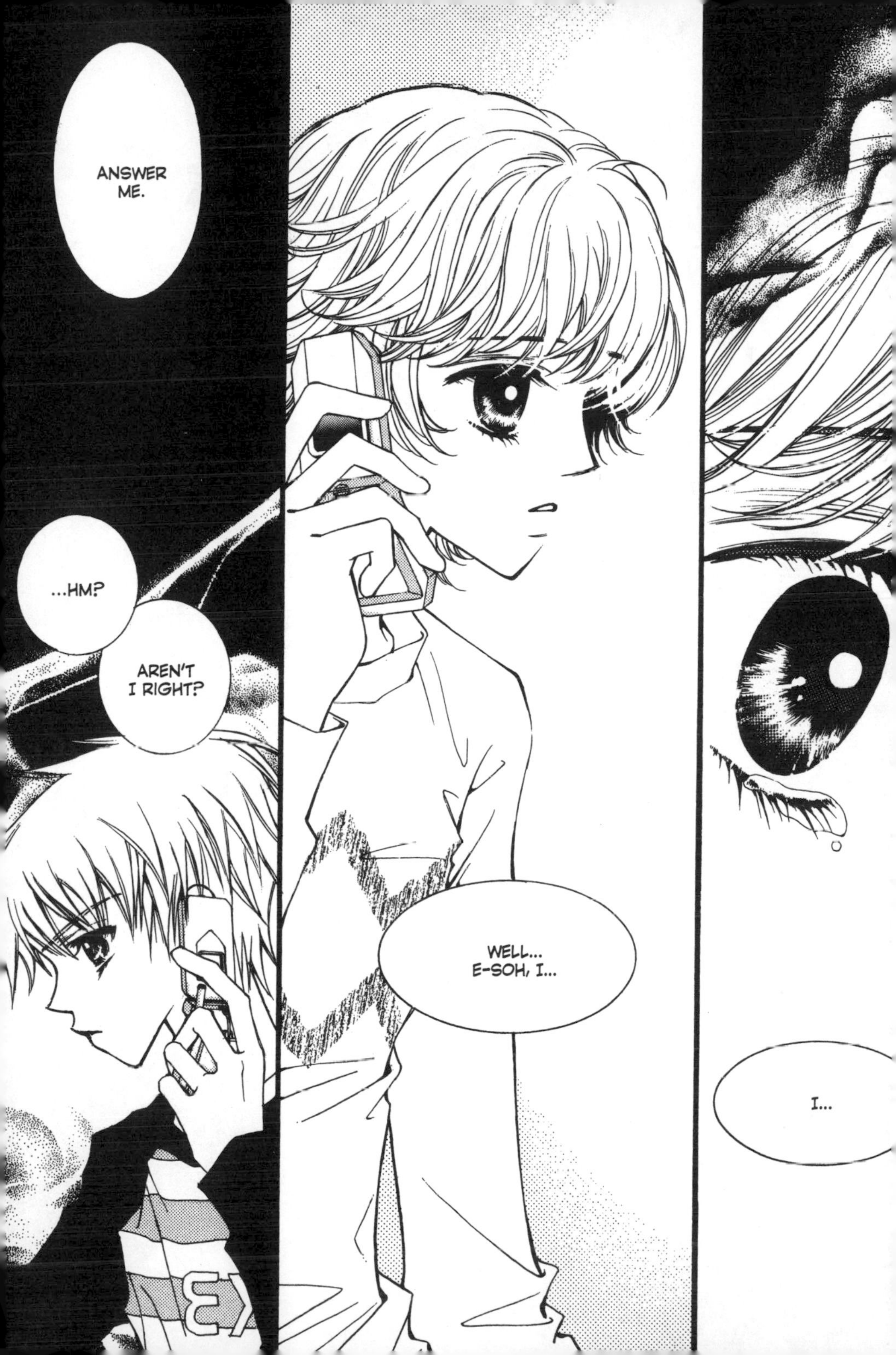
ANSWER ME.
...HM?
AREN'T I RIGHT?
WELL... E-SOH, I...
I...

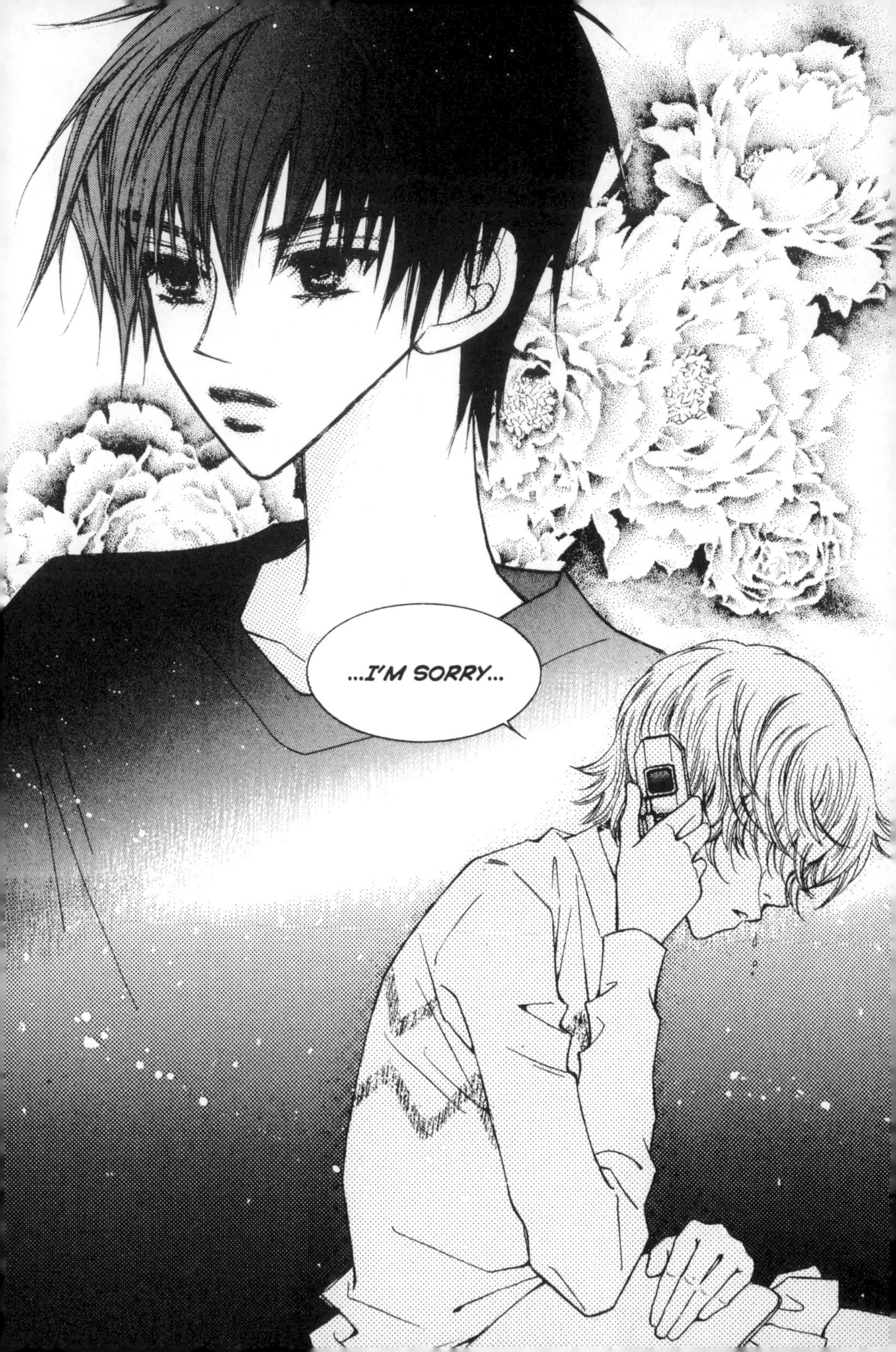
...I'M SORRY...

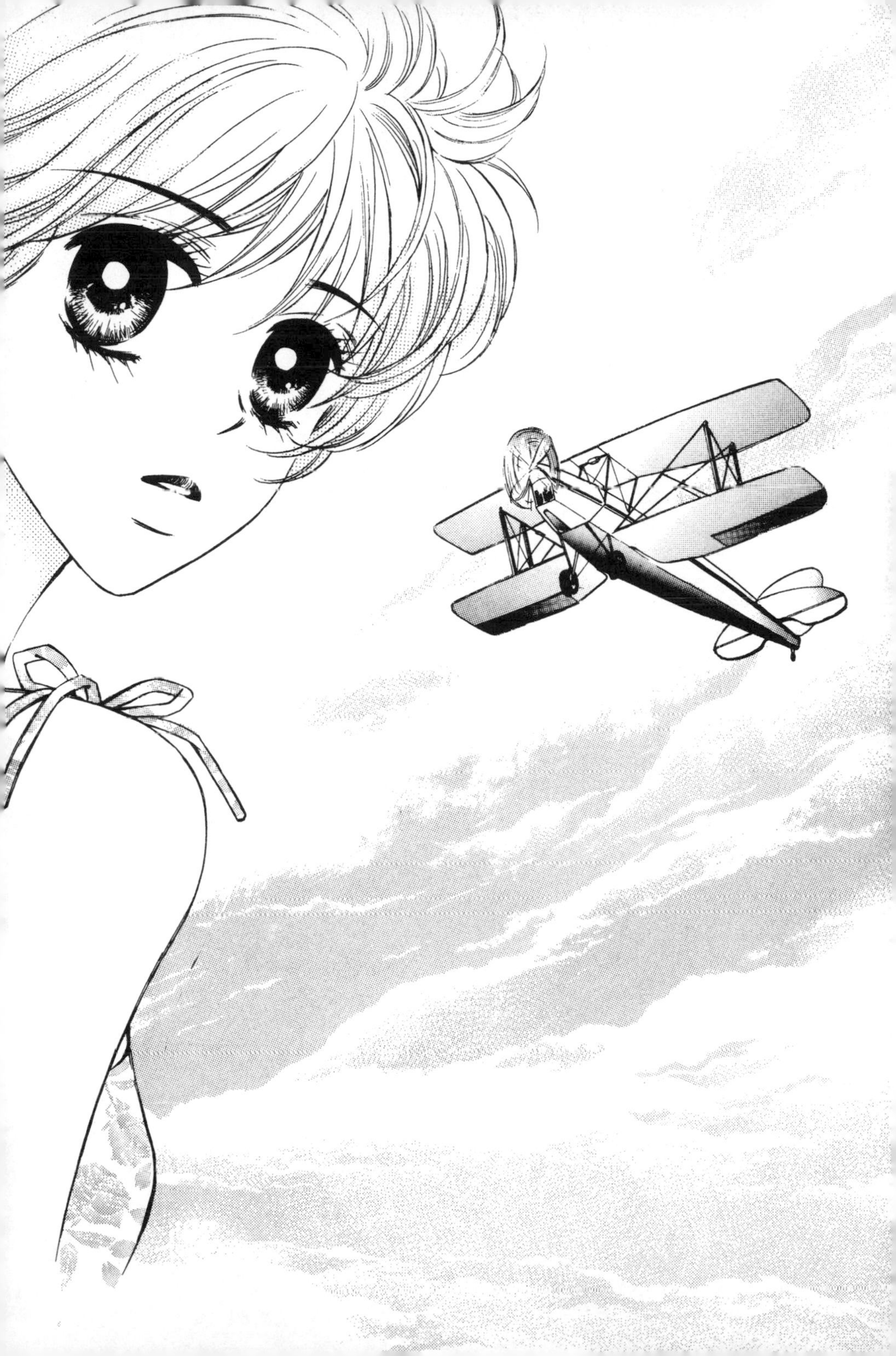

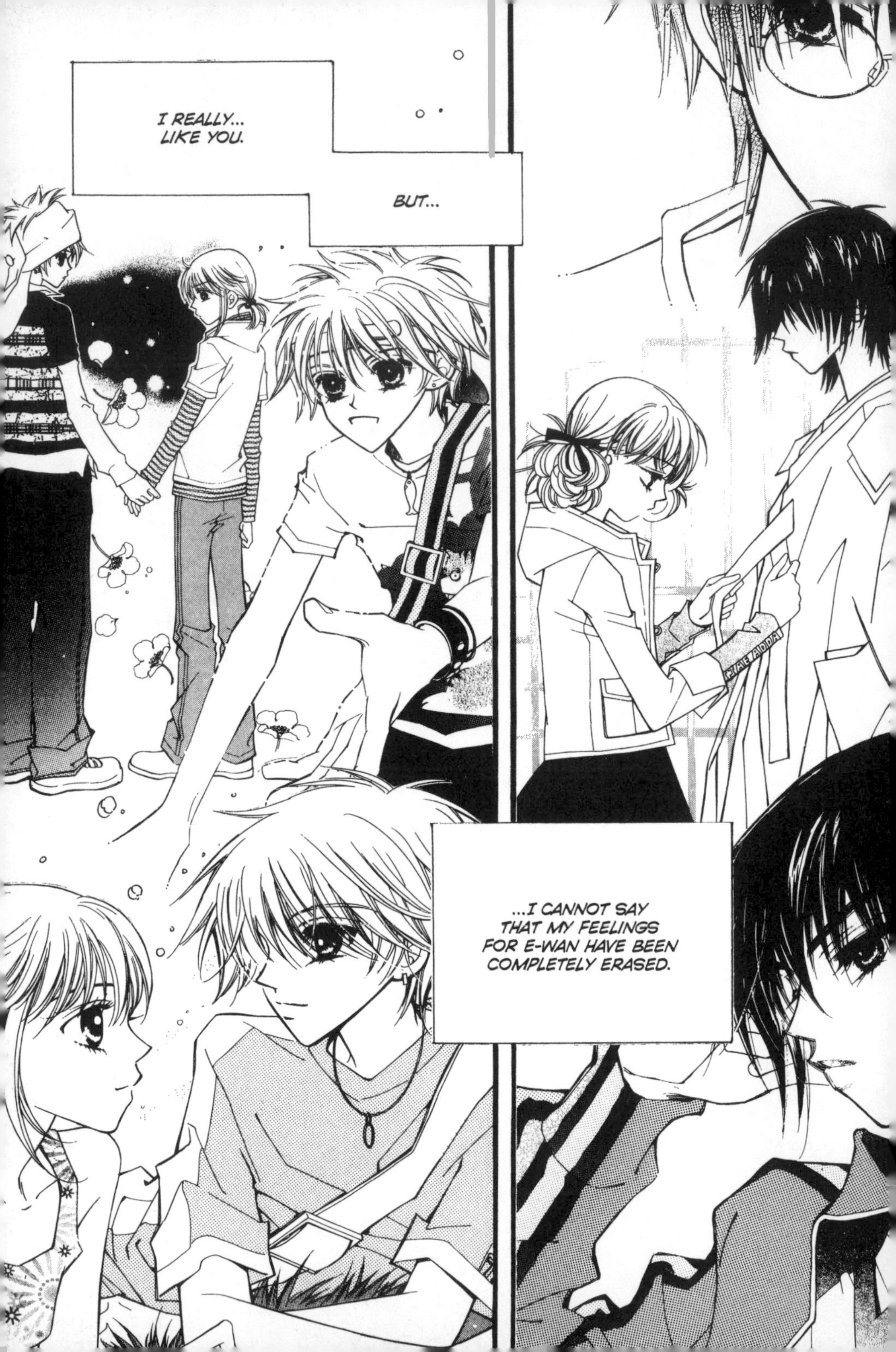
I REALLY... LIKE YOU.
BUT...
...I CANNOT SAY THAT MY FEELINGS FOR E-WAN HAVE BEEN COMPLETELY ERASED.

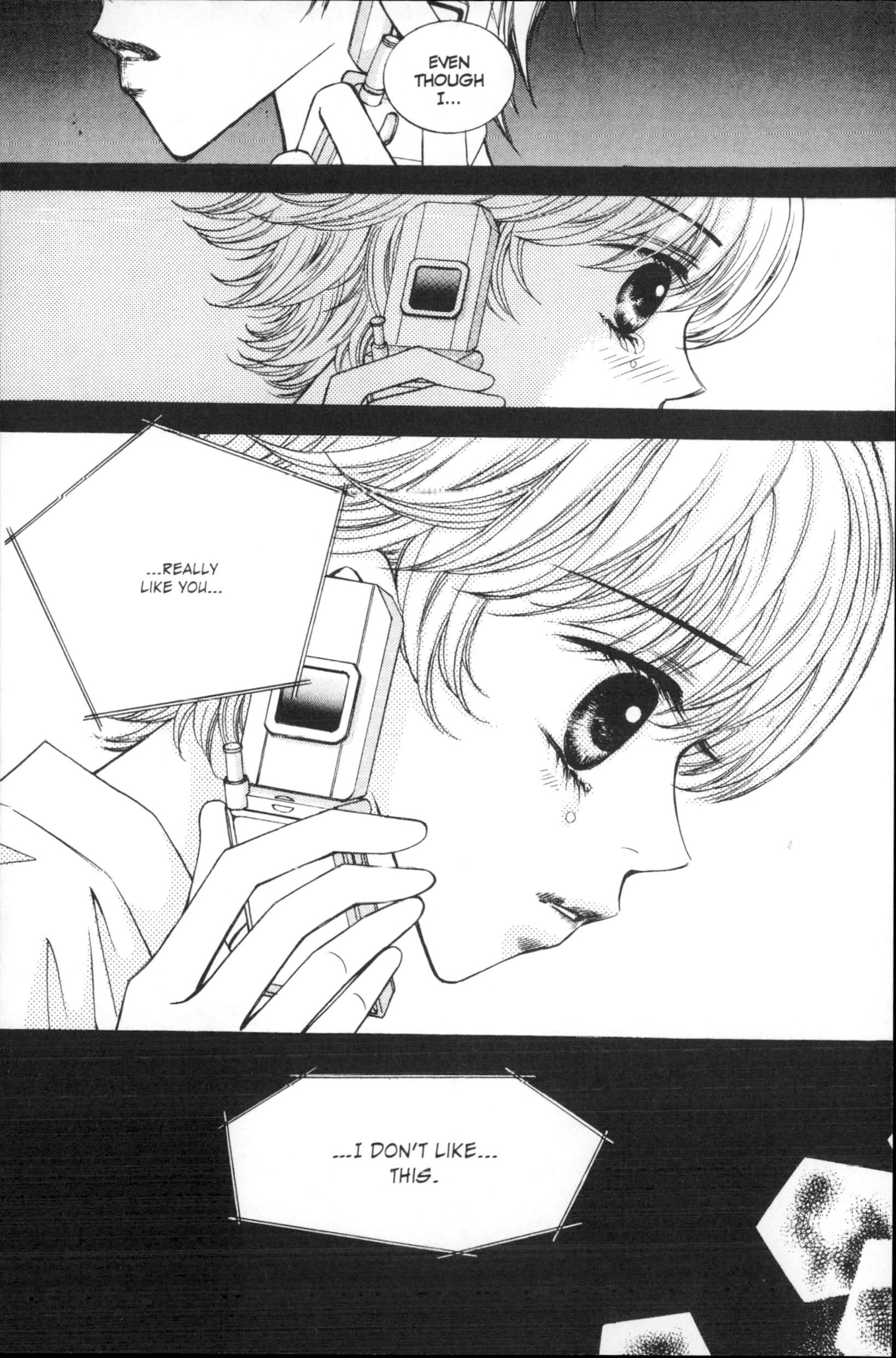
EVEN THOUGH I...
...REALLY LIKE YOU...
...I DON'T LIKE... THIS.

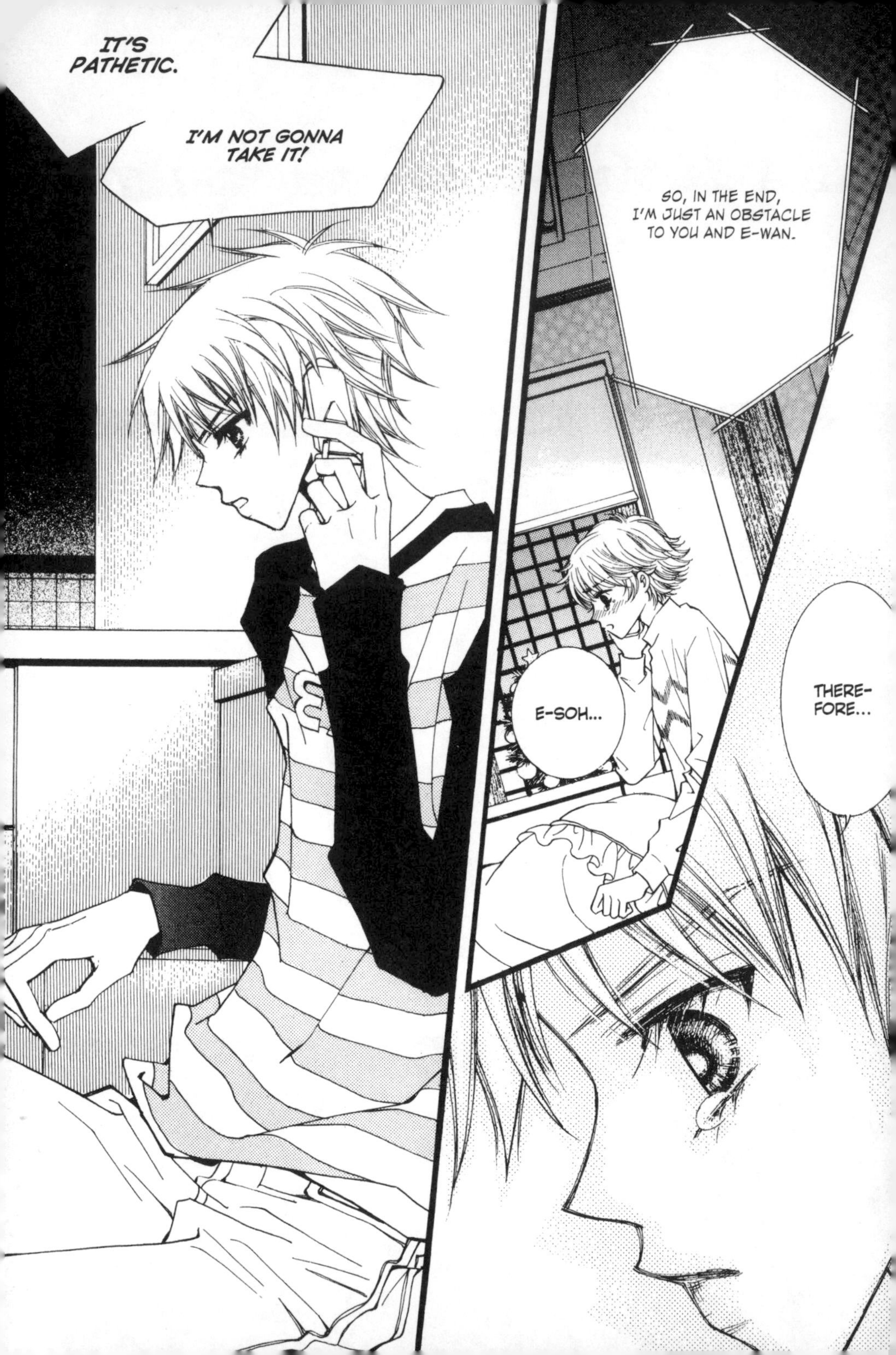
IT'S PATHETIC.
I'M NOT GONNA TAKE IT!
SO, IN THE END, I'M JUST AN OBSTACLE TO YOU AND E-WAN.
E-SOH...
THERE-FORE...

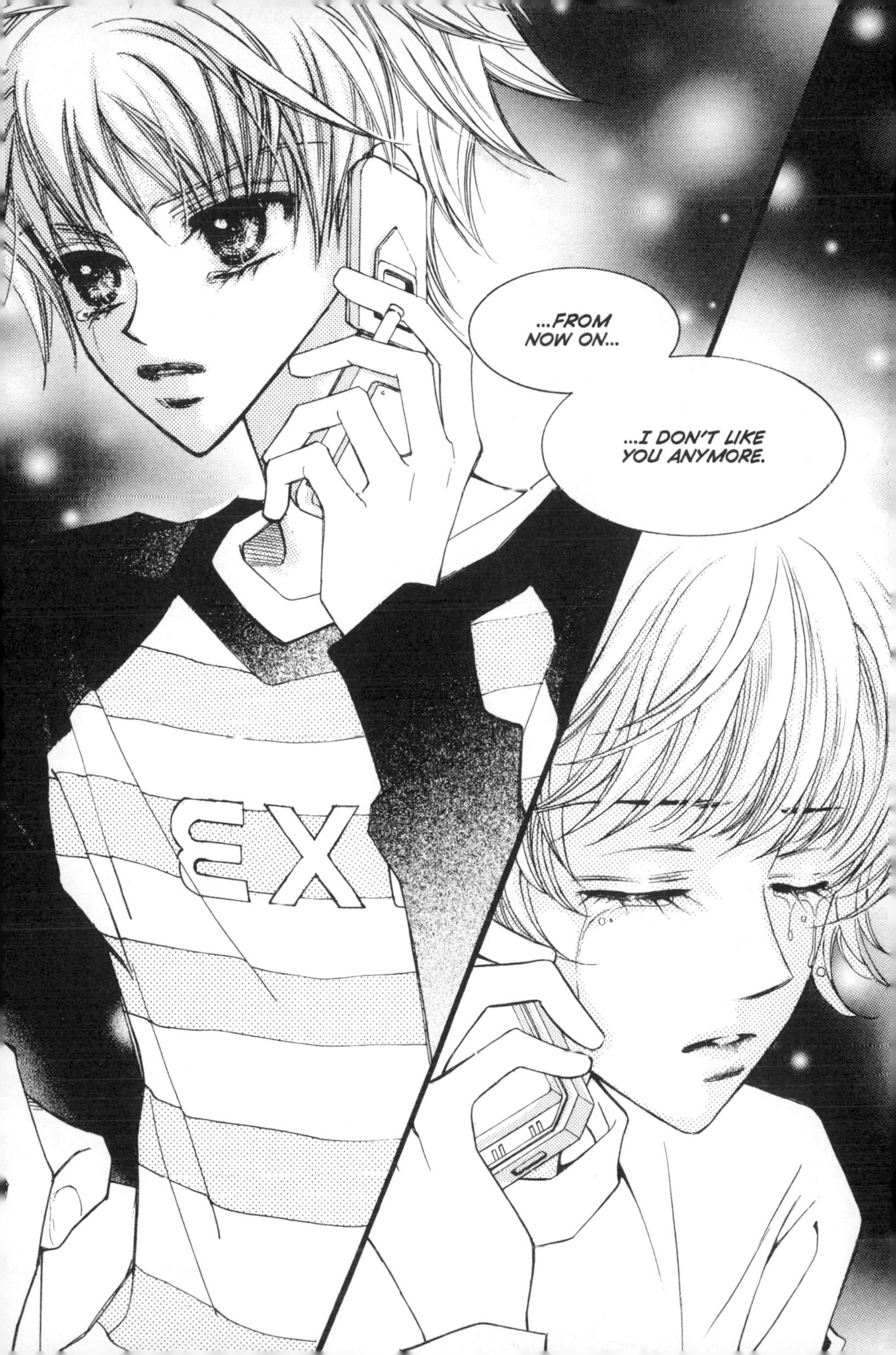
...FROM NOW ON...
...I DON'T LIKE YOU ANYMORE.
EX

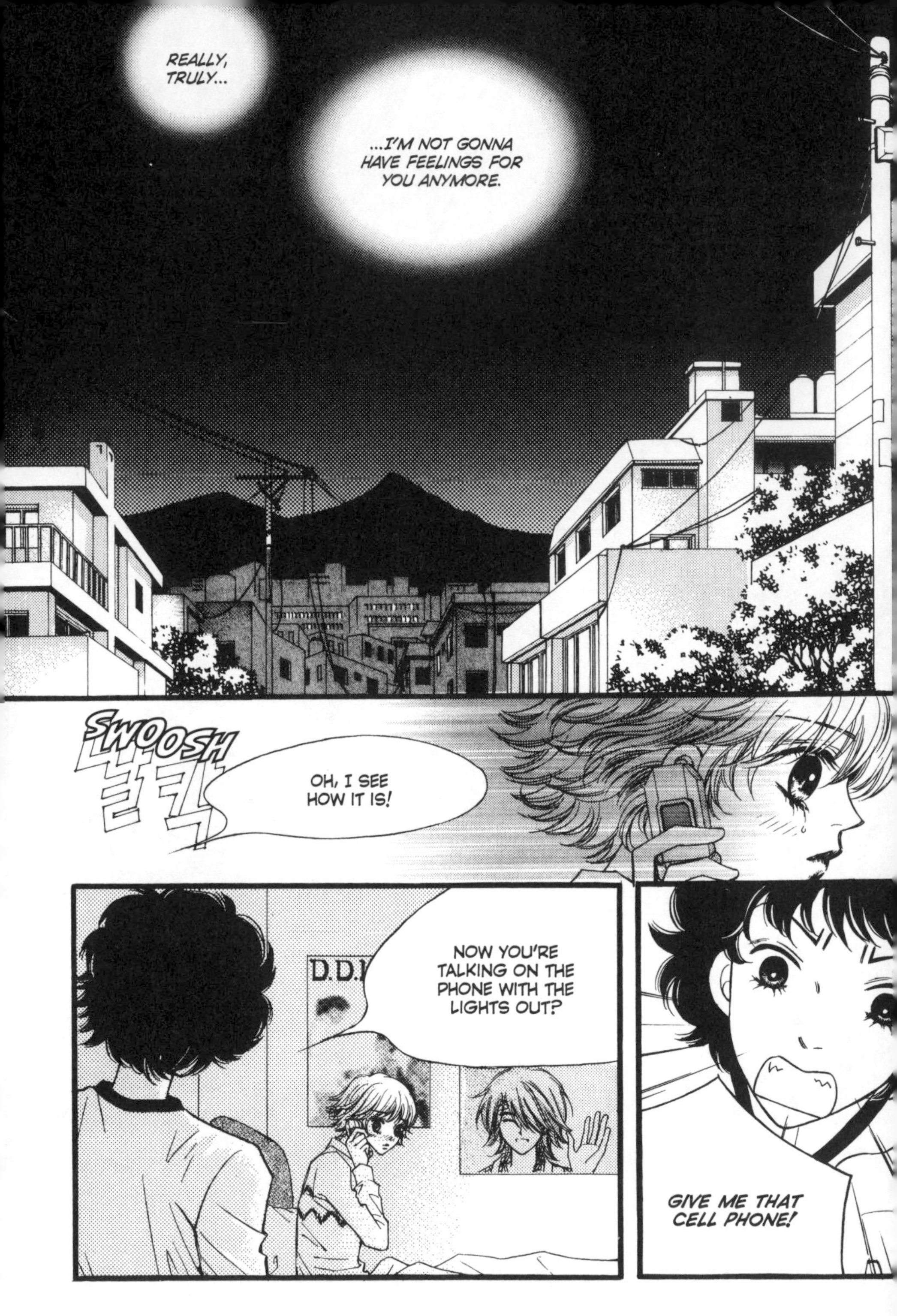
REALLY, TRULY...
...I'M NOT GONNA HAVE FEELINGS FOR YOU ANYMORE.
SWOOSH
OH, I SEE HOW IT IS!
NOW YOU'RE TALKING ON THE PHONE WITH THE LIGHTS OUT?
D.D.
GIVE ME THAT CELL PHONE!

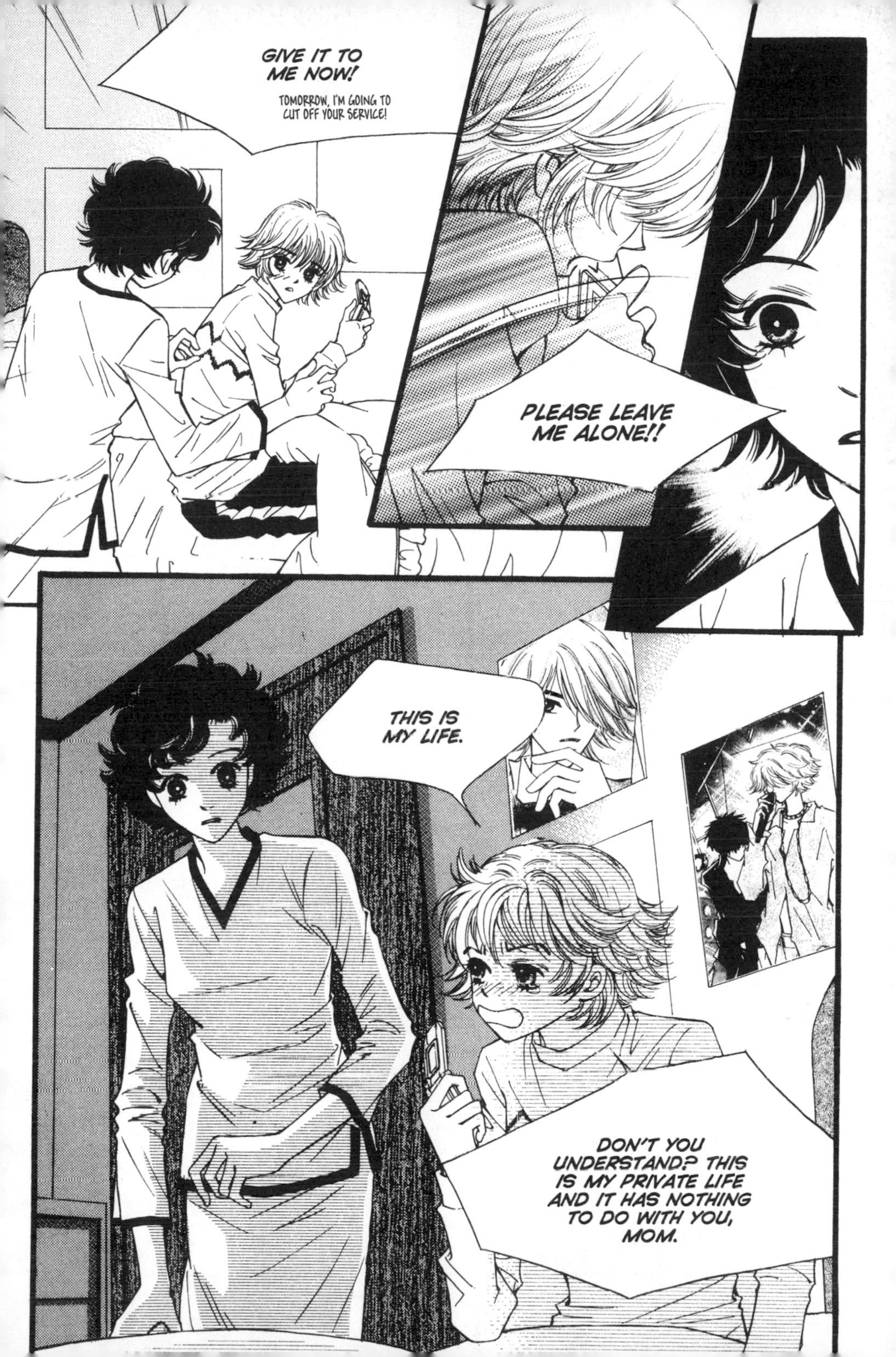
GIVE IT TO ME NOW!
TOMORROW, I'M GOING TO CUT OFF YOUR SERVICE!
PLEASE LEAVE ME ALONE!!
THIS IS MY LIFE.
DON'T YOU UNDERSTAND? THIS IS MY PRIVATE LIFE AND IT HAS NOTHING TO DO WITH YOU, MOM.

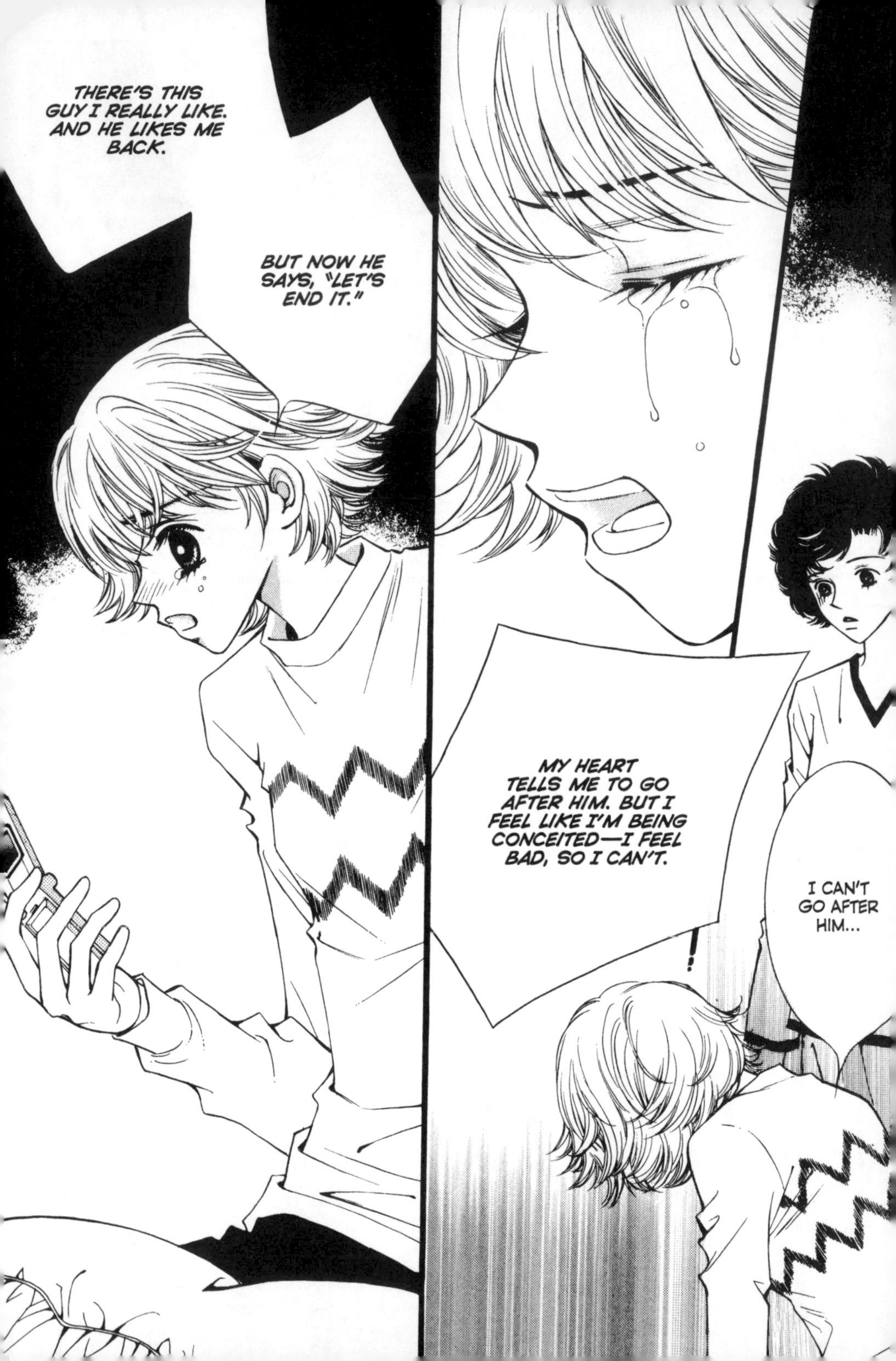
THERE'S THIS GUY I REALLY LIKE. AND HE LIKES ME BACK.
BUT NOW HE SAYS, "LET'S END IT."
MY HEART TELLS ME TO GO AFTER HIM. BUT I FEEL LIKE I'M BEING CONCEITED—I FEEL BAD, SO I CAN'T.
!
I CAN'T GO AFTER HIM...

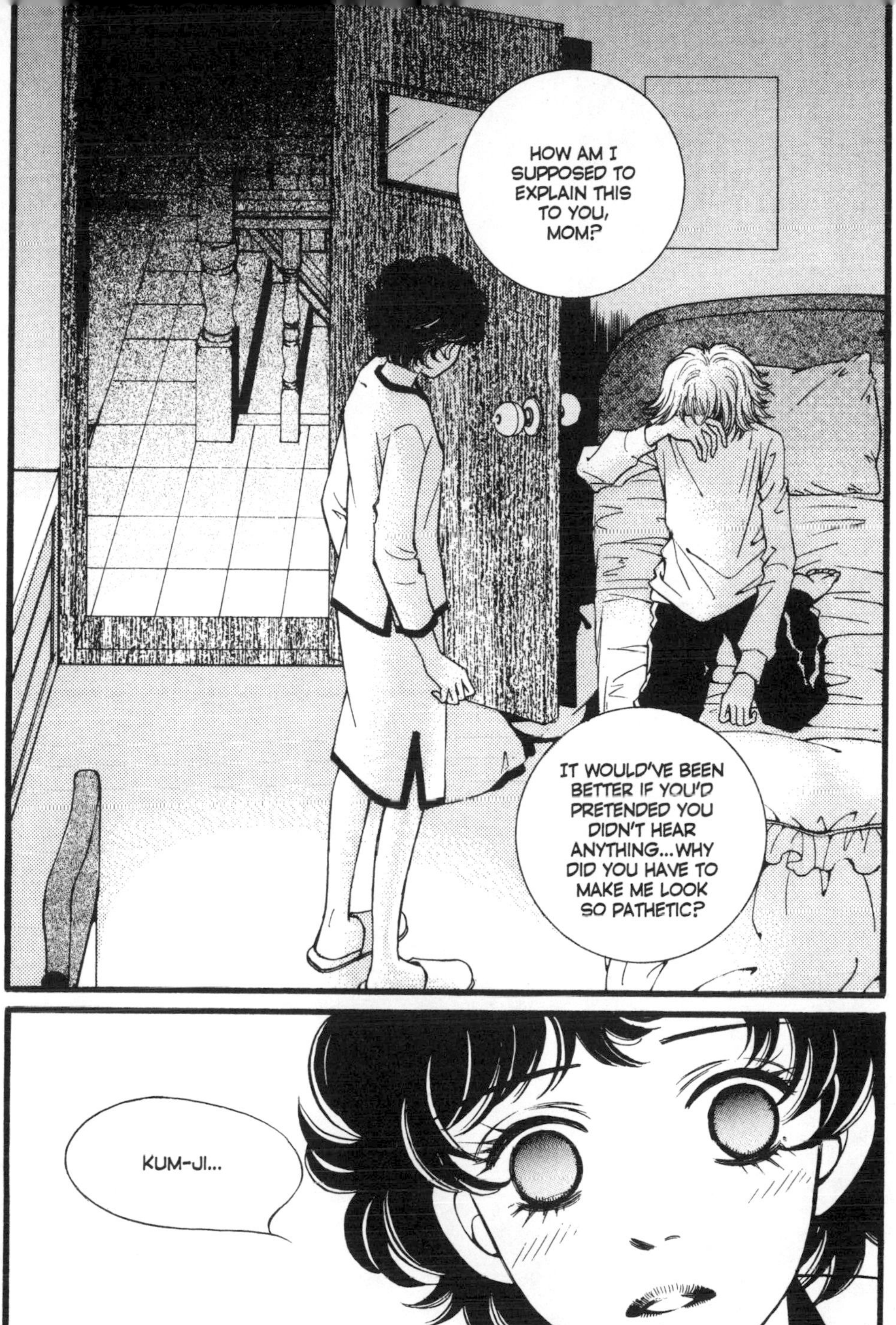
HOW AM I SUPPOSED TO EXPLAIN THIS TO YOU, MOM?
IT WOULD'VE BEEN BETTER IF YOU'D PRETENDED YOU DIDN'T HEAR ANYTHING...WHY DID YOU HAVE TO MAKE ME LOOK SO PATHETIC?
KUM-JI...

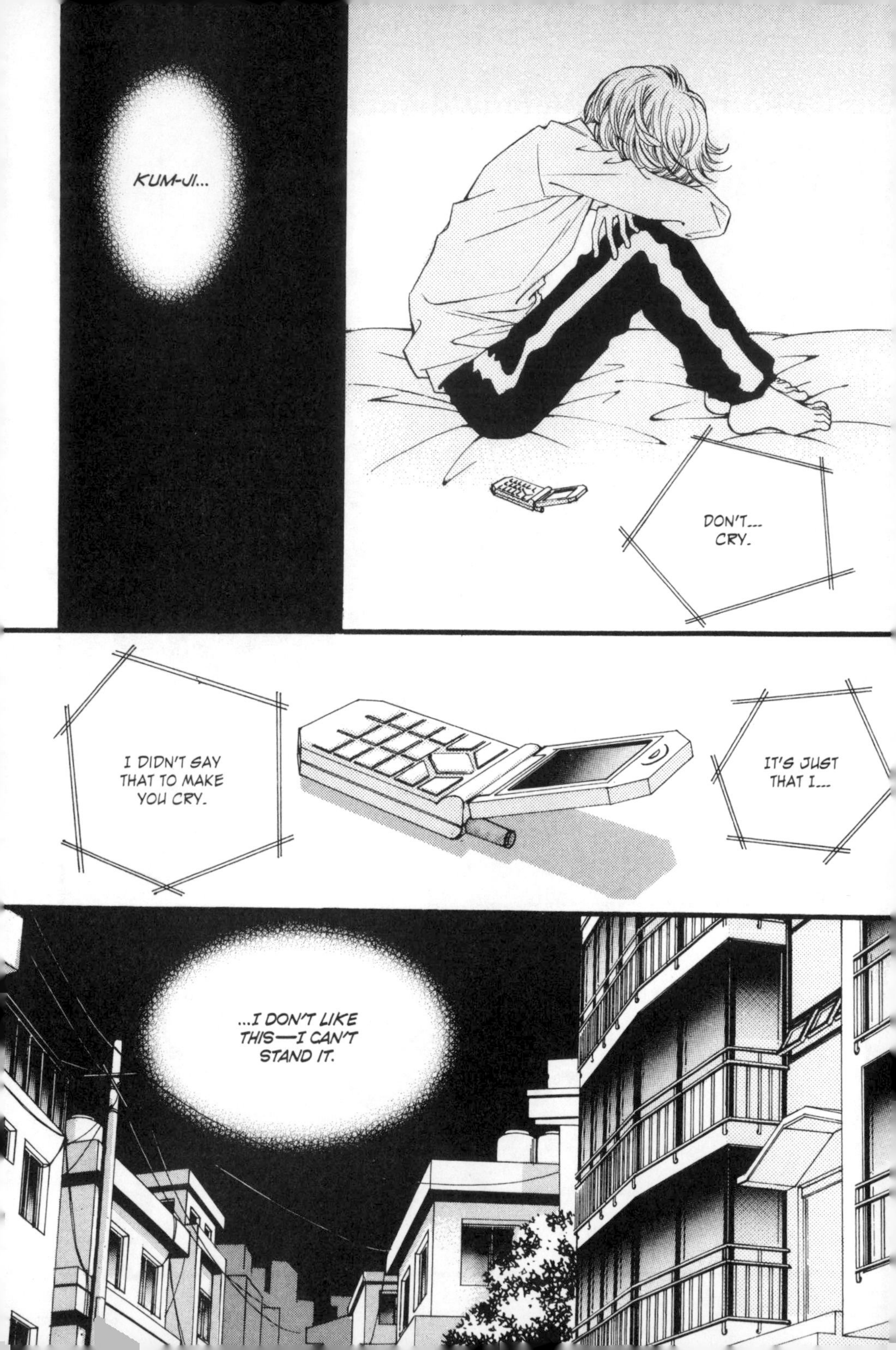
KUM-JI...
DON'T... CRY.
I DIDN'T SAY THAT TO MAKE YOU CRY.
IT'S JUST THAT I...
...I DON'T LIKE THIS—I CAN'T STAND IT.

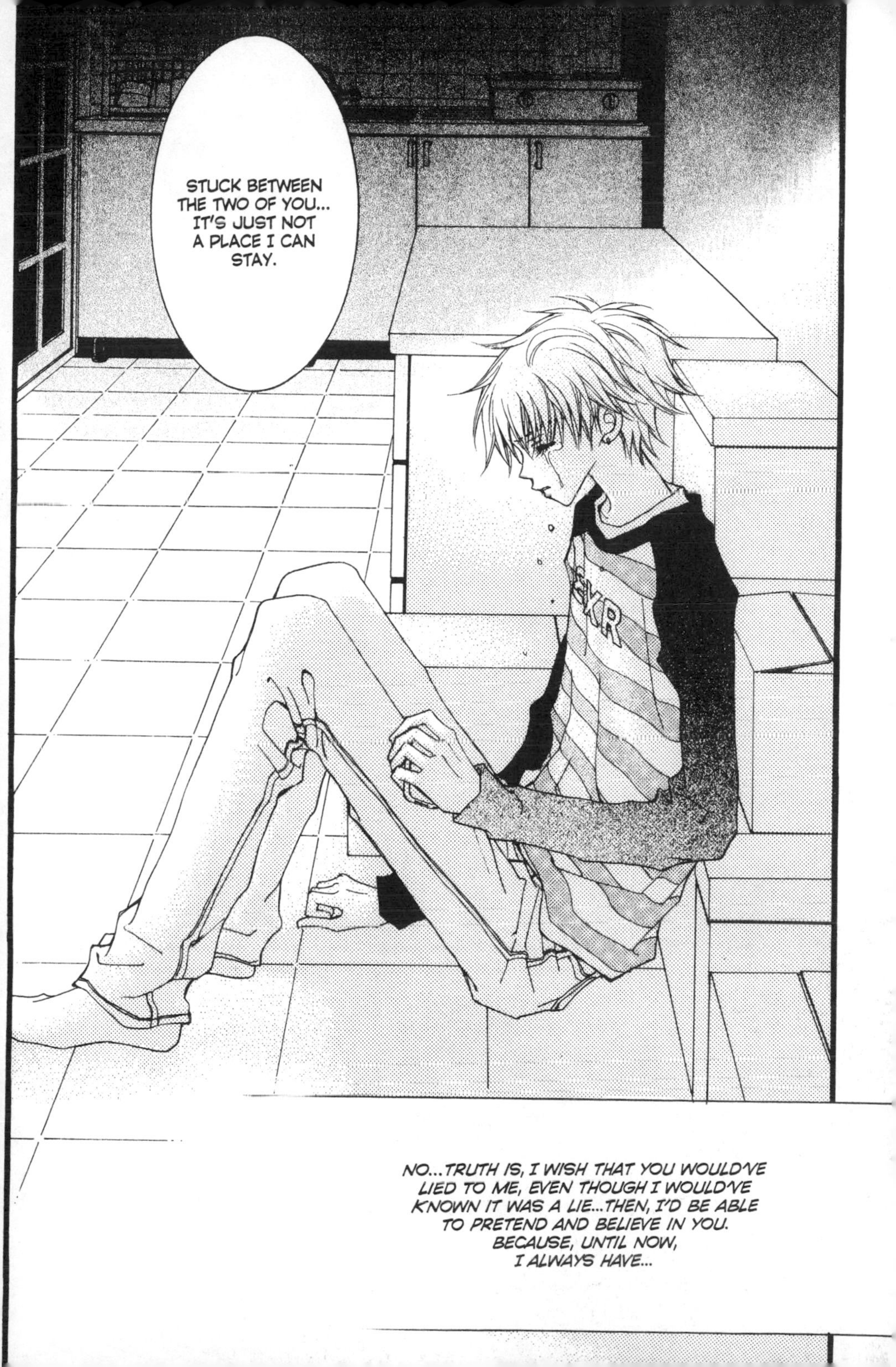
STUCK BETWEEN THE TWO OF YOU... IT'S JUST NOT A PLACE I CAN STAY.
NO...TRUTH IS, I WISH THAT YOU WOULD'VE LIED TO ME, EVEN THOUGH I WOULD'VE KNOWN IT WAS A LIE...THEN, I'D BE ABLE TO PRETEND AND BELIEVE IN YOU. BECAUSE, UNTIL NOW, I ALWAYS HAVE...

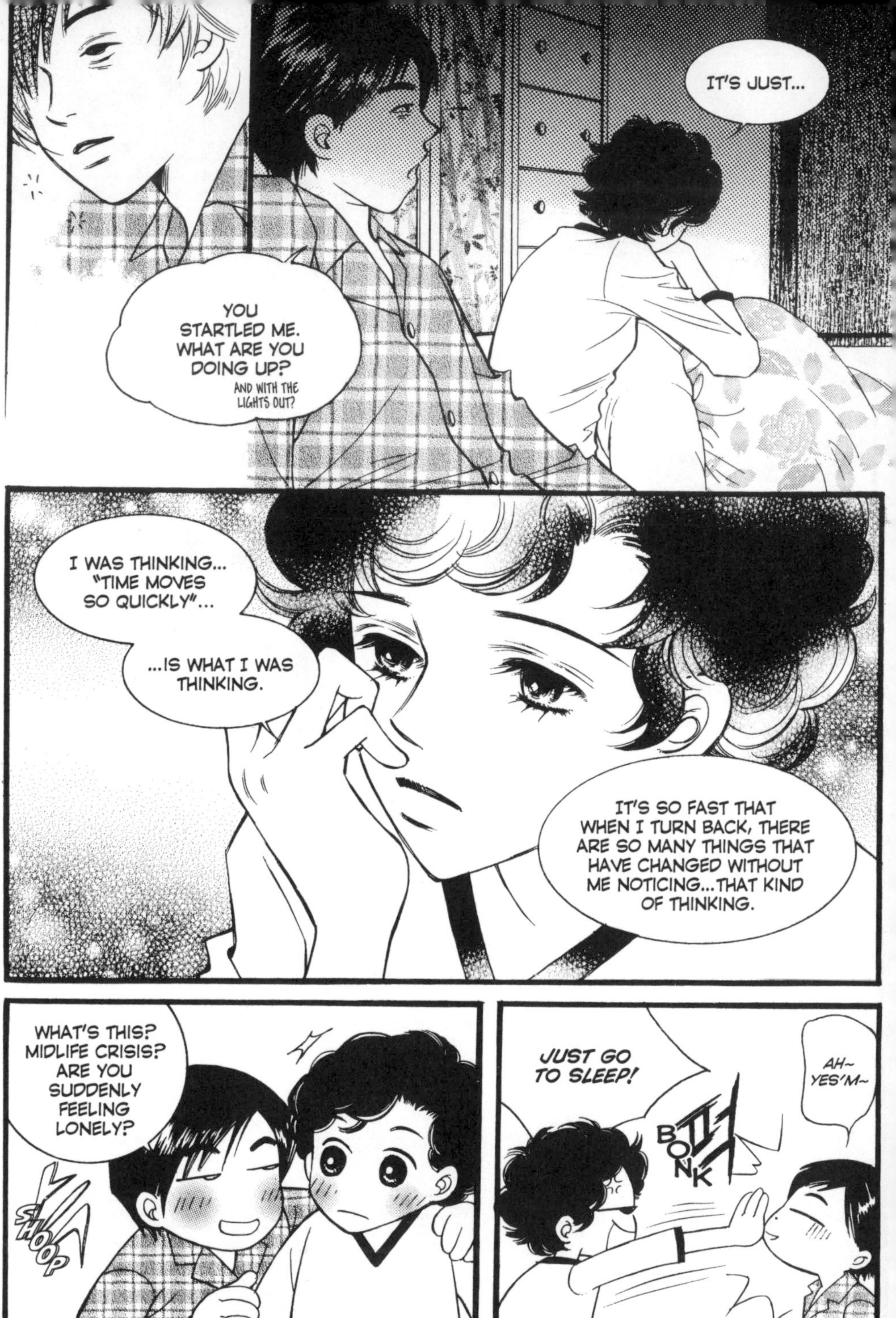
IT'S JUST...
YOU STARTLED ME. WHAT ARE YOU DOING UP?
AND WITH THE LIGHTS OUT?
I WAS THINKING... "TIME MOVES SO QUICKLY"...
...IS WHAT I WAS THINKING.
IT'S SO FAST THAT WHEN I TURN BACK, THERE ARE SO MANY THINGS THAT HAVE CHANGED WITHOUT ME NOTICING...THAT KIND OF THINKING.
WHAT'S THIS? MIDLIFE CRISIS? ARE YOU SUDDENLY FEELING LONELY?
SHOOP
JUST GO TO SLEEP!
BONK
AH~ YES'M~

......

IS THERE A KID JUST LIKE ME LIVING ON THAT STAR TOO?

SHE WAS ONCE...SUCH A LITTLE GIRL...

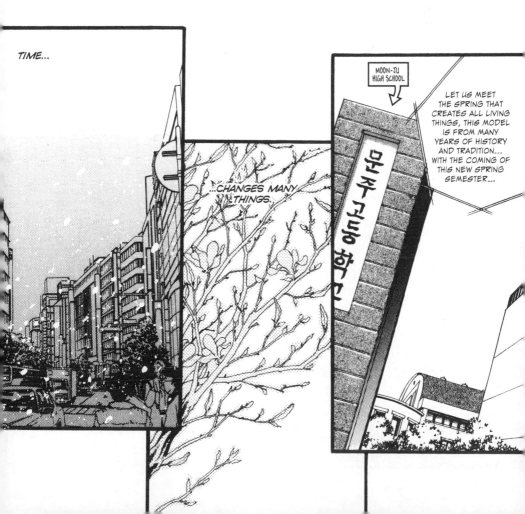

TIME...

...CHANGES MANY THINGS.

MOON-JU HIGH SCHOOL

문주고등학교

LET US MEET THE SPRING THAT CREATES ALL LIVING THINGS, THIS MODEL IS FROM MANY YEARS OF HISTORY AND TRADITION... WITH THE COMING OF THIS NEW SPRING SEMESTER...

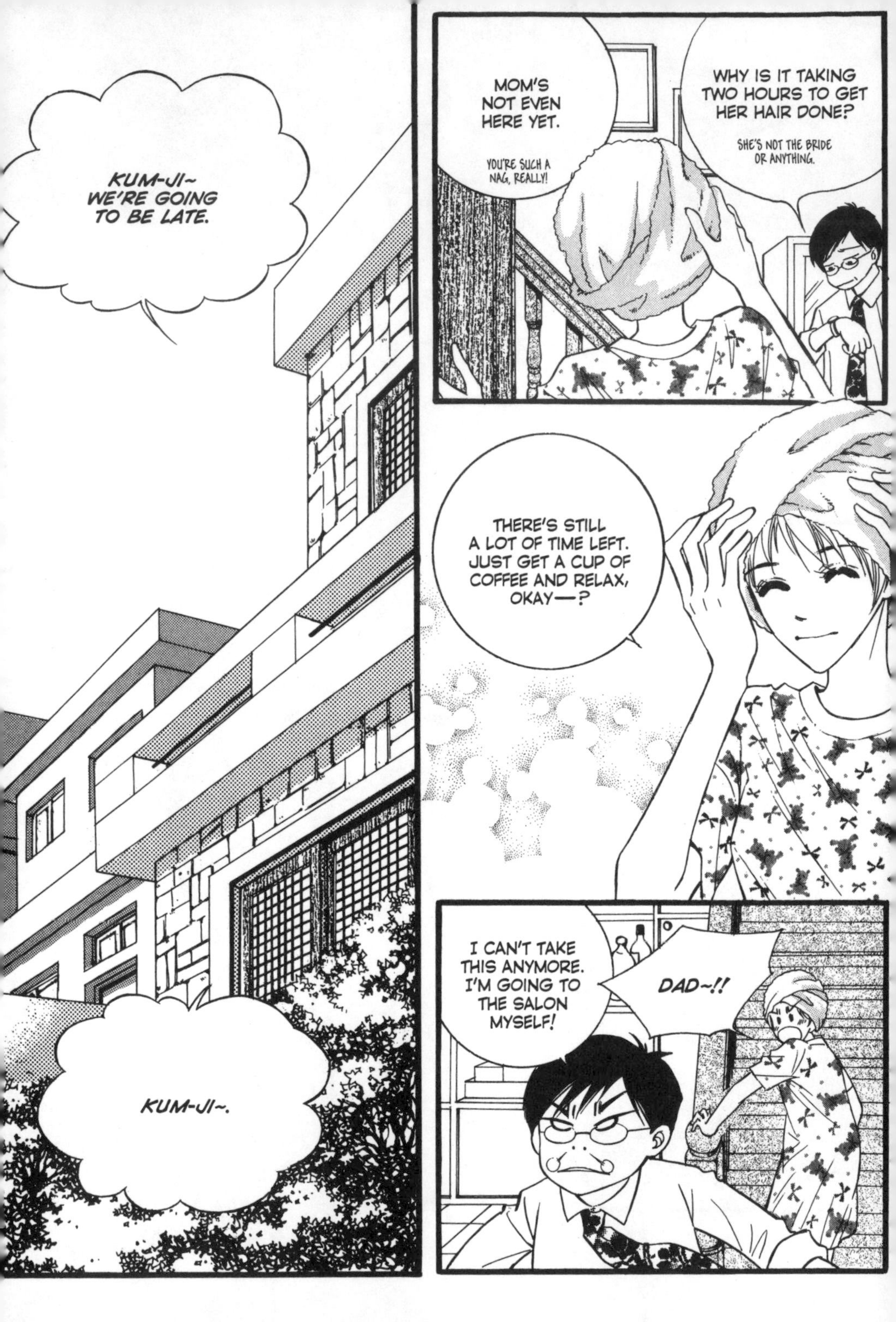
KUM-JI~ WE'RE GOING TO BE LATE.
KUM-JI~.
MOM'S NOT EVEN HERE YET.
YOU'RE SUCH A NAG, REALLY!
WHY IS IT TAKING TWO HOURS TO GET HER HAIR DONE?
SHE'S NOT THE BRIDE OR ANYTHING.
THERE'S STILL A LOT OF TIME LEFT. JUST GET A CUP OF COFFEE AND RELAX, OKAY—?
I CAN'T TAKE THIS ANYMORE. I'M GOING TO THE SALON MYSELF!
DAD~!!

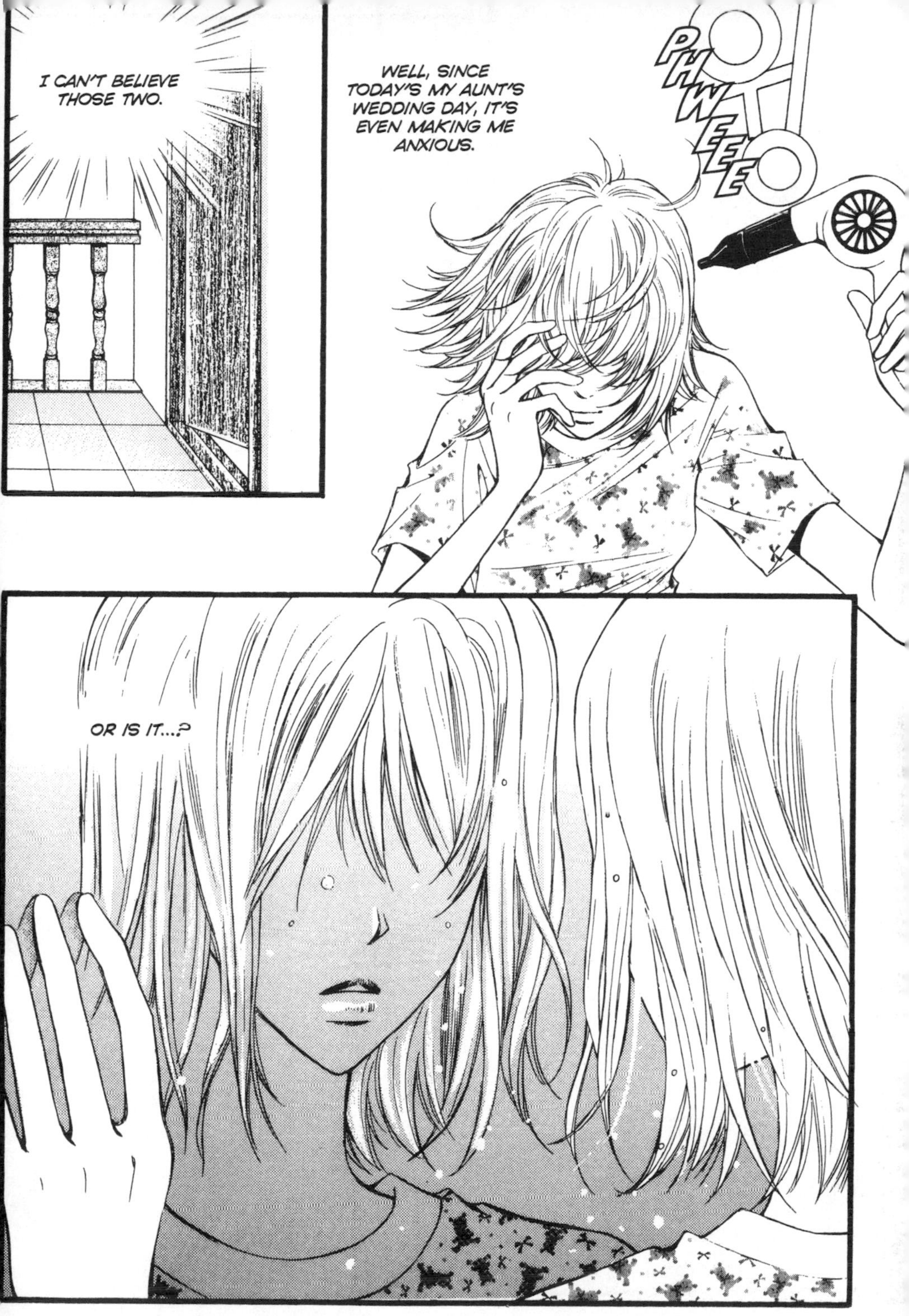
I CAN'T BELIEVE THOSE TWO.
WELL, SINCE TODAY'S MY AUNT'S WEDDING DAY, IT'S EVEN MAKING ME ANXIOUS.
PHWEEE
OR IS IT...?

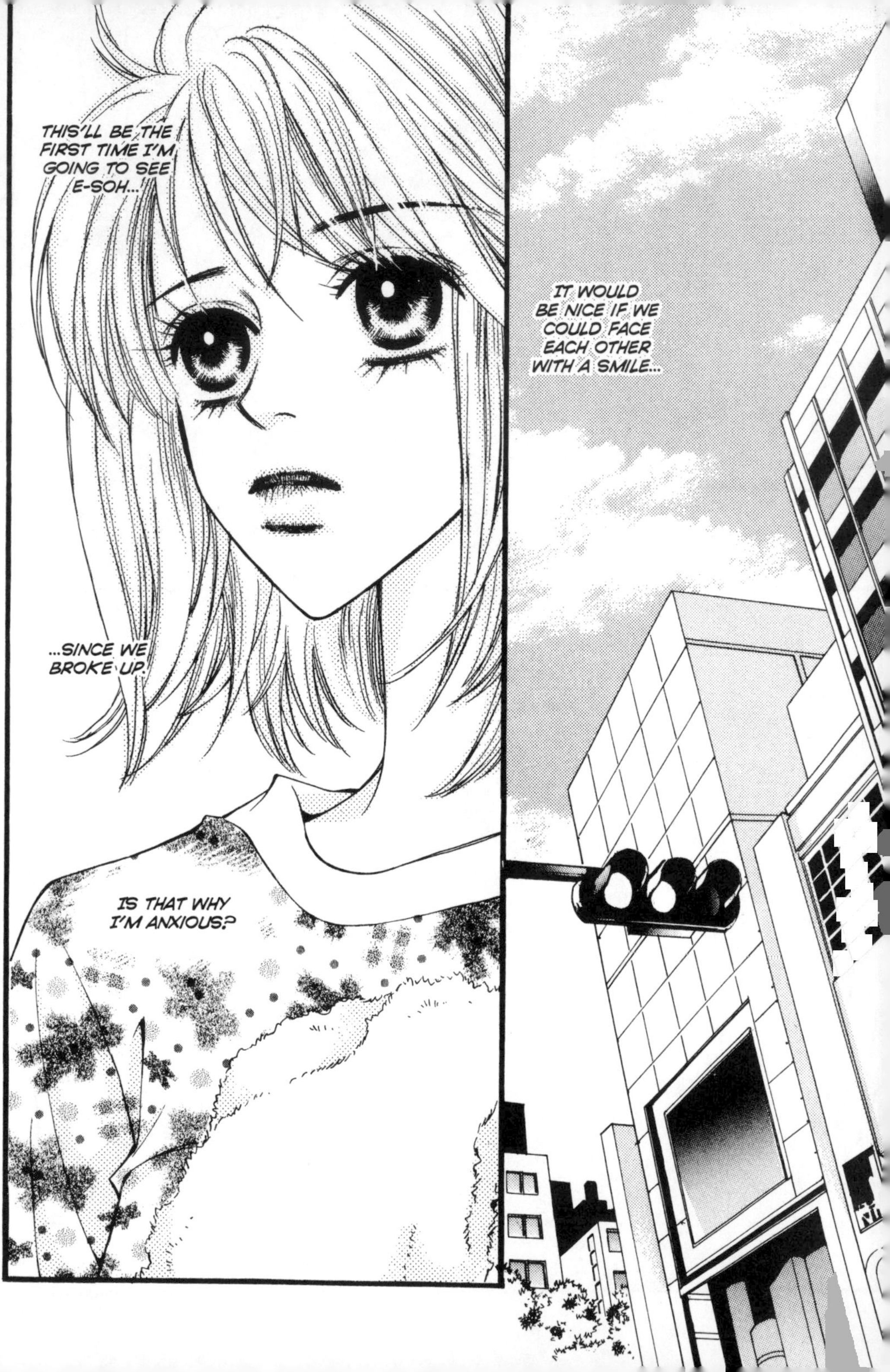
THIS'LL BE THE FIRST TIME I'M GOING TO SEE E-SOH...
...SINCE WE BROKE UP.
IS THAT WHY I'M ANXIOUS?
IT WOULD BE NICE IF WE COULD FACE EACH OTHER WITH A SMILE...

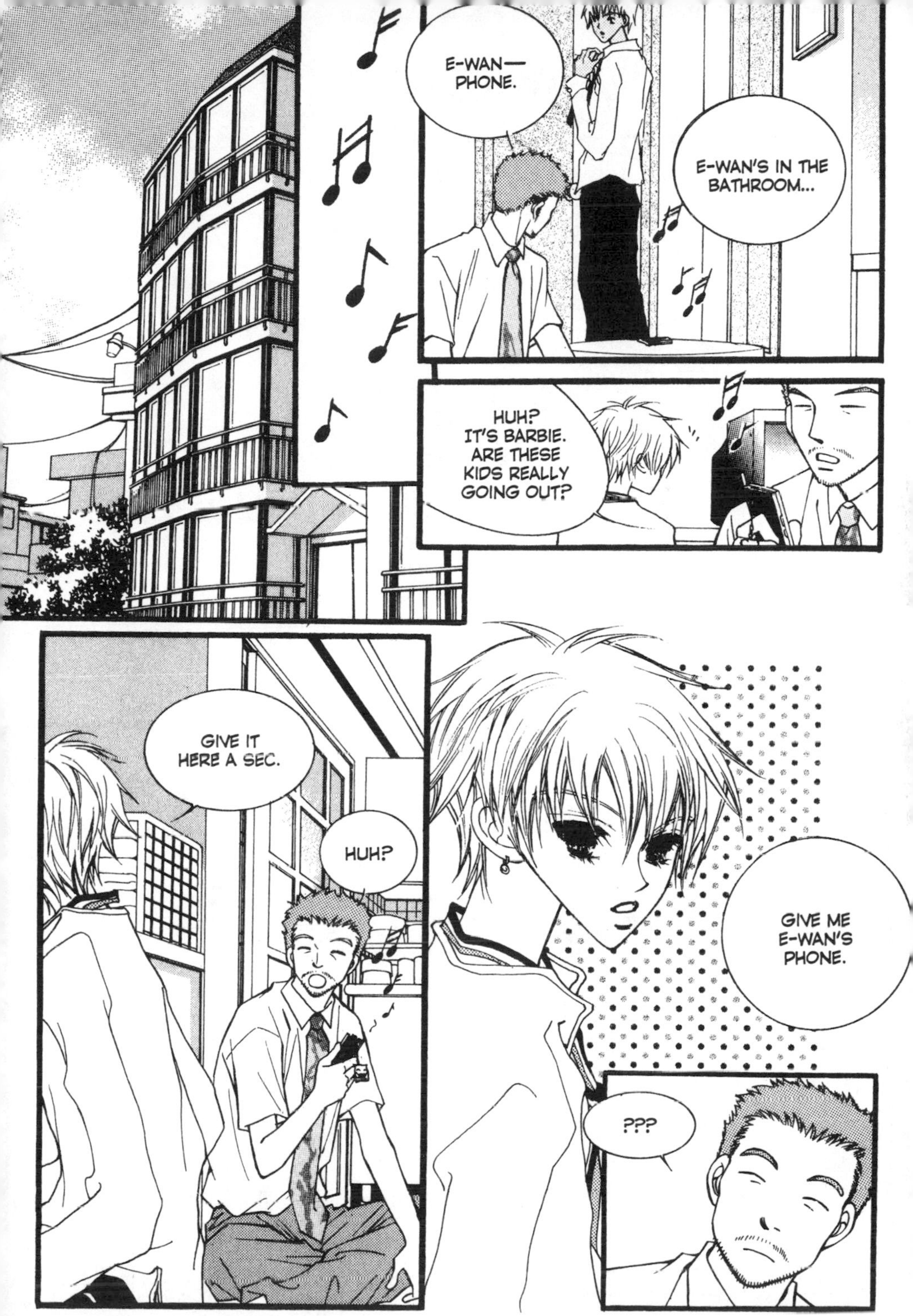
E-WAN—
PHONE.
E-WAN'S IN THE BATHROOM...
HUH? IT'S BARBIE. ARE THESE KIDS REALLY GOING OUT?
GIVE IT HERE A SEC.
HUH?
GIVE ME E-WAN'S PHONE.
???

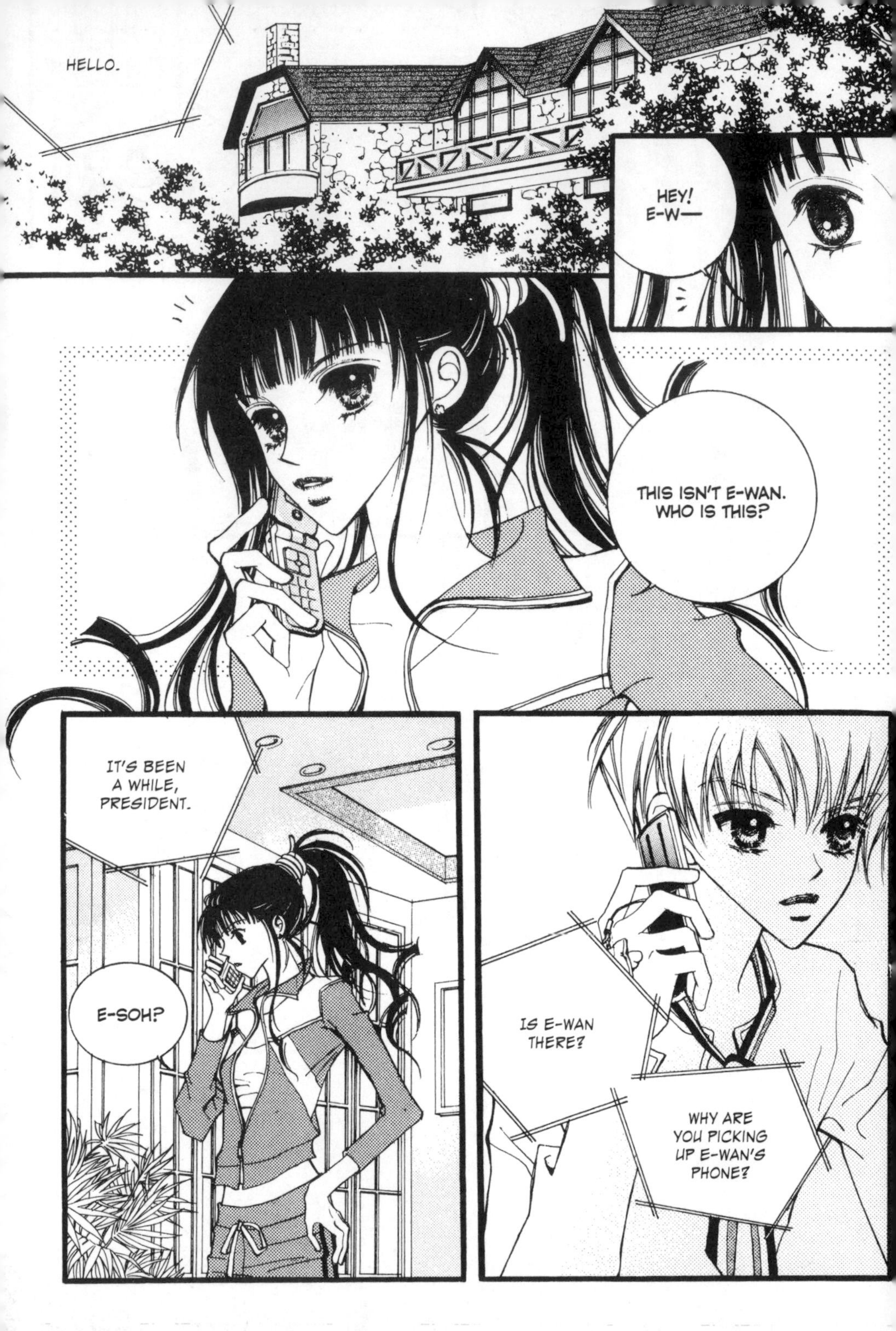
HELLO.
HEY! E-W—
THIS ISN'T E-WAN. WHO IS THIS?
IT'S BEEN A WHILE, PRESIDENT.
E-SOH?
IS E-WAN THERE?
WHY ARE YOU PICKING UP E-WAN'S PHONE?

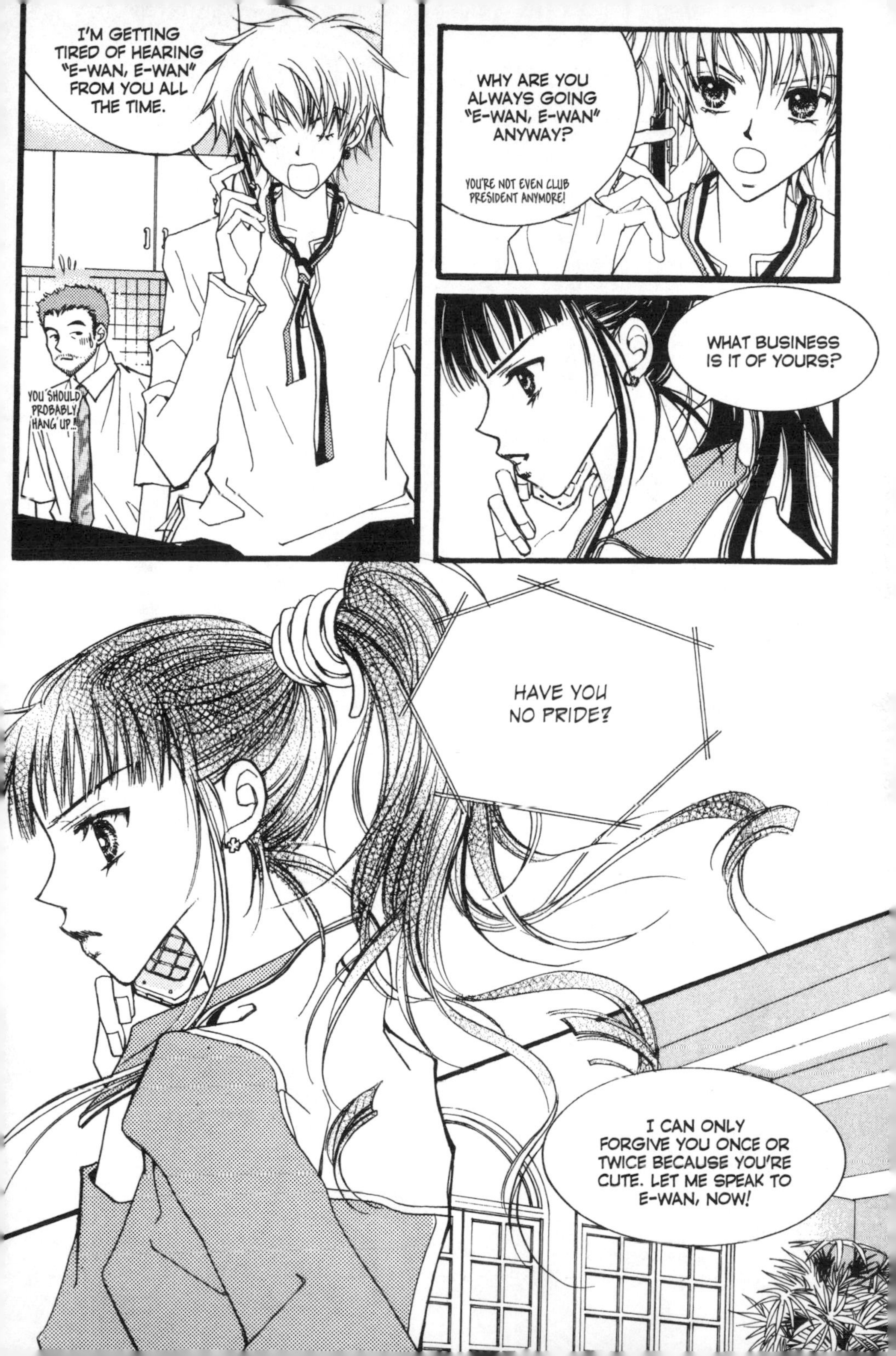
I'M GETTING TIRED OF HEARING "E-WAN, E-WAN" FROM YOU ALL THE TIME.
YOU SHOULD PROBABLY HANG UP...
WHY ARE YOU ALWAYS GOING "E-WAN, E-WAN" ANYWAY?
YOU'RE NOT EVEN CLUB PRESIDENT ANYMORE!
WHAT BUSINESS IS IT OF YOURS?
HAVE YOU NO PRIDE?
I CAN ONLY FORGIVE YOU ONCE OR TWICE BECAUSE YOU'RE CUTE. LET ME SPEAK TO E-WAN, NOW!

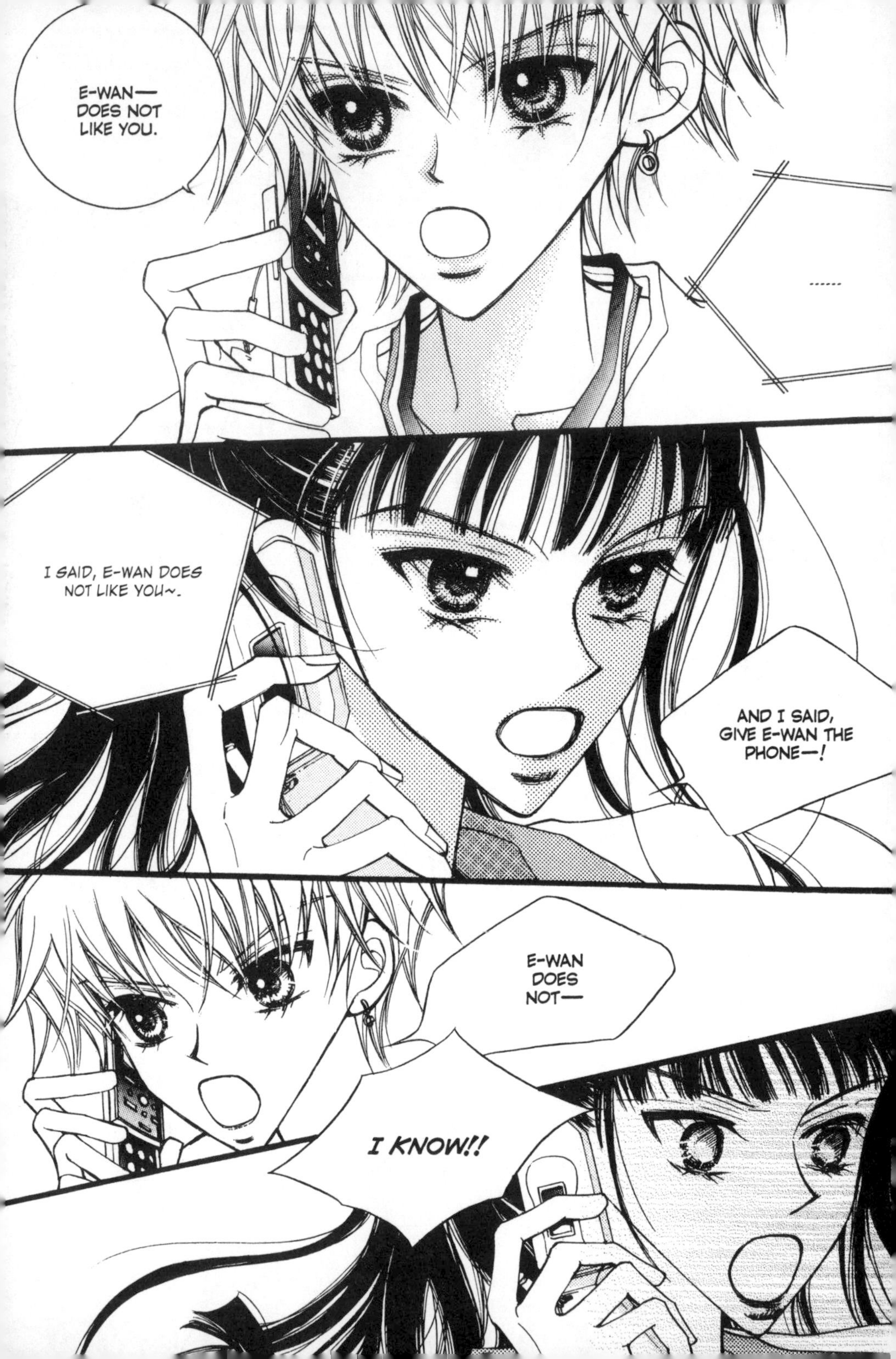
E-WAN— DOES NOT LIKE YOU.
......
I SAID, E-WAN DOES NOT LIKE YOU~.
AND I SAID, GIVE E-WAN THE PHONE—!
E-WAN DOES NOT—
I KNOW!!

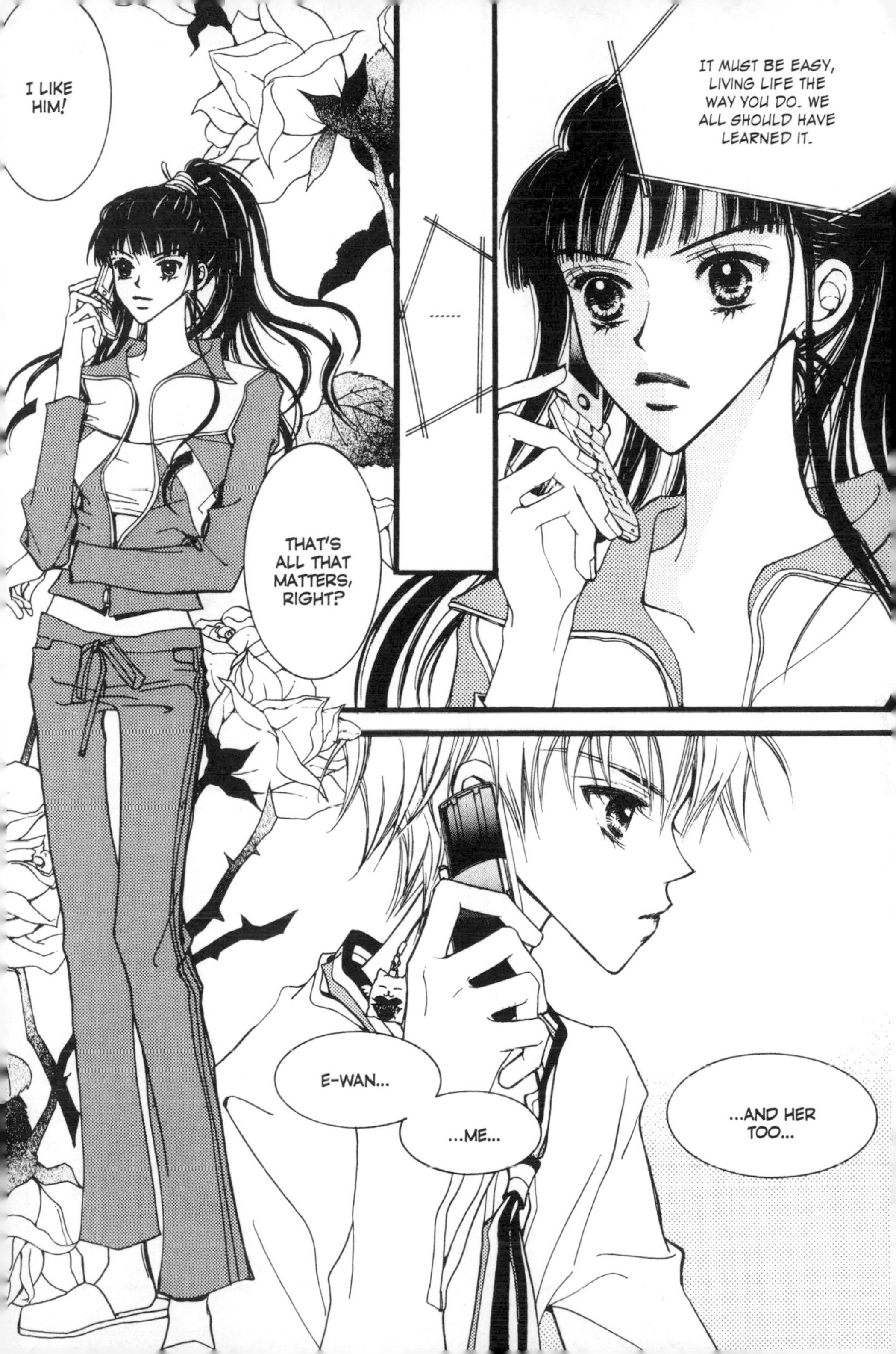
I LIKE HIM!
THAT'S ALL THAT MATTERS, RIGHT?
......
IT MUST BE EASY, LIVING LIFE THE WAY YOU DO. WE ALL SHOULD HAVE LEARNED IT.
E-WAN...
...ME...
...AND HER TOO...

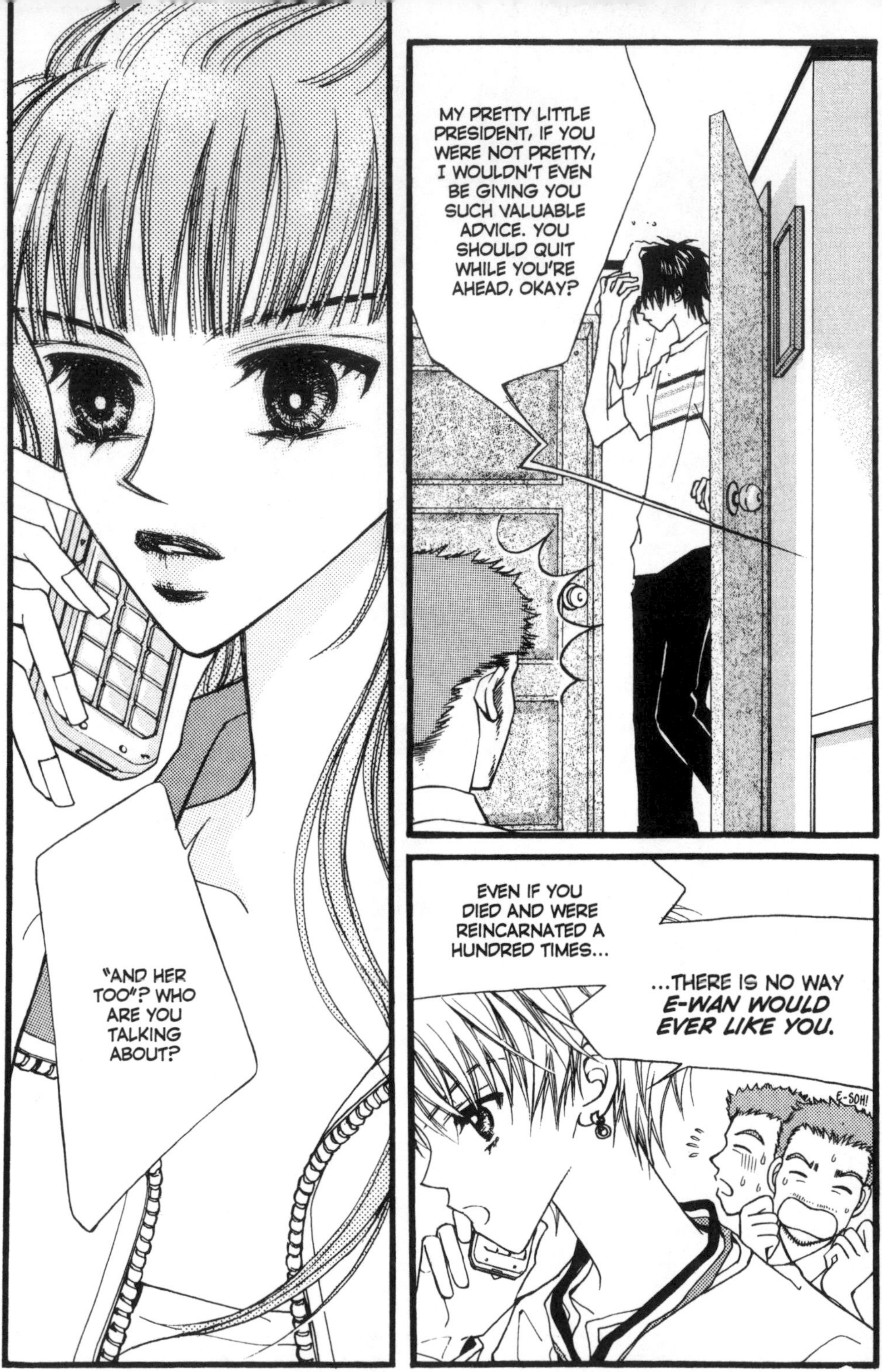
"AND HER TOO"? WHO ARE YOU TALKING ABOUT?
MY PRETTY LITTLE PRESIDENT, IF YOU WERE NOT PRETTY, I WOULDN'T EVEN BE GIVING YOU SUCH VALUABLE ADVICE. YOU SHOULD QUIT WHILE YOU'RE AHEAD, OKAY?
EVEN IF YOU DIED AND WERE REINCARNATED A HUNDRED TIMES...
...THERE IS NO WAY *E-WAN WOULD EVER LIKE YOU.*
E-SOH!

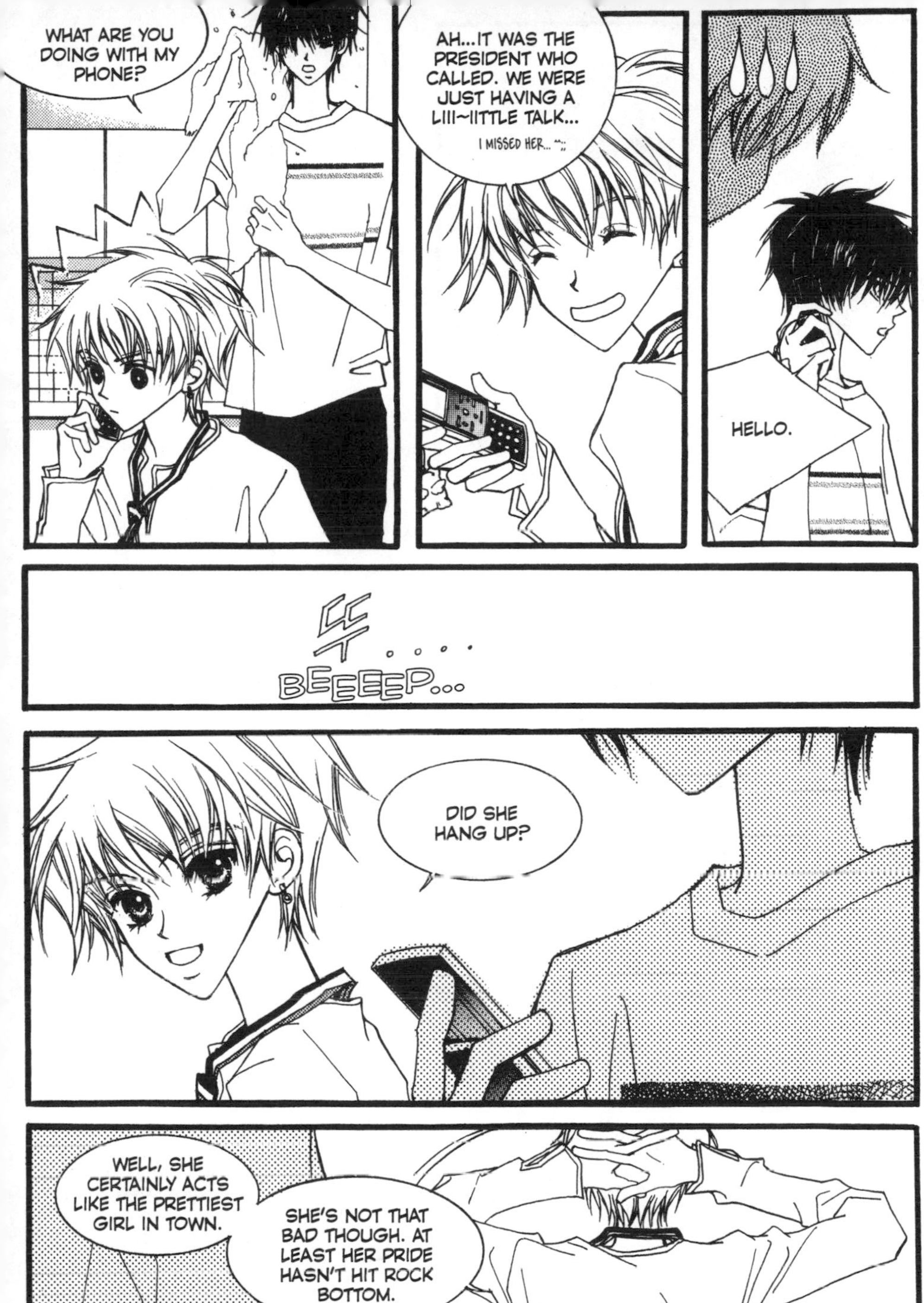
WHAT ARE YOU DOING WITH MY PHONE?
AH...IT WAS THE PRESIDENT WHO CALLED. WE WERE JUST HAVING A LIII~IITTLE TALK...
I MISSED HER...
HELLO.
BEEEEEP...
DID SHE HANG UP?
WELL, SHE CERTAINLY ACTS LIKE THE PRETTIEST GIRL IN TOWN.
SHE'S NOT THAT BAD THOUGH. AT LEAST HER PRIDE HASN'T HIT ROCK BOTTOM.

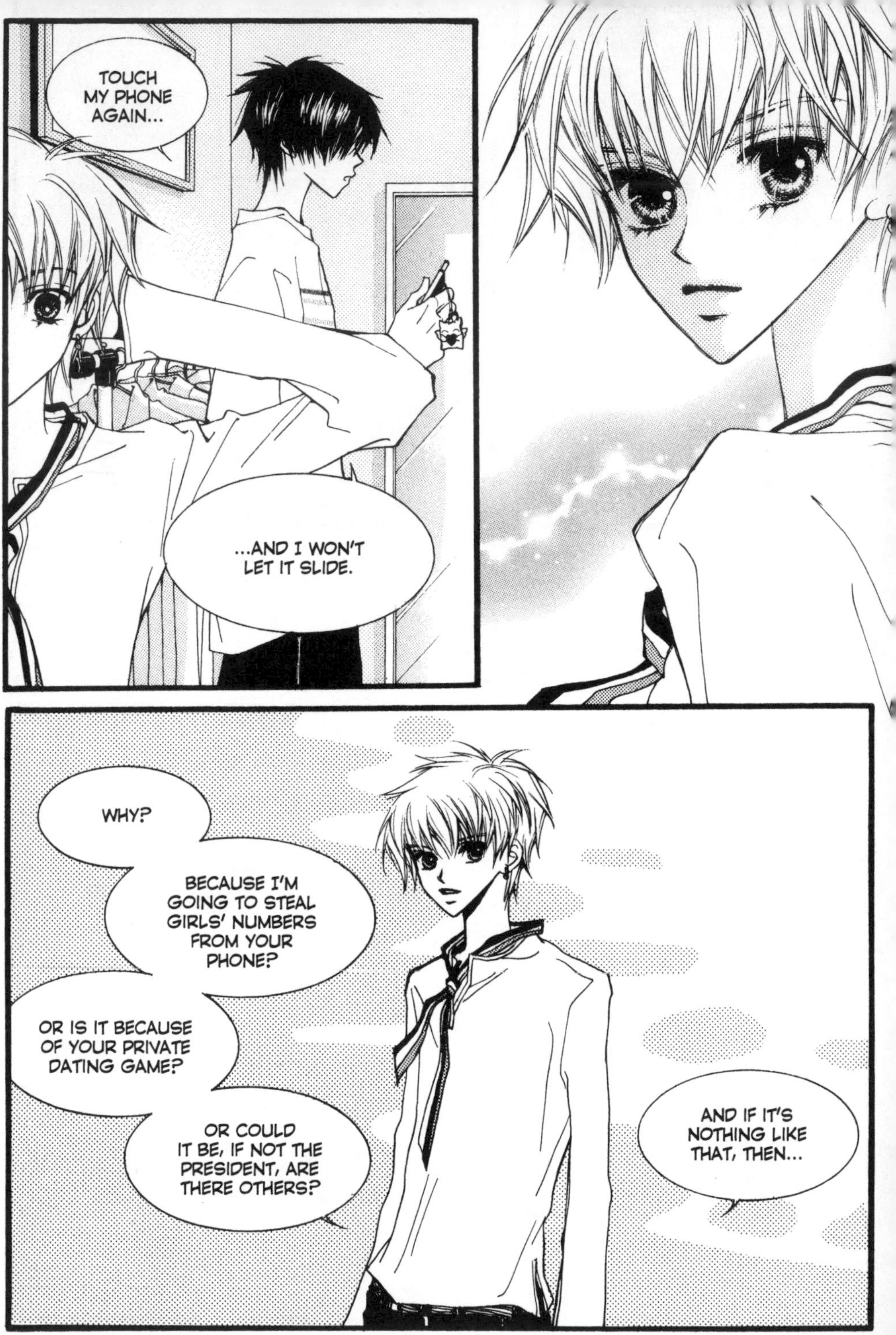
TOUCH MY PHONE AGAIN...
...AND I WON'T LET IT SLIDE.
WHY?
BECAUSE I'M GOING TO STEAL GIRLS' NUMBERS FROM YOUR PHONE?
OR IS IT BECAUSE OF YOUR PRIVATE DATING GAME?
OR COULD IT BE, IF NOT THE PRESIDENT, ARE THERE OTHERS?
AND IF IT'S NOTHING LIKE THAT, THEN...

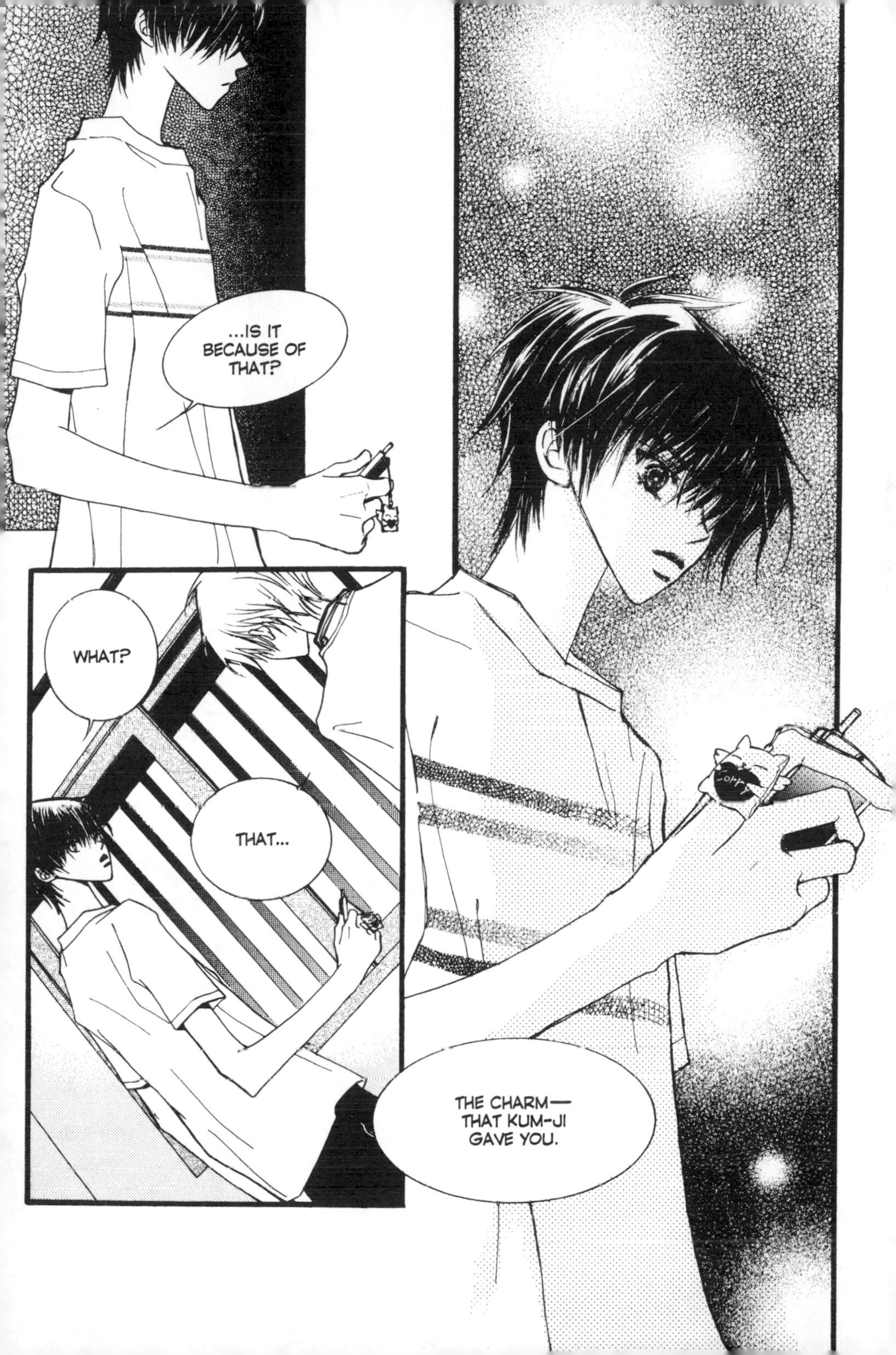
...IS IT BECAUSE OF THAT?
WHAT?
THAT...
THE CHARM—THAT KUM-JI GAVE YOU.

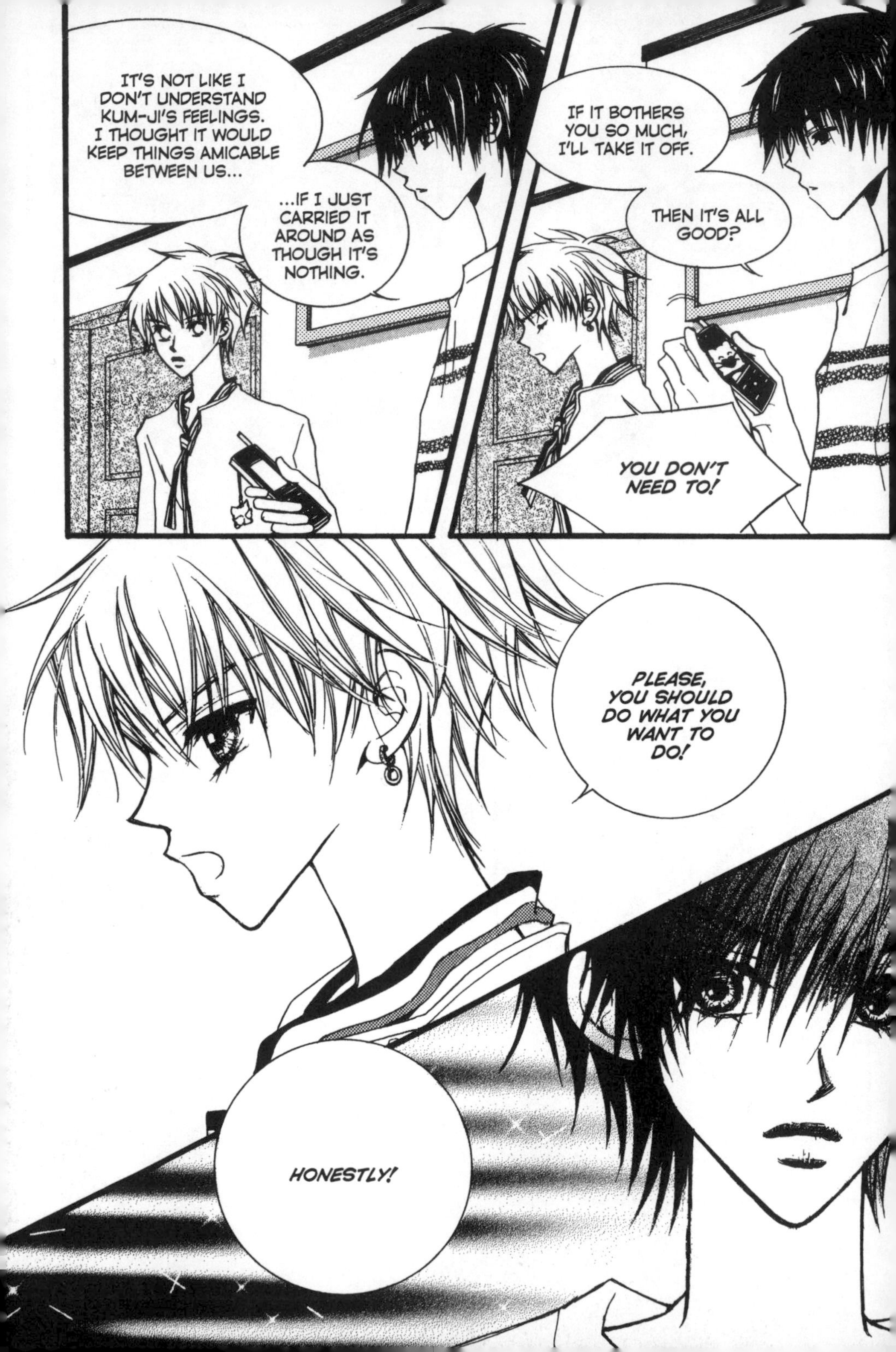
IT'S NOT LIKE I DON'T UNDERSTAND KUM-JI'S FEELINGS. I THOUGHT IT WOULD KEEP THINGS AMICABLE BETWEEN US...
...IF I JUST CARRIED IT AROUND AS THOUGH IT'S NOTHING.
IF IT BOTHERS YOU SO MUCH, I'LL TAKE IT OFF.
THEN IT'S ALL GOOD?
YOU DON'T NEED TO!
PLEASE, YOU SHOULD DO WHAT YOU WANT TO DO!
HONESTLY!

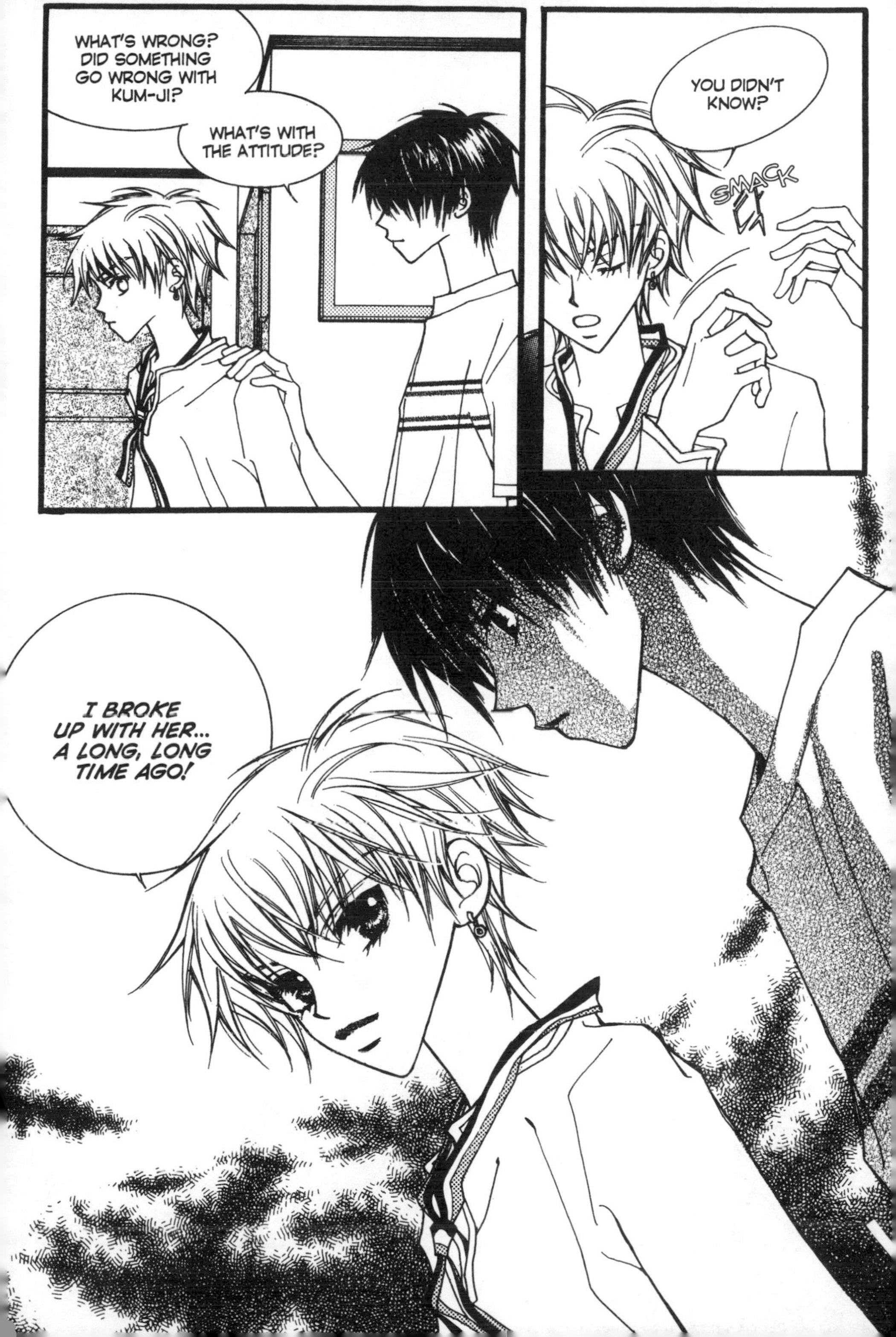
WHAT'S WRONG? DID SOMETHING GO WRONG WITH KUM-JI?
WHAT'S WITH THE ATTITUDE?
YOU DIDN'T KNOW?
SMACK
I BROKE UP WITH HER... A LONG, LONG TIME AGO!

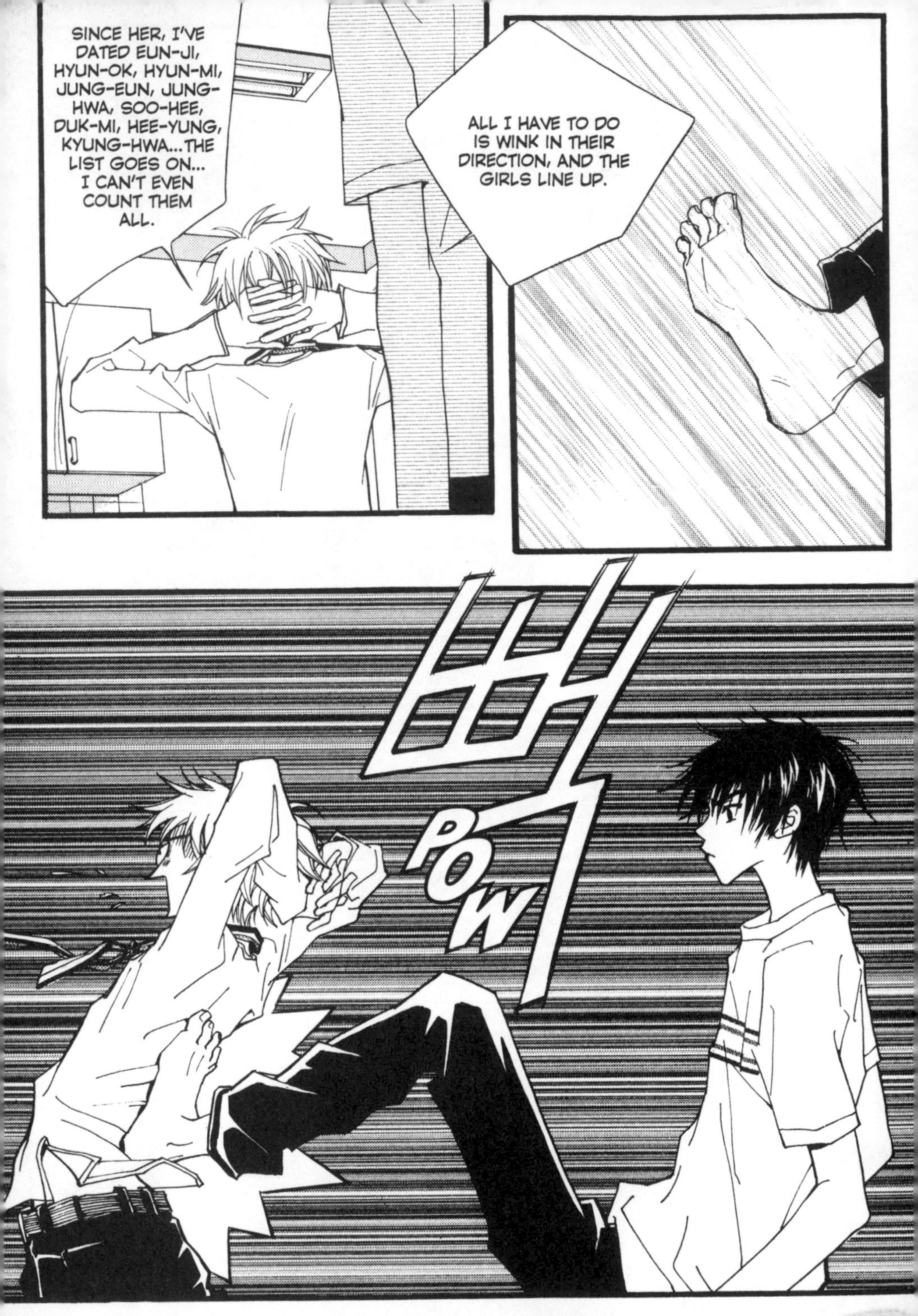
SINCE HER, I'VE DATED EUN-JI, HYUN-OK, HYUN-MI, JUNG-EUN, JUNG-HWA, SOO-HEE, DUK-MI, HEE-YUNG, KYUNG-HWA...THE LIST GOES ON... I CAN'T EVEN COUNT THEM ALL.
ALL I HAVE TO DO IS WINK IN THEIR DIRECTION, AND THE GIRLS LINE UP.
POW

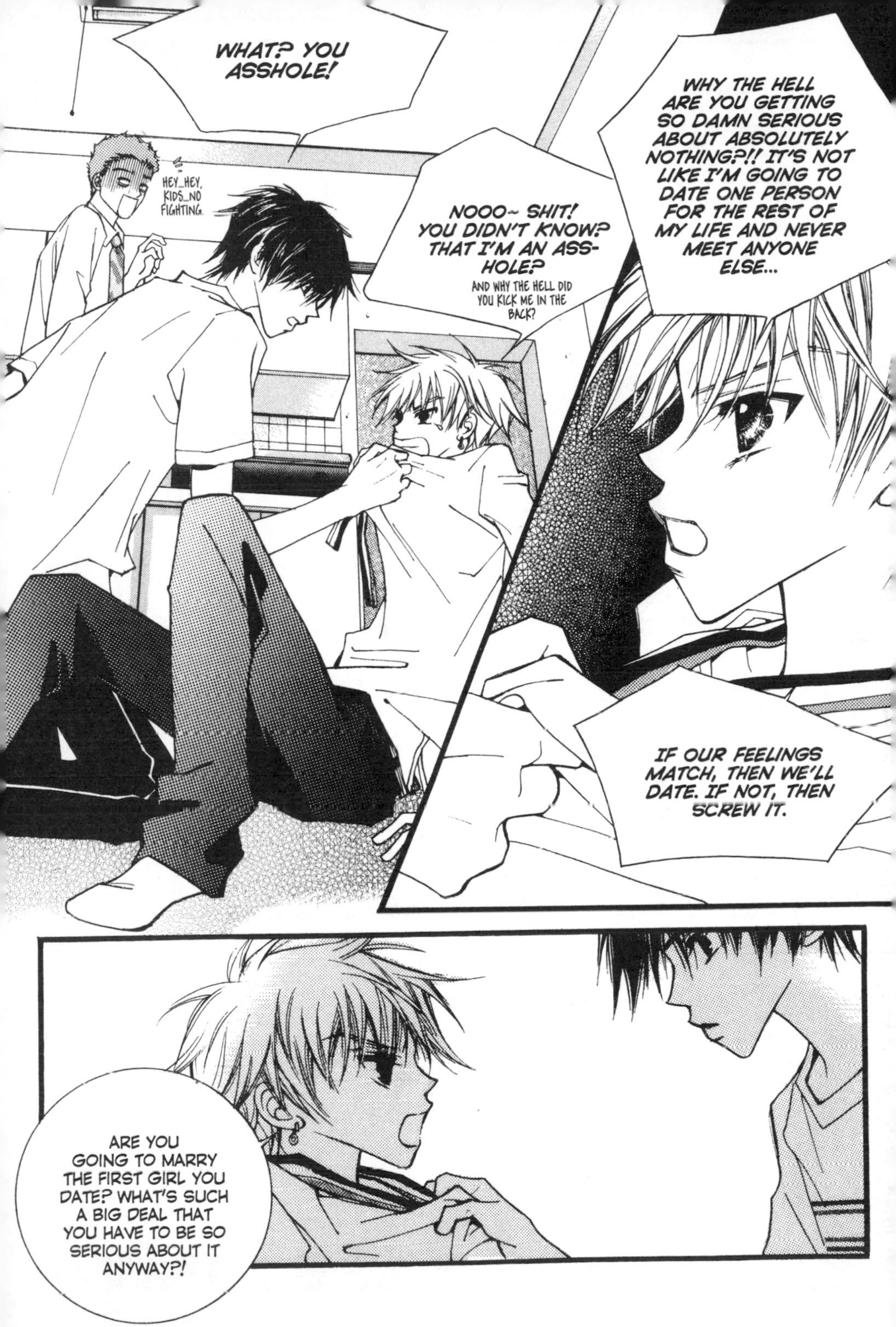
WHAT? YOU ASSHOLE!
HEY...HEY, KIDS...NO FIGHTING.
NOOO~ SHIT! YOU DIDN'T KNOW? THAT I'M AN ASS-HOLE?
AND WHY THE HELL DID YOU KICK ME IN THE BACK?
WHY THE HELL ARE YOU GETTING SO DAMN SERIOUS ABOUT ABSOLUTELY NOTHING?!! IT'S NOT LIKE I'M GOING TO DATE ONE PERSON FOR THE REST OF MY LIFE AND NEVER MEET ANYONE ELSE...
IF OUR FEELINGS MATCH, THEN WE'LL DATE. IF NOT, THEN SCREW IT.
ARE YOU GOING TO MARRY THE FIRST GIRL YOU DATE? WHAT'S SUCH A BIG DEAL THAT YOU HAVE TO BE SO SERIOUS ABOUT IT ANYWAY?!

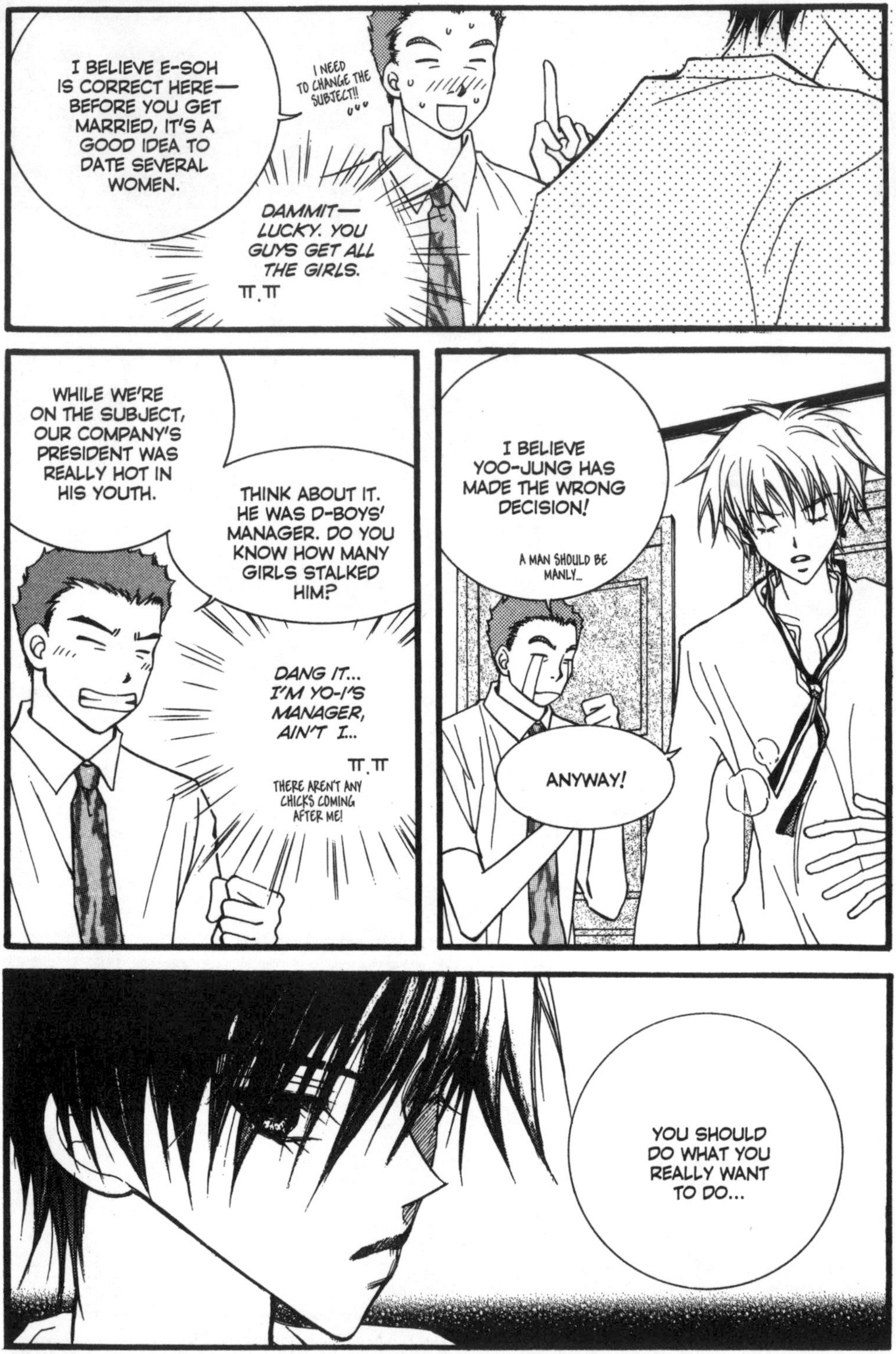

I BELIEVE E-SOH IS CORRECT HERE—BEFORE YOU GET MARRIED, IT'S A GOOD IDEA TO DATE SEVERAL WOMEN.
I NEED TO CHANGE THE SUBJECT!!
DAMMIT—LUCKY. YOU GUYS GET ALL THE GIRLS.
π.π
WHILE WE'RE ON THE SUBJECT, OUR COMPANY'S PRESIDENT WAS REALLY HOT IN HIS YOUTH.
THINK ABOUT IT. HE WAS D-BOYS' MANAGER. DO YOU KNOW HOW MANY GIRLS STALKED HIM?
DANG IT... I'M YO-I'S MANAGER, AIN'T I...
π.π
THERE AREN'T ANY CHICKS COMING AFTER ME!
I BELIEVE YOO-JUNG HAS MADE THE WRONG DECISION!
A MAN SHOULD BE MANLY...
ANYWAY!
YOU SHOULD DO WHAT YOU REALLY WANT TO DO...

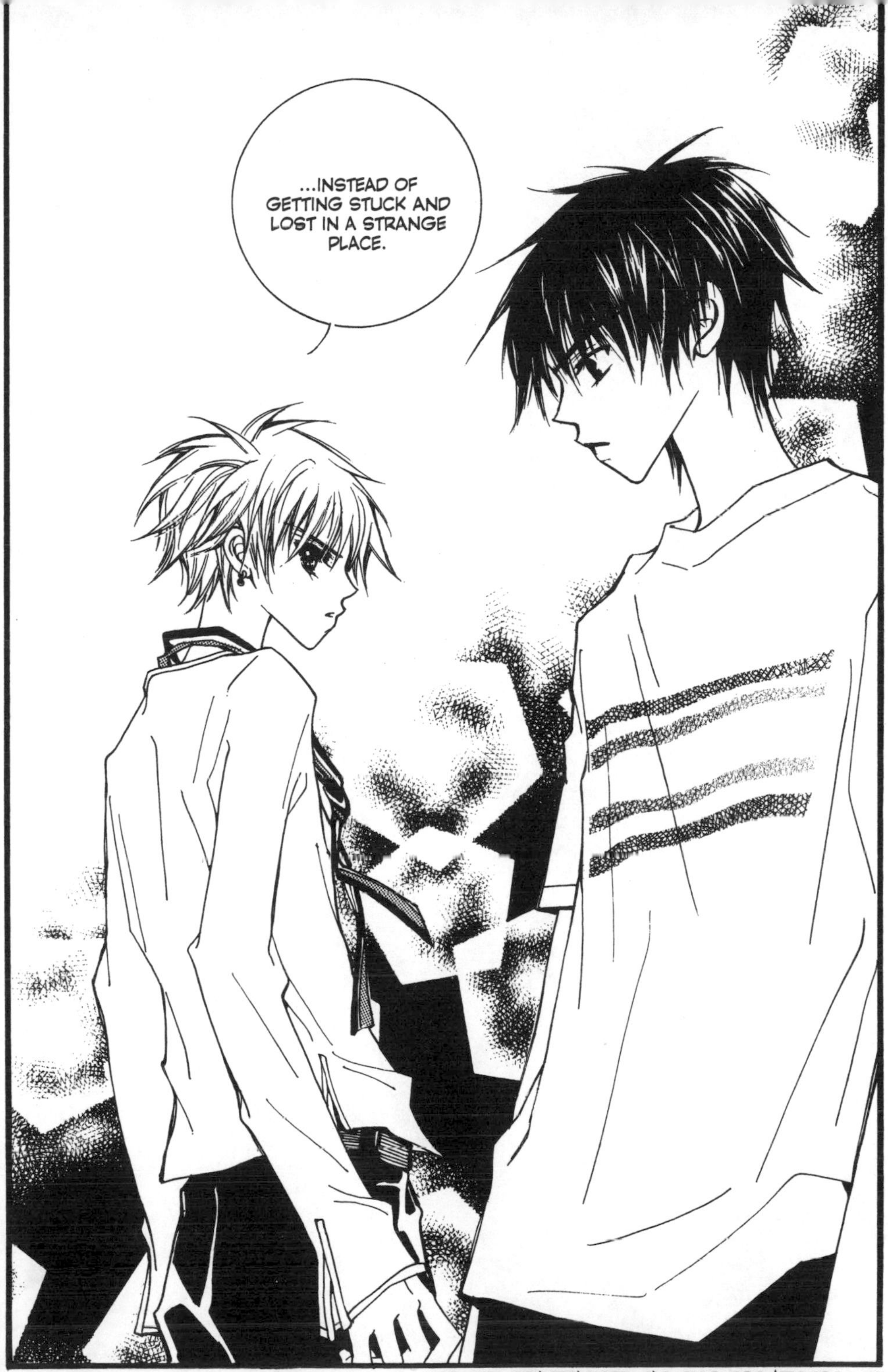
...INSTEAD OF GETTING STUCK AND LOST IN A STRANGE PLACE.

TO BE CONTINUED IN CHOCOLAT VOL. 8!

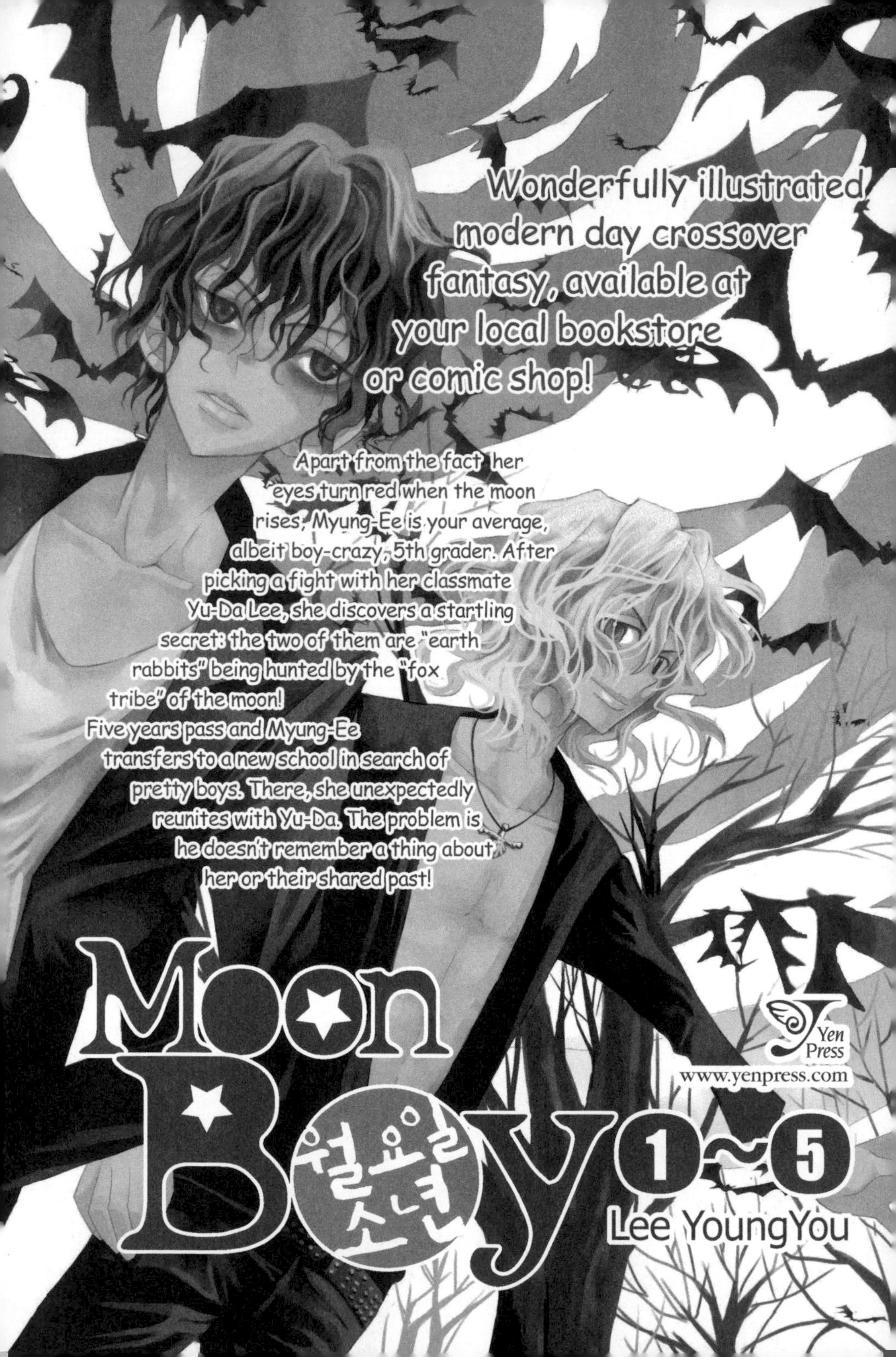
Wonderfully illustrated modern day crossover fantasy, available at your local bookstore or comic shop!
Apart from the fact her eyes turn red when the moon rises, Myung-Ee is your average, albeit boy-crazy, 5th grader. After picking a fight with her classmate Yu-Da Lee, she discovers a startling secret: the two of them are "earth rabbits" being hunted by the "fox tribe" of the moon!
Five years pass and Myung-Ee transfers to a new school in search of pretty boys. There, she unexpectedly reunites with Yu-Da. The problem is he doesn't remember a thing about her or their shared past!
Moon Boy 1~5
월요일 소년
Lee YoungYou
Yen Press
www.yenpress.com

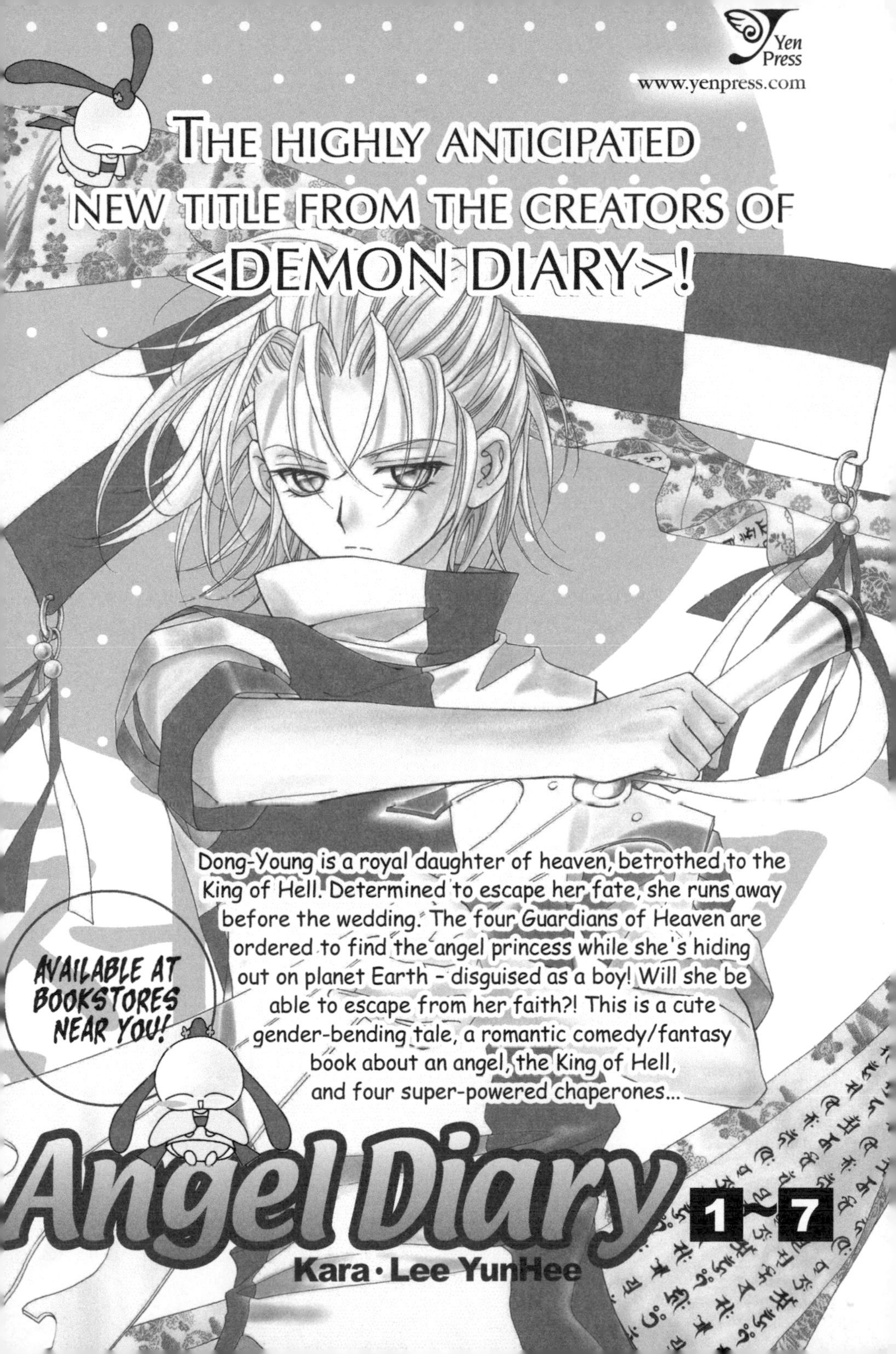
Yen Press
www.yenpress.com
THE HIGHLY ANTICIPATED NEW TITLE FROM THE CREATORS OF <DEMON DIARY>!
Dong-Young is a royal daughter of heaven, betrothed to the King of Hell. Determined to escape her fate, she runs away before the wedding. The four Guardians of Heaven are ordered to find the angel princess while she's hiding out on planet Earth – disguised as a boy! Will she be able to escape from her faith?! This is a cute gender-bending tale, a romantic comedy/fantasy book about an angel, the King of Hell, and four super-powered chaperones...
AVAILABLE AT BOOKSTORES NEAR YOU!
Angel Diary 1~7
Kara · Lee YunHee

Chocolat vol. 7

Story and art by JiSang Shin · Geo

Translation: Jackie Oh
English Adaptation: Jamie S. Rich
Lettering: Terri Delgado

CHOCOLAT, Vol. 7 © 2004 JiSang Shin · Geo. All rights reserved. First published in Korea in 2004 by SIGONGSA Co., Ltd.

English translation © 2008 Hachette Book Group, Inc.

Yen Press
Hachette Book Group
237 Park Avenue, New York, NY 10017

Visit our Web sites at www.HachetteBookGroup.com and www.YenPress.com.

Yen Press is an imprint of Hachette Book Group, Inc. The Yen Press name and logo are trademarks of Hachette Book Group, Inc.

First Yen Press Edition: December 2008

ISBN-13: 978-0-7595-3009-6

10 9 8 7 6 5 4 3 2 1

BVG

Printed in the United States of America